Lecture Notes of the Institute
for Computer Sciences, Social Informatics
and Telecommunications Engineering 610

Editorial Board Members

Ozgur Akan, *Middle East Technical University, Ankara, Türkiye*
Paolo Bellavista, *University of Bologna, Bologna, Italy*
Jiannong Cao, *Hong Kong Polytechnic University, Hong Kong, Hong Kong*
Geoffrey Coulson, *Lancaster University, Lancaster, UK*
Falko Dressler, *University of Erlangen, Erlangen, Germany*
Domenico Ferrari, *Università Cattolica Piacenza, Piacenza, Italy*
Mario Gerla, *UCLA, Los Angeles, USA*
Hisashi Kobayashi, *Princeton University, Princeton, USA*
Sergio Palazzo, *University of Catania, Catania, Italy*
Sartaj Sahni, *University of Florida, Gainesville, USA*
Xuemin Shen ⓘ, *University of Waterloo, Waterloo, Canada*
Mircea Stan, *University of Virginia, Charlottesville, USA*
Xiaohua Jia, *City University of Hong Kong, Kowloon, Hong Kong*
Albert Y. Zomaya, *University of Sydney, Sydney, Australia*

The LNICST series publishes ICST's conferences, symposia and workshops.
   LNICST reports state-of-the-art results in areas related to the scope of the Institute.
   The type of material published includes

- Proceedings (published in time for the respective event)
- Other edited monographs (such as project reports or invited volumes)

   LNICST topics span the following areas:

- General Computer Science
- E-Economy
- E-Medicine
- Knowledge Management
- Multimedia
- Operations, Management and Policy
- Social Informatics
- Systems

Kebe Cheikh M. F. Kebe · Assane Gueye ·
Ababacar Ndiaye · Ndèye Awa Sene ·
Amadou-Seidou Maiga
Editors

Innovations and Interdisciplinary Solutions for Underserved Areas

7th International Conference, InterSol 2024
Dakar, Senegal, July 3–4, 2024
Proceedings

Editors
Kebe Cheikh M. F. Kebe
Université Cheikh Anta Diop de Dakar
Dakar-Fann, Senegal

Assane Gueye
Carnegie Mellon University Africa
Kigali, Rwanda

Ababacar Ndiaye
Université Cheikh Anta Diop de Dakar
Dakar-Fann, Senegal

Ndèye Awa Sene
Université Cheikh Anta Diop de Dakar
Dakar-Fann, Senegal

Amadou-Seidou Maiga
Université Gaston Berger de Saint Louis
St. Louis, Senegal

ISSN 1867-8211 ISSN 1867-822X (electronic)
Lecture Notes of the Institute for Computer Sciences, Social Informatics and Telecommunications Engineering
ISBN 978-3-031-86492-6 ISBN 978-3-031-86493-3 (eBook)
https://doi.org/10.1007/978-3-031-86493-3

© ICST Institute for Computer Sciences, Social Informatics and Telecommunications Engineering 2025

This work is subject to copyright. All rights are solely and exclusively licensed by the Publisher, whether the whole or part of the material is concerned, specifically the rights of translation, reprinting, reuse of illustrations, recitation, broadcasting, reproduction on microfilms or in any other physical way, and transmission or information storage and retrieval, electronic adaptation, computer software, or by similar or dissimilar methodology now known or hereafter developed.
The use of general descriptive names, registered names, trademarks, service marks, etc. in this publication does not imply, even in the absence of a specific statement, that such names are exempt from the relevant protective laws and regulations and therefore free for general use.
The publisher, the authors and the editors are safe to assume that the advice and information in this book are believed to be true and accurate at the date of publication. Neither the publisher nor the authors or the editors give a warranty, expressed or implied, with respect to the material contained herein or for any errors or omissions that may have been made. The publisher remains neutral with regard to jurisdictional claims in published maps and institutional affiliations.

This Springer imprint is published by the registered company Springer Nature Switzerland AG
The registered company address is: Gewerbestrasse 11, 6330 Cham, Switzerland

If disposing of this product, please recycle the paper.

Preface

The seventh edition of InterSol was held in Dakar, Sene[...] Anta Diop University of Dakar hosted this annual inter[...] Sol 2024 was once again a meeting place for scientists fr[...] it provided a framework for participants to present th[...] and problems of the world, but more particularly th[...] areas.

Through InterSol, researchers are making their co[...] of populations living in these unserved and underserve[...] energy, water, climate, health and ICT as an enabler, [...]

However, it is clear that the solutions proposed ca[...] effective when they integrate an interdisciplinary dim[...] combine different disciplines while taking into acco[...] and environmental specificities, among others. All th[...] and it has established itself on the African and eve[...] interdisciplinary research, given the number, diversi[...]

InterSol 2024 brought together researchers, tea[...] and NGOs from a wide range of African backgrour[...]

This volume presents the papers presented at I[...] cation. It also includes selected papers presented [...] in Computer Science and its Applications (CNRIA[...] May 2 to 4, 2024 at the Université Cheikh Anta [...] together scientists from Africa and Europe.

This volume presents 29 papers, 16 of which c[...] 2024. The 29 articles can be broadly classified u[...] Computing, Electronics, Social Sciences, Telecon[...]

We believe that this volume will enable the [...] 2024 and CNRIA 2024 to be widely disseminat[...] solutions proposed by the scientists who took part [...] primarily to the problems of unserved areas.

Kebe Cheikh M. F. Kebe · Assane Gueye ·
Ababacar Ndiaye · Ndèye Awa Sene ·
Amadou-Seidou Maiga
Editors

Innovations and Interdisciplinary Solutions for Underserved Areas

7th International Conference, InterSol 2024
Dakar, Senegal, July 3–4, 2024
Proceedings

Editors
Kebe Cheikh M. F. Kebe
Université Cheikh Anta Diop de Dakar
Dakar-Fann, Senegal

Assane Gueye
Carnegie Mellon University Africa
Kigali, Rwanda

Ababacar Ndiaye [iD]
Université Cheikh Anta Diop de Dakar
Dakar-Fann, Senegal

Ndèye Awa Sene
Université Cheikh Anta Diop de Dakar
Dakar-Fann, Senegal

Amadou-Seidou Maiga
Université Gaston Berger de Saint Louis
St. Louis, Senegal

ISSN 1867-8211   ISSN 1867-822X (electronic)
Lecture Notes of the Institute for Computer Sciences, Social Informatics
and Telecommunications Engineering
ISBN 978-3-031-86492-6   ISBN 978-3-031-86493-3 (eBook)
https://doi.org/10.1007/978-3-031-86493-3

© ICST Institute for Computer Sciences, Social Informatics and Telecommunications Engineering 2025

This work is subject to copyright. All rights are solely and exclusively licensed by the Publisher, whether the whole or part of the material is concerned, specifically the rights of translation, reprinting, reuse of illustrations, recitation, broadcasting, reproduction on microfilms or in any other physical way, and transmission or information storage and retrieval, electronic adaptation, computer software, or by similar or dissimilar methodology now known or hereafter developed.
The use of general descriptive names, registered names, trademarks, service marks, etc. in this publication does not imply, even in the absence of a specific statement, that such names are exempt from the relevant protective laws and regulations and therefore free for general use.
The publisher, the authors and the editors are safe to assume that the advice and information in this book are believed to be true and accurate at the date of publication. Neither the publisher nor the authors or the editors give a warranty, expressed or implied, with respect to the material contained herein or for any errors or omissions that may have been made. The publisher remains neutral with regard to jurisdictional claims in published maps and institutional affiliations.

This Springer imprint is published by the registered company Springer Nature Switzerland AG
The registered company address is: Gewerbestrasse 11, 6330 Cham, Switzerland

If disposing of this product, please recycle the paper.

Preface

The seventh edition of InterSol was held in Dakar, Senegal from July 3 to 4, 2024. Cheikh Anta Diop University of Dakar hosted this annual international scientific meeting. InterSol 2024 was once again a meeting place for scientists from several countries. Once again, it provided a framework for participants to present their work, which addresses issues and problems of the world, but more particularly those of unserved and underserved areas.

Through InterSol, researchers are making their contribution to tackling the problems of populations living in these unserved and underserved areas in several sectors including energy, water, climate, health and ICT as an enabler, just to name a few.

However, it is clear that the solutions proposed can only be sustainable, relevant and effective when they integrate an interdisciplinary dimension. In other words, they need to combine different disciplines while taking into account geographical, social, economic and environmental specificities, among others. All these elements make InterSol unique, and it has established itself on the African and even international scientific scene for interdisciplinary research, given the number, diversity and quality of the participants.

InterSol 2024 brought together researchers, teacher-researchers, doctoral students and NGOs from a wide range of African backgrounds.

This volume presents the papers presented at InterSol2024 and selected for publication. It also includes selected papers presented at the 14th Conference on Research in Computer Science and its Applications (CNRIA 2024). CNRIA 2024 was held from May 2 to 4, 2024 at the Université Cheikh Anta Diop in Dakar, Senegal, and brought together scientists from Africa and Europe.

This volume presents 29 papers, 16 of which concern InterSol 2024 and 13 CNRIA 2024. The 29 articles can be broadly classified under the following headings: Energy, Computing, Electronics, Social Sciences, Telecoms, Networks, Health and Water.

We believe that this volume will enable the scientific work presented at InterSol 2024 and CNRIA 2024 to be widely disseminated. It will also help to popularize the solutions proposed by the scientists who took part in these two scientific events dedicated primarily to the problems of unserved areas.

Kebe Cheikh M. F. Kebe
Assane Gueye
Ababacar Ndiaye
Ndèye Awa Sene
Amadou-Seidou Maiga

Organization

Steering Committee

Cheikh M. F. Kebe   Université Cheikh Anta Diop de Dakar/École Supérieure Polytechnique de Dakar, Senegal

Assane Gueye   Carnegie Mellon University Africa, Rwanda

Organizing Committee

General Chair

Cheikh M. F. Kebe   Universite Cheikh Anta Diop de Dakar, Senegal

General Co-chairs

Cheikh Ahmadou Bamba Guèye   Université Cheikh Anta Diop de Dakar, Senegal

TPC Chair and Co-chairs

Assane Gueye   Carnegie Mellon University Africa, Rwanda
Abdulhameed Mambo   Nile University of Nigeria, Nigeria
Abdelkader Outzourhit   Université Cadi Ayyad, Morocco
Amadou-Seidou Maiga   Université Gaston Berger de Saint Louis, Senegal
Narcisse Talla   Université de Dschang, Cameroun

Sponsorship and Exhibit Chair

Pape Ibrahima Ndiaye   Université Alioune Diop de Bambey, Senegal

Local Chair

Ndèye Awa Sène   Université Cheikh Anta Diop de Dakar/École Supérieure Polytechnique de Dakar, Senegal

Workshops Chair

Youssou Faye   Université Assane Seck de Ziguinchor, Senegal

Publicity and Social Media Chair

Ndèye Fatima Faye   Université Cheikh Anta Diop de Dakar/École Supérieure Polytechnique de Dakar, Senegal

Publications Chair

Ababacar Ndiaye   Université Cheikh Anta Diop de Dakar/École Supérieure Polytechnique de Dakar, Senegal

Web Chair

Adama Sarr   École Supérieure Polytechnique de Dakar, Senegal

Posters and PhD Track Chair

Aida Gaye   École Supérieure Polytechnique de Dakar, Senegal

Panels Chair

Malick Diouara   Université Cheikh Anta Diop de Dakar/École Supérieure Polytechnique de Dakar, Senegal

Demos Chair

Babacar Mbaye Ndiaye   Université Cheikh Anta Diop de Dakar, Senegal

Tutorials Chair

Abdelkader Outzourhit   Université Cadi Ayyad, Morocco

Technical Program Committee

Bamba Gueye	UCAD, Senegal
Jessica P. R. Thorn	University of York, UK/ACDI, South Africa/AIMS, Rwanda
Narcisse Talla Tankam	University of Ngaoundere, Cameroon
Assane Gueye	UADB, Senegal/UMCP, USA
Gaoussou Camara	UADB, Senegal
Francois Pazisnewende Kabore	Jesuit University Institute, Ivory Coast/GU, USA
Cheikh M. Fadel Kebe	UCAD, Senegal
Melissa Densmore	UCT, South Africa
Alassane Diop	UVS, Senegal
Ghada Bassioni	Ain Shams University, Egypt
Moustapha Diop	UMBC, USA
Senghane Mbodji	UADB, Senegal
Rabab El Sherif	Cairo University, Egypt
Tembine Hamidou	NYU, USA
Ababacar Ndiaye	UCAD, Senegal
Abdulhameed Mambo	Nile University of Nigeria, Nigeria
Charif Mahmoudi	NIST, USA
Abdelkader Outzourhit	Université Cadi Ayyad, Morocco
Malick Diouara	Université Cheikh Anta Diop de Dakar - École Supérieure Polytechnique de Dakar, Senegal
Aida Gaye	École Supérieure Polytechnique de Dakar, Senegal
Adama Sarr	École Supérieure Polytechnique de Dakar, Senegal
Youssou Faye	Université Assane Seck de Ziguinchor, Senegal
Ndèye Awa Sene	Université Cheikh Anta Diop de Dakar - École Supérieure Polytechnique de Dakar, Senegal
Amadou-Seidou Maiga	Université Gaston Berger de Saint Louis, Senegal

Contents

Energy and Environment

Study of the Impact of Solar Pumping Solutions on Agricultural
Production in Senegal: The Case of Small Farms in the Niayes Area (Thiès
Region) 3
   Ibrahima Seck, Julien Potron, and Audrey Kakpohoue

Public Participation in Municipal Solid Waste Management: A Mobile
Persuasive App 9
   *Irene Arinaitwe, Ssemakula Jonathan, Agnes Nakakawa,
and Gilbert Maiga*

A Risk-Based Pedestrian Crossing Decision Model for Traffic Simulation
in African Urban Traffic 26
   Modou Gueye, Ndiouma Bame, and Mamadou Thiongane

Modelling and Optimization of the Electrical Parameters of an $In_xGa_{1-x}N$
Solar Cell Under Dynamic Frequency Illumination 38
   *Baboucar Fickou, Moussa Camara, Moustapha Thiame, Issa Faye,
Landing Diatta, and Mamadou Faye*

Assessment of Pavement Damage Caused by Speed Bumps Along
Nyanya – Jikwoyi Road Abuja 47
   Ukinvore Ushiki Adamu, Abubakar Dayyabu, and Abdulhameed Mambo

Analyzing Water's Characteristics Health Impact with Classification
Algorithms 59
   Khadim Gueye, Ndiouma Bame, and Aliou Boly

Information Technology

Optimizing Coverage in a Wireless Sensors Network by Selecting the Best
Sensors 71
   Absa Lecor, Mohamed Mejri, and Senghane Mbodji

Towards a Single-Sign-On Authentication Architecture Based on OpenID
Connect Protocol and Blockchain Technology 87
   *Assane Ilboudo, Didier Bassole, Justin Pegdwindé Kouraogo,
Gouayon Koala, and Oumarou Sie*

An Experimental 5G Standalone Testbed for Rural Connectivity 100
    Mahamadou Diawara and Andre Faye

An Application of the Hough Transform and Convolutional Neural
Networks to Detect Straight Lines 115
    Moussa Bamogo and Abdoulaye Sere

A Slotted Random Access Algorithm for Efficient Transmission in White
Area: Case of Artisanal Fishing in West Africa 126
    Fatoumata Awa Yandé Diouf, Madoune R. Seye, Moussa Diallo,
    and Bamba Gueye

A New Delay History Predictor for Multi-skill Call Center 139
    Mamadou Thiongane, Mohamed M. Ould Deye, Modou Gueye,
    and Mbaye Séne

Retrieving Data from Social Network Platforms: A State-of-Art Review 151
    Harriet Sibitenda, Awa Diattara, Assitan Traore, and B. A. Cheikh

Strabismus Diagnosis and Angular Deviation Calculation Based
on Artificial Intelligence Approaches: A Review 167
    Madior Gueye, Ousmane Khoum, Mandicou Ba, Idy Diop,
    Alassane Bah, Doudou Dione, Regina Esi Turkson, and Aly Mb Kâ

Towards the Implementation of a Dynamic IDS for IoT: Anomaly
Detection in MQTT Traffic 183
    Abdoulaye Diallo, Lionel Affognon, Chérif Diallo, and Eugène C. Ezin

ICT Enabler

Straight-Line Recognition in a Virtual Hexagonal Grid Using Hough
Transform 197
    Moïse Ouedraogo and Abdoulaye Sere

Predicting the Rate of Aflatoxin Contamination in the White Corn Value
Chain 214
    Mahugnon Géraud Azehoun Pazou, Julian Adjibi,
    Régis Donald Hontinfinde, Elognissè Erasme Guérin Agossadou,
    Vidédji Naéssé Adjahossou, Christian Djidjoho Akowanou,
    and Macaire B. Agbomahena

The Impact of Agents Heterogeneous in Call Center Performance Measures ... 228
    Mamadou Thiongane, Mohamed M. Ould Deye, Modou Gueye,
    and Ndiouma Bame

Towards a Mobile, Intelligent, Personalized and Adaptive E-learning
System Considering Learners' Context in Semi-nomadic and Conflict
Zones 240
   *Alhoudourou Almaimoune Maiga, Richard Hotte, Gaoussou Camara,
Mariem Abid, and Anis Masmoudi*

Comparative Study of Machine Learning Models for the Detection
of Abusive Messages: Case of Wolof-French Codes Mixing Data 252
   Ibrahima Ndao, Khadim Dramé, Gorgoumack Sambe, and Gayo Diallo

Towards an Ontology-Based Platform for Integrating Infectious Disease
Simulation Models 264
   Papa Alioune Cisse

AI-Based Control Approach of .SN Reserved Domain Names (aIDN.SN) 275
   *Evrard Cabrel Nguemeyou Tchouangang, Ahmadou Ndiaye,
Bassirou Kassé, Alex Corenthin, and Idrissa Sarr*

Efficient Combination of Deep Learning Models for Skin Disease Detection ... 287
   Mohamed Massamba Sene, Ndeye Fatou Ngom, and Michel Seck

Agricultural and Land Management Using AI: A Case Study of Rice Plot
Identification in Senegal 299
   Mariama Drame, Seydina Moussa Ndiaye, and Moussa Lo

Beqi: Revitalize the Senegalese Wolof Language with a Robust Spelling
Corrector 311
   Derguene Mbaye and Moussa Diallo

Important Predictors for Covid-19 Vaccine Hesitation 326
   *Mireille Fangueng, Mamadou Thiongane, Idrissa Sarr,
and Bitsha-kitime D. Kabkia*

Ensemble Machine Learning Methods to Predict Oil Production 338
   *M. D. Adewale, I. A. Adeyanju, J. Oju, O. C. Ubadike, U. I. Muhammed,
and S. T. Omisakin*

AI-Powered Corn Disease Classification Using Deep Transfer Learning 358
   *Moussa Mahamat Boukar, Assia Aboubakar Mahamat,
Hassane Hamdan, and Usman Abubakar Bello*

Author Index 373

Energy and Environment

Study of the Impact of Solar Pumping Solutions on Agricultural Production in Senegal: The Case of Small Farms in the Niayes Area (Thiès Region)

Ibrahima Seck(✉), Julien Potron, and Audrey Kakpohoue

Nadji.Bi Senegal Monitoring and Evaluation Department, Place du Martyr Mamadou Diop, 23000 Mbour, Senegal
ibrahima.seck@nadjibi.com

Abstract. The Niayes region represents Senegal's principal horticultural zone, contributing approximately 80% of the country's total horticultural production. A survey was conducted to investigate the impact of the distribution of solar pumps on farmers in this region. The transition enabled farmers to achieve an average savings of 713.24 USD in fuel costs. Moreover, the adoption of the solar water pump led to an 8% increase in agricultural production and a 5% increase in income per hectare. The initial six-month period of pump operation resulted in a total avoidance of 137.5 tonnes of CO_2 emissions. The findings demonstrate the beneficial impact of solar pumping solutions on the environment, agricultural productivity, and economic viability in the Niayes region.

Keywords: Agriculture · Solar Water Pump · Senegal · Niayes region

1 Introduction

In many African countries, Sustainable Development Goal (SDG) 2, ending hunger, is an important catalyst for the achievement of many other SDGs. In Senegal, it is the most critical for development. According to the World Food Programme, around 1.3 million people in Senegal faced acute food insecurity during the lean season in 2023 [1]. The development of local agriculture is essential for reducing food insecurity. However, the lack of effective, sustainable, profitable, and environmentally-friendly practices and tools among the majority of farmers is hindering this process.

The Niayes agricultural zone in Senegal covers some 2,759 km^2 [2, 3], and is reputed to be the main market-gardening area responsible for the production of almost 80% of the country's vegetables [4]. In 2023, our study on 545 market garden plots in the Niayes revealed that 62.8% of these plots use diesel-powered pumps. In 2022, the solar energy company Nadji.Bi Senegal, in partnership with USAID-funded West Africa Trade & Investment Hub (Trade Hub) and La Banque Agricole, launched a new product, Woomal

Mbay, designed to promote connected solar pumping and irrigation solutions in the Niayes area. This initiative is part of the drive to promote modern and green agriculture.

The following section presents the results of our study on the impact of the distribution of Woomal Mbay solar pumps in the Niayes region of Senegal. This study was conducted using data collected through interviews with farmers who were using the Woomal Mbay solution. The interviews were conducted at six-month intervals between 2023 and 2024. A total of 68 interviews on 53 farmers using a total of 57 pumps were the subjects of the data collection. The IoT data was used to evaluate the energy consumption of the pumps (Fig. 1).

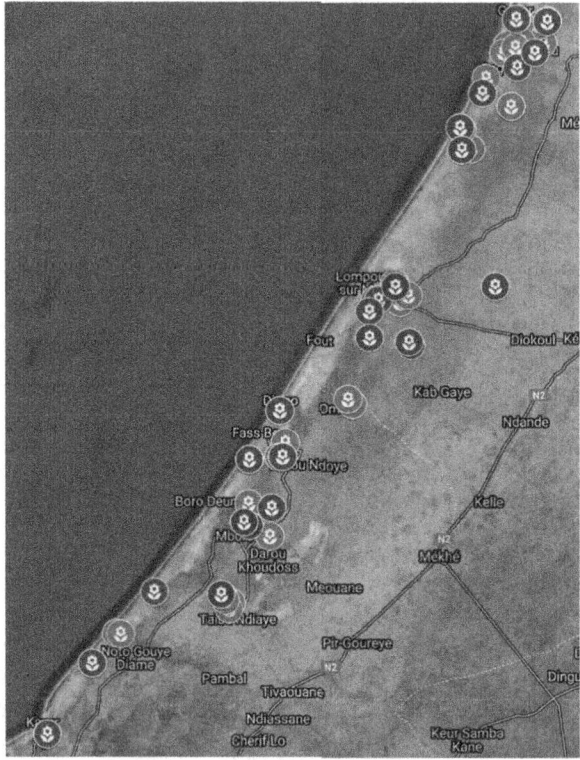

Fig. 1. Distribution of solar pumps installed in the different localities of the Niayes area, as studied in the framework of our research (source: Nadji.Bi Senegal Database).

2 Presentation of Solar Water Pumping System

Solar water pumping systems are composed of three principal components: the hydraulic pump, the inverter, and the solar panels. Nadji.Bi Senegal provides farmers with three system options, each designed for surfaces ranging from 1 to 3 hectares. The system is proposed to the farmer following a system selection study. This study involves the assessment of the water requirement and the suitability of the pump for the farm. The following data is collected for this purpose: the type of crop, the dimensions and depth of the borehole, the presence of particles in the water (e.g., iron and salt), and the size of the cultivated area (including the highest point, geographical coordinates, and surface area). The selection process is typically conducted with the objective of attaining a performance of around 10 m3/h/ha for an average head of 20 m, with a daily operational period of five to six hours under clear skies (Table 1 and Figs 2, 3).

Table 1. Performance table for Solar Water Pumping Systems

System no1	Power (kW)	Flow rate (m3/h)	7	10	17	20	28	30
1	1.1	Manometric head (m)	29	20				
2	2.2		39.5	38	28	22		
3	3		33	32	30	28	24	22

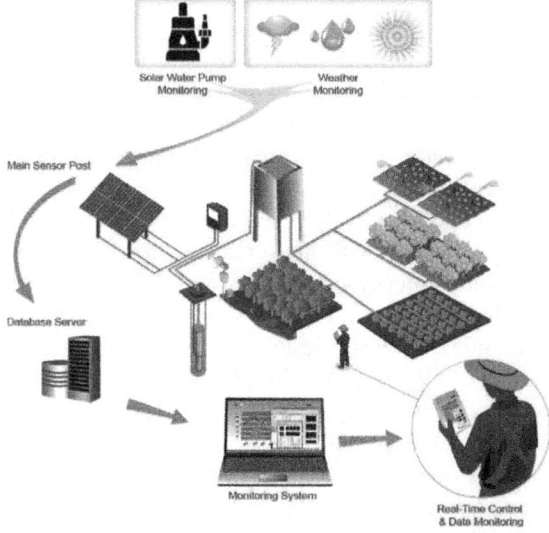

Fig. 2. Solar pumping system (source: Nadji.Bi Senegal Database).

3 Results

The age range of farmers surveyed was 23 to 71, with an average age of 47 and an average working experience of 18 years. With an average of four different crops per farmer, the most widespread of the 21 different crops identified are onions (51%), bitter eggplants (43%) and potatoes (40%). Of the 53 farmers surveyed, 17% were women.

Fig. 3. Woomal Mbay System No. 1 used by the farmer, replacing the previous diesel-powered motor pump system in the background (source: Nadji.Bi Senegal Database).

The survey of 53 farmers revealed that the crops generate 212 full-time jobs. The average age of these workers is 29.2 years, and there is an average of 1.80 full-time jobs per hectare. The number of part-time jobs created during harvest periods, which typically last for an average of four days, is 1,804. This is equivalent to 1,274 full-time jobs for a period of one month. The majority of these workers are women (62.20%), while a significant proportion are young people (42.96%).

45 sites were already under cultivation before the installation of the pump and their area was estimated to be 91.75 ha, with an average area per site of 2.03 ha. We observed that in 22 of these sites, the farmers used the solar water pump to increase their cultivated area by 30.75 ha, which represents an average increase in cultivated area of 33.52% for these 45 sites. The remaining 12 sites invested in the solar water pump to start cultivation on a new area, for a total of 19.5 hectares. In total, the solar water pump allowed the 57 surveyed sites to increase their cultivated area from 91.75 ha to 142 ha, an increase of 54.77%, with an average cultivated area of 2.49 ha.

A total of 1,375 tons of vegetables have been harvested since the installation of the solar water pump, resulting in a total turnover of 420,279,800 FCFA (approximately 691,671 USD). The respondents indicated that their agricultural production had increased overall by 8% per hectare as a result of the solar water pump. This translates into a 5% increase in farm income per hectare.

The majority of farmers surveyed indicated that they perceived solar pumping solutions as a more sustainable alternative to diesel pumps. This perception was supported by the survey results, which showed that out of 44 responding farmers, 63.6% had replaced their diesel pumps with solar water pumps. In addition, 36.4% of respondents indicated that they had replaced their pumping systems (solar or grid electricity) for performance reasons.

The substitution of diesel pumps with solar pumps by farmers led to a reduction in costs of 440,000 FCFA (approximately 713.24 USD) per hectare and per cropping period. The survey of 53 farmers indicated that 60.4% of them cultivate crops twice a year, while 39.6% cultivate them three times. Eleven farmers have attested to an increase in the number of periods during which crops are cultivated throughout the year, as a consequence of the utilization of solar pumps.

A survey of 58 connected solar water pumps revealed that these pumps are used for an average of 4.07 h per day, with a daily output of 45.5 m^3 of water. Data collected (IoT data) from the 57 farmers surveyed showed an average consumption of 4,794 kWh per solar pump since installation. The average reduction in CO_2 emissions is 4.5 tons per pump, for a total reduction of 258.9 tons of CO_2 for the monitored pumps.

A total of 53 interviews were conducted and analyzed to assess the customer satisfaction rate (CSAT) of the Woomal Mbay solar water pump across all categories. The overall CSAT score is considered satisfactory, with an average customer satisfaction score of over 80%. The associated SamaPump Android application, which allows farmers to monitor their pump, the performance of the solar water pumps, and the after-sales service provided by the company were rated by respondents as satisfactory, with an average customer satisfaction score of over 80%, and the quality of the installation and study services provided for the solar water pump was rated as very satisfactory, with an average customer satisfaction score of over 90%.

4 Discussion

The results of this study on the use of solar pumps in the Niayes region of Senegal, via the Woomal Mbay project, demonstrate a notable shift from the use of diesel pumps to solar solutions. A substitution rate of 63.6% was observed among the farmers surveyed. This figure is consistent with trends observed in other parts of Africa, such as Morocco, where a significant majority (96%) of farmers expressed a desire to switch to solar pumps [5]. This convergence serves to illustrate a common recognition of the economic and environmental benefits of solar solutions, as evidenced by previous studies [5, 6]. Despite the initial challenge of high installation costs, the long-term benefits are clear [7].

From an economic standpoint, the utilization of solar water pumps has the potential to result in considerable annual cost savings for farmers. As evidenced in [5], the projected payback period for these pumps ranges from 2.7 to 3.6 years, with the adoption of solar pumps leading to an increase in profit margins, which have been estimated to range from 765.04 to 1137.50 USD per hectare.

Following the installation of solar pumps in the Niayes region, there has been an increase observed in the irrigated area and yields. These findings are also presented in [5, 8], where an extension of the irrigated area, the introduction of intercropping and an increase in the water supply for the same crops grown in areas of water scarcity have been noted. This increase in productivity is attributed to improved water availability and accessibility, which has enabled the expansion of cultivated areas.

A notable proportion of respondents expressed a high level of appreciation for solar water pumps. This sentiment was particularly evident in [9], where it was expressed by over 80% average customer satisfaction score. This indicates that solar pumping solutions are well-suited to the needs of farmers, as they can be easily adapted to suit a variety of circumstances.

In addition, Solar pumps also provide significant environmental benefits. During the initial deployment of solar pumps in the Niayes region, a total of 137.5 tons of CO_2 emissions were avoided over a six-month period. This reduction in greenhouse gas emissions is consistent with the results of other studies showing that solar energy is instrumental in promoting sustainable and environmentally responsible agricultural practices, thereby increasing Senegal's food self-sufficiency. Moreover, the adoption of solar solutions serves to stem the rural exodus by contributing to the creation of green jobs, which in turn reduces the unemployment rate in rural areas, as our results have shown.

5 Conclusion

The results of our study show that the installation of solar pumps in the Niayes region has led to significant changes. The Woomal Mbaye project has facilitated an increase in farmers' incomes and the adoption of more effective agricultural practices. The Woomal Mbaye project is a valuable contribution to improving food security in Senegal. Further research would be beneficial to assess the challenges associated with the widespread adoption of solar pumps in the Niayes region and to determine the potential consequences of using this technology on water resources.

References

1. World Food Programme Homepage. https://www.wfp.org/countries/senegal#:~:text=In%20total%2C%201.3%20million%20people,as%20deforestation%20in%20the%20south. Accessed 24 June 2024
2. Gaye, A.T., Lo, H.M., Sakho-Djimbira, S., Fall, M.S., Ndiaye, I.: Sénégal Revue du Contexte Socioéconomique, Politique et Environnemental. IED (Senegal) (2015)
3. Ministère de L'Environnement et de la Protection de la Nature: Rapport National Sur L'état de L'environnement Marin et Côtier. MEPN, Senegal (2002)
4. DIVECOSYS Homepage. https://www.divecosys.org/terrains/senegal/les-niayes. Accessed on 24 June 2024
5. Water, Energy & Food Security Resource Platform. https://www.water-energy-food.org//fr/resources/pompage-solaire-investigation-de-l-impact-des-installations-de-pompage-solaire-sur-la-consommation-d-eau-et-la-situation-socio-economique-d-un-agriculteur-dans-3-zones-pilotes-au-maroc. Accessed on 27 June 2024
6. Eclairages marché GET.invest. Sénégal: Les énergies renouvelables dans les chaînes de valeur agricoles / Modèle d'analyse de rentabilité. Pompage d'eau à l'énergie solaire photovoltaïque pour un programme d'irrigation à grande échelle répondant à une forte demande d'eau (2019)
7. Raïs, I., Faysse, N., Lejars, C.: Impacts d'un changement de politiques énergétiques sur les exploitations irriguées: éclairage sur la base d'un échantillon d'exploitations dans le Saiss (Maroc) (2016)
8. Gupta, E.: The impact of solar water pumps on energy-water-food-nexus: evidence from Rajasthan, India. Energy Policy 129, 598–609 (2019). https://doi.org/10.1016/j.enpol.2019.02.008
9. Liu, H., et al.: Technical modelling of solar photovoltaic water pumping system and evaluation of system performance and their socio-economic impact (2023). https://doi.org/10.1016/j.heliyon.2023.e16105

Public Participation in Municipal Solid Waste Management: A Mobile Persuasive App

Irene Arinaitwe[(✉)], Ssemakula Jonathan, Agnes Nakakawa, and Gilbert Maiga

School of Computing and Informatics Technology, Makerere University, Kampala, Uganda
`irenedats@gmail.com`

Abstract. Effective waste management relies on active public participation, yet engaging citizens in sustainable waste management remains a challenge. This study introduces a novel approach by developing a mobile application to support public involvement in waste management processes. Drawing upon the Persuasive Systems Design (PSD) framework, the application incorporates persuasive strategies to motivate users to adopt responsible waste handling behaviors. The developed mobile application features a set of functionalities aimed at facilitating user engagement and behavior change. These include a leaderboard to foster competition and motivation among users, a chat room for community interaction, a sorting guide for proper waste categorization, and a module for locating nearby waste collectors, thereby promoting accessibility. To assess the effectiveness and user satisfaction of the application, a structured walkthrough evaluation method was employed, complemented by questionnaire items based on the Attention, Relevance, Confidence, and Satisfaction (ARCS) model. Through this evaluation process, the study measured users' attention to the application's features, the relevance of its content to their needs, their confidence in using the application, and their overall satisfaction with the experience. The findings of the evaluation demonstrate the potential of the mobile application in effectively engaging users and promoting positive changes in waste management behaviors.

Keywords: waste management · public participation · persuasive technologies

1 Introduction

1.1 Background to the Study

Municipal solid waste (MSW) management has become a major worldwide concern with broad consequences for public health, urban development, and environmental sustainability (Hoornweg & Bhada-Tata 2012; Kaza et al. 2018). Globally, the rates at which municipal garbage is generated have significantly increased due to factors such as population growth, rapid urbanization, and changing consumer habits. According to World Bank projections, the amount of MSW generated worldwide is expected to soar by 70% between 2016 and 2050, reaching an estimated 3.4 billion tons annually by that time (Kaza et al. 2018). This increase is especially noticeable in emerging nations, such as those in sub-Saharan Africa, where urbanization is happening at a rate never seen before. Urbanization rates in sub-Saharan Africa have surpassed the development of waste management infrastructure, creating significant issues for the processing of municipal waste (Pai et al. 2013; Paul et al. 2019). Inadequate garbage collection services, careless dumping, and open burning of rubbish characterize the ensuing situation, which worsens environmental contamination and poses serious risks to public health (Alfthan et al. 2016; Parrot et al. 2009). Many developing countries in the region confront waste management difficulties that are exacerbated by inadequate financial resources and ineffective policies (Parrot et al. 2009; Wilson 2007). The environmental and health risks associated with improper waste disposal are of particular concern. Open burning of waste releases harmful pollutants into the air, contributing to respiratory diseases and air quality degradation (Awino & Apitz 2023). Improperly managed landfills can contaminate soil and water, posing long-term risks to ecosystems and human populations (Parrot et al. 2009). These challenges underscore the urgency of developing sustainable waste management strategies, especially in the context of developing countries where the impacts are most pronounced.

Public participation one of strategies for tackling the difficulties associated with managing municipal solid waste (Kaza et al. 2018). Involving communities in waste management initiatives promotes awareness, accountability, and group effort. However, ensuring public participation is a difficult task, especially in developing nations due to lack of knowledge and instruction on waste management techniques (Kaza et al. 2018; Wilson 2007), poor attitude towards waste management initiatives (Tennakoon et al. 2023) and lack of enforcement of policies (McAllister 2015). To overcome these obstacles and enable communities to actively participate in sustainable waste management practices, innovations and approaches related to behavioral change need to be explored. In the realm of Information communication technologies (ICT), persuasive technologies have a potential to motivate behavioral change to adopt sustainable practices without coercion or deception (B. J. Fogg 2003a).

The integration of persuasive technologies into waste management strategies presents a promising avenue for enhancing public participation. Persuasive technologies leverage principles from behavioral psychology and human-computer interaction to influence attitudes and behaviors (B. J. Fogg, 2003a). Mobile applications, in particular, have become ubiquitous and provide a convenient platform for delivering persuasive interventions (Aldenaini et al. 2020). By leveraging the reach and accessibility of mobile platforms, persuasive applications can effectively communicate information, provide real-time feedback, and encourage positive behavior change related to waste management practices. Therefore, this study seeks to explore the potential of a mobile persuasive application to enhance public participation in municipal solid waste management. Specifically, the study addressed the following specific objectives; To identify persuasive strategies based on behavioral theories that are implemented in mobile persuasive interventions. To develop a mobile persuasive application that support public participation in municipal solid waste management.

The rest of the paper is organized as follows; Sect. 2 presents related work. Section 3 presents materials and methods, Sect. 4 presents results, Sect. 5 concludes the paper.

2 Related Literature

2.1 Waste Management in the Post COVID-19 Era

The advent of the COVID-19 pandemic has significantly altered the landscape of municipal solid waste (MSW) management, introducing novel challenges and opportunities that warrant close examination. According to (Torkashvand et al. 2021) there is a need for adaptive strategies to navigate the complexities of waste management in the post-COVID. A notable effect of the epidemic has been an increase in the production of medical waste. The amount of infectious waste generated has increased as a result of people using personal protective equipment (PPE), disposable masks, and other medical items more frequently (Torkashvand et al. 2021). This calls for a reassessment of waste management techniques to take into account the particular difficulties associated with the sustainable and safe disposal of medical waste. Also, lockdowns and changes in consumer behavior during the pandemic have further influenced waste composition and generation patterns. Patrício Silva et al. (2020) highlight that altered consumption habits, increased reliance on home deliveries, and shifts in product packaging have led to changes in the types and amounts of waste being generated. This dynamic shift requires waste management systems to be agile and responsive to evolving patterns, prompting the need for innovative approaches to waste collection, sorting, and disposal. In addition, Singh et al. (2022) advocate for the development of resilient waste management systems capable of withstanding shocks and disruptions, such as those caused by a global health crisis. Resilience in waste management involves not only the ability to adapt to sudden changes in waste streams but also to withstand systemic challenges, ensuring the continuity of essential waste management services. Therefore, the post-COVID era calls for a comprehensive re-evaluation of waste management policies.

2.2 Municipal Solid Waste Management

Managing municipal solid waste (MSW) is one of the core services that any municipal authority should offer to the citizens. However, in the context of urban governance, offering sustainable MSW services is a challenging due to several interconnected factors, such as population growth, urbanization, and shifting consumption habits amidst poor infrastructure, inadequate funds and poor attitude towards waste management initiatives (Kaza et al. 2018; McAllister 2015). As noted by Parrot et al. (2009) most developing countries are characterized by inadequate infrastructure to manage the growing volumes of waste generated in urban areas. Also, the rate of urbanization is faster than the development of waste management infrastructure, leading to insufficient waste collection services and inefficient disposal techniques. The absence of infrastructure is particularly apparent in developing countries, such those in sub-Saharan Africa, where the region's meagre waste management capabilities are being taxed by an increasing number of urban residents (Pai et al. 2013). In addition, insufficient funding for waste collection, recycling initiatives, and the establishment of proper disposal facilities hinders the implementation of sustainable waste management practices in regions with limited economic resources (Wilson 2007). Finally, inconsistent and poorly enforced waste management policies contribute to a lack of standardization and coordination in waste disposal practices (Parrot et al.

2009). Thus, the absence of robust regulations can foster unregulated dumping and open burning of waste, further intensifying environmental pollution and jeopardizing public health.

The challenges in MSW management extend beyond mere logistical and infrastructural concerns. Thus, (Parrot et al. 2009), noted that there is a need for a nuanced approach that addresses the social and economic dimensions of waste management. Recognizing waste management as a complex socio-technical system, they advocate for a comprehensive understanding of local contexts, including the livelihood implications and community dynamics associated with waste management practices. This perspective aligns with the broader recognition that addressing MSW challenges requires integrated solutions that consider the cultural, economic, and social fabric of the communities involved (Daniel Hoornweg et al. 2013).

2.3 Persuasive Technologies Design

The field of persuasive technologies has evolved as a powerful tool for positively influencing user behavior through thoughtful and strategic design. Central to this evolution is Fogg's Behavior Model (B. J. Fogg 2003a), which lays the foundation for understanding the factors that drive behavior change through technology. Fogg's Behavior Model identifies three primary components that contribute to behavior change: motivation, ability, and triggers. Motivation refers to the user's desire to perform a behavior, ability involves the user's capability to execute the behavior, and triggers act as the catalysts that prompt the behavior (B. J. Fogg 2003a). Successful persuasive technology design leverages these components to create interventions that are not only effective but also engaging and user-friendly. In addition, designing persuasive technologies involves the intentional integration of design principles tailored to specific behaviors, motivations, and contexts as outlined in the persuasive systems design (PSD) framework (Oinas-Kukkonen & Harjumaa 2009). Thus, the persuasive systems design framework (PSD) is a valuable tool in persuasive technology design. PSD outlines several persuasive strategies that should implement in a persuasive intervention. The PSD 28 principles are categorized into four groups based on the task the principle is set to accomplish. The principles and their respective categories are described in Table 1.

User-centered approaches are also important in persuasive technology design because they ensure that interventions resonate with the target audience. Understanding the motivations, preferences, and challenges of users is fundamental to crafting persuasive strategies that align with their needs (Oinas-Kukkonen & Harjumaa, 2009). This involves conducting thorough user research to gather insights into the context in which the technology will be used and the behaviors it seeks to influence. In addition, feedback mechanisms play a crucial role in persuasive technology design, providing users with real-time information about their actions and progress. Positive reinforcement through feedback enhances user engagement and motivation by offering a sense of accomplishment and recognition (Chatterjee et al. 2009). Incorporating persuasive strategies such as reminders, rewards, and social influence further enhances the efficacy of these interventions. Reminders prompt users to perform desired behaviors, rewards provide incentives for compliance, and social influence leverages the power of social connections to foster behavior change (Oinas-Kukkonen & Harjumaa, 2009).

Table 1. Principles in PSD framework

Primary task support	Dialogue Support	Social support	System credibility support
Reduction	praise	Social learning	Trustworthiness
Tunneling	rewards	Social comparison	Expertise
Tailoring	reminders	Social facilitation	Surface credibility
personalization	Suggestion	Normative influence	Real world feel
Simulation	Similarity	cooperation	Authority
Self-monitoring	Liking	Competition	Third part endorsement
	Social role	Recognition	Verifiability

2.4 Application of Persuasive Technologies in Waste Management

Persuasive technology applications in waste management are still in infancy stages, with lots of potential for encouraging positive behavioral changes. Particularly, mobile persuasive applications have become powerful instruments that may encourage recycling, reduce waste, and enhance waste management practices generally (Bocken et al. 2014; Bretter et al. 2023). Persuasive technologies in waste management leverages social norms, gamification elements, and customized feedback to support environmentally friendly waste management practices (Bretter et al. 2023; Nkwo et al. 2018). For instance, gamification incorporates gaming features, such contests, challenges, and prizes, into waste management applications to boost user enthusiasm and involvement (Helmefalk & Rosenlund 2019). Therefore, gamification approaches transform waste reduction and recycling duties into enjoyable and competitive experiences that encourage community engagement and a sense of accomplishment. In addition, social norms play a pivotal role in shaping individual behaviors, and persuasive technologies leverage this influence to drive positive change. By highlighting and reinforcing socially desirable waste management practices, applications can create a sense of collective responsibility and encourage users to align their behaviors with accepted norms within their communities (Bretter et al. 2023). Finally, personalized feedback mechanisms within persuasive technologies provide users with tailored information about their waste management behaviors, fostering self-awareness and accountability (Suruliraj et al. 2020).

Successful implementation of persuasive technologies in waste management necessitates a comprehensive understanding of the local context, waste generation patterns, and community dynamics. Tailoring interventions to specific cultural and socioeconomic conditions ensures that persuasive strategies resonate with the target audience, increasing the likelihood of sustained behavior change (Thaler & Sunstein 2009). Also, iterative design processes, guided by user feedback and ongoing evaluation, are essential for the continuous improvement of persuasive technologies. This adaptive approach was employed by Suruliraj et al. (2020) to develop an initial medium-fidelity and also high-fidelity prototype of Bota App.

2.5 Behavioral Theories and Persuasive Strategies

In the design of persuasive technologies, several behavioral theories such as the Theory of Planned Behavior (TPB), Fogg's Behavioral Model (FBM), and the Transtheoretical model (TTM) have been used to analyze factors that motivate behavioral change. In this study we reviewed of persuasive strategies associated TPB and FBM. TPB has been used to influence attitudes and behaviors in the design of persuasive technologies. For example, (Sanabrian et al. (2023) used TPB to understand the determinants of physical activity in a HIV self-management intervention. In their study, self-monitoring/tracking, encouragement and achievement of goals were some of the persuasive strategies related to attitude, social norms and behavioral intention respectively. On the other hand, FBM has been used as a guiding framework to motivate target behaviors in various areas of persuasive technologies, such as smoking cessation (Abdul Karim et al. 2017) and banking (Lockton et al. 2010). Commonly employed persuasive strategies based on FBM includes; reminders that are associated with the trigger factor, simplifying a task (reduction) that is associated with ability factor and social learning that is related to motivation (Fogg 2009). TPB and FBM were adopted in this study because they are well established theories studying behavior change (Won 2018). Table 2 presents a review of persuasive strategies based on these theories.

Table 2. Persuasive strategies.

Theory	Persuasive strategies
Fogg's Behavioral Model (FBM)	**Triggers** Kairos (Fogg 2009), Reminders, pop-messages and auditory cues (Mallawaarachchi et al. 2023) **Ability** Simplification (Fogg 2003; Mallawaarachchi et al. 2023), Suggestions, repetitive tasks (Mallawaarachchi et al. 2023) **motivation** Reinforcement, rewards, social acceptance (Mallawaarachchi et al. 2023; Fogg 2003)
Theory of Planned Behavior (TPB)	**Emotional support** Tailoring, Liking, Reward, Similarity Surface, Credibility and Praise (Won 2018) **Social support** Authority, Expertise, Real-world feel, 3rdParty endorsements, Verifiability, Social Comparison, Normative Influence, Social learning, Recognition, Cooperation, Social facilitation, Competition, Surveillance (Won 2018) **Ability support** Tunneling, Reduction, Self-Monitoring, Simulation, Personalization, Rehearsal, Conditioning, Suggestion, Prompt, Call to action, Reminder, Cue, Request Offer, feedforward, feedback, Kairos (Won 2018), Social clues (Parmar et al. 2008)

3 Materials and Methods

3.1 Requirements Gathering

The process of developing a mobile persuasive application for supporting public participation in municipal solid waste management presented in this study started with gathering the functional requirements. Based on the persuasive strategies presented in Table 2, we reviewed literature to identify the system features that align with those persuasive strategies. Therefore, following functional requirements were identified and subsequently integrated into the application:

- Leaders Board: The application includes a leaders' board that not only ranks the highest-performing waste collectors but also provides detailed statistics and achievements for each collector. Leaderboards leverage principles of social comparison and competition to motivate users to engage more with the application (Hamari et al. 2014; Sánchez-Martín et al. 2017).
- Sorting Guide: In its commitment to promoting responsible waste disposal, the application features a highly informative sorting guide. This guide comprehensively educates users on the various waste types, their associated environmental impacts, and the recommended colours of bins for proper waste segregation. This feature is based on tailoring strategy (Oinas-Kukkonen, H., & Harjumaa 2009).
- Locate Nearby Collectors: The user-friendly app employs geolocation technology to assist users in locating nearby waste collectors who specialize in specific types of waste. Users can select collectors based on their proximity and specialization, ensuring that their waste is handled responsibly and expediently. This feature is based on the reduction persuasive strategy (Suruliraj et al. 2020; Nkwo et al. 2020)
- Schedule Pickup: Recognizing the importance of convenience and timeliness in waste management, the application offers a scheduling option. Users can set a date for waste collection, specifying their preferred time. When the scheduled date approaches, the app sends proactive notifications to remind the user to request a waste collector. This feature is based on the reduction and reminders strategy proposed by Fogg, (2003) and Oinas-Kukkonen & Harjumaa (2009).
- Chat Forum: To foster a sense of community and knowledge sharing among users and waste collectors, the application hosts a robust and moderated chat forum. Users can engage in discussions, share valuable tips and insights, and collectively address challenges related to waste collection. This feature is based on the social facilitation persuasive strategy (Nkwo et al. 2020).
- Impact Reporting: In an era where transparency and accountability are paramount, the application empowers waste collectors to provide comprehensive impact reports. Waste collectors can use the app to document what has been done with the waste they have collected, including whether it has been recycled, repurposed, or otherwise responsibly managed. This reporting feature not only promotes transparency but also encourages waste collectors to prioritize sustainable waste disposal practices.
- Rate Us Page: User feedback is integral to enhancing the application's quality and functionality continually. To facilitate this, the application includes a dedicated "Rate Us" page. Here, users can provide detailed feedback, suggestions, and ratings based on their experiences. These ratings and comments are displayed within the app, providing transparency and demonstrating a commitment to continuous improvement.

3.2 System Design and Implementation

The development of a mobile app presented in this study leverages the Flutter framework for the front-end and Firebase for the back-end infrastructure. The user interface design, facilitated by Flutter's flexibility and cross-platform capabilities, prioritized user experience through collaborative efforts with waste management experts and potential users (citizens), resulting in an intuitive and visually appealing interface. Key aspects included user-centered design, visually appealing aesthetics, responsive layouts, and accessibility features to ensure inclusivity for all users, while the robust back-end powered by Firebase facilitated real-time database interactions, secure user authentication, and efficient cloud functions.

Furthermore, specialized features such as the sorting guide, scheduling feature, and chat forum moderation were implemented in collaboration with environmental experts and waste management professionals. These features enhance user engagement and contribute to the application's differentiation by providing valuable resources on waste sorting, seamless scheduling capabilities, and fostering a supportive community within the chat forum. Overall, the application's development process prioritized both functionality and user experience, resulting in a comprehensive solution poised to address contemporary waste management challenges effectively.

4 Presentation of Results (Mobile App)

This section offers an in-depth overview of the application's key features, functions, and its overarching objective of transforming waste management practices by actively involving both waste collectors and the wider public.

Leaders Board: Fostering Healthy Competition
The achievements of waste collectors. This feature serves not only as a source of motivation but also as a mechanism to encourage healthy competition within the community. Waste collectors can view their rankings, track their progress, and vie for the top spots, ultimately driving them to collect more waste and contribute to a cleaner environment. Figure 1 presents a leader board implemented in this study.

Sorting Guide: Promoting Proper Waste Disposal
The Sorting Guide feature provides users with invaluable information about different waste types and the corresponding colours of bins for proper waste segregation. By equipping users with knowledge, this feature plays a pivotal role in mitigating the environmental impact of waste mismanagement. Figure 1 presents a sorting guide.

Locate Nearby Collectors: Facilitating Convenient Waste Disposal
Users seeking to dispose of specific types of waste can effortlessly locate nearby waste collectors specialized in handling their particular waste category. The integration of geolocation technology ensures the accuracy of results, connecting users with collectors in their vicinity. This feature streamlines waste disposal, making it more efficient and convenient for the public. This feature is shown in Fig. 2.

Public Participation in Municipal Solid Waste Management 17

a) leaders board   b) sorting guide

Fig. 1. A leader board and a sorting guide

Schedule Pickup: Timely and Hassle-Free Waste Collection

The Scheduling feature empowers users to set waste collection dates at their convenience. As the scheduled date approaches, the application issues notifications to remind users to request a waste collector. This proactive approach to waste collection ensures that waste is disposed of in a timely and hassle-free manner, contributing to cleaner neighborhoods.

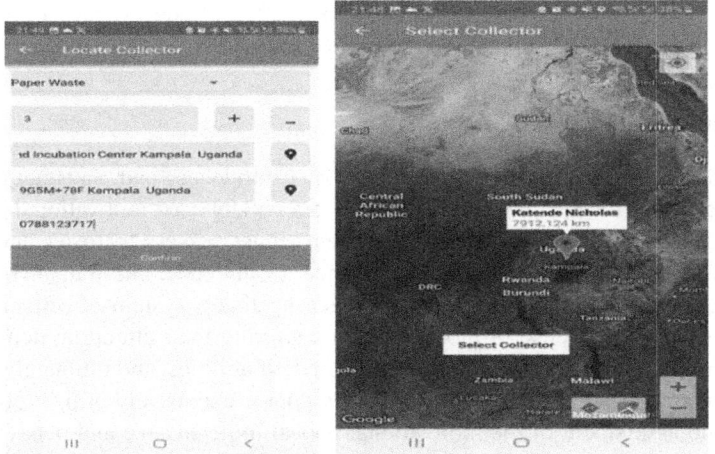

c) locating waste collector

Fig. 2. Locating a waste collector and scheduling pickup.

Chat Forum: Community Collaboration and Knowledge Sharing

The Chat Forum fosters a sense of community among waste collectors. It serves as a virtual space where collectors can engage in discussions, share tips, and address challenges related to waste collection. This collaborative environment not only empowers collectors with valuable insights but also strengthens the bonds within the waste management community. The chat room feature is presented in Fig. 3.

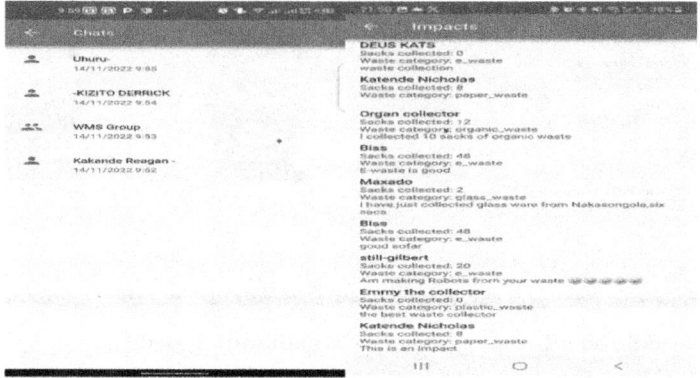

d) The chat room and impact rating feature

Fig. 3. The chat room

The login screen is designed to cater to users' preferences, offering personalized options for logging in using either their email address, or phone number. Additionally, new users have the flexibility to sign up using their email, phone number, or Facebook accounts. This approach ensures that users can access the application through their preferred method of authentication, whether it be via social media credentials or traditional email and phone authentication methods. This method of authentication leverages the tailoring strategy. The login feature is presented in Fig. 4.

4.1 Evaluation of the App

This study adopted the (Attention, Relevance, Confidence, and Satisfaction) ARCS model to evaluate the app. The ARCS model is a widely used motivational model that emphasizes four essential qualities that systems must possess to foster and maintain motivation in individuals: Attention, Relevance, Confidence, and Satisfaction (Keller 1987). These components are integral in ensuring that a system effectively engages users and cultivates a sense of motivation by capturing their attention, demonstrating relevance to their needs, instilling confidence in their abilities, and ultimately satisfying their desires or goals. The ARCS motivation model is extensively utilized to guide the creation and assessment of the motivational appeal in persuasive and behavior change systems (Derbali & Frasson 2010).

A.

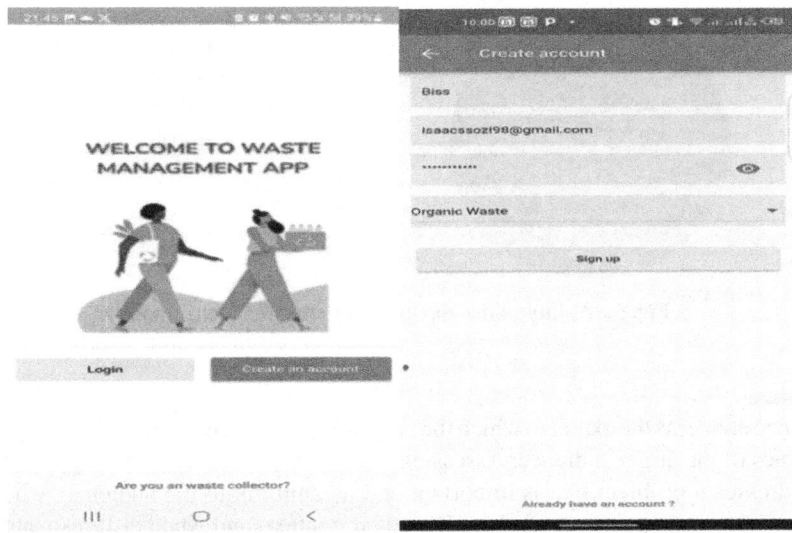

e) creating an account

Fig. 4. Login page

A total of 50 participants were conveniently sampled from the students of Makerere University, college of computing and information sciences to participate in the evaluation of the app. Participants were given the opportunity to interact with the system independently for a period of three weeks. Following this period, two walkthrough sessions were conducted by the researcher and a research assistant, each lasting 45 min. During the sessions, participants explored all app features and completed tasks such as locating waste collectors, engaging in chat room discussions with fellow participants, and brainstorming on the waste sorting guide.

After the walkthrough sessions, participants completed online survey questionnaire, which included questions about the app's ability to capture their attention, the relevance of the information provided, their level of satisfaction with app features, and their confidence in the app. The study adopted a motivational appeal questionnaire based on the ARCS model proposed by Orji et al. (2019). A total of 31 responses were downloaded and analysed. The subsequent subsections present the results from the evaluation of the prototype.

In this section we present findings of prototype evaluation. The findings are arranged based on ARCS model constructs as follows.

Attention

In persuasive applications, the attention concerns attracting and engaging the target audience to persuade them effectively. It involves using visual and multimedia elements, emotional appeal, intriguing questions or challenges, personalization and relevance, as well as attention-grabbing headlines and openings to stimulate curiosity, evoke emotions. The study responses in relation to the ability of the app to user's attention is presented in Fig. 5.

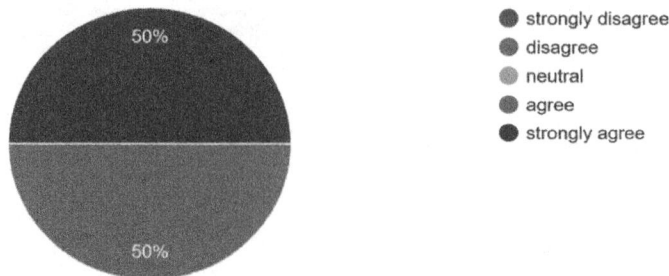

Fig. 5. Ability of the app to capture the user's attention.

Relevance

Relevance concerns the extent to which the persuasive app aligns with the needs, interests, and values of the target audience. Assessing relevance involves considering whether the app addresses a problem that is important and meaningful to the audience, whether it provides information that are applicable to their context, and whether it resonates with their beliefs, attitudes, and priorities. The study findings on the relevance of the app are presented in Fig. 6.

Fig. 6. Relevance of the app

Based on the findings illustrated in Fig. 6, 25% of the respondents expressed strong agreement regarding the application's relevance and its effective addressing of significant issues. Additionally, 50% of the respondents indicated agreement that the app provided crucial and pertinent information. Meanwhile, another 25% of the respondents remained neutral in their assessment.

Confidence

Confidence refers to the level of trust and assurance that users have in the app's effectiveness, reliability, and usability. Assessing confidence involves examining factors such as the app's functionality, ease of use, security measures, and the credibility of the information provided. Users need to feel confident that the app will accurately collect and process data, provide valuable insights or solutions, and facilitate meaningful contributions to waste management efforts. The study findings in relation to how participants felt confident in using the app is presented in Fig. 7.

Fig. 7. Users perceived confidence in the app

The findings presented in Fig. 7 show that all the respondents agreed that the app had the necessary functionalities and was easy to use.

Satisfaction
Satisfaction refers to the degree to which users feel content and fulfilled with their experience using the app. Evaluating satisfaction in this study involved assessing user experience, ease of navigation, responsiveness, and the effectiveness of features in addressing users' needs and preferences. Users should feel satisfied with the app's performance, functionality, and the value it provides in facilitating their engagement in waste management activities. The study findings on ease of use and pleasure and enjoyment interacting with the app are presented in Fig. 8 and Fig. 9 respectively.

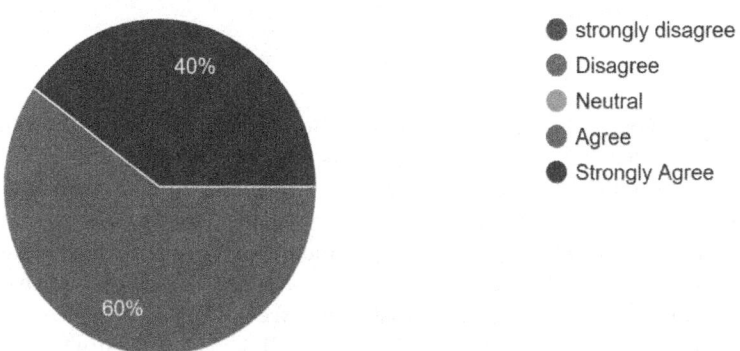

Fig. 8. Ease of use of the app

Based on the study findings in Fig. 8, 40% of the respondents strongly agreed that the app was easy to use. Also, 60% of the participants agreed that the system was easy to use.

The study findings depicted in Fig. 9 reveal that 20% of the participants found pleasure and enjoyment in using the app. Conversely, 80% of the participants remained neutral in their assessment.

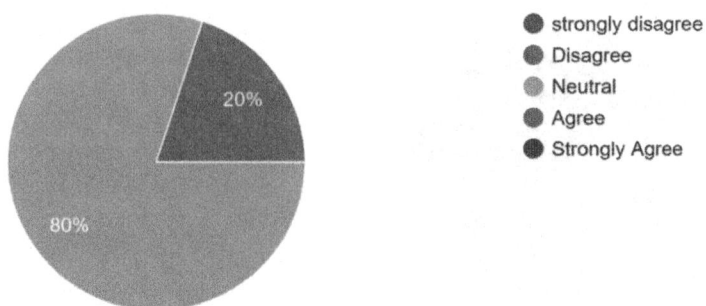

Fig. 9. Enjoyment using the app

5 Limitations and Future Work

The features incorporated into the mobile application detailed in this study were drawn from a review of existing apps in relevant literature. However, there remains a necessity to further refine this application by incorporating both functional and non-functional requirements identified during field studies. Additionally, customization of the application is essential to address contextual challenges specific to engaging citizens in municipal waste management processes.

The evaluation of the application was conducted among university students from the College of Computing and Information Sciences, who possessed computing knowledge. Nonetheless, to comprehensively assess its effectiveness, further evaluation is required involving citizens and municipal authorities' staff in major cities across Uganda.

6 Conclusion

The development of a mobile persuasive application aimed at supporting citizen involvement in waste management represents a significant stride towards leveraging technology to address pressing environmental challenges. Persuasive solutions can take various forms, ranging from mobile applications like the one developed in this study to interactive websites, social media campaigns, and community-based initiatives. These solutions capitalize on behavioral theories and persuasive strategies to induce positive changes in attitudes and behaviors towards sustainable practices. By integrating features derived from literature on persuasive strategies, specifically aligned with constructs from the theory of planned behavior and Fogg's behavioral model, the application offers a nuanced approach to promoting pro-environmental behaviors. The evaluation of the application through a walkthrough session and Likert scale questionnaire yielded promising results, indicating favorable perceptions among participants regarding attention, relevance, confidence, and satisfaction levels—essential components of the ARCS model. This positive reception underscores the potential efficacy of employing persuasive technology in fostering meaningful engagement with waste management practices. As we continue to explore the intersection of technology and behavior change, it becomes increasingly evident that mobile applications hold immense potential as vehicles for promoting positive environmental stewardship. By harnessing the principles of persuasion and leveraging insights from behavioral theories, such applications can empower individuals to make informed choices and contribute meaningfully to the collective effort towards waste reduction and environmental sustainability.

References

Abdul Karim, N. S., AlHarbi, A., AlKadhi, B., AlOthaim, N.: Mobile Application on Smoking Cessation Based on Persuasive Design Theor, (2017)

Aldenaini, N., Alqahtani, F., Orji, R., Sampalli, S.: Trends in persuasive technologies for physical activity and sedentary behavior: a systematic review. Front. Artif. Intell. **3**, 7 (2020)

Alfthan, B., et al.: Waste Management Outlook for Mountain Regions Sources and Solutions (UNEP, GRID-Arendal, & ISWA. (eds.)). Arendal and Vienna (2016). www.iswa.org

Awino, F.B., Apitz, S.E.: Solid waste management in the context of the waste hierarchy and circular economy frameworks: an international critical review. In: Integrated Environmental Assessment and Management. John Wiley and Sons Inc. (2023). https://doi.org/10.1002/ieam.4774

Bocken, N.M.P., Short, S.W., Rana, P., Evans, S.: A literature and practice review to develop sustainable business model archetypes. In: Journal of Cleaner Production, vol. 65, pp. 42–56 (2014). https://doi.org/10.1016/j.jclepro.2013.11.039

Bretter, C., Unsworth, K.L., Russell, S.V., Quested, T.E., Kaptan, G., Doriza, A.: Food waste interventions: Experimental evidence of the effectiveness of environmental messages. J. Cleaner Prod. **414** (2023). https://doi.org/10.1016/j.jclepro.2023.137596

Chatterjee, S., ACM Digital Library.: Proceedings of the 4th International Conference on Persuasive Technology. ACM (2009)

Hoornweg, D., Bhada-Tata, P., Kennedy, C.: Waste production mustpeak this century. Nature**502**(615)

Derbali, L., Frasson, C.: Prediction of players motivational states using electrophysiological measures during serious game play. In: 2010 10th IEEE International Conference on Advanced Learning Technologies, pp. 498–502 (2010)

Fogg, B.: A behavior model for persuasive design. ACM Int. Conf. Proc. Ser. **350** (2009). https://doi.org/10.1145/1541948.1541999

Fogg, B.J.: Persuasive technology : using computers to change what we think and do. Morgan Kaufmann Publishers (2003a)

Fogg, B.J.:Persuasive Technology: Using Computers to Change What We Think and Do. Morgan Kaufmann Publishers Inc (2003b)

Hamari, J., Koivisto, J., Sarsa, H.: Does gamification work?--a literature review of empirical studies on gamification. In: 2014 47th Hawaii International Conference on System Sciences, pp. 3025–3034 (2014)

Helmefalk, M., Rosenlund, J.: Make waste fun again! A gamification approach to recycling. In: International Conference on ArtsIT, Interactivity and Game Creation, pp. 415–426 (2019)

Hoornweg, D., Bhada-Tata, P.:What a Waste : A Global Review of Solid Waste Management. Urban development series. World Bank (2012)

Kaza, S., Yao, L., Bhada-Tata, P., Van Woerden, F., Kaza, S., Yao, L.: At a Glance: a global picture of solid waste management. In: What a Waste 2.0: A Global Snapshot of Solid Waste Management to 2050 (2018). https://doi.org/10.1596/978-1-4648-1329-0_ch2

Keller, J.M.: Development and use of the ARCS model of instructional design. J. Instr. Dev. **10**(3), 2 (1987). https://doi.org/10.1007/BF02905780

Lockton, D., Harrison, D., Stanton, N.A.: The design with intent method: a design tool for influencing user behaviour. Appl. Ergon. **41**(3), 382–392 (2010)

McAllister, J.: Factors influencing solid-waste management in the developing world (2015)

Nkwo, M., Orji, R., Ugah, J.: Mobile persuasion: promoting clean and sustainable environment. ACM Int. Conf. Proc. Ser. 259–262 (2018). https://doi.org/10.1145/3283458.3283515

Nkwo, M., Suruliraj, B., Orji, R., Ugah, J.: Socially-oriented persuasive strategies and sustainable behavior change: implications for designing for environmental sustainability. PERSUASIVE (Adjunct) (2020)

Oinas-Kukkonen, H., Harjumaa, M.: Persuasive systems design: Key issues, process model, and system features. In: Communications of the Association for Information Systems, pp. 28–40 (2009)

Oinas-Kukkonen, H., Harjumaa, M.: Persuasive systems design: Key issues, process model, and system features. Commun. Assoc. Inf. Syst. **24**(1), 485–500 (2009). https://doi.org/10.17705/1cais.02428

Orji, R., Reilly, D., Oyibo, K., Orji, F.A.: Deconstructing persuasiveness of strategies in behaviour change systems using the ARCS model of motivation. Behav. Inf. Technol. **38**(4), 319–335 (2019)

Pai, R.R., Rodrigues, L.L.R., Hebbar, S.: Impact of urbanization on municipal solid waste management: a system dynamics approach manipal academy of higher education (2013). https://www.researchgate.net/publication/293061721

Parrot, L., Sotamenou, J., Dia, B.K.: Municipal solid waste management in Africa: strategies and livelihoods in Yaoundé Cameroon. Waste Manag. **29**(2), 986–995 (2009). https://doi.org/10.1016/j.wasman.2008.05.005

Patrício Silva, A.L., et al.: Rethinking and optimising plastic waste management under COVID-19 pandemic: policy solutions based on redesign and reduction of single-use plastics and personal protective equipment. Sci. Total Environ. **742** (2020). https://doi.org/10.1016/j.scitotenv.2020.140565

Paul, S.-M., Kwaku, O.-O., Albert, A.A., Theophilus, K.A., Richard, T.O.: Solid waste management in urban communities in Ghana: a case study of the Kumasi metropolis. Afr. J. Environ. Sci. Technol. **13**(9), 342–353 (2019). https://doi.org/10.5897/ajest2019.2713

Sanabria, G., Bushover, B., Ashrafnia, S., Cordoba, E., Schnall, R.: Understanding physical activity determinants in an HIV self-management intervention: qualitative analysis guided by the theory of planned behavior. JMIR Form. Res.**7**(1), (2023)

Sánchez-Martín, J., Cañada-Cañada, F., Dávila-Acedo, M.A.: Just a game? Gamifying a general science class at university: collaborative and competitive work implications. Thinking Skills Creativ. **26**, 51–59 (2017)

Kaza, S., Yao, L., Bhada-Tata, P., Van Woerden, F.: What a Waste 2 . 0A Global Snapshot of Solid Waste Management to 2050 (2018)

Singh, E., Kumar, A., Mishra, R., Kumar, S.: Solid waste management during COVID-19 pandemic: recovery techniques and responses. Chemosphere 288 (2022). https://doi.org/10.1016/j.chemosphere.2021.132451

Suruliraj, B., Olagunju, T., Nkwo, M., Orji, R.: Bota: a personalized persuasive mobile app for sustainable waste management. IN: CEUR Workshop Proceedings, vol. 2629 (2020)

Tennakoon, G.A., Rameezdeen, R., Chileshe, N.: Identifying factors affecting the low uptake of reprocessed construction materials: a systematic literature review. Waste Manage. Res. **41**(4), 781–800 (2023)

Thaler, R.H., Sunstein, C.: NUDGE: Improving Decisions About Health, Wealth, and Happiness (2009). http://www.cihr-irsc.gc.ca/e/42882.html

Torkashvand, J., Jafari, A. J., Godini, K., Kazemi, Z., Kazemi, Z., Farzadkia, M.: Municipal solid waste management during COVID-19 pandemic: a comparison between the current activities and guidelines (2021). https://doi.org/10.1007/s40201-020-00591-9/Published

Wilson, D.C.: Development drivers for waste management. Waste Manage. Res. **25**(3), 198–207 (2007). https://doi.org/10.1177/0734242X07079149

Won, J.: PSPB (Persuasive service design strategies based on the theory of planned behavior) methodology for user behavior modification. Arch. Des. Res. **31**(3), 17–30 (2018)

A Risk-Based Pedestrian Crossing Decision Model for Traffic Simulation in African Urban Traffic

Modou Gueye(✉), Ndiouma Bame, and Mamadou Thiongane

Université Cheikh Anta Diop, Dakar, Senegal
{modou2.gueye,ndiouma.bame,mamadou.thiongane}@ucad.edu.sn

Abstract. Traffic jams are a particularly difficult global problem. They cause considerable economic losses. These losses are particularly significant for large cities in developing countries such as Dakar. Hence the need to optimize urban traffic by studying the impact of the various factors determining traffic flow.

Traffic simulators are an inexpensive way of studying and improving traffic flow. However, most existing simulators are adapted to the traffic context of cities in developed countries, for which they were primarily created. Their use in African cities such as Dakar would be ineffective if they were not adapted to the local context, where pedestrian crosswalks are almost non-existent.

In this work, we propose a pedestrian decision model for crossing the road in illegal locations. We demonstrate its effectiveness through three simulation scenarios using SUMO, an open-source, microscopic, and very popular traffic simulation package designed to handle large networks.

Keywords: Traffic Simulation · Pedestrian Crossing · Behavior Modeling

1 Introduction

The growing urbanization of the world's major cities poses enormous challenges for transport systems. A significant proportion of the economic losses is directly linked to poorly performing transport systems, which causes numerous traffic jams on the roads [4,18]. This loss is particularly significant for large cities in developing countries such as Dakar, where it is estimated to 235 billion West African CFA francs[1]. Hence the need to optimize urban traffic by studying the impact of the various factors determining traffic flow. For instance, Bhardwaj *et al.* find that Nairobi, the capital of Kenya, experiences three times the mean jam time per road segment as compared to São Paulo and New York City [3]. They assert that chaotic driving patterns and traffic mismanagement in the developing

---

[1] https://shorturl.at/eqELS.

world cities lead to tighter traffic curves, more intense jams and overall lower road capacity utilization, which explains their observed data. Thus they conclude that the problem of traffic congestion in developing countries cannot be solved entirely by building new infrastructure, but also requires smart management of existing road infrastructure.

Since experimenting traffic on a real environment is not practical, computer simulation is widely used to study the flow of traffic at least since 1955 [16]. Indeed the use of numerical simulations enables the benchmarking of several scenarios for organizing transport systems at lower cost, and provides a clear view of the impact of any future road or other development. Thus many urban traffic simulators have been designed and proposed [8,15].

Through the years they have evolved to use better simulation paradigms, better models and eventually cover whole traffic networks instead of specific locations [19]. However, it should be noted that they are almost all designed for the highly organized transport systems of developed countries which have different operating modes compared to cities in developing countries. Examples include reserved lanes for two-wheelers or buses, the presence of crosswalks and traffic lights at most intersections.

As a result, the use of traffic simulators primarily made for developed countries in a less regulated context proves less effective, unless adapted [17]. Some authors have already tackled the issue of adapting simulators to the urban traffic context of several cities. Most have focused on modeling driving styles that can vary from one country to another [17]. Fewer have focused on pedestrian behavior and the factors determining road crossing decisions [9,10]. Moreover they focus on modeling pedestrian behavior at signalized crossings or regularized crosswalks [9] and thus do not consider the behavior of pedestrians crossing a road at a location other than a designated crossing. In addition they use a gap acceptance model that represents how a pedestrian decides when to cross a road, based on the frequency and speed of approaching vehicles, while considering the spacing between them. The aim of this work is to develop a pedestrian model more suited to cities lacking organization and crosswalks. In this context, several factors contribute to the pedestrian crossing decision. Our model takes into account most of the decision factors cited in the literature, including age, gender, impatience, speed and distance of approaching vehicles. We demonstrate the effectiveness of our model by simulating it with real traffic data collected in Dakar. The sequel of this paper is organized as follows. In Sect. 2, we present a brief review on related works on pedestrian crossing decision models. Section 3 details our pedestrian crossing decision model based on risk-taking relative to sociodemographic factors and pedestrian waiting time, on the one hand, and traffic conditions, on the other. We address also the integration of the model with a popular traffic simulator we used. Then in Sect. 4, we expose the simulation scenarios we ran with our model and discuss the results we obtained. Three scenarios are considered in this section. Finally, in Sect. 5 we conclude the paper.

2 Literature Review

As cities continue to grow, increasingly complex, high-performance transportation systems are being developed. Computer simulation is therefore widely used in research into urban traffic modeling, planning and transport system development.

Traffic simulation models are generally classified according to their field of application: microscopic, mesoscopic or macroscopic modeling. Macroscopic models are models of traffic in a continuous flow, mesoscopic models consider individual vehicles, while microscopic models capture the behavior of vehicles and drivers in detail. The latter can take into account a vehicle's interactions with other vehicles and pedestrians, its lane changes, its reaction to incidents and its load-dependent behavior. As a result, microscopic models are better suited to simulating pedestrian behavior models, as they enable a very fine simulation of traffic [8,15].

As we said in our introduction, most microscopic simulators use a simple decision model for pedestrians at crosswalks. The behavior of pedestrians crossing a road at a location other than regular crosswalks is not well taking into account: a pedestrian wishing to cross the street at an uncontrolled intersection can only do so if its expected time slot for using the intersection does not interfere with that of an approaching vehicle [1,9].

Recent research has thus been carried out to improve this behavior by integrating more realistic decision models that consider additional factors motivating the decision of pedestrians to cross at red lights or in areas without regular crosswalks [1,5,10,12].

In [10], Garrido *et al.* used Unity3D to create an external 3D representation of a running simulation, they are able to create and control pedestrians. This also opened the possibility to use virtual reality immersed subjects to participate in the simulation, but it is limited to manage only a few number of pedestrians. Amini *et al.* used a game theoretic approach to model pedestrian road crossings [1]. A safety level is embedded into their model to evaluate the collision risk depending on a wide range of factors such as pedestrians' group size and density, number of vehicles approaching the crossing, and approaching lane for both pedestrians and vehicle.

Lawrence *et al.* utilize a simpler model based on a gap acceptance model that represents how a pedestrian decides when to cross a road, based on the frequency and speed of approaching vehicles, while considering the spacing between them [12]. Therefore their gap acceptance model allows the pedestrians to choose to cross all lanes in one go, when safe to do so, known as *Double Gap* or *one stage crossing*. Cai *et al.* propose to use machine learning to optimize and improve pedestrian crossing predictions in intelligent transportation systems, where the crossing process is vital to pedestrian crossing behavior [5]. They applied OpenCV image recognition and machine learning methods to analyze the mechanisms of pedestrian crossing behaviors. However they do not consider pedestrians' gender and age category in their work.

Like [5], our proposal uses machine learning to take decision but it differs from all these cited works in the fact that we consider sociodemographic factors (e.g., gender and age) in addition to pedestrians' group influence and traffic state. This is the greatest difference between our work and theirs.

3 A Risk-Based Pedestrian Crossing Decision Model

Like many cities in developing countries, Dakar lacks regular crosswalks on several streets, particularly in its suburbs. As a result, crossing the carriageway is a big risk for pedestrians, who have to decide on the right timing to start crossing. In the literature, a number of studies have focused on the factors influencing pedestrians' decisions. It goes without saying that pedestrians base their decision to cross on the risk of collision, given their speed and that of vehicles. For instance, this is the basis of the current model implements into SUMO, an open source, microscopic and very popular traffic simulation package [9]. This model is not adapted to African urban traffic where the lack of crosswalks leads pedestrians who do not want to wait longer to take more risks.

Moreover the literature shows that age and gender are the two individual factors that primarily determine the degree of risk-taking by pedestrians, in addition to the length of time they spend waiting at the roadside [11]. Added to this is the influence of other pedestrians during the crossing [13]. Pedestrians tend to join those crossing if they are not far away. In this way, they take few risks by taking advantage of the slower speed of cars to avoid pedestrians.

This work want to consider all these factors to build an efficient decision model. Therefore, our contribution consist in three items: i) collection data about pedestrian crossing decision in real traffic for our learning process, ii) designing and evaluating a risk-based crossing model by using machine learning algorithms and iii) simulating urban traffic with the model and evaluating its efficiency.

3.1 Data Collection

To build our risk-based decision model which takes more account of the pedestrian sociodemographic characteristics and pedestrian flow, we first collected pedestrian crossing data using video camera as illustrated in Fig. 1 where one can see a group of pedestrians illegally crossing the road on one of Dakar's main avenues.

We collected nearly ten hours of video over three days at peak traffic times. In a second step, we analyze the videos and manually build a structured dataset with the following information:

- the pedestrian gender (man or woman)
- the pedestrian age category (visually estimated among: young, adult, senior)
- the pedestrian waited time (in seconds)
- fastest vehicle speed to arrive (calculated from the videos, in m/s)
- the distance of the vehicle (estimated from the videos, in meters)

Fig. 1. Illegal pedestrian crossings.

- the number of pedestrians who are currently crossing the road
- and the pedestrian decision to cross or not the road

Table 1 shows a sample of 1850 rows we prepared for our machine learning phase.

Table 1. A sample of the dataset

Gender	Age	Waiting	Car Speed	Car Distance	Crossing Ped.	Decision
woman	adult	2	10	50	0	crossing
man	adult	1	17	25	0	waiting
man	young	4	5	37	0	crossing

3.2 Modeling Pedestrian Crossing via the Risk of Accidents

Once the data was collected, we compared the performance of eight machine learning models: logistic regression (LR), support vector machines (SVM), k-nearest neighbors (KNN), naive Bayes (NB), decision trees (DT), random forests (RF), gradient boosting (GB) and multilayer perceptrons (MLP).

We have splitted the dataset into training and testing data (75% and 25% respectively). We then tested the performance of each of the machine learning models ten times, renewing the training and test data each time. The Table 2 shows their average accuracies over all experiments.

From our testing, SVM models appear better than the rest in predicting pedestrian crossing probabilities. We used it for pedestrian crossing prediction in our traffic simulations.

Table 2. Average accuracies of the machine learning models

LR	SVM	KNN	NB	DT	RF	GB	MLP
90.33%	91.67%	83.33%	75%	58.33%	66.67%	75%	85.67%

3.3 Simulation of Urban Mobility (SUMO)

For our simulation, we decide to use Eclipse SUMO [14]. The reason is that SUMO is an open source, highly portable, microscopic and continuous multi-modal traffic simulation package designed to handle large networks. It is widely used [10]. SUMO allows modeling of inter-modal traffic systems - including road vehicles, public transport and pedestrians. Despite its popularity, it was only in 2014 that SUMO included pedestrian modeling in its package. Its model, called stripping model, allows a pedestrian wishing to cross the street at an uncontrolled intersection to only do so if its estimates it has enough time to cross the road without the arrival of coming vehicles [9].

SUMO offers several tools which automate core tasks for designing a road network, creating a simulation data and making traffic simulations. Therefore it allows network imports from GIS platforms like OpenStreetMap, the visualization of simulations and the calculation of many output data like CO_2 emission or lost time on a road. To end, SUMO can integrate custom models and provides various APIs to remotely control the simulation.

Along these APIs, we cite the Traffic Control Interface (TRACI) which leverages the use of external application in combination with SUMO in order to manipulate the simulation states and variables in real time and so enables the control of vehicles and pedestrians through its interface. We used TRACI to control the pedestrian crossing decisions in our simulation.

Figure 2 presents the architecture of our simulation. In one side, we have SUMO core functionalities which run the traffic simulation. SUMO integrates also the TraCI server which uses TCP communication. The latter combines our risk-based decision model with the TraCI client API via Python scripts.

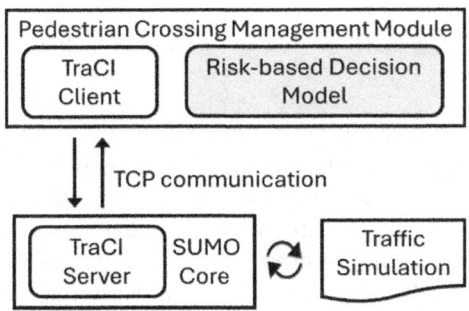

Fig. 2. Simulation architecture.

4 Experimentation

In order to demonstrate the suitability of our decision model to the traffic context of cities such as Dakar, we carried out a series of simulations and compared the performance of our model with that currently implemented in the SUMO simulator.

In this section, we first describe the configuration of our simulation and then present the results we obtained and their analysis.

4.1 Simulation Setup

Road Network. For our study, we chose a section of one of the heavily used highway of Dakar, called the VDN (Voie de Dégagement Nord). The configuration of Dakar makes this highway often busy. Indeed, the suburbs are located to the north and northeast of the peninsula, while economic activity is mainly concentrated to the south, with the administrative center and Dakar port. Figure 3(a), taken from the work of [6], illustrates the bimodal nature of the region.

The section corresponds to the part of VDN highway covering the west side of Keur Gorgui quarter, as highlighted in Fig. 3(b).

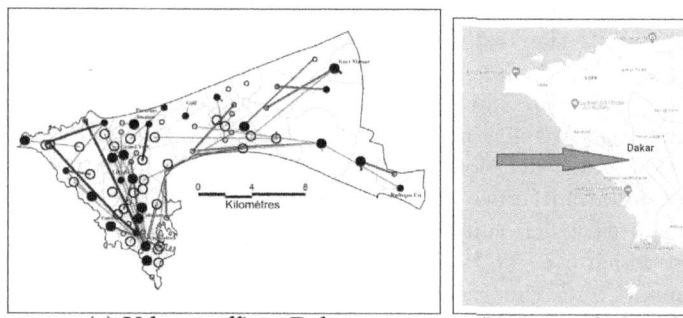

(a) Urban traffic at Dakar   (b) Located place for the simulation

Fig. 3. Dakar region and urban mobility.

As the city is economically very dynamic, many employees work there and take public transport to go working. Out of laziness or ignorance, many of them do not cross the road at the crosswalk under the autobridge. They prefer to illegally cross the road at the stop where they are. Figure 4 shows in green the position of the crosswalk to be used by pedestrians, in orange the area most used by pedestrians to illegally cross the freeway, and in red the stretch of road directly impacted by these illegal crossings. In the following, we will refer to this road stretch by *Edge 1*.

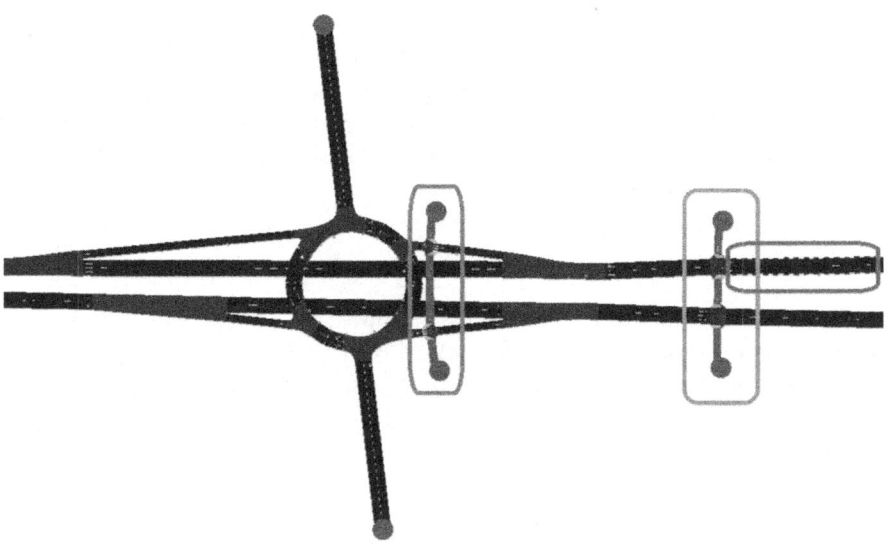

Fig. 4. Studied road network section.

Traffic Data. We used data from the Dakar urban master plan by 2035 [7]. Chapter 12 of this report deals with the project to improve junctions on the VDN highway. This chapter alone provides sufficient information on the current traffic. In particular, it includes statistics on the daily number of vehicles at normal hours at the junction. Similarly, on page 252 of the same document, traffic evolution forecasts are drawn up for the year 2035^2.

On the basis of all these data and the breakdown of the Senegalese vehicle fleet as established in chapter 13 of ANSD report on the economic and social situation in Senegal from 2017 to 2018, published in July 2020 [2], we estimated a number of vehicles to consider during our experimental time slot corresponding to the peak hour between 8am and 9am.

Finally, we validated the reliability of our values by comparing them with traffic survey data collected in July 2016 by students of the graduate school of applied economics (ESEA) as part of a project with the Dakar urban transport executive board (CETUD). As a reminder, the main goal of the survey was to collect data on the frequency of public transport vehicles and their occupancy rate on certain Dakar roads [6]. The local types of vehicle targeted were *Dakar Dem Dikk* buses, *Tata* minibuses and *Ndiaga Ndiaye* and *Car Rapide* vans. Private vehicles and cabs were not included. Over 160 surveyors were stationed in different parts of Dakar department for a week. Their task was to fill in a form collecting information on several observation variables, including the time of passage of the target vehicle, its type and its occupancy level.

---

[2] https://pdudakar.sec.gouv.sn/PDU-Dakar-et-environs-a-l-horizon-2034.html.

Three Simulation Scenarios. We carried out three simulation scenarios. In the first scenario (sim1), we assume that all pedestrians take the regular crosswalk dedicated to crossing the road. They have the right of way when crossing. In the next two scenarios, two-thirds of pedestrians illegally cross the road. In the first case, we use the simulator's default decision model (sim2), and in the second, our proposed model (sim3) is used.

4.2 Results and Discussion

It follows from all our results that traffic is slowest on *Edge 1*, as shown in Fig. 5. The time lost on this section represents 92% of the time taken by the bulk of the traffic using the autobridge. This lost time is greatly due to illegal pedestrian crossings.

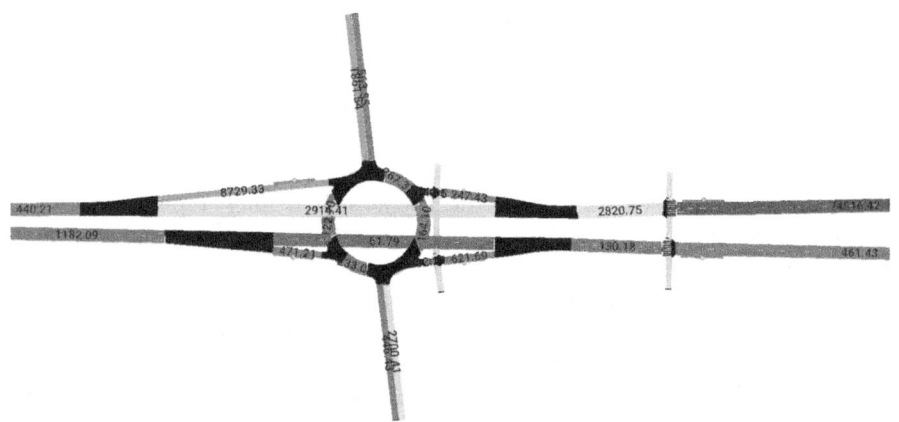

Fig. 5. Average time lost on different sections of the road.

Table 3 details the results of the three simulation scenarios on the impact of pedestrian crossings on the traffic. For each scenario, the table reports the number of vehicles having completed their travels, their average travel time and the average time that they lost during slowdowns. The first row shows data for the traffic on the overall network, while the second row shows data only on *Edge 1* where their are illegal pedestrian crossings. It is easy to see that cars waste more time in their travels with the second scenario (sim2). Fewer and fewer cars reach the end of their path. The third scenario (sim3) wastes less time with our decision model.

Table 4 gives the average waiting time for pedestrians at the illegal crossing position in *Edge 1* before deciding to engage. It also shows the number of vehicles' emergency braking on this road section. One can see that the average time with our decision model is five times lower than the one with the basic SUMO simulator model. With the latter, some pedestrians may indeed wait several

Table 3. Simulation output data on vehicles

Road Section	Nb Arrived Vehicles			Travel Time (s)			Time Loss (s)		
	sim1	sim2	sim3	sim1	sim2	sim3	sim1	sim2	sim3
Global road	3690	3397	3648	57.24	64.39	58.46	26.8	34.65	27.83
Edge 1	1870	1570	1835	52.63	75.21	47.01	39	61.52	40.12

Table 4. Simulation output data on pedestrian waiting time and vehicle emergency braking

Waiting Time (s)			Emergency Braking		
sim1	sim2	sim3	sim1	sim2	sim3
1.69	46.85	8.54	114	90	117

minutes for a safe slot, while they do not necessarily take advantage of the momentum of other pedestrians crossing the road.

Our model is more consistent with reality. Indeed, as studied by Zafri et al. in [20], pedestrians did not want to wait more than 20 to 30 s to cross the road in case of waiting. They find that the waiting time of the pedestrians varied with intersection control type, gender, age, minimum gap, waiting location, and vehicle flow. The average time of 46.85 s seems so too exaggerated. For the first scenario (sim1), the average waiting time is less than one second, since in this scenario pedestrians use the legal crosswalk and therefore have priority over vehicles.

A second element confirming the effectiveness of our decision model is the increase in emergency braking on *Edge 1* compared with the simulator's base model. In the latter, pedestrians prefer to wait as long as necessary to cross safely, whereas our model seeks to reproduce the logic of many pedestrians, based on the fact that drivers will see them from a distance and reduce their speed to avoid them.

5 Conclusion

In this paper, we presented a road crossing decision model for pedestrians based on risk judgment. The model is specifically designed for African urban traffic, as we collected data from a busy economic activity location in Dakar. We explained how we integrated our model into SUMO using the TRACI API.

We then carried out three urban traffic simulation scenarios. The results highlight the effectiveness of the model compared to the native SUMO model.

As part of our future work, we aim to collect more data on pedestrian behaviors when crossing the road illegally at different locations, at different times of the day and in different weather conditions, in order to improve and to generalize our decision model. Second, we intend to study a larger portion of Dakar's road network, which will allow us to truly understand the impact of multiple pedestrians crossing a road in dispersed locations.

References

1. Amini, R.E., Dhamaniya, A., Antoniou, C.: Towards a game theoretic approach to model pedestrian road crossings. Transp. Res. Procedia **52**, 692–699 (2021)
2. ANSD: Situation économique et social du sénégal. Agence Nationale de la Statistique et de la Démographie (2020). https://wwwansd.sn/ressources/ses/SES_2017-2018_fin.pdf
3. Bhardwaj, A., Iyer, S.R., Ramesh, S., White, J., Subramanian, L.: Understanding sudden traffic jams: from emergence to impact. Dev. Eng. **8**, 100105 (2023)
4. Muneera, C.P., Karuppanagounder, K.: Economic impact of traffic congestion-estimation and challenges. Eur. Transp. Trasporti Europei (2018)
5. Cai, J., Wang, M., Wu, Y.: Research on pedestrian crossing decision models and predictions based on machine learning. Sensors **24**(1) (2024). https://doi.org/10.3390/s24010258. https://www.mdpi.com/1424-8220/24/1/258
6. Colloque, A., Ndonky, A., Ibrahima, N.: Cartographie de la mobilité intra-urbaine á Dakar, pp. 131–153 (2023)
7. Dakar, P.: Plan directeur durbanisme de dakar et ses environs horizon 2035. Rapport Final **1**, 103 (2014)
8. Ejercito, P.M., Nebrija, K.G.E., Feria, R.P., Figueroa, L.L.: Traffic simulation software review. In: 2017 8th International Conference on Information, Intelligence, Systems & Applications (IISA), pp. 1–4 (2017). https://api.semanticscholar.org/CorpusID:3923377
9. Erdmann, J., Krajzewicz, D.: Modelling pedestrian dynamics in sumo (2015). https://api.semanticscholar.org/CorpusID:13885326
10. Garrido, D., Jacob, J., Silva, D., Rossetti, R.: Pedestrian simulation in sumo through externally modelled agents, pp. 111–118 (2021). https://doi.org/10.7148/2021-0111
11. Holland, C., Hill, R.: The effect of age, gender and driver status on pedestrians intentions to cross the road in risky situations. Accid. Anal. Prev. **39**(2), 224–237 (2007)
12. Lawrence, P., Pellacini, V., Blackshields, D., Filippidis, L.: The development of pedestrian gap acceptance and midblock pedestrian road crossing behavior utilizing sumo. In: SUMO Conference Proceedings, vol. 2, p. 3351 (2022). https://doi.org/10.52825/scp.v2i.90. https://www.tib-op.org/ojs/index.php/scp/article/view/90
13. Leden, L.: Pedestrian risk decrease with pedestrian flow. a case study based on data from signalized intersections in hamilton, ontario. Accid. Anal. Prev. **34**(4), 457–464 (2002). https://doi.org/10.1016/S0001-4575(01)00043-4. https://www.sciencedirect.com/science/article/pii/S0001457501000434
14. Lopez, P.A., et al.: Microscopic traffic simulation using sumo. In: The 21st IEEE International Conference on Intelligent Transportation Systems. IEEE (2018). https://elib.dlr.de/124092/
15. Martinez-Estupiñan, Y., Baza, N., Velasquez-MartíÂŋnez, R., Torres-Bohórquez, C., Poliziani, C.: Traffic simulation with open-source and commercial traffic microsimulators: a case study. Commun. Sci. Lett. Univ. Zilina **24**, 49–62 (2022). https://doi.org/10.26552/com.C.2022.2.E49-E62

16. Pursula, M.: Simulation of traffic systems: an overview (1998). https://api.semanticscholar.org/CorpusID:16548346
17. Sashank, Y., Navali, N.A., Bhanuprakash, A., Kumar, B.A., Vanajakshi, L.: Calibration of SUMO for Indian heterogeneous traffic conditions. In: Arkatkar, S.S., Velmurugan, S., Verma, A. (eds.) Recent Advances in Traffic Engineering. LNCE, vol. 69, pp. 199–214. Springer, Singapore (2020). https://doi.org/10.1007/978-981-15-3742-4_13
18. Shlyakhtin, A., Nugaev, F., Mustafin, A.: Traffic jam influence on the economic losses to society as exemplified by the city of Kazan. J. Econ. Econ. Educ. Res. **17**, 157–162 (2016)
19. Young, W., Sobhani, A., Lenné, M.G., Sarvi, M.: Simulation of safety: a review of the state of the art in road safety simulation modelling. Accid. Anal. Prev. **66**, 89–103 (2014)
20. Zafri, N.M., Rony, A.I., Adri, N.: Analysis of pedestrian crossing speed and waiting time at intersections in Dhaka. Infrastructures **4**(3) (2019). https://doi.org/10.3390/infrastructures4030039. https://www.mdpi.com/2412-3811/4/3/39

Modelling and Optimization of the Electrical Parameters of an $In_xGa_{1-x}N$ Solar Cell Under Dynamic Frequency Illumination

Baboucar Fickou, Moussa Camara, Moustapha Thiame(✉), Issa Faye, Landing Diatta, and Mamadou Faye

Assane Seck University of Ziguinchor, LCPM, Ziguinchor, Senegal
{m.camara1696,m.faye20160903}@zig.univ.sn, {mthiame, issa.faye}@univ-zig.sn

Abstract. In this article, we propose a modelling and optimization of an $In_xGa_{1-x}N$ based PV solar cell in the frequency-dynamic regime under monochromatic illumination.

We first elaborated a mathematical model of the $In_xGa_{1-x}N$ based solar cell in order to study its behaviour when subjected to monochromatic illumination in the frequency-dynamic regime. We were able to establish the electrical parameters as a function of the pulsation and wavelength of the illumination.

Next, we optimized the indium proportion as a function of the nature of the illumination by simulating the efficiency of the PV solar cell, for different wavelength of the illumination and values of the pulsation, as a function of the indium fraction. This enabled us to obtain, for an illumination pulsation ranging from 0 to 10^6 rad.s^{-1}, the optimum values for the indium fraction, which are $x_{op} = 0.28$ and $x_{op} = 0.26$ respectively for wavelengths of 0.5 µm and 0.9 µm, corresponding to optimum efficiencies of 28.7% and 26.6% respectively. Above a pulsation of 10^6 rad.s^{-1}, the increase in pulsation leads to an increase in the indium fraction, resulting in a decrease in efficiency for both short and long wavelengths.

Keywords: Frequency · Optimization · Efficiency · Wavelength · Optimum indium fraction

1 Introduction

Fossil fuels, which emit high levels of carbon dioxide (CO_2), account for the vast majority of the world's energy consumption. These fuels account for almost 85% of the world's energy consumption. Renewable energies (wind, photovoltaic) account for around 3% of global consumption [1]. To reduce the use of these polluting energies, the share of renewable energies in the energy mix should be considerably increased. Huge efforts are currently being made worldwide to develop these 'clean' renewable energies.

There are many expectations in the photovoltaic (PV) sector: increased conversion efficiency, lower production costs, reduced environmental impact, and so on. Currently, the PV filière is largely dominated by crystalline silicon technology, with almost 93% of global production in 2016 [2]. However, the production of silicon-based PV solar cells remains costly and requires a large quantity of materials. In addition, silicon solar cells currently have a maximum laboratory efficiency of 25.6% [3], which is very close to the maximum theoretical limit for a single-junction cell [4]. As a result, the growing need for photovoltaic energy has prompted research into the use of other alternative materials, although this in no way means that research in the silicon field has come to a halt. Today, this wide-ranging research is focused mainly on thin-film technologies. These include technologies based on III-V materials, which are highly promising in terms of efficiency. InGaN alloys have a direct and variable band gap from 3.42 eV to 0.76 eV that covers the entire solar spectrum. They have a very high coefficient of absorption (10^5 cm-1) so that a few hundred nanometers of thickness are sufficient for absorbing the majority of incident light. This alloy began to emerge as a promising material for PV applications after its considerable developments for light-emitting diode (LED) blues [5]. With the aim of contributing to the optimization of the electrical parameters of InGaN-based solar cells, we propose in this work the modelling and optimization of an $In_xGa_{1-x}N$-based solar cell under monochromatic illumination in a dynamic frequency regime. A mathematical model will be proposed to obtain the various parameters of the solar cell.

Finally, using simulation, we will propose an optimization method to
Obtain the best performance from the solar cell.

2 Mathematical Modelling

2.1 Introducing the Solar Cell

In this study, we consider a solar cell as shown in Fig. (1). The parameter H designates the thickness of the cell base. In practice, the dimensions of the base along the axes perpendicular to the z axis are very large compared with the depth of the solar cell. Thus, the current is neglected by these directions. By hypothesis, the diffusion coefficient of the minority carriers in the emitter is considered negligible compared with that of the base. Thus, our analysis is developed only on the base of the solar cell. We also take the origin of our reference frame from the emitter of the solar cell [6].

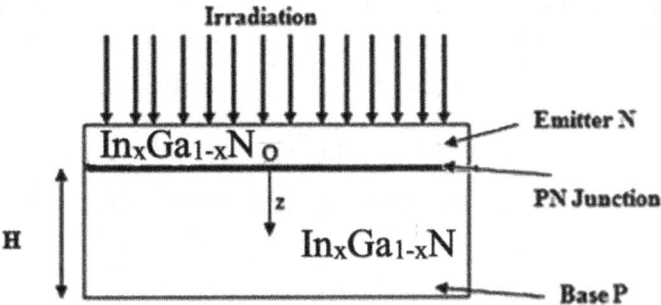

Fig. 1. Presentation of the $In_xGa_{1-x}N$ based solar cell subjected to frequency illumination

2.2 Optical Parameters

Our study is based on ($In_xGa_{1-x}N$), where the magnitude x represents the indium fraction. The solar energy band gap is related to the indium fraction as follows [7].

$$Eg = x \cdot Eg^{InN} + (1-x) \cdot Eg^{GaN} - b \cdot x \cdot (1-x) \quad (1)$$

where the energy of the band gap of l'InN (Eg^{InN}) et GaN (Eg^{GaN}) are respectively 0,7 eV et 3,42 eV et b = 1,43 eV.

The absorption coefficient is also given as a function of the indium fraction and the incident photon as follows [8]:

$$\alpha(\lambda, x) = 10^5 \sqrt{C(x)(E_{ph} - E_g(x)) + D(x)(E_{ph} - E_g(x))^2} \quad (2)$$

where $E_{ph} = 1,24/\lambda$ represents the energy of the photon and λ the wavelength.

$$c = 3,525 - 18,29 \cdot x + 40,22 \cdot x^2 - 37,52 \cdot x^3 + 12,77 \cdot x^4 \quad (3)$$

$$D = -0,6651 + 3,616 \cdot x - 2,46 \cdot x^2 \quad (4)$$

The refractive index of the solar cell is given as a function of the photon energy and the indium fraction as follows [9, 10]:

$$N(\lambda, x) = \sqrt{A(x) \cdot \left(\frac{E_g}{E_{ph}}\right)^2 \cdot \left[2 - \sqrt{1 + \frac{E_{ph}}{E_g}} - \sqrt{1 - \frac{E_{ph}}{E_g}}\right] + B(x)} \quad (5)$$

where

$$A(x) = 13,55 \cdot x + 9,31 \cdot (1-x); B = 2,05 \cdot x + 3,03 \cdot (1-x) \quad (6)$$

2.3 Electronic Parameters

The concentration of intrinsic carriers is also given by the indium fraction and takes the following form [10]:

$$n_i = \sqrt{N_c \cdot N_v} \cdot e^{\frac{-E_g}{2 \cdot K_b \cdot T}} \quad (7)$$

With Nc and Nv being the density of state in the conduction band and valence band respectively. Their expressions are given respectively in the form:

$$N_c = (0,9 \cdot x + 2,3 \cdot (1-x)) \cdot 10^9 (IV - 8) \quad (8)$$

$$N_v = (5,3 \cdot x + 1,8 \cdot (1-x)) \cdot 10^{19} \quad (9)$$

The follows equation give the expression of the carrier's effective mass [8]

$$m_n = (0,12 \cdot x + 0,2 \cdot (1-x)) \cdot m_0 \quad (10)$$

The intrinsic diffusion coefficient used in the simulation is [10]:

$$D_0 = \frac{K_b \cdot \tau \cdot T}{(0,12 \cdot x + 0,2 \cdot (1-x)) \cdot m_0} \quad (11)$$

2.4 Continuity Equation

The equation governing the variation in the density of photo-generated minority charge carriers in the base of a photovoltaic cell in static equilibrium is [11]:

$$D(\omega) \times \frac{\partial^2 \delta(z, t)}{\partial z^2} - \frac{\delta(z, t)}{\tau} = -G(z, \alpha, w, t) + \frac{\partial \delta(z, t)}{\partial t} \quad (12)$$

With:
$\delta(z, t)$ is the minority carrier density as a function of space z and time.

$$\delta(z, t) = \delta(z) \cdot e^{-j \cdot \omega \cdot t} \quad (13)$$

$G(z, \alpha, \omega, t)$ is the generation rate of carriers.

$$G(z, \alpha, \omega, t) = g(z, \omega) \cdot e^{-j \cdot \omega \cdot t} \quad (14)$$

with.

$$g(z, \omega) = \alpha(\lambda, x) \cdot I_0(\lambda) \cdot (1 - R(\lambda, x)) \cdot e^{-\alpha(\lambda, x) \cdot Z} \quad (15)$$

where:
$I_0(\lambda)$ is the intensity of the incident monochromatic light.
$R(\lambda, x)$ and $\alpha(\lambda, x)$ are the reflection and absorption coefficients respectively.
The continuity equation becomes, by replacing the Eq. (14) and (15) in (16):

$$\frac{\partial^2 \delta(z, t)}{\partial z^2} - \frac{\delta(z, t)}{L^2(\omega)} = -\frac{g(z, \omega)}{D(\omega)} \quad (16)$$

$L(\omega)$ is the complex of the diffusion length in the base [7],

$$L(\omega) = \sqrt{\frac{D(\omega) \cdot \tau}{1 + j \cdot \omega \cdot \tau}} \quad (17)$$

The solution to this equation gives:

$$\delta(z, \omega) = A \cdot \cosh\left(\frac{z}{L(\omega)}\right) + B \cdot \sinh\left(\frac{z}{L(\omega)}\right) + K \cdot e^{-\alpha(\lambda, x) \cdot z} \quad (18)$$

with:

$$K = \frac{\alpha(\lambda, x) \cdot I_0(\lambda, x) \cdot (1 - N(\lambda, x)) \cdot [L(\omega)]^2}{D(\omega) [L(\omega)^2 \cdot \alpha^2 - 1]} \quad (19)$$

The coefficients A and B are determined through the boundary conditions [10]:
- At the junction:

$$D(\omega) \cdot \left.\frac{\partial \delta(z, \omega)}{\partial Z}\right|_{z=0} = S_f \cdot \delta(z, \omega)\big|_{z=0} \quad (20)$$

- on Back face:

where Sf and Sb are the recombination speeds at the junction and at the back of the solar cell, respectively.

$$D(\omega) \cdot \left. \frac{\partial \delta(z, \omega)}{\partial z} \right|_{z=H} = -S_b \cdot \delta(z, \omega)|_{z=H} \quad (21)$$

As a function of the minority carrier density in the base, the photocurrent density is given by the expression (22) [11]:

$$J_{ph} = q \cdot D(\omega) \cdot \left. \frac{\partial \delta(z, \omega)}{\partial z} \right|_{z=0} \quad (22)$$

When the solar cell is illuminated, a photovoltage is produced, the expression for which is given by Boltzmann's Eq. (23) [12]:

$$V_{ph} = V_T \cdot \ln \cdot \left(1 + \frac{N_b}{n_0^2} \cdot \partial \delta(z, \omega) \Big|_{z=0} \right) \quad (23)$$

The diode current is a leakage current which characterizes the losses of charge carriers.

photogenerated. It is given by the following relationship [13]:

$$Id(S_f, \omega) = q \cdot S_f \cdot \frac{n_0^2}{N_b} \left(e^{\left(\frac{V_{ph}(S_f, w)}{V_T} \right)} - 1 \right) \quad (24)$$

Equations (22), (23) and (24) give the expression for the electrical power supplied by the solar cell for monochromatic illumination:

$$P(Sf, \omega) = \left(\text{Jph}((Sf, \omega) - Id(S_f, \omega) \right) \times V_{ph}(Sf, \omega) \quad (25)$$

3 Results and Discussion

3.1 Power Study

Figure (2) shows the power as a function of the recombination rate for different frequency values.

These power profiles as a function of the recombination rate Sf can be analysed along three axes:

- For values of Sf between 0 and 2.10^2 cm.s^{-1} the power is almost zero, which can be explained by the fact that at this speed range the photocurrent density is low or even zero due to the proximity of the open circuit [6].

- From 3.10^2 to 4.10^4 cm.s^{-1} the power increases progressively until it reaches its maximum value, which corresponds to the maximum power of the solar cell.

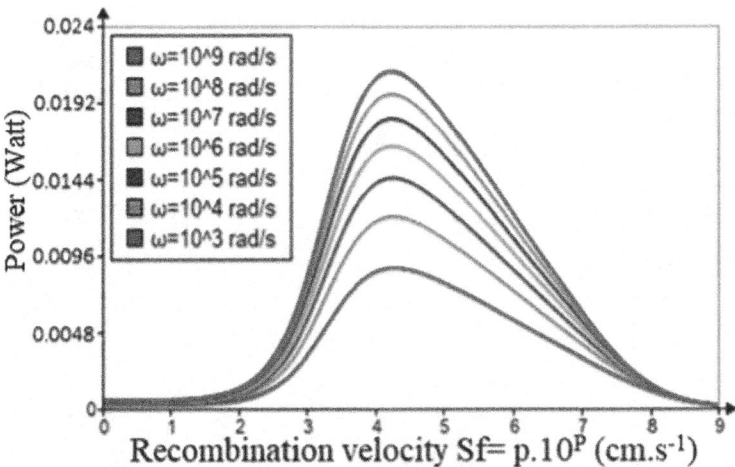

Fig. 2. Power as a function of recombination speed for different modulation frequency values (H = 3 μm, λ = 0,5 μm, x = 0,3, Sb = 2.10^2 $cm.s^{-1}$).

- Above 4.10^4 $cm.s^{-1}$ the power decreases sharply until it is completely cancelled out. This can be explained by the fact that as the solar cell approaches the short-circuit operating point, the voltage will tend towards zero [12].

We can also see that the maximum power value decreases with frequency. So we can say that an increase in frequency leads to a decrease in power.

3.2 Optimization of the Indium Fraction as a Function of the Pulsation and Wavelength of the Illumination

Our approach consists of simulating the efficiency of our solar cell for a wavelength λ equal to 0.5 μm and 0.9 μm as a function of the indium fraction for different frequency values. This method will enable us to obtain the optimum values for the indium fraction and the frequency, which will give the highest efficiency.

Figures (3) and (4) show the variation of the photocell efficiency as a function of the indium fraction for different values of the frequency for wavelengths λ = 0.5 μm and λ = 0.9 μm respectively.

In Figs. (3, 4), as the indium fraction increases, we note an increase in the efficiency until it reaches a maximum which corresponds to its optimum value for a fixed frequency and wavelength. We also note that the maximum efficiency decreases as the frequency increases beyond 10^6 $rad.s^{-1}$. This is because high frequencies do not allow minority carriers to diffuse, as many of them will be recombined either in the bulk or on the surface of the solar cell. This explains the decrease in the diffusion coefficient [12], which means that the maximum efficiency decreases with frequency.

For a given frequency, the optimum indium fraction is obtained when the conversion efficiency reaches its maximum. Tables 1 and 2 summarise the optimum values for the indium fraction at wavelengths of 0.5 μm and 0.9 μm respectively, as well as the optimum electrical parameters of the solar cell as a function of pulsation: short-circuit

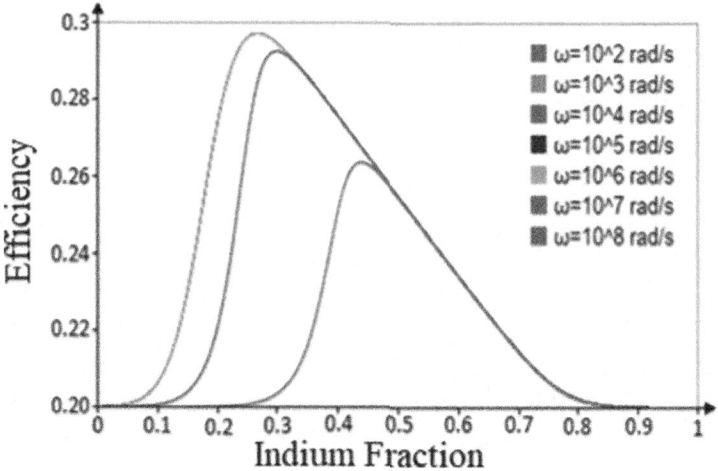

Fig. 3. Cell efficiency as a function of indium fraction for different frequency values ($\lambda = 0.5$ μm, H = 3 μm, Sf = 6.10^6 cm.s^{-1}, Sb = 2.10^2 cm.s^{-1}.)

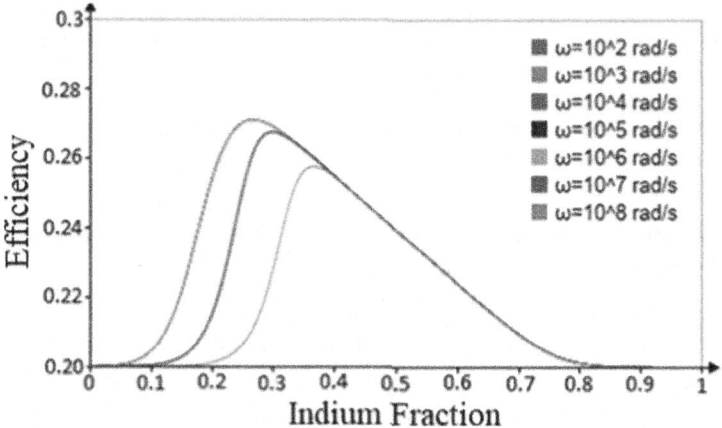

Fig. 4. Efficiency as a function of indium fraction for different frequency values ($\lambda = 0.9$ μm, H = 3 μm, Sf = 6.10^6 cm.s^{-1}, Sb = 2.10^2 cm.s^{-1}).

current, open-circuit voltage, series and shunt resistances and conversion efficiency, for different frequencies of illumination.

We note that for both wavelengths, we have an increase in the optimum indium fraction for frequencies above 10^6 rad. s^{-1}. This corresponds to a decrease in the efficiency of the solar cell. On the other hand, for pulses ranging from 10^2 to 10^6, the optimum indium fraction is independent of frequency but decreases slightly as the length increases from 0.5 μm to 0.9 μm.

We also note that the optimum indium fraction is more sensitive to higher frequencies when the wavelength is short.

Table 1. Optimum values for the indium fraction and electrical parameters for $\lambda = 0.5$ μm

ω(rad/s)	X_{op}	Jcc_{op}(A/cm^2)	Vco_{op}(V)	Rsh_{op} (Ω.cm^3)	Rs_{op} (Ω.cm^2)	η (%)
10^2 to 10^6	0.28	0.071	3.8	8.5 10^4	0.3	28.7
10^7	0.30	0.048	3.6	5.5 10^4	0.26	28.6
10^8	0.44	0.033	2.7	2.6 10^4	0.18	26.3

Table 2. Optimum values for the indium fraction and electrical parameters for $\lambda = 0.9$ μm

Ω (rad/s)	X_{op}	$Jccop$ (A/cm^2)	Vco_{op}(V)	Rsh_{op} (Ω.cm^3)	Rs_{op} (Ω.cm^2)	η (%)
10^2 to 10^6	0.26	0.061	3.1	4,5 10^4	0.28	26.6
10^7	0.31	0.035	2.8	2.7 10^4	0.20	26.4
10^8	0.36	0.022	1.7	1.6 10^4	0.10	26.3

4 Conclusion

In this paper we have modelled the electrical parameters of a thin-film solar cell based on indium gallium nitride as a function of the pulsation and wavelength of the illumination. Simulation of the power as a function of the recombination rate at the junction for different pulsations shows that as the recombination rate increases, the productivity of the cell decreases.

We simulated the effect of the light modulation frequency and wavelength on the optimum indium fraction and on the power and efficiency of the solar cell.

For wavelengths equal to 0.5 μm and 0.9 μm, we obtained optimum values for the indium fraction x_{opt} equal to 0.28 and 0.26 respectively, corresponding to efficiencies equal to 28.6% and 26.6% respectively.

References

1. British Petroleum. BP statistical review of world energy. London: British Petroleum, 1 (2017)
2. Fraunhofer, I.S.E.: Photovoltaics report. Fraunhofer ISE, Freiburg **1**, 12–15 (2017)
3. Martin. A., Emery, G.K., Hishikawa, Y., Warta, W., Dunlop, E.D.: Solar cell efficiency tables (version 48). Progr. Photovolt.: Res. Appl. **24**(7), 905–913 (2016)
4. Shockley, W., Queisser, H.J.: Detailed balance limit of efficiency of p-n junction solar cells. J. Appl. Phys. **32**(3), 510–519 (1961)
5. Bhuiyan, A.G., Sugita, K., Hashimoto, A., et Yamamoto, A.: InGaN solar cells: present state of the art and important challenges, IEEE J. Photovolt.**2**(3), 276-293 (2012)
6. Ly, I., et al.: Techniques de détermination des paramètres de recombinaison et le domaine de leur validité d'une photopile bifaciale au silicium polycristallin sous éclairement multi spectral constant en régime statique. Revue des Energies Renouvelables (15), 187–206 (2012)
7. Benmoussa, D., Hassane, B., Abderrachid, H.: Simulation of $In_{0.52}Ga_{0.48}N$ Using AMPS ResearchGate, pp.1–5 (2017)

8. Mesrane, A., Rahmoune, F., Mahrane, A., et Oulebsir, A.: Design and Simulation of InGaN p - n Junction Solar Cell. Int. J. Photoenergy **2015**, 1–9 (2015)
9. Nawaz, M., Ahmad, A.: A TCAD-based modeling of GaN/InGaN/Si solar cells. Semicond. Sci. Technol. **27**(3), 019–035 (2012)
10. Pelap, F.B., Tagne, E.K., Kenfack, A.D.K.: Numerical optimization of a tandem solar cell based on InGaN. J. Renew. Energ. **24**, 25–39 (2021)
11. Ndiaye, M., et al.: Capacite de Diffusion d'une photopile au Silicium à Multijonction Verticales Connectées en Série sous Eclairement Monochromatique en Modulation de Fréquence : Effet du Taux de dopage de la Base. Int. J. Adv. Res. 10(4), 556–572 (2022)
12. Ly Diallo, H., et al.: Determination of the Recombination and Electrical Parameters of a Vertical Multijunction Silicon Solar Cell, pp.1–6 (2020)
13. Sow, O., Zerbo, I., Mbodji, S., Ngom, M.I., Diouf, M. S., Sissoko, G.: Silicon solar cell under electromagnetic waves in steady state: electrical parameters determination using the I-V and P-V characteristics. Int. J. Sci. Environ. Technol. **1**, 230–246 (2012)

Assessment of Pavement Damage Caused by Speed Bumps Along Nyanya – Jikwoyi Road Abuja

Ukinvore Ushiki Adamu[1(✉)], Abubakar Dayyabu[1], and Abdulhameed Mambo[2]

[1] Department of Civil Engineering, Nile University, Abuja, Nigeria
Ukinvoreushiki@gmail.com, adayyabu@nileunversity.edu.ng
[2] Faculty of Environmental Sciences, Nile University, Abuja, Nigeria
abdulhameed.mambo@nileuniversity.edu.ng

Abstract. Unauthorized speed bumps installed by communities contribute to various problems such as road accidents, passenger discomfort, and potential pavement deterioration. This study focused on assessing pavement damage and the compliance of these speed bumps with design standards along the Nyanya – Jikwoyi road in Abuja utilizing the Pavement Condition Index (PCI) and a design guideline for traffic calming devices based on the City of Federal Heights, Colorado, the study examined variables including speed bump geometry, pavement distress types, severity levels, and their locations. Survey results revealed a significant interplay between speed bumps and pavement health, with 75% of sections showing moderate to high distress levels and an average PCI of 26.625, indicating poor pavement condition. Analysis indicated that 11 out of 34 speed bumps failed to meet the minimum spacing requirement of 121.92 m, highlighting design discrepancies. Additionally, only four surveyed locations had proper speed bump warning signs, suggesting a lack of adherence to safety standards. Recommendations include involvement of urban planners and traffic engineers in speed bump placement is suggested, along with routine pavement maintenance, especially in areas with high concentrations of speed bumps. Moreover, integrating speed bump placement into pavement design stages to deter unauthorized installations is proposed. In conclusion, this study underscores the importance of adhering to guidelines and involving professionals in speed bump placement to enhance road safety and pavement integrity.

Keywords: Pavement damage · Speed bumps · Road infrastructure · Pavement Condition Index (PCI) · Design standards · Traffic calming devices · Pavement integrity

1 Introduction

1.1 Background of Study

Speed bumps are crucial road traffic safety features designed to enhance pedestrian and vehicle safety, finding utility in various locations. The speed breaker, characterized by a rounded shape and a width wider than most vehicles' wheelbases, serves as a surface over the roadway. Positioned in areas where speed control is essential, a speed breaker acts as a potent stimulus to engage brain activity. In comparison to visual stimuli, audible and tactile cues prompt quicker reaction times in drivers, leading them to instinctively decrease their speed [1].

The Institute of Traffic Engineers (ITE) defines traffic calming as the combination of primarily physical interventions that improve conditions for non-motorized road users, alter driver behavior, and reduce the adverse effects of motor vehicle use [2]. The objective of traffic calming is to decrease traffic speeds and volumes to acceptable levels, thereby enhancing road safety. Various traffic calming devices, including speed humps, speed bumps, speed tables, roundabouts, transverse rumble strips, optical speed bars, textured pavement, and cat-eye reflectors, are employed for this purpose.

Speed humps and speed bumps are widely employed as common measures to prevent speeding and enhance road safety for vulnerable road users in urban areas globally [3]. In addition to decreasing speed by 20 to 40%, these devices are effective in reducing the occurrence of traffic accidents by 50–79%, particularly those involving pedestrians and cyclists, and lessening their impact. Furthermore, they help in decreasing traffic congestion, discouraging overtaking, and promoting changes in driving behavior. [4] These devices are known for their ease of installation and maintenance, resulting in low overall costs. [5–8].

Despite the mentioned benefits, the utilization of traffic calming devices comes with certain drawbacks. These include reduced driving comfort for all road users, potential delays for emergency and public transport vehicles (up to 10 s per obstacle), risks of vehicle damage and associated repair expenses, extended travel times and traffic congestion, challenges in snow clearance during winter, the formation of ruts and potholes around these obstacles, increased fuel consumption (by 40–50%), amplified traffic noise, and the emission of harmful gases due to braking and acceleration (e.g., CO increasing by approximately 60%, HC by around 50%, and CO_2 by about 25%) [3, 9, 5 6, 7, 8]. Consequently, these traditional traffic calming measures are frequently criticized by urban road users worldwide [4].

1.2 Statement of Problem

Communities randomly install unauthorized speed bumps on roads, leading to road accidents, vehicle damage, discomfort for passengers, and potential deterioration of the pavement.

1.3 Aim and Objectives

This study aims at assessing asphalt damage caused by speed bumps along Nyanya – Jikwoyi Road Abuja by analyzing the interaction between vehicles and speed bumps.

To accomplish this goal, the ensuing objectives are established:

i. To determine the pavement condition in sections with speed bumps
ii. To determine the compliance of the speed bumps placement according to standards of design and specifications

2 Literature Review

Previous studies have made diverse contributions to understanding the relationship between speed bump characteristics and factors influencing pavement deterioration in various global regions. Studies have explored the geometry of speed bumps, its impact on highway safety, and its potential for causing pavement damage. However, there exists a contextual research gap in the specific case of the Nyanya–Jikwoyi road. To address this gap, the present study focused on evaluating the condition of areas where speed bumps are situated in the case study. The objective is to provide valuable insights into the state of these areas and propose mitigations to address the identified issues. This research contributes to the understanding and improvement of road conditions affected by speed bumps.

2.1 Theoretical Review

The Pavement Condition Index (PCI) is a depreciation model defined on a scale of 0–100. A rating of 100 indicates that the pavement is considered to be in perfect condition, while a score of 0 signifies a completely failed section. The PCI is determined by assuming an initial perfect condition (PCI of 100) for the pavement and then subtracting Deduct Values (DV) assigned to each observed distress. These Deduct Values are based on the type, and extent of severity of each distress. The Deduct Value provides relative weights, indicating the importance of distress severity levels concerning pavement performance. Shahin and Kohn developed the PCI model in 1981. This initiative aims to collect ground information for parking lots, streets, and roadways using visual inspection to assess road surface conditions. The effectiveness of the assessment is based on its capacity to identify different kinds of roadway problems and link them to the corresponding causes. Understanding the causes of current issues is an important part of this process since it helps you select the best maintenance or restoration strategy [10].

A research study was conducted on the effects of speed hump characteristics on pavement conditions in Sohag, Egypt, specifically on a two-lane, two-road scenario. The findings indicated that the availability of speed humps led to significant accelerations and decelerations before and after these road features. Consequently, this resulted in increased travel time, potential vehicle damage, passenger discomfort, elevated fuel consumption, heightened pollution, and a decline in pavement condition [11]. Additionally, the study identified significant and strong correlations between the Pavement Condition Index (PCI) and the characteristics of the examined speed humps. Interestingly, there was a positive link found between PCI and both the width of the speed hump and its spacing from the previous hump. The speed bumps height, on the other hand, showed a negative link with PCI. The researchers utilized regression analysis to establish the most significant relationships between PCI and speed hump variables. This study generated several models, with the most effective being the multivariate model incorporating three independent variables (bump height, spacing from the previous bump, and hump width). They emphasized the utility of this model, suggesting its application for pavement quality assessments based on characteristics of speed bump [11].

Due to insufficient guidelines and instances of illegal speed hump placements, a research study on the geometry of speed humps was carried out. The objective was to establish a model using multiple linear regression to define the criteria for designing speed humps, focusing on a particular 85th percentile speed reduction and degree of discomfort. Their study concentrated on residential streets and collector roads, which usually had speed limits of 50 km/h or less [12].

The Alexandria Governorate's pavements' performance was assessed in a research study, finding the predominant patterns of pavement deterioration and examining the possible effects of unlawful speed bumps on pavement conditions were the key goals. The Pavement Condition Index (PCI) of parts with speed bumps is substantially lower than that of sections without speed bumps, the researcher concluded. The pavements with and without speed bumps had different conditions, averaging around 24 PCI points apart [13].

3 Materials and Method

3.1 Study Area

The case study is a dual carriageway that connects Nyanya and Jikwoyi settlement within the Abuja Municipal Area Council (AMAC) of the Federal capital Territory-Abuja, which goes further to Karshi (Fig. 1), as a case study. The road measures approximately 5 km in total length. It runs straight through a level terrain without sharp turns or unusual sight distances. The choice of this particular road for the study was based on the presence of a significant number of speed humps that vary in their characteristics. Along the entirety of the road, there are a total of 34 speed humps, with 19 positioned on the right-hand side and the remaining 15 on the left-hand side. These bumps were constructed with concrete asphalt and exhibit domed shapes, featuring varying heights and widths.

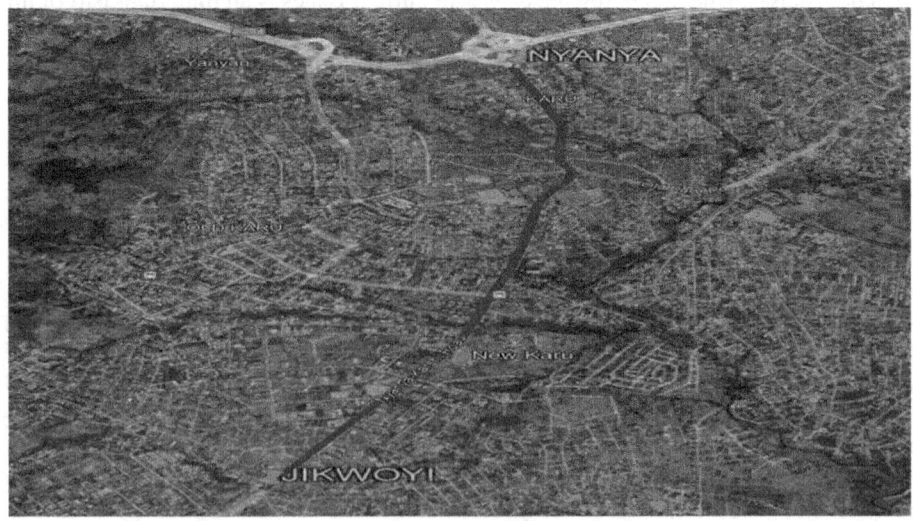

Fig. 1. Nyanya – Jikwoyi road (source; Google Earth)

3.2 Data Analysis

Pavement Section

To provide a uniform area for each portion under consideration, the road stretch was divided into 16 sections of equal area (900 m^2). This was done in order to capture the distresses surrounding the speed bumps.

The road data such as Speed bump geometry and spacings were collected at sections where speed bumps or speed breakers are found.

Pavement Distress

ASTM D6433-11 provides a comprehensive distress identification manual, wherein the degree of distress within a pavement segment is assessed based on the nature of the distress. Measurement is done using a variety of measurements, including linear meters (m), square meters (m^2), and the number of occurrences.

This approach allows for a detailed and standardized evaluation of various distress types within the pavement, considering their specific characteristics and impact on pavement performance.

Pavement Condition Index
Guide for computing PCI of flexible pavement

The PCI was determined by utilizing the data gathered through the manual examination method. The following procedure were taken to determine the PCI and PCR:

According to ASTM, the procedure used to determine PCI for a pavement section can be divided into following four steps:

1. Convert raw data to distress density (%) using area of surveyed section as denominator;
2. Find deduct value (DV) using DV-Density graph;
3. Sum the largest 7 DVs resulting in total deduct value (TDV);
4. Find corrected deduct value (CDV) using CDV-TDV graph and PCI equal to 100-CDV.

4 Result and Discussion

4.1 Pavement Distress

Distresses in Asphalt Pavement: Table 4.1 lists the 19 different types of distress for AC pavements in alphabetical order (Table 1).

TYPE OF DISTRESSES MEASURED IN THIS STUDY

1. Alligator cracking
2. Longitudinal & Transverse cracking
3. Patching & Utility patch
4. Potholes
5. Raveling

Table 1. Alphabetical arrangement of asphalt pavement distress [14].

S/N	Types of distress
1	Alligator/Fatigue cracking
2	Bleeding
3	Block cracking
4	Bumps and sags
5	Corrugation
6	Depression
7	Edge cracking
8	Reflection cracking
9	Lane shoulder drop
10	Longitudinal & Transverse
11	Patching & Utility patch
12	Polished Aggregate
13	Potholes
14	Rutting
15	Railroad crossing
16	Shoving
17	Slippage
18	Swell
19	Raveling & Weathering

4.2 Site Survey

The results from the site survey are represented in Table 2 showing the sections, locations of speed bumps, pavement distresses represented in numbers according to ASTM D 6344 with their respective level of severity, speed bump heights & weights, spacing between each bump and warning signs. The measurements and observations were all carried out using manually inspection method (Tables 2 and 3).

Pavement Survey Result for Sect. 1 RHS
The PCI was determined by utilizing the data gathered through the manual examination method. The following procedure were taken to determine the PCI and PCR:

1. Determine distress types and severity levels

The sample units were surveyed and the distress data, including types and severity, were meticulously recorded on a data report form, as illustrated in Table 4.

2. Find the deduct values:

The overall quantity of every distress at various severities were summed and then computed with formulas for calculating density of distress as discussed in the previous

Assessment of Pavement Damage Caused   53

Table 2. Results from site survey and measurements

SECTION	STATION	BUMP	DISTRESS AND SEVERITY	DIRECTION - BOTH SIDES	HEIGHTS (cm) 7.62 - 10.16	WIDTHS (M)	SPACING BETWEEN BUMPS	DISTANCE FROM INTERSECTION	WARNING SIGN
	0+000	NIL							
	0+412	1		RHS	10	1.2			
	0+439	2	1 M, 10 L, 13 L,	RHS	10	0.5	27		NO
1	0+451	3	11 H, 19M	RHS	10	0.5	12		
	0+612	4	1 H, 10 H, 10	RHS	6	0.8	161		NO
2	0+651	5	M, 11 L, 13 L,	RHS	6	0.8	39		
3	0+711	6	10 L, 10 M, 11 L, 13 L, 13 H, 19 M	RHS	6	0.8	60		NO
	1+107	7	10 M, 13 L, 13	RHS	6	0.8	396		NO
4	1+125	8	M, 13 H, 19 M	RHS	6	0.8	18	16.45	
	1+238	9	10 M, 13 L, 13	RHS	6	0.8	113		NO
5	1+259	10	M, 13 H, 19 M	RHS	6	0.8	21	16.86	
	1+503	11		RHS	8	0.8	244		
	1+516	12		RHS	8	0.8	13		
	1+542	13		RHS	8	0.8	26		NO
	1+557	14	1 M, 1 H, 10 L,	RHS	8	0.8	15		
6	1+569	15	10 M, 19 M	RHS	8	0.8	12	196.32	
	2+235	16	1 M, 10 L, 10	RHS	10	0.8	666		YES
7	2+251	17	M, 11 H, 11 L,	RHS	10	0.8	16	4.36	
	2+644	18	1 M, 10 L, 10	RHS	8	0.8	393		YES
8	2+662	19	H, 13 L, 13 M,	RHS	8	0.8	18	10.37	

Table 3. Results from site survey and measurements cont.

SECTION	STATION	BUMP	DISTRESS AND SEVERITY	DIRECTION - BOTH SIDES	HEIGHTS (cm) 7.62 - 10.16	WIDTHS (M)	SPACING BETWEEN BUMPS	DISTANCE FROM INTERSECTION	WARNING SIGN
	0+656	1	13 L, 13 H, 19	LHS	4			111.86	NO
1	0+682	2	M	LHS	8	0.8	26		
	1+173	3		LHS	8	0.8	491	26.75	NO
2	1+194	4	10 L, 13 L, 19 M	LHS	8	0.8	21		
	1+307	5	10 L, 10 L, 13 L,	LHS	8	0.8	113	20	NO
3	1+334	6	19 M	LHS	8	0.8	27		
	1+569	7	10 L, 13 L, 13	LHS	8	0.8	235		NO
4	1+597	8	M, 19 M, 1 M	LHS	8	0.8	28		
	2+285	9	13 L, 13 M, 19	LHS	8	0.8	688	9.19	YES
5	2+297	10	M, 1 M	LHS	8	0.8	12		
	2+718	11		LHS	10	1.5	421	15	YES
6	2+742	12	10 L, 13 L, 19 M	LHS	8	0.8	24		
7	3+201	13	10 L, 19 M	LHS	8	0.8	459		NO
	4+187	14		LHS	8	0.8	986		NO
8	4+204	15	10 L	LHS	8	0.7	17		

chapter. ASTM D 6433 supplied distress deduct value curves from which the DV of all distress types and severity combinations was determined.

Table 4. Evaluation sheet for sample 1.

MODIFIED DATA SHEET FOR EVALUATION AND CONDITION SURVEY							100m 9m		
ROAD: NYANYA SAMPLE UNIT: SECTION 1 RHS									
SURVEYED BY: GROUP DATE: NOV-2023									
1. Alligator Cracking	5. Depression			11. Patching & Utility Cut Patching			16. Shoving		
2. Bleeding	7. Edge Cracking			12. Polished Aggregate			17. Slippage Cracking		
3. Block Cracking	8. Lane/Shoulder Drop Off			13. Potholes			18. Swell		
4. Bumps and Sags	9. Jt. Reflection Cracking			14. railroad Crossing			19. Weathering/Ravelling		
5. Corrugation	10. Long & Trans Cracking			15. Rutting					
DISTRESS SEVERITY	QUANTITY						TOTAL	DENSITY	DEDUCT VALUE
10 L	65						65	7.22	13
13 L	5						5	0.56	48
11 H	0.5						0.5	0.127	8
19 M	900						900	100	44
1 M	4						4	0.44	14

Table 5. Calculation for corrected deduct value.

M = 1+(9/98)*(100-48) = 5.77551

NO	DEDUCT VALUE							Total	q	CDV
1	48	44	14	13	6.16			125.16	5	66
2	48	44	14	13	2			121	4	70
3	48	44	14	2	2			110	3	68
4	48	44	2	2	2			98	2	70
5	48	2	2	2	2			56	1	56

Max CDV = 70
PCI = 100 - Max CDV = 30
Rating =   Poor

3. Determine the corrected deduct value (CDV):

If none or only one individual deduct is greater than two, the total value was used in place of the maximum CDV in determining the PCI; otherwise, maximum CDV must be determined. The individual deduct values were listed in descending order, the allowable number of deducts **m**, was calculated using the following formula:

$$M = 1 + (9/98) * (100 - HDV) \leq 10 \quad (4.1)$$

where:

m = allowable number of deducts including fractions (must be less than or equal to ten).

HDV = highest individual deduct value. For example:

$$m = 1 + (9/98)(100 - 48) = 5.77$$

The number of individuals deduct values was reduced to the '**m**' largest deduct values, including the fractional part. For the example in Table 5 the values are 48, 44, 14, 13 and 6.16. (the 6.16 is obtained by multiplying 8.0 by (5.77-5.0) = 6.16)).

4. The total deduct value was calculated by aggregating individual deduct values.
5. 'q' was established as the count of deducts with a value exceeding 2.0.
6. The DVs were replicated from the present line to the subsequent line, with the modification of the smallest DV exceeding two being set to two. This process was iterated until 'q' equaled 1.
7. The CDV was calculated from the summation of deduct values and 'q' by referring to the corresponding correction curve for AC pavements.
8. The PCI was calculated by subtracting the maximum CDV from 100 [15]

The PCI of the sections of the road under consideration, as outlined in Fig. 2, delineates the outcomes for the road under evaluation.

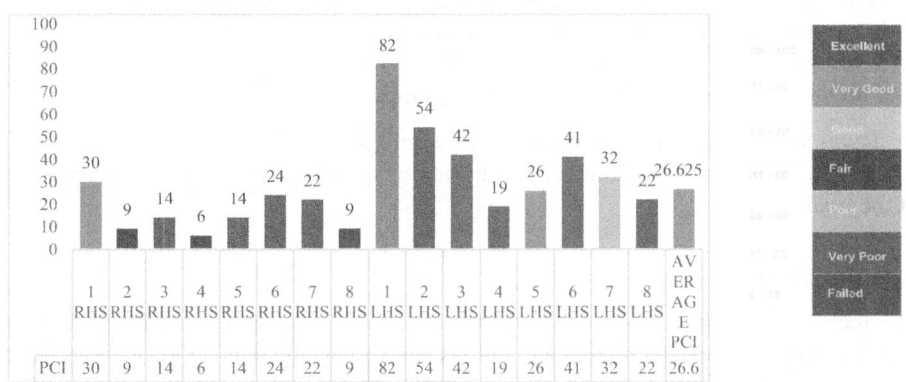

Fig. 2. Bar chart showing the summary of results for all sections with legend.

The highest PCI for the sections calculated is 82 which is rated very good, and it was noted that the section contained only one speed bump unlike the sections with PCIs of 6 and 9 which were rated as failed all contained more than one speed bump and also had poor spacing of bumps in-between them. The mean PCI for all sixteen Sects. (16) calculated is 26.625 which was rated as Poor according to the ASTM D6433 rating scale. It can be noted that, the availability of speed bumps on a road can reduce the life cycle of the road due to its effects on pavement integrity as seen in the pavement condition index values.

4.3 Speed Bump Characteristics

The following parameters will be used in the analysis of the compliance of placement and geometry of speed bumps in the study area in accordance with [16].

1. Height and width of the speed bump
2. Spacing between speed bumps

3. Distance from intersections
4. Speed bump sign before or at the location of the bump

4.4 Summary of Results for the Speed Bump Compliance to Standards

The road at intersections already had traffic lights and so the need for having speed bumps very close to intersections is not necessary as the traffic lights already function as a traffic management system which eliminates the need for speed bumps at those locations. It was observed that the speed bumps were not installed at regular intervals in accordance with standards. Here is further breakdown of the results:

1. From the results of speed bump geometry measured from the road it was discovered that they were in line with the specifications provided.
2. The spacing between the bumps were not in line with the specifications as different locations had multiple bumps within a short radius. Eleven (11) out of thirty-four (34) speed bumps passed the minimum spacing of 121.92m.
3. Four (4) out the twelve (12) bumps located near intersections passed the minimum specification of 60m away from an intersection.
4. There were only four speed bump signs at the various locations which is not in line with the specification of placing of speed bumps.

It was also observed that the road had no streetlights, posing a potential danger when traveling at night due to the high concentration of speed bumps and the poor condition of the road.

4.5 Discussion

The analysis of results from the study shed light on the significant impact of speed bumps on pavement integrity. Through a meticulous site survey and data collection process, it was revealed that the Pavement Condition Index (PCI) for the road sections inspected indicated a poor rating, with most sections ranging from Fair to Failed due to the presence of speed bumps.

The study highlighted that while the geometry of the speed bumps generally met specifications, issues arose concerning the spacing between bumps, their proximity to intersections, and the lack of proper signage. These factors contributed to the accelerated deterioration of the pavement, emphasizing the need for better adherence to design standards and guidelines for speed bump placement.

Furthermore, the results underscored the importance of strategic planning and professional oversight in the installation of traffic calming devices which highlights the critical need for a holistic approach to road design and maintenance that considers the impact of speed bumps on pavement condition.

5 Conclusion and Recommendation

5.1 Conclusion

Based on the findings presented in the thesis, it is evident that the condition of the road sections inspected is poor, with ratings ranging from Fair to Failed due to the presence of speed bumps. The study revealed that the spacing between speed bumps did not adhere to specifications, leading to accelerated pavement deterioration. Furthermore, the absence of speed bump signs at most locations and their proximity to intersections highlighted the need for better traffic calming measures. In conclusion, the installation of speed bumps along the Nyanya - Jikwoyi Road has significantly impacted the pavement integrity, as reflected in the Pavement Condition Index values.

The assessment of pavement damage caused by speed bumps along Nyanya - Jikwoyi Road in Abuja has provided valuable insights into how speed bumps affect pavement integrity. Significant findings were uncovered through the systematic evaluation of pavement condition index (PCI) and adherence to design standards.

Pavement conditions on the sections of road inspected ranged from Fair to Failed, indicating substantial damage near speed bump locations. Out of sixteen sections assessed, 15 were rated Fair to Failed, with an average Pavement Condition Index of 26.625, indicating extensive deterioration caused by the presence of speed bumps.

A further key discrepancy was found in the placement of speed bumps, with only two out of ten bumps near intersections meeting the specified distance of 60 m and 11 out of 34 bumps meeting the minimum spacing requirement of 121.92 m. As an added indication of non-compliance with design standards, most locations did not have speed bump signs. The results emphasize the urgent need for improved management and design of speed bumps to minimize pavement damage and ensure road safety. It is possible to significantly improve the longevity and performance of roads pavements by implementing the study's recommendations, such as utilizing alternative traffic calming devices and improving maintenance practices.

Overall, this research contributes valuable numerical insights to the field of Civil Engineering, particularly Highway and Transport Engineering, by quantifying the extent of pavement damage caused by speed bumps and providing a basis for informed decision-making to enhance the sustainability and efficiency of urban road networks.

5.2 Recommendations

The following recommendations not only address the challenges uncovered in this research but also pave the way for a more sustainable and economical installation of speed bumps within the urban areas:

1. The development and implementation of innovative speed bump designs that prioritize road safety without compromising pavement integrity with considerations to materials, shapes, and dimensions that distribute impact forces more evenly.
2. Only Urban Planners and Traffic Engineers should be allowed to plan, design and install speed bumps, considering factors like traffic flow, road type, and proximity to sensitive infrastructure.
3. Speed bumps placement should be incorporated right from the design stage of a pavement in a bid of reducing illegal placement of speed bumps.
4. Routine and proactive pavement maintenance should be carried out particularly in areas of high concentration of speed bumps.
5. Streetlights should be installed on roads to aid visibility and promote safety of road users.
6. Street bumps should be placed at standard interval of 120m for better traffic management.

References

1. Sinoconcept (2022). https://www.sinoconcept.co.uk/purchasing-guides/everything-about-speed-bumps/
2. Faheem, H.: Effectiveness of using cat-eye reflectors as warning and traffic calming devices in local roads and highways. In: 3rd International Conference on Road Safety and Simulation, Indianapolis, vol. 2011 (2011)
3. Al-Haji, G., Fowler, S., Granberg, T.A.: Smart Traffic Calming Measures for Smart Cities – a pre-study: CARER rapport Nr 22 2017, Linköpings universitet (2018)
4. Džambas, T., Ivancev, A.C., Dragcevic, V., Vujevic, I.: Safety and environmental benefits of intelligent speed bumps. Transp. Res. Proc. **73**, 159–166 (2023). https://doi.org/10.1016/j.trpro.2023.11.904
5. Damsere-Derry, J., Lumor, R., Bawa, S., Tikoli, D.: Effects of traffic calming measures on mobility, road safety and pavement conditions on Abuakwa-Bibiani Highway. Front. Sustain. Cities **2**(26) (2020). https://doi.org/10.3389/frsc.2020.00026
6. Džambas, T., Dragčević, V., Lakušić, J.: Impact of vertical traffic calming devices on environmental noise. Građevinar **72**(12), 1131–1143 (2020). https://doi.org/10.14256/JCE.3022.2020
7. Mei, J., Wang, J.: An intelligent dynamic speed hump. In: 2021 IEEE 4th International Conference on Automation, Electronics and Electrical Engineering (AUTEEE), Shenyang, China (2021). https://doi.org/10.1109/AUTEEE52864.2021.9668805
8. Lin, H., Ho, C.: Adaptive speed bump with vehicle identification for intelligent traffic flow control. IEEE Access **10**, 68009–68016 (2022). https://doi.org/10.1109/ACCESS.2022.3186010
9. Plămădeală, V.: Modern road safety elements of the pedestrians. J. Eng. Sci. **26**(1), 47–60 (2019). https://doi.org/10.5281/zenodo.2640037
10. Walker, D.: Pavement Surface Evaluation and Rating, University of Wisconsin–Madison (2002)
11. Abdel-Wahed, T., Hassan, H.I.: Effect of speed hump characteristics on pavement condition. J. Traff. Transp. Eng. **4**, 103–110 (2017)
12. Zainuddin, N., Adnan, M., Md Diah, J.: Optimization of speed hump geometric design: case study on residential streets in Malaysia. J. Transp. Eng. **140**(3), 9 (2013)
13. Bekheet, W.: Short term performance and effect of speed humps on pavement condition of Alexandria governorate roads. Alex. Eng. J. **53**(4), 855–861 (2014)
14. Cline, D.G., Shahin, M., Burkhalter, J.: Automated data collection for pavement condition index survey (2002)
15. ASTM Designation: D6433-11. Standard Practice for Roads and Parking Lots Pavement Condition Index Surveys, ASTM International
16. Standards and specifications for the design and construction of public improvements volume 1. City of Federal Heights, Colorado (2010)

Analyzing Water's Characteristics Health Impact with Classification Algorithms

Khadim Gueye(✉), Ndiouma Bame, and Aliou Boly

Dept. Mathématiques et Informatique, Cheikh Anta Diop University, BP 5005, Dakar Fann, Senegal
{khadim40.gueye,ndiouma.bame,aliou.boly}@ucad.edu.sn

Abstract. The water crisis is compounded by a number of factors, including population growth. In order to assess water potability, several indicators need to be taken into account during water quality evaluation. The World Health Organisation (WHO) sets concentration standards for each parameter to ensure that it is fit for drinking. The aim of this work is to take an in-depth look at these various water parameters, which have a significant impact on human health, and to understand how they influence water quality by using advanced machine learning techniques. The methodology consists on the one hand, to build a model for predicting the potability of water and on the other hand to study the impact of certain physico-chemical factors related to human health in this potability. The study was based on the use of three machine learning algorithms, namely Decision Tree, XGBoost and Random Forest, to analyze the impact of parameters such as pH, chlorine, chlorides, turbidity, nitrates, conductivity and fluoride. The results for the prediction model are promising especially for the Random Forest algorithm which gives the best performances. Regarding the impact of physico-chemical factors in the potability, all the algorithms place pH and chlorine at the top. Other parameters such as chlorides and turbidity are also significant, although their contribution is slightly lower than that of the previous characteristics.

Keywords: Anomaly detection · water quality · machine learning algorithms · health parameters · impact of physico-chemical parameters

1 Introduction

Water scarcity is a major global crisis, resulting in the death of 297,000 children under the age of five each year due to diarrheal diseases. Eighty percent of industrial and municipal activities discharge their wastewater into the environment without prior treatment[1,2]. Water quality is assessed based on several parameters to ensure its safety for human consumption. Nitrate, arsenic, chlorine, pH,

[1] Unisef rapport 2019.
[2] Unesco rapport 2021.

lead, fluoride, and turbidity are among the substances found in water, with maximum recommended concentrations set by the World Health Organization (WHO)[3]. The emergence of machine learning algorithms presents an opportunity to establish effective systems for monitoring and ensuring the quality of drinking water [1,4]. These tools provide an innovative approach to analyzing and predicting water quality, enabling informed decision-making by policymakers and water resource managers. In this context, our study aims to explore the water parameters that most significantly impact human health and to examine how these parameters affect water quality assessment using machine learning algorithms. We will detail our exploration of essential drinking water parameters and conduct an in-depth analysis of water anomaly detection, emphasizing the specific advantages of machine learning algorithms in this domain. Finally, we will conclude by identifying future research perspectives related to this issue.

2 Drinking Water Parameters

For water to be drinkable, it must comply with more than 60 parameters grouped into five main groups: organoleptic parameters, microbiological parameters, physico-chemical parameters, toxic substance parameters and undesirable substance parameters [5,6,10]. Some of these physico-chemical parameters have a significant impact on human health. In this section, we will examine some key water parameters, looking at their impact on health and the concentrations recommended by the World Health Organisation (WHO).

2.1 Chlorine (Cl^-)

Chlorine (Cl^-) disinfects water by eliminating pathogenic microorganisms such as bacteria, viruses, and parasites, and also acts as an oxidant to reduce unpleasant odors and tastes. However, high exposure to chlorine can cause skin and eye irritations, respiratory issues, and even long-term carcinogenic risks (See footnote 3)[4]. The WHO recommends a limit of 5 mg/L of chlorine in drinking water.

2.2 Hydrogen Potential (pH)

The pH of water is crucial for human health and overall water quality. Extreme pH levels, either too acidic or too basic, can promote the growth of microorganisms such as bacteria, fungi, and algae, potentially leading to health issues (See footnotes 3 and 4). To ensure the quality of drinking water and public health, it is essential to maintain the pH within an optimal range, typically between 6.5 and 8.5.

---

[3] WHO: Guidelines for Drinking-Water Quality: 4th ed. Incorporating First Addendum.
[4] WHO: Guidelines for Drinking-Water Quality: Fourth Edition Incorporating the First and Second Addenda.

2.3 Turbidity (NTU)

The turbidity of water measures the amount of suspended particles, such as organic matter, bacteria, viruses, and algae (See footnotes 3 and 4). High turbidity in drinking water can indicate the presence of harmful contaminants like pathogenic microorganisms, chemicals, or heavy metals. Quality standards recommend a maximum limit of 5 nephelometric turbidity units (NTU) to ensure the safety of drinking water.

2.4 Electrical Conductance (EC)

Electrical conductivity measures the water's ability to conduct electricity. This capacity is linked to the presence of dissolved salts in the water, such as sodium, calcium, magnesium, chloride, and sulfate ions. The presence of dissolved salts in water can affect its taste, odor, color, and turbidity (See footnotes 3 and 4). The WHO sets a maximum limit of 1000 microsiemens per centimeter (µS/cm) for the electrical conductivity of drinking water.

2.5 Nitrate (NO_3^-)

Nitrates (NO_3^-), primarily from excessive use of nitrogen fertilizers in agriculture, pose a major concern in water. At high levels, they can convert to nitrites in the body, disrupting the blood's ability to carry oxygen (See footnote 3). This is particularly concerning for infants, who may develop methemoglobinemia, commonly known as blue baby syndrome (See footnote 4). The WHO recommends a maximum limit of 50 mg per liter (mg/L) of nitrates in drinking water to ensure safety.

2.6 Fluorine (F^-)

Fluoride (F^-) is often naturally present in water, but at excessive levels it can cause dental fluorosis (stains on the teeth) and, at much higher concentrations, fluoride can cause bone problems such as bone fluorosis, which manifests itself as changes in bone structure (See footnotes 3 and 4). The WHO requires an optimum concentration of fluoride in drinking water of between 0.5 and 1.5 milligrams per litre (mg/L), with a maximum permissible concentration of 1.5 mg/L.

2.7 Trihalomethane (THM)

Trihalomethanes are a concern due to their carcinogenic potential and effects on human health. Prolonged exposure to high concentrations of trihalomethanes in drinking water has been associated with an increased risk of bladder, kidney, and colon cancer (See footnotes 3 and 4). Additionally, they can affect the respiratory system and cause skin problems. To safeguard public health, the WHO has established a maximum limit of 0.1 mg/L for trihalomethanes in drinking water.

Although the WHO issues international guidelines, each country may have its own standards and regulations regarding water quality, including maximum allowable concentrations (MAC) for contaminants. These standards can vary based on environmental conditions, agricultural practices, water resource availability, and country-specific public health considerations.

3 State of the Art on Water Anomaly Detection

Anomaly detection methods include a variety of approaches such as statistical models, supervised and unsupervised machine learning, signal processing techniques and deep learning-based methods. These techniques aim to extract unusual behaviour or aberrant patterns in data, enabling organisations to react quickly and take preventive action. Many researchers have explored machine learning algorithms to accurately assess the potability of water. This trend is widely documented in the scientific literature.

- In [11] Dorado-Guerra et al., the study employed Random Forest (RF) and XGBoost algorithms to analyze nitrate concentrations. The input data were divided into training (70%) and test (30%) sets, encompassing nineteen variables that span various climatic, hydrological, ecological, and anthropogenic aspects. The algorithms demonstrated high correlations (0.93 for RF and 0.92 for XGBoost). Predictions of nitrate concentrations were accurate with both methods, evaluated using the KGEM index ranging from 0.85 to 0.90 for RF and from 0.77 to 0.80 for XGBoost.
- In [12] Chinnappan et al., the study by presents a water quality monitoring system integrating sensors such as temperature, flow, and chlorine, connected to a Raspberry Pi 3 microcontroller. This system uses a decision tree to predict chlorine levels based on variables like temperature and pH. Data is preprocessed to remove outliers and normalize it. Fuzzy rules describe the relationship between input variables and chlorine levels, with a fuzzy algorithm adjusting the solenoid valve accordingly. The chlorine sensor measures in PPM, and the model defines ranges to interpret chlorine levels. Model performance includes a recall of 90%, precision of 92%, F-score of 89%, and an AUC of 91%.
- The study [13] by Ivan Ivanov, Borislava Toleva examines a dataset on the potability index of water with a dataset available on Kaggle. Missing values are filled in using the mean of the corresponding variable. To avoid overfitting, the data are randomly mixed. The input variables are standardised using the StandardScaler method, and the data are divided into training (72%) and test (28%) sets. Various classification models, such as SVM, DT and Random Forest (RF), are fitted. The paper evaluates the performance of the algorithms using measures such as precision, recall and f1 score. In particular, the Random Forest model has a precision of 0.81, a recall of 0.81 and an f1 score of 0.81.

In these studies, several machine learning algorithms are used. In [11] Dorado-Guerra et al. successfully employed the powerful XGBoost and Random Forest (RF) algorithms to assess nitrate concentration, obtaining satisfactory results. In [12] Chinnappan et al. opted for a decision tree to determine chlorine concentration, following predefined rules, and obtained highly conclusive accuracies. In [13] Ivan Ivanov and Borislava Toleva explored various classification models, including SVM, DT, and Random Forest, to assess the overall potability of water, achieving their best results using RF. In summary, algorithms such as Random Forest, Decision Tree, and XGBoost are frequently used in water potability assessment, providing satisfactory results.

However, although determination and detection are general, the impact of each individual parameter is not specified. Knowing this information would enable managers to focus more sharply on the parameters that have the greatest impact on water potability.

4 Our Proposition Methodology

In this section, we present the objective of our proposition and we detail the adopted methodology, starting with a study of the algorithms. We will then present the dataset used and the experimentation, before concluding with a discussion of the obtained results.

4.1 Objective

Our research is committed to taking an in-depth look at the various water parameters that have a significant impact on human health. We aim to understand how these parameters influence water quality using advanced machine learning techniques. The objective is to identify the influence of these parameters on the accurate assessment of water potability.

4.2 Machine Learning Algorithms

There are several machine learning algorithms in the literature, but some stand out from the rest in terms of anomaly detection based on the frequency, rarity and proportion of anomalies in the dataset. These algorithms include the Decision Tree (DT), XGBoost and Random Forest [7–9], which are widely used for anomaly detection.

Decision Tree (DT): A decision tree is a supervised learning method that progressively divides the dataset into smaller subsets based on feature values. The goal is to create a model that predicts the value of the target variable by learning simple decision rules derived from the data's features.

eXtreme Gradient Boosting (XGBoost): XGBoost is an advanced implementation of the gradient boosting algorithm used to build prediction models by sequentially adding base models, typically weak decision trees. The primary objective is to optimize the loss function at each step to minimize overall prediction error. This method works by sequentially adding trees to adjust the residuals of the existing model, thereby minimizing the loss function. XGBoost employs efficient optimization techniques such as gradient computation and variance reduction to accelerate the learning process.

Random Forest (RF): Random Forests are decision tree-based algorithms used to detect anomalies in water. They create multiple trees from random data samples, with variable randomization at each node to prevent overfitting. While effective for large datasets and robust against outliers, interpreting them can be challenging due to the numerous trees and parameters to adjust, and they may be sensitive to imbalanced data.

4.3 Dataset

In order to determine the impact of physico-chemical parameters of water on the determination of its potability and having dangerous consequences on human health, we use a dataset available on the Kaggle platform. The dataset contains 2140 records with 15 input parameters including pH, nitrate, fluoride, conductivity, chlorine and chloride and a binary output parameter which is potability. Missing values can compromise the quality of a model's results. We opted to use the SimpleImputer function to replace missing values with the mean, an approach commonly used in data pre-processing. Next, the SMOTE method is applied to manage class imbalance. Finally, we split the dataset into a training set (80%) and a test set (20%) before moving on to implementation.

4.4 Results and Discussion

To evaluate the proposition, metrics such as precision, recall and F-score are used to study the performance of classification models.

Results: Table 1 contains the performance of three classification algorithms: Decision Tree, XGBoost and Random Forest in determining the potability of water. Each algorithm is evaluated in terms of precision, recall and F-score. Overall, it can be seen that the Random Forest and XGBoost algorithms outperform the Decision Tree in all metrics. This suggests that these two algorithms have a greater ability to classify data correctly than to detect anomalies compared with the Decision Tree.

The importance of the different water parameters in the dataset as a function of the different types of algorithm is presented in Table 2.

Table 1. Algorithms performances

Classifier	Precision	Recall	F-score
Decision Tree	80.00	69.86	74.59
XGBoost	87.14	79.91	83.37
Random Forest	86.69	82.53	84.56

Table 2. Importance of parameters on the potability of water (%)

Classifier	DT	RF	XGBoost
pH	23.98	20.82	21.61
Chlorine	15.93	15.98	15.72
Chloride	14.98	15.41	14.80
Turbidity	15.19	14.53	14.50
Nitrate	12.24	14.05	12.96
Fluoride	10.35	11.57	10.81
Conductivity	07.29	08.23	08.96

The results obtained from the importance of the characteristics for each model (Random Forest, XGBoost and Decision Tree) provide valuable information on the relative contribution of each characteristic to the prediction of water potability.

Discussion: In all three models, pH is the most important characteristic, with importance values ranging from 20.82% to 23.98%. This suggests that the pH level of the water is a crucial factor in determining its potability. High or low pH values can indicate potentially undrinkable water due to its extreme acidity or alkalinity. Chlorine is also an important characteristic in all models, with importance values of 15.93%, 15.72% and 15.98% for the Decision Tree, XGBoost and random Forest respectively. This is consistent with the fact that chlorine is commonly used as a disinfectant in drinking water treatment to remove microbial contaminants. Chloride is also considered important in all three models with importance values ranging from 14.80% to 15.41%, although its contribution is slightly less than that of chlorine. Chloride levels in water can come from natural sources or from water treatment processes, and high levels can indicate contamination by soluble salts. Water turbidity, a measure of water clarity based on the presence of suspended particles, is also important in all models. High levels of turbidity can indicate undrinkable water due to the presence of unwanted particles. Nitrate, Fluoride and Conductivity are also important but have a slightly lower contribution than the previous characteristics. High levels of nitrate can come from agricultural or industrial sources, while the presence of fluoride can be controlled to avoid excessive concentration. Conductivity can be related to the amount of dissolved salts in the water, which may indicate the presence of certain minerals. These results underline the importance of monitoring a varied set of characteristics to assess the potability of water. pH, chlorine, chloride, turbidity and other characteristics play critical roles in determining the quality of drinking water, and monitoring them regularly is essential to ensure public health. Different machine learning methods provide consistent insights into the factors important to water potability, boosting confidence in water treatment recommendations and decisions.

5 Conclusion and Perspectives

The study focused on analysing the influence of water characteristics on human health, with particular emphasis on predicting the potability of water by assessing the parameters that have a direct impact on human health. Through the analysis of many works dealing with the potability of water and the use of machine learning algorithms such as random forest, XGBoost and decision tree, we evaluate the effectiveness of these models and determine the importance of each parameter. The obtained results, expressed in terms of precision, recall and F1-score, showed that the XGBoost and Random Forest algorithms outperformed the Decision Tree in terms of predictive performance. In addition, analysis of the specific results for different parameters such as pH, chlorine, chloride, turbidity, nitrates, fluoride and conductivity revealed significant variations in the contribution of these factors to the prediction of water potability. By analysing the results, we observed that pH, chlorine and turbidity have a predominant influence on the prediction of water potability, while other parameters such as nitrate and fluoride also play a significant role. These results can inform decision makers and health professionals in their efforts to ensure a safe, high-quality water supply for all. Particular attention should be paid to identifying the most relevant combinations of parameters for predicting drinking water quality. This may require in-depth analyses, such as correlation studies and data mining techniques, to determine the most significant relationships between different parameters. By developing models that take into account the conjunction of several parameters, it will be possible to gain a better understanding of the mechanisms underlying water potability and identify effective strategies for mitigating the associated risks. This combination of parameters could play a crucial role in water quality management, helping to ensure universal access to safe drinking water.

References

1. Ainapure, B., Baheti, N., Buch, J., Appasani, B., Vidyakant, J., Srinivasulu, A.: Drinking water potability prediction using machine learning approaches: a case study of Indian rivers. Water Pract. Technol. (2023)
2. Mondal, A., Dubey, S.: Machine learning-based water potability prediction: model evaluation, and hyperparameter optimization. In: Tripathi, A.K., Shrivastava, V. (eds.) Advancements in Communication and Systems, SCRS, India, pp. 37–54 (2024)
3. Gao, H., Li, Y., Lu, H., Zhu, S.: Water Potability Analysis and Prediction. Highlights in Science, Engineering and Technology, pp. 70–77 (2022)
4. El Fadel, D.: Water resources evaluation and potability in north-east of Algeria. Alger J. Eng. Archit. Urban **5**(4), 192–198 (2021)
5. Soulounganga, P., Ndjeri-Ndjouhou, M., Ngohang, F.: Drinking water consumption habits and perception of the organoleptic quality of tap water by the population of Greater Libreville (Gabon). Int. J. Biol. Chem. Sci. 1117–1130 (2023)
6. Josiane, C., et al.: Physico-chemical and bacteriological characteristics of river waters. Afrique Sci. **23**(2), 50–64 (2023)

7. Didavi, K., Agbokpanzo, R., Agbomahena, M.: Comparative study of decision tree, random forest and XGBoost performance in forecasting the power output of a photovoltaic system. In: Proceedings of a Conference, pp. 1–5 (2021)
8. Meric, E., Ozer, C.: Symptom Based Health Status Prediction via Decision Tree, KNN, XGBoost, LDA, SVM, and Random Forest, pp. 193–207 (2023)
9. Helmud, E., Fitriyani, F., Romadiana, P.: Classification comparison performance of supervised machine learning random forest and decision tree algorithms using confusion matrix. Jurnal Sisfokom (Sistem Informasi dan Komputer) **13**, 92–97 (2024)
10. Melin, J.: Occurrence and fate of metabolites of four pesticide families (neonicotinoids, carbamates, organophosphates, phenylpyrazoles) in drinking water resources and drinking water treatment plants (PhD thesis) (2020)
11. Dorado-Guerra, D.Y., Corzo-Pérez, G., Paredes-Arquiola, J., Pérez-Martín, M.Á.: Machine learning models to predict nitrate concentration in a river basin. Environ. Res. Commun. **4**(12), 125012 (2023)
12. Chinnappan, C.V., et al.: IoT-enabled chlorine level assessment and prediction in water monitoring system using machine learning. Electronics **12**, 1458 (2023)
13. Ivanov, I., Toleva, B., Taylor, G.: Predicting the water potability index using machine learning. Environ. Ecol. Res. **11**, 537–542 (2023)

Information Technology

Optimizing Coverage in a Wireless Sensors Network by Selecting the Best Sensors

Absa Lecor[1(✉)], Mohamed Mejri[2], and Senghane Mbodji[1]

[1] Université Alioune Diop de Bambey, Bambey, Senegal
{absa.lecor,senghane.mbodji}@uadb.edu.sn
[2] Laval University, Quebec City, Canada
mohamed.mejri@ift.ulaval.ca

Abstract. The challenges imposed by wireless sensor networks can be attributed to several factors such as a severe energy constraints, the limited processing and communication capabilities, the dynamic deployment of the environment, the unique data dissemination model, and the quality of service required at the application level. The routing protocol is considered as an important service. It allows to the routing of data packets captured to shift from the sensors to the base station. The choice of the path taken is made according to the performance standards such as energy consumption, reliability, transmission delay, etc. In this work, we will look for the best sensors and the best path to choose in order to set up our sensor network properly. As well, we will optimize the type of sensors for purchasing and the routing of the packets as far as possibility. And consequently, we use a multi-objective function for this purpose. The first part will consist of making the choice between different sensors. As a result, we have the group of sensors which has a minimum communication radius with a cheaper cost, a high throughput, and low-energy consumption. Our results are more optimal in terms of cost, energy, and transfer rate compared to other approaches. The optimization results obtained give us a minimum value for the cost of sensor deployment in the area equal to 218586 FCFA, a minimum value of 1609120 W/h, and a maximum value for the transmission rate equal to 47.82 bit/s. This optimization ensures 91.03% coverage with the square octagon network model.

Keywords: Routing protocol · Optimization · Wireless Sensors Network · Coverage

1 Introduction

Advances in microelectronics, micromechanics, and wireless communication technologies over the past few decades have made it possible to produce components with a volume of just a few cubic millimeters at reasonable cost. These components, known as microsensors, contain a sensing unit that detects physical quantities (heat, humidity, and vibration) and converts them into digital data. Sensors are thus true embedded systems. A wireless sensor network is the use of a large number of battery-powered sensors to autonomously collect and transmit environmental data to one or more collection points. They are becoming increasingly popular in a variety of fields. Despite their many advantages, wireless sensor networks are limited by the battery power, processor power, and communication capacity of the sensors.

Therefore, it's important to make an optimal choice of sensor types and how to deploy them in a wireless sensor network. In our work, we present the best sensor available on the market based on a set of criteria. We made a comparative study of a set of sensors based on their energy, communication range, transmission power, and price. The result is a set of sensors with minimum communication range, lower cost, higher throughput and lower energy consumption. For each optimization case, we implemented a sensor deployment pattern in square, hexagon and square-octagon shapes. In this way, we optimized the network while ensuring maximum coverage in the working area. The results are shown in Fig. 5, Fig. 6, and Fig. 7.

2 State of the Art of Routing Protocols in Wireless Sensors Networks

The routing in wireless sensor networks, is a field which is very much explored by researchers. They give specific characteristics of this type of network. The energy and computing limits of power of the sensors require consequently a new generation of protocols completely different from those of wired and wireless networks. This difference is explained by the fact that the sensors have limited energy in computing power and in storage capacity which one requires an efficient management of resources. As for the literature's side, there are several researchers who have oriented their works in this same field. We can name among them, [1–10]. Afterward, in this part, we will then lay out the different types of routing protocols, the importance energy and quality of service in wireless sensor networks.

2.1 Routing Protocols in WSNs

According to the sensor network topology, Mammeri and al have developed three types of routing protocols in theirs work [11] which are listed as the flat routing protocol, the hierarchical routing protocol and the geographic routing protocol. In theirs works [5] and [12], the authors have explained that hierarchical routing is the most effective in terms of energy efficiency. In fact, it is based on the concept of standard node, master node and base station. The standard nodes itself routes the messages to the masters ones, which then route the standard nodes through the network via others master nodes until the base station called (sink). Among the hierarchical routing protocols, there are those that follow the hierarchy in a grouped manner called (clustering) that are elaborated in work

[5] done by AnnushaKumar and al. In addition, there are those that follow the routing protocols which are in the chained hierarchy which is established in work [1] done by Es-Sabery and al.

Hierarchical Routing Protocols. In the work [8], by Seedha Devi and al, they have established the technique of hierarchical system which is usually divided the network into subsets in the purpose of facilitating its management and typically to optimize the routing which is carried out at several levels. In this type of protocols, we distinguish two types of node groups where the network's architecture is situated named the zone and the cluster. Malisetti and al. have defined a cluster in work [13] as a set of nodes which has a node named node-head or Cluster Head (CH) and the role of the CH is to be a relay directly between the nodes of the cluster and the base station or others CHs. Generally, the CH has greater energy resources than the other nodes in the network. Then, Vinitha and al have shown in their work [10] that the CH is elected according to different criteria and information on the network. Which are the energy level of a sensor, the connection with other sensors and the geographical position, etc. So every area is defined by a set of nodes which does not have a head node (or CH). Thus, obviously a cluster is a subclass of an area.

Figure 1 this technique presented the Hierarchical topology.

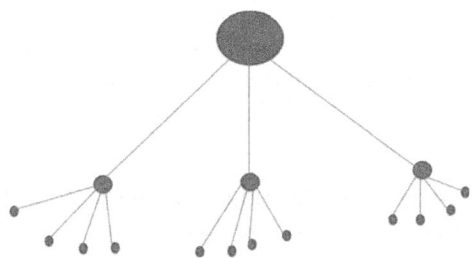

Fig. 1. Hierarchical topology.

2.2 Transmission Algorithms in WSN

The approach proposed in work [14] by Yemeni and al. have run the Kalman filter for redundancy reduction. The Kalman filter is an infinite impulse response filter which estimates the states of a dynamic system from a series of incomplete or noisy measurements. The technique based on the traveling salesman problem and clustering is presented by Velusamy and al in work [6]. In order to ensure low-power consumption for data transmission in sensor networks. A quantum annealing approach is used in work [15] by Nikouei and al in order to improve the cost of system deployment by minimizing the number of sinks and SDN controllers needed. In work [8], Seedha Devi and al. have elaborated a data aggregation scheme based on cluster heads to reduce latency and packet's loss. They also placed an aggregation system directly at the base station. The work of Vinitha and al. in [10] addressed the issue regarding energy and provided energy efficient multi-hop routing in WSNs. The author have used an energy-efficient multi-hop routing named Taylor which in based on Cat Salp Swarm Algorithm (Taylor C-SSA) by shifting the C-SSA with Taylor series.

The work of AnnushaKumar and al. in [5] address the issue of energy and provide an efficient Clustering-like routing protocol for sensor energy conservation and lifetime with high throughput. The authors used a new routing protocol based on the hybrid cuckoo search algorithm combined with the genetic algorithm. In work [9], Singh and al. proposed an application of three algorithms:

- Algorithms 1: Consisted of the placement of the receiver node (sink) by optimizing the swarm of particles.
- Algorithms 2: the route between the sensors and the sink uses the tree of minimum range (spanning tree), which is then optimized by the technique of bee colonies.
- Algorithms 3: it is about the opportunistic transmission of packets to neighbors.

In work [8], Seedha Devi and al propose latency reduction and packet loss in WSNs. They propose a data aggregation scheme based on clusters and consists two phases.

- Phase 1: Each cluster head applies compressional aggregation. Then, the aggregation tree is built by the receiver using the minimum spanning tree.
- Phase 2: The Packet loss rate and the latency are considered when prioritizing and allocating time slots.

As for the maintenance and adjustment of knots, the work of Ouyang and al. in [7] showed a drone-based scheme with automatic transmission and reception. This system is based on a special drone coupled with the GNSS-RTK platform (Global Navigation Satellite System, Real - Time Kinematic). Table 1: compares the algorithms covered at the level of the state of the art with full respect for the working criteria. Which are the deployment strategy, the structure of the network, the type of routing, the transmission protocol used and lastly the objective expected.

Table 1 compares the algorithms covered at the level of the state of the art with respect to the working criteria which are: the deployment strategy, the structure of the network, the type of routing, the transmission protocol used and the objective expected.

3 Preliminaries

In order to simplify the presentation of our approach, we start by introducing some key models that we use in the rest of our document such as: network model, energy model and radio model.

Table 1. Comparison of approaches

Protocol approach	Deployment strategy	Network structure	Routing type	Sensor node	Transmission protocol	objectif
[14]	random on square grids	Flat topology	end-node level and sink-node level	Active and passive	Kalman filter	Reduces data redundancy
[6]	Polygons (vorony diagram)	hierarchical	UAVs	CH, NCH, VCH	Trade Seller (ESDCS)	Reduces energy
[15]	Dynamics (methaheuristics)	hierarchical	multi-sink multi-controller node	SDN	quantum annealing	Reduce the cost
[10]	Random	hierarchical	multi hop routing	CH	Taylor C-SSA	Reduce energy, delay
[5]	random	hierarchical	clustering	CH level 1 and level 2	Cuckoo combined with GA(TEEN)	Long life, high throughput
[16]	Deployment in hexagon	hierarchical	Clustering	CH, target nodes	CSMA/CA	Fusion of real-time data, collision, energy
[17]	dynamic	hierarchical	multi-hop def routing	SDN	Mobile well(ODGRP)	Reduces energy
[9]	random	hierarchical	multi-hop and multi-sink	CH	coding, spanning tree	Reduces redundancy, energy
[8]	-	hierarchical	multi hop routing	multi-level CH	spanning tree, slot	Reduce pck loss
[7]	By point of interest	hierarchical	UAVs	Asset	3G 4G 5G	-

3.1 Network Model

We assume that each sensor is omnidirectional and has 360° coverage. Each sensor is represented by a circle with center I and radius R which mean the communication radius of the sensor. A defined number of sensors will be placed in the search area. It is divided into square-octagon patterns. Each pattern consists of two octagons and a square with equal sides. Thus, each sensor is placed in the center of each octagon (see Fig. 2).

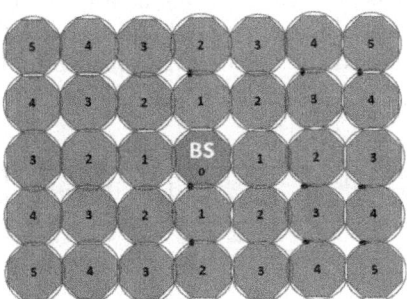

Fig. 2. Cutting in a square-octagon pattern.

The network topology is centralized. Each sensor node is identified by its label number and its position within frame which takes as its origin from the center of the base station. In our architecture, the distance between two consecutive sensors is identified by the Euclidean distance between the center of two consecutive sensors. Then The value is equal twice the communication radius of the sensor presented by Lecor al. in [18]. The author defines the value d of the Euclidean distance between two consecutive sensors in (1). The author also defines the network cost as a function of R in Eq. (2).

$$\begin{cases} d = 2*R*\cos(T) \\ T = \frac{2\pi}{8} \\ d = 2*R*\cos(\frac{\pi}{4}) \\ d = R*\sqrt{2} \end{cases} \quad (1)$$

$$Cost(N,x) = a(N) * \frac{1}{3.82*R(x)^2} * price(x) \quad (2)$$

The cost equation takes as input a network N and sensors x. We have $a(N)$ the total area of the network, $price$ the price of a sensor and $\frac{1}{3.82*R(x)^2}$ the area of an octagon containing a sensor x.

3.2 Energy Model

The sensor node consumes energy to perform three main tasks which followed: detection, communication and data processing. In [1], Es-Sabery and al show that the energy used for revealing the physical phenomenon is negligible. Besides, the energy used for processing is less than the communication's energy. In [19], Sharma and al show that energy's efficiency represents a significant metric performance because it straightly influences the durability of the network. In [13], Malisetti and al systematically underline that the radio model is used to communicate the information between the receiver and the transmitter. The energy is conveyed by the transmitters to operate the power amplifier and the electronic circuits of the transmitter and the receiver in Fig. 3. The power's consumption at the time when the data bits are received and transmitted and at any distance between the transmitter and the receiver, is represented by Eq. (3) and Eq. (5).

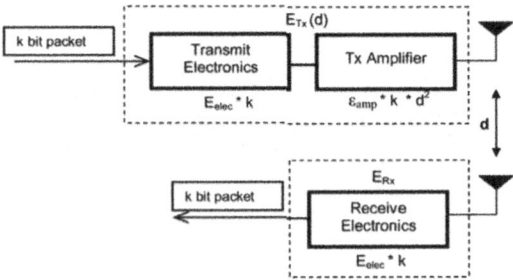

Fig. 3. Energy consumption model [3].

In the energy model, Wang and al showed in [20] that the energy used by each node to transmit, is proportional to d^2 if the distance between the transmitter and the receiver is less than the threshold distance d_0, otherwise it is proportional to d^4. The total energy required by each node to transmit $k-bit$ data is:

$$E_{tx}(k,d) = \begin{cases} k[E_{elec} + E_{amp} * d^2] & \text{si } d < d_0 \\ k[E_{elec} + E_{amp} * d^4] & \text{si } d > d_0 \end{cases} \quad (3)$$

$$d_0 = \sqrt{\frac{e_{fs}}{e_{mp}}} \quad (4)$$

$$E_{rx}(k,d) = E_{elec} * k \quad (5)$$

With a full consideration of k the number of bits to be transmitted, d being the Euclidean distance between the transmitter and the receiver, and E_{elec} is a hardware parameter of energy consumed during the operation of the transmission channel. It amplifies energy for the free space model e_{fs} and for the multi-path model e_{mp}, which are two parameters of energy consumption by the amplifier E_{amp} and d_0 which is a distance threshold between two successive nodes.

3.3 Wireless Model

In their work titled [21], Gungor and al showed that the wireless channel is modeled using a log-normal path loss model by shading and combining analytical and empirical methods. This model is used for large and small coverage systems and for indoor wireless environments with obstructions. In this model, the signal-to-noise ratio $S_B(d)$ at a distance d from the transmitter is given by Eq. (6):

$$S_B(d)_{dB} = P_t - P_l(d_0) - 10 * n * \log_{10}(\frac{d}{d_0}) - X_\alpha - X_n \quad (6)$$

where P_t is the transmit power in dBm, $P_L(d_0)$ is the path loss at a reference distance d_0, n is the path loss exponent, X_α is a variable zero-mean Gaussian random with standard deviation α, and P_n is the noise power in dBm. In [22], Shannon gave in 1998 the formula for the transmission capacity of the communication channel of k bits over a distance d by Eq. (7)

$$C_{tx}(k,d) = W * \log_2(1 + S_B) \quad (7)$$

With W the bandwidth, $S_B(d)$ the signal to noise ratio, k is the number of bits to be transmitted over a distance d.

3.4 Communication Model

This section introduces the Bluetooth, UWB, ZigBee, and Wi-Fi protocols, which correspond to the IEEE 802.15.1, 802.15.3, 802.15.4, and 802.11a/b/g standards respectively. The main objective of this part is to set forth a comparison of the four main short-range wireless networks in Fig. 4.

Standard	Bluetooth	UWB	Zigbee	Wi-Fi
IEEE spec..	802.15.1	802.15.3a	802.15.4	802.11a/b/g
Frequency band	2.4GHz	3.1-10.6 GHz	868/915 MHz; 2.4 GHz	2.4 GHz; 5 GHz
Max signal rate	1 Mb/s	110Mb/s	250kb/s	54Mb/s
Nominal range	10 m	10 m	10-100 m	100 m
Nominal TX power	0 - 10 dBm	-41.3 dBm/MHz	(-25) - 0 dBm	15 - 20 dBm
Number of RF channels	79	(1-15)	1/10;16	14(2.4GHz)
Channel bandwidth	1MHZ	500MHz-7.5GHz	0.3/0.6 MHz; 2 MHz	22MHz
Modulation type	GFSK	BPSK, QPSK	BPSK (+ ASK), O-QPSK	BPSK, QPSK COFDM, CCK, M-QAM
Spreading	FHSS	DS-UWB, MB-OFDM	DSSS	DSSS, CCK, OFDM
Coexistence mechanism	Adaptive freq. hopping	Adaptive freq. hopping	Dynamic freq. selection	Dynamic freq. selection transmit power control (802.11h)
Basic cell	Piconet	Piconet	Star	BSS
Extension of the basic cell	Scatternet	Peer-peer	Cluster tree-mesh	ESS
Max number of cell nodes	8	8	> 65000	2007
Data protection	16-bit CRC	32-bit CRC	16-bit CRC	32-bit CRC

Fig. 4. Comparison table of the main short-range wireless networks [23].

Bluetooth and ZigBee are protocols intended for low-speed and short-range portable products. They have a limited energy life (battery). Therefore, the power's consumption must be very low. UWB is offered for short-range and high-speed applications. And Wi-Fi is designed for longer range connection and supports devices with power supply. Bluetooth and ZigBee protocols consume less power than UWB and Wi-Fi protocols. To conclude, Bluetooth and ZigBee are suitable for low data rate applications with limited battery (such as mobile devices and sensor networks running on battery), due to their low-power consumption which gives them a long service life. While, for high-speed applications (like audio/video surveillance systems), UWB and Wi-Fi would be better solutions.

4 Approach

In our approach, we note that there are several categories of sensors on the market with different performances. These differ on criteria such as: cost, power to transmit captured data, coverage and collection radius, and energy. It is necessary to make a good choice of these sensors in order to optimize the coverage and performance of our WSN. The main goal of our work is to choose the least expensive sensors in terms of energy and transmission power to ensure coverage and data transmission in our wireless network. To optimize the network paths, we need to find the minimum distance between two consecutive sensors. To do this, we use three functions representing cost, energy, and transmission rate, respectively. These three functions have in common a variable called d, which is the Euclidean distance between two consecutive sensors. In our approach, the network topology we use defines the d value of the distance between two sensors. This value is defined in Eq. (8).

$$d = 2 * R * \cos(\frac{\pi}{4}) = R * \sqrt{2} \qquad (8)$$

4.1 Formalization of the Problem

Given:

- N a network with an area denoted by $a(N)$
- S a set of sensors where each sensor x in S is characterized by its price, denoted by $price(x)$, its communication radius, denoted by $R(x)$, its electrical energy, denoted by $E_{elec}(x)$, its amplification energy, denoted by $E_{amp}(x)$, its width of bandwidth, denoted by $W(x)$ and its transmission power, denoted by $Pr(x)$.
- E_{tr}: a maximum energy threshold not to be exceeded
- C_r: a maximum network cost threshold not to be exceeded
- D_r: a minimum threshold of the transmission rate
- K: the number of bits to transmit

We are looking for the sensor that minimize the following function.

$$\min_{x \in S} \text{Cost}(N, x, E_{tr}, D_r, K)$$

such that:
$$\begin{cases} \text{Cost}(N, x, E_{tr}, D_r, K) \leq C_r \\ \\ \text{EnergyTotal}(x, K) \leq E_{tr} \\ \\ \text{TransmissionRate}(N, x) \geq D_r \end{cases}$$

With

$$\begin{cases} \text{Cost}(N, x) = a(N) * \frac{1}{3.82 * R(x)^2} * price(x) \\ \\ EnergyTotal(x, K) = K * [2E_{elec}(x) + E_{amp}(x) * (2R(x)\cos(\frac{\pi}{4}))^2] \\ \\ TransmissionRate(x) = W(x) * \log_2(1 + S_B(x)) \\ \\ S_B(x) = 10^{\frac{(P_t(x) - 20 * \log_{10}(\frac{4\pi * d(x)}{\lambda}))}{10}} \end{cases} \qquad (9)$$

Details on these formulas are given in the next section.

4.2 Network Cost Function

It evaluates the cost of all the sensors that are placed in the network. Each sensor node has a price and all the nodes in the network have a total cost. It takes as variable R the communication radius of the sensor x.

$$Cost(N, x) = a(N) * \frac{1}{3.82 * R(x)^2} * price(x) \tag{10}$$

According to our working criteria, the cost of the network must not exceed the threshold value C_r. Therefore, the communication radius of a sensor is given by the following equation.

$$R(x) \geq \sqrt{\frac{a(N) * price(x)}{C_r * 3.82}} \tag{11}$$

4.3 Network Energy Function

It evaluates the transmission energy and the reception energy between two neighboring sensors. When a sensor transmits data to another sensor, they provide transmit energy and receive energy. The sum of these two energies is called $EnergyTotal$. It takes as variable R the communication radius of a sensor x.

$$EnergyTotal(x, k) = k * [2 * E_{elec}(x) + E_{amp}(x) * (2 * R(x) * \cos(T))^2]$$

$$EnergyTotal(x, k) = k[2E_{elec}(x) + E_{amp}(x) * (R(x)\sqrt{2})^2] \tag{12}$$

4.4 Network Transmission Rate Function

It evaluates the transmission power between two consecutive sensors of the network at a distance d. It takes as variable $R(x)$ the communication radius of the sensor x.

$$TransmissionRate(N, x, S_B(x)) = W * \log_2(1 + S_B(x)) \geq D_r$$

$$S_B(x) = P_t(x) - P_L(x)$$

$$P_L(x) = 20 * \log_{10}(\frac{4\pi * d(x)}{\lambda})$$

$$S_B(x)(d)_{dB} = P_t(x)_{dB} - 20 * \log_{10}(\frac{4\pi * d(x)}{\lambda})$$

$$S_B(x)(d) = 10^{\frac{(P_t(x)_{dB} - 20*\log_{10}(\frac{4\pi*d(x)}{\lambda}))}{10}}$$

$$TransmissionRate(N, x, S_B(x)) = W(x) \log_2(1 + S_B(x)(d)) \tag{13}$$

5 Case Studies

- Given the wireless transmission modules with their characteristics in the table below Table 2.

$$\min_{x \in S} \text{Cost}(N, x, E_{tr}, D_r, K)$$

such that:
$$\begin{cases} \text{Cost}(N, x, E_{tr}, D_r, K) \leq C_r \\ \text{EnergyTotal}(x, K) \leq E_{tr} \\ \text{TransmissionRate}(N, x) \geq D_r \end{cases}$$

Table 2. Sensor choice minimize $\text{Cost}(N, x, E_{tr}, D_r, K)$

Sensor/data	N	Price(x)	R(x)	$P_t(x)$	$E_{elec}(x)$	$E_{amp}(x)$	W(x)	C_R	K	E_{tr}	λ	Dr
Digi XBee Cellular 3G	(200,100)	77185.9	100	3.3*0.702	8333.69	0.0013	2.4	40411	2	30	0.125	250M
Bluetooth V3 module TEL0026	(200,100)	14.630	10	3.6*0.05	648	0.0013	2.4	765960	2	2.59	0.125	2M
ESP8266 Wi-Fi IoT	(200,100)	31675	50	3.3*0.5	5940	0.0013	2.4	66335	2	25	0.125	54M
Digi XBee 3 Zigbee	(200,100)	22260	20	3.6*0.04	518.4	0.0013	2.4	296596	2	2.07	0.125	250k
RF ZigBee ETRX357	(200,100)	16700	20	3.6*0.031	648	0.0013	2.4	218586	2	2.59	0.125	250k

- Given the wireless transmission modules with their characteristics in the table below Table 3.

$$\min_{x \in S} \text{EnergyTotal}(x, K)$$

such that:
$$\begin{cases} \text{EnergyTotal}(x, K) \leq E_{tr} \\ \text{Cost}(N, x, E_{tr}, D_r, K) \leq C_r \\ \text{TransmissionRate}(N, x) \geq D_r \end{cases}$$

Table 3. Sensor choice minimize $TotalEnergy$

Sensor/data	N	Price(x)	R(x)	$P_t(x)$	$E_{elec}(x)$	$E_{amp}(x)$	W(x)	C_R	K	E_{tr}	λ	Dr
Digi XBee Cellular 3G	(200,100)	77185.9	100	3.3*0.702	8333.69	0.0013	2.4	40	2	33361120	0.125	250M
Bluetooth V3 module TEL0026	(200,100)	14.630	10	3.6*0.05	648	0.0013	2.4	40	2	2594080	0.125	2M
ESP8266 Wi-Fi IoT	(200,100)	31675	50	3.3*0.5	5940	0.0013	2.4	40	2	23762080	0.125	54M
Digi XBee 3 Zigbee	(200,100)	22260	20	3.6*0.04	518.4	0.0013	2.4	40	2	2074080	0.125	250k
RF ZigBee ETRX357	(200,100)	16700	20	3.6*0.031	648	0.0013	2.4	40	2	1609120	0.125	250k

- Given the wireless transmission modules with their characteristics in the table below Table 4.

$$\min_{x \in S} \text{TransmissionRate}(N, x)$$

such that:
$$\begin{cases} \text{EnergyTotal}(x, K) \leq E_{tr} \\ \text{Cost}(N, x, E_{tr}, D_r, K) \leq C_r \\ \text{TransmissionRate}(N, x) \geq D_r \end{cases}$$

Table 4. Sensor choice maximize $TransmissionRate$

Sensor/data	N	$Price(x)$	$R(x)$	$P_t(x)$	$E_{elec}(x)$	$E_{amp}(x)$	$W(x)$	C_R	K	E_{tr}	λ	$Dr(b)$
Digi XBee Cellular 3G	(200,100)	77185.9	100	3.3*0.702	8333.69	0.0013	2.4	40	2	33.4	0.125	1.91
Bluetooth V3 module TEL0026	(200,100)	14.630	10	3.6*0.05	648	0.0013	2.4	40	2	2.5	0.125	191.31
ESP8266 Wi-Fi IoT	(200,100)	31675	50	3.3*0.5	5940	0.0013	2.4	40	2	23.7	0.125	7.65
Digi XBee 3 Zigbee	(200,100)	22260	20	3.6*0.04	518.4	0.0013	2.4	40	2	2.07	0.125	47.82
RF ZigBee ETRX357	(200,100)	16700	20	3.6*0.031	648	0.0013	2.4	40	2	1.6	0.125	47.82

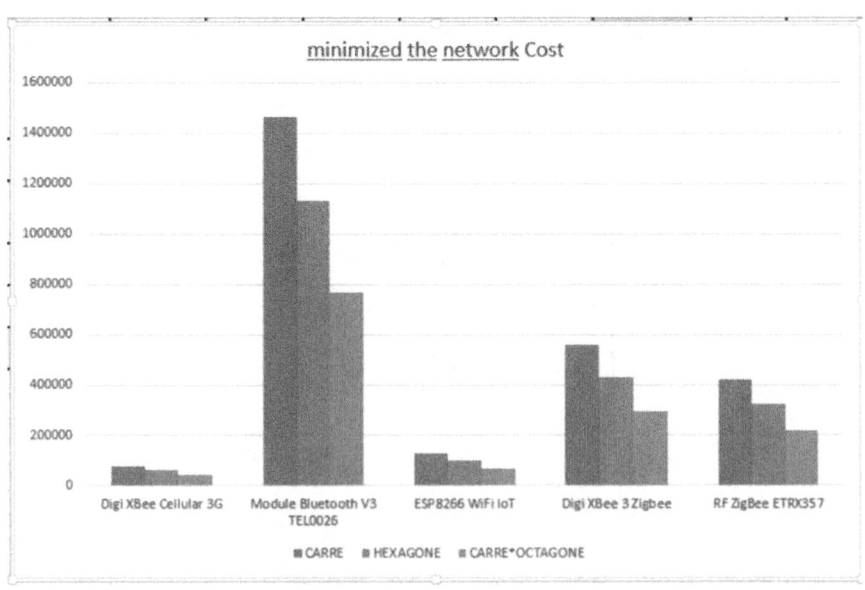

Fig. 5. Minimized the network $Cost$.

Based on optimization criteria, Fig. 5 shows that network cost is highest with Bluetooth, 3G and WiFi are cheaper and Zigbee is average.

According to the optimization criteria, Fig. 6 shows that the energy consumed in the network is highest with 3G followed by WiFi, Bluetooth consumes less energy and transmission with Zigbee requires low energy.

According to the optimization criteria, Fig. 7 shows that the transmission rate is lower with 3G and WiFi, Zigbee has an average rate and Bluetooth uses the highest transmission rate.

5.1 Assessment

We evaluated a number of sensors on the market for different scenarios. This multi-objective study was based on three basic functions. They have a common variable called d, which is the Euclidean distance between two consecutive sensors. The functions we used are: the $Cost$ function, the $EnergiTotal$ function, and the $TransmissionRate$ function. We maximized the network $TransmissionRate$ function and minimized the network $Cost$ and $EnergiTotal$ functions. After a comparative study of a set of sensors based on our three functions, we obtained as results three tables presented in Tables 2, 3, 4.

The analysis of our results shows that sensors using the IEEE 802.4 communication protocol and the ZIGBEE ETRX357 RF type offer better performance than other sensors. So we'll use this type of sensor to improve the performance of our data sensor network.

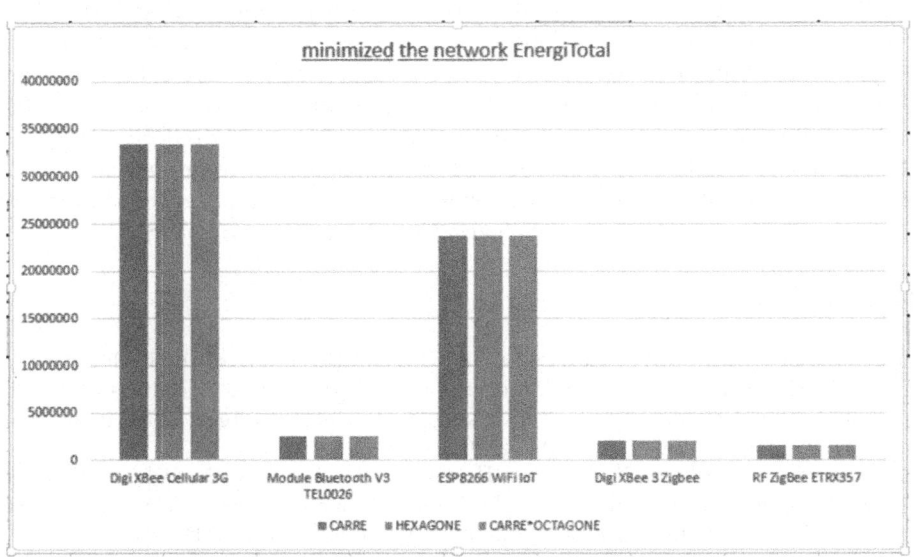

Fig. 6. Minimized the network $EnergiTotal$.

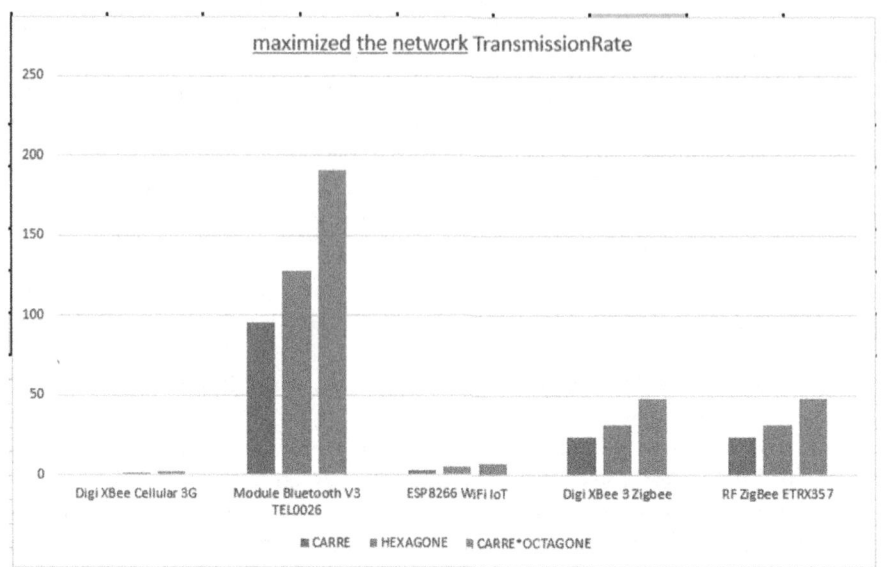

Fig. 7. Maximized the network $TransmissionRate$.

6 Conclusion

In summary, we conducted a comparative study of a number of sensors on the market. This multi-objective study was based on a number of criteria. Each constraint is represented as a function, so we used three functions. We have a function that represents the cost of the network, we also have a function that represents the total energy of the network and finally we have the function that gives us the transmission rate of the network. In summary, ZIGBEE ETRX357 RF sensors with IEEE 802.4 protocol will be implemented in our wireless sensor network. Again with the aim of increasing network performance, we will propose a linear routing algorithm for data packet transmission in our WSN.

References

1. Es-Sabery, F., Hair, A.: Evaluation and comparative study of the both algorithm LEACH and PEGASIS based on energy consumption. In: Proceedings of the 3rd International Conference on Networking, Information Systems & Security, Marrakech, Morocco, pp. 1–6. ACM (2020)
2. Isaac, S.J., Hancke, G.P., Madhoo, H., Khatri, A.: A survey of wireless sensor network applications from a power utility's distribution perspective. In: IEEE Africon 2011, Victoria Falls, Livingstone, Zambia, pp. 1–5. IEEE (2011)
3. Somauroo, A., Bassoo, V.: Energy-efficient genetic algorithm variants of PEGASIS for 3D wireless sensor networks. Appl. Comput. Inform. **19**(3/4), 186–208 (2020)
4. Meghanathan, N.: Use of tree traversal algorithms for chain formation in the PEGASIS data gathering protocol for wireless sensor networks. KSII Trans. Internet Inf. Syst. **3**(6), 612–627 (2009)

5. AnnushaKumar, G.R., Padmathilagam, V.: Comparison of hybrid GACS – TEEN with fuzzy – TEEN and GA – TEEN in hierarchical routing protocol for WSN. Mater. Today Proc. S2214785321003229 (2021)
6. Karunanithy, K., Velusamy, B.: Energy efficient cluster and travelling salesman problem based data collection using WSNs for intelligent water irrigation and fertigation. Measurement **161**, 107835 (2020)
7. Ouyang, F., et al.: Automatic delivery and recovery system of wireless sensor networks (WSN) nodes based on UAV for agricultural applications. Comput. Electron. Agric. **162**, 31–43 (2019)
8. Seedha Devi, V., Ravi, T., Baghavathi Priya, S.: Cluster based data aggregation scheme for latency and packet loss reduction in WSN. Comput. Commun. **149**, 36–43 (2020)
9. Singh, A., Nagaraju, A.: Low latency and energy efficient routing-aware network coding-based data transmission in multi-hop and multi-sink WSN. Ad Hoc Netw. **107**, 102182 (2020)
10. Vinitha, A., Rukmini, M.S.S., Dhirajsunehra: Secure and energy aware multi-hop routing protocol in WSN using Taylor-based hybrid optimization algorithm. J. King Saud Univ. Comput. Inf. Sci. S131915781930878X (2019)
11. Mammeri, M.Z., Rodrigues, M.J.: Routage pour la Gestion de l'Energie dans les Réseaux de Capteurs Sans Fil, p. 147 (2010)
12. Makableh, A.H., Samara, G.: Impact of node clustering on power consumption in WSN. In: The 7th International Conference on Information Technology, pp. 266–269. Al-Zaytoonah University of Jordan (2015)
13. Malisetti, N.R., Pamula, V.K.: Performance of quasi oppositional butterfly optimization algorithm for cluster head selection in WSNs. Procedia Comput. Sci. **171**, 1953–1960 (2020)
14. Yemeni, Z., Wang, H., Ismael, W.M., Wang, Y., Chen, Z.: Reliable spatial and temporal data redundancy reduction approach for WSN. Comput. Netw. **185**, 107701 (2021)
15. Nikouei, R., Rasouli, N., Tahmasebi, S., Zolfi, S., Faragardi, H., Fotouhi, H.: A quantum-annealing-based approach to optimize the deployment cost of a multi-sink multi-controller WSN. Procedia Comput. Sci. **155**, 250–257 (2019)
16. Achroufene, A., Chelik, M., Bouadem, N.: Modified CSMA/CA protocol for real-time data fusion applications based on clustered WSN. Comput. Netw. **196**, 108243 (2021)
17. Faheem, M., Butt, R.A., Raza, B., Ashraf, M.W., Ngadi, M.A., Gungor, V.C.: Energy efficient and reliable data gathering using internet of software-defined mobile sinks for WSNs-based smart grid applications. Comput. Stand. Interfaces **66**, 103341 (2019)
18. Lecor, A., Ngom, D., Mejri, M., Mbodji, S.: A new strategy for deploying a wireless sensor network based on a square-octagon pattern to optimizes the covered area. In: Faye, Y., Gueye, A., Gueye, B., Diongue, D., Nguer, E., Ba, M. (eds.) CNRIA 2021. LNICST, vol. 400, pp. 61–76. Springer, Cham (2021). https://doi.org/10.1007/978-3-030-90556-9_6
19. Sharma, D., Tomar, G.S.: Enhance PEGASIS algorithm for increasing the life time of wireless sensor network. Mater. Today Proc. **29**, 372–380 (2020)
20. Jin Wang, Yu., Gao, X.Y., Li, F., Kim, H.-J.: An enhanced PEGASIS algorithm with mobile sink support for wireless sensor networks. Wirel. Commun. Mob. Comput. **2018**, 1–9 (2018)

21. Gungor, V.C., Bin, L., Hancke, G.P.: Opportunities and challenges of wireless sensor networks in smart grid. IEEE Trans. Industr. Electron. **57**(10), 3557–3564 (2010)
22. Shannon, C.E.: Communication in the presence of noise. Proc. IEEE **86**(2) (1998)
23. Lee, J.-S., Su, Y.-W., Shen, C.-C.: A comparative study of wireless protocols: Bluetooth, UWB, ZigBee, and Wi-Fi. In: IECON 2007 - 33rd Annual Conference of the IEEE Industrial Electronics Society, Taipei, Taiwan, pp. 46–51. IEEE (2007)

Towards a Single-Sign-On Authentication Architecture Based on OpenID Connect Protocol and Blockchain Technology

Assane Ilboudo[✉], Didier Bassole, Justin Pegdwindé Kouraogo, Gouayon Koala, and Oumarou Sie

Laboratoire de Mathématiques et d'Informatique, Université Joseph Ki-Zerbo, Ouagadougou, Burkina Faso
assaneilboudo1998@gmail.com
https://www.ujkz.bf

Abstract. OpenID Connect is a delegated authentication protocol used in web and mobile applications. It emphasizes the crucial role of third-party applications, also known as Relying Parties, which securely request information from an identity provider. In this article, we have proposed an approach based on the Ethereum blockchain to enhance the authentication process and user account privacy within the OpenID Connect protocol. This mechanism adds an additional layer of protection.

Keywords: Authentication · Security · Blockchain · OpenID Connect

1 Introduction

Nowadays, the number of internet users continues to grow globally. According to estimates from the second half of 2022, based on global Internet usage statistics, there are now over 4.95 billion active Internet users[1] among the eight (08) billion inhabitants of the planet[2]. This significant increase can be attributed to the growing proliferation of online services and remarkable advancements in network technologies [1]. However, this expansion comes with a proliferation of identification data for each user, exacerbating the inherent risk of losing or forgetting this information.

In this context, the adoption of Single Sign-On (SSO) systems emerges as a relevant solution to address various issues associated with user authentication on the web. The single sign-on system offers practical advantages by allowing users to access a multitude of applications with a single authentication [2]. Users only need to remember one set of credentials to access various services, thereby reducing cognitive load and mitigating the frustration associated with managing multiple passwords.

---

[1] https://fr.statista.com/statistiques/985232/nombre-utilisateurs-internet-monde/.
[2] https://www.un.org/fr/global-issues/population.

In the single sign-on system, each user has an account managed by an Identity Provider (IdP) [3]. When a user logs into a service, they are redirected to the identity provider to authenticate. The IdP serves as a trusted third party for service providers and users. However, the identity provider may be vulnerable to certain attacks, such as sophisticated phishing attacks and identity theft, leading to data leaks and compromising users' privacy [2,4,5].

Furthermore, single sign-on authentication also poses potential security issues, including the risk of session hijacking and authentication token interception [3,6–8]. The robustness and confidentiality challenges in single sign-on authentication systems are currently a major concern for the computer security research community.

The main goal of this work is to enhance the robustness of the authentication process within the OpenID Connect protocol by proposing a secure architecture that integrates a decentralized multi-factor authentication mechanism based on the Ethereum blockchain.

The remainder of this article is organized as follows: in Sect. 2, we discuss the related works; in Sect. 3, we conduct a comparative study of different SSO protocols. Section 4 discusses our methodological approach and we conclude this work in Sect. 5.

2 Related Works

The widely used Single Sign-On protocols nowadays include OpenID Connect, supported by major digital companies such as Microsoft, Amazon, Google, Meta, PayPal, Verizon, Salesforce, Oracle, VMWare, IBM, WordPress, Yahoo, GitHub, and Twitter. OpenID Connect is also considered the new standard for Single Sign-On systems [9,10]. According to Zhang et al. [11], over a million websites support Single Sign-On (SSO) through OpenID Connect. Despite its widespread adoption on the web, mobile devices, cloud, Internet of Things (IoT), and SSO systems, OpenID Connect has a weakness. It inadequately verifies authenticity, merely validating the parameters of a request without confirming the identity of the request sender. Consequently, attackers can gain unauthorized access to restricted resources by exploiting theft, insufficient protection, and/or incomplete token validation.

To address these vulnerabilities, Yousra et al. [12] proposed a new model aimed at enhancing the security of OpenID Connect using blockchain technology and non-fungible tokens. Despite these improvements, it is important to note that vulnerabilities still exist. For example, if a legitimate user's credentials (username and password) fall into the hands of an attacker, they can use them to log in without the system effectively detecting the impersonation of the legitimate user's identity. This illustrated deficiency needs to be examined to strengthen the security of the conventional authentication process, which encompasses traditional methods such as the use of usernames and passwords, one-time codes, or security questions. These methods are employed to verify a user's identity before granting access to a system or information. Thus, how can the robustness of the authentication process within the OpenID Connect protocol be strengthened? Yuki Ezawa et al. [13] presented an authentication system based on a blockchain-based PKI structure and smart contracts via a verification and authentication server, providing enhanced security during identity authentication. However, it is important to note that this approach requires the user to enter sensitive information such as the public key certificate, a random number, and a signature on the mobile login screen. In case of mobile loss, the user will no longer be able to authenticate, as the mobile is necessary to generate the required key certificate for authentication. In 2020, Mustafa [14] developed a Single Sign-On authentication system based on a private blockchain. In this system, each user has a pair of public and private addresses defined on the private blockchain network. This system relies on the OAuth2 protocol and uses a two-factor authentication method via a specifically developed mobile application, enhancing user information security. However, the creation of the public and private address pair via a mobile application before logging into a website poses a challenge. In case of mobile loss, the user will no longer be able to authenticate, as the mobile is necessary to generate the required key certificate for authentication. Also, in 2023, Shuhan et al. [15] introduced a federated identity system based on blockchain technology. Federated identity systems based on SAML face centralization issues by depending on a single identity provider within the federation, creating a single point of failure. To address this problem, the authors opted for a decentralized model based on the blockchain. In 2023, Yawalkar et al. [16] developed a federated identification and audit system based on blockchain technology. This system, relying on the SAML protocol, offers a decentralized approach to grant and control federated identities, allowing users to access online services provided by marketplace business partners. The framework is powered by smart contracts executed on the blockchain, ensuring secure and transparent management of federated identity creation and validation processes. Additionally, the system integrates an audit mechanism, enabling users and business partners to closely monitor all activities associated with the use of federated identities. The fundamental goal of this research is to provide a robust and effective solution for managing identities and transactions on a marketplace platform, leveraging the benefits of blockchain to ensure the integrity and efficiency of the process. In 2020, Nikos Fotiou et al. [17] proposed the creation of a new type of OAuth 2.0 token backed by distributed ledger technology, specifically blockchain. This proposal aims to enhance the security and management of OAuth 2.0 tokens used in online authorization protocols. This solution leverages Ethereum to store information for audits and verify token integrity. Ethereum smart contracts simplify revocation, separation of authorization servers and resource servers, enable token delegation, and offer opportunities for token exchange for fungible assets. In 2023, Fugkeaw [18] introduced a D2-IAM (Decentralized and Distributed Identity and Access Management) system based on blockchain supporting SSO authentication, authorization, and preventive access control with a supervisor in the cloud computing domain. All these features are orchestrated by a series of smart contracts, resulting in more autonomous and traceable access control procedures.

SSO authentication relies on token usage, reducing communication overhead between multiple systems. The D2-IAM system is based on OAuth2.

3 Comparative Study of Single Sign-On Protocols

3.1 Criteria and Comparison

In this section, we will conduct a comparative study of the protocols used in Single Sign-On systems, based on the following criteria (Table 1):

- Authorization and Authentication
- Token Format
- Data Integrity/Non-Repudiation
- Data Confidentiality/Privacy
- Support for Web Applications and Native Mobile Applications
- Lightweight Standard/Protocol

Table 1. Comparative analysis of Single Sign-On protocols

Criteria	SAML [19]	OAuth2 [19]	OIDC [19]
Authorization and Authentication	Mainly focused on authentication, with some authorization features	Emphasizes authorization, does not provide authentication	Combines authentication with the OAuth2 authorization framework
Token Format	XML	XML, JSON, JWT	JSON, JWT
Data Integrity/Non-Repudiation	Ensures data integrity with XML signatures	Security depends on the underlying transport (e.g., HTTPS)	Uses JSON Web Tokens (JWT) signatures to ensure data integrity
Data Confidentiality/Privacy	Assertions can be encrypted for confidentiality	Confidentiality depends on secure transport TLS	JWTs can be encrypted for confidentiality
Support for Web Applications and Native Mobile Applications	Primarily designed for web applications	Supports both web and native mobile applications	Supports both web and native mobile applications
Lightweight Standard/Protocol	Heavy due to the use of XML	Lighter	Lighter

In order to enhance the authentication process within the Single Sign-On system, some researchers, such as Mustafa [14] and Ezawa [13], have opted for a second-factor authentication (2FA) based on an application installed on a smartphone. However, in the event of a lost smartphone, the user would be unable to access their account. Similarly, in the case of a smartphone being stolen by a malicious individual, it could be used to impersonate the legitimate user and gain access to their account.

In contrast, author Yousra [12] did not integrate a second-factor authentication (2FA) into their Single Sign-On authentication system. Given that in Single Sign-On systems, the user relies on a single set of credentials, namely their username and password, Yousra's system presents an increased risk in the event of credential theft by a malicious actor, potentially compromising access to all accounts.

We have chosen the OpenID Connect protocol, in line with Yousra's prior use of this protocol, who also integrated blockchain technology into their Single Sign-On system. To enrich our contribution, we plan to build upon Yousra's advancements by incorporating a second-factor authentication (2FA) mechanism. This mechanism will be based on blockchain technology, and the user will be able to perform the second-factor authentication (2FA) using either their smartphone, their computer, or both, thus providing increased flexibility.

3.2 Description of the Operation of OpenID Connect

Operation of the OpenID Connect Protocol

OpenID Connect is a widely used authentication and authorization protocol that enables users to securely authenticate across various online applications and services. It is built on OAuth 2.0 [17], an authorization protocol, and adds an authentication layer, making it a popular choice for modern authentication systems. The OpenID Connect protocol offers three distinct flows to authenticate the end user with a Relying Party (RP): the authorization code flow, the implicit flow, and the hybrid flow. Among these three options, the authorization code flow is the most widely used for OpenID Connect protocol authentication due to its robustness and security.

To start using the services of the OpenID Connect protocol as an end user, the RP must first undergo a registration process with the Identity Provider (IdP). This registration involves configuring the necessary parameters and information to establish the connection between the RP, IdP, and the user. This registration process ensures a smooth and secure interaction among the parties involved in OpenID Connect authentication. It is designed to establish a standardized framework, allowing users to log in to multiple online services while preserving their security and privacy. The operation of the OpenID Connect protocol is illustrated in Fig. 1.

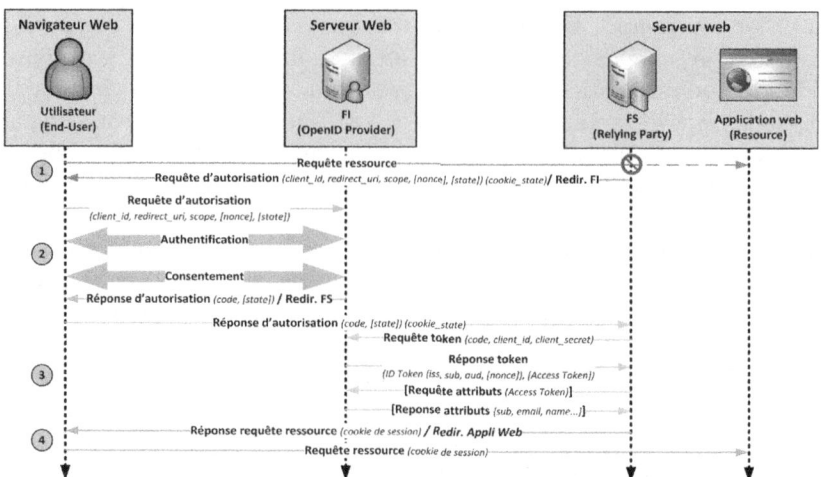

Fig. 1. Operation of the OpenID Connect protocol [20]

Some Parameters Used in the OpenID Connect Protocol Flow

- **client_id**: Unique identifier of the Service Provider with the Identity Provider. This is a public value, typically generated randomly by the Identity Provider,
- **client_secret**: This value is optional, but it is commonly used to authenticate the Service Provider when retrieving an authorization code from the Identity Provider. It must remain confidential and be known only to the two parties,
- **redirect_uri**: URL belonging to the domain of the Service Provider, used by the Identity Provider after user authentication to send the authorization response back to the Service Provider (via the user).
- **scope**: Lists the user's resources protected by the Identity Provider that the Service Provider wishes to access. This typically includes additional identity information such as email address.

Phase 1: An unauthenticated user seeks to access a protected resource. Their request is intercepted by the Service Provider, triggering an authorization request initiated by the Service Provider. This request is then sent back to the user, who presents it to their Identity Provider for validation.

Phase 2: The Identity Provider reviews the authorization request and prompts the user to log in to prove their identity. Once authenticated, the user is prompted to give consent to share the information required by the Service Provider (SP), defined in the "scope" parameter. After obtaining user consent, the Identity Provider sends an authorization response to the Service Provider (SP) via the user's browser. This response includes an essential authorization code.

Phase 3: The Service Provider (SP) verifies the authorization response submitted by the user and retrieves the authorization code. Subsequently, the service system sends this code to the Identity Provider through a token request. This message is authenticated using the client credentials (client_ID and client_secret) and is transmitted via the token endpoint. The Identity Provider authenticates the Service Provider, verifies the authorization code, and in return sends the Service Provider the identity token (ID Token) corresponding to the authenticated user. At this stage, it is also possible for the Service Provider to obtain an access token to acquire additional identity information by sending an attribute request.

Phase 4: The Service Provider examines the ID Token, identifies the user, and performs a verification to control their access. If the user is authorized to use the requested service, the Service Provider finally grants them access to the initially requested resource. When a user wants to access secure data, a Relying Party (RP) requests approval from the Identity Provider (IdP) via the OpenID Connect protocol, but implementation errors can expose this request to attacks. Security must be strengthened by using TLS, following OpenID Connect, and blockchain technology can offer an additional layer of protection.

4 Methodological Approach

Our system is based on an existing reference model aimed at enhancing security and preserving privacy within OpenID Connect systems integrating the Ethereum blockchain and Non-Fungible Tokens (NFTs) [12]. This existing reference model takes a comprehensive approach, ensuring the integrity, availability, and confidentiality of OpenID Connect protocol security parameters, while limiting their access to authorized entities through a robust verification process.

By merging and expanding the definitions of Bal and Ner [21], Regner et al. [22], and Leech [23], we define a Non-Fungible Token (NFT) as "a cryptographically unique, indivisible, irreplaceable, and verifiable token representing a given asset, whether digital or physical, on a blockchain." Currently, the vast majority of NFTs are built on the Ethereum blockchain network and are therefore Ethereum tokens. For example, suppose we want to acquire gold without becoming its owner [23]. Someone could create a token whose value changes based on the price of gold. Instead of physically owning gold, we hold a representation in the form of tokens. This means that we do not own tangible, fungible gold, but rather a representation through tokens. These tokens are considered more secure because it is much more difficult to hack an Ethereum token than to break into someone's physical possession. The blockchain enables this by being immutable; once a transaction is validated, it cannot be modified [24]. We use these NFTs to enhance the security of access tokens to the account.

4.1 Strengthening Authentication Through 2F

Trust in technology has been seriously compromised by the alarming rise in online fraud cases, phishing attacks, and cybercrime [25]. The rapid growth and increasing sophistication of cybercrime have rendered traditional authentication mechanisms (username and password) ineffective in safeguarding users' private data. To address this situation, OTPs (One-Time Passwords) and single sign-on systems have emerged as preferred solutions to counteract these fraudulent activities [26–28]. OTP represents a type of two-factor authentication mechanism. Simply put, an OTP is a time-based access token provided by the bank or application, containing numerical or alphanumeric values.

Various means are employed to deliver OTPs to users, such as software tokens through mobile applications, hardware tokens (like key fobs), and on-demand OTPs via SMS or emails [29]. Before completing the transaction, the user is prompted to enter the OTP received on their registered phone number, email address, or both. Once the correct OTP is entered by the user, the transaction is finalized. However, even with the OTP mechanism, the possibility of SIM cloning persists, allowing fraudulent access to the OTP and the execution of transactions on behalf of the user [30]. Another conceivable scenario is the loss of the user's phone, resulting in the inability to receive the OTP and consequently, the impossibility of completing the transaction [31].

To address this issue encountered by existing MFA (Multi-Factor Authentication) systems, we have decided to integrate a decentralized multi-factor authentication mechanism into our approach. Indeed, this multi-factor authentication mechanism will be based on smart contracts. The user will receive a transaction via their wallet, which they must confirm by signing it with their private key. Then, this transaction will be sent back to the smart contract for verification. If the transaction is valid, the user's identity is confirmed. The wallet can be installed either on the computer's browser, the smartphone, or both, i.e., the computer's browser and the smartphone.

4.2 Integration of a Decentralized Multi-factor Authentication Mechanism into the Reference Model

To address the Broken En-User Authentication attack issue faced by the reference model, we are incorporating a decentralized multi-factor authentication mechanism within it, as illustrated in Fig. 2. By integrating a multi-factor authentication mechanism, our model specifically tackles the challenge posed by the previously mentioned Broken En-User Authentication attacks. By requiring multiple factors for authentication, we significantly complicate the task for attackers attempting to compromise a user's identity. Moreover, the decentralization of this mechanism ensures that user identity validation is not dependent on a single central point. This approach significantly enhances the system's resilience by minimizing risks associated with isolated vulnerabilities or attacks directed at a centralized point.

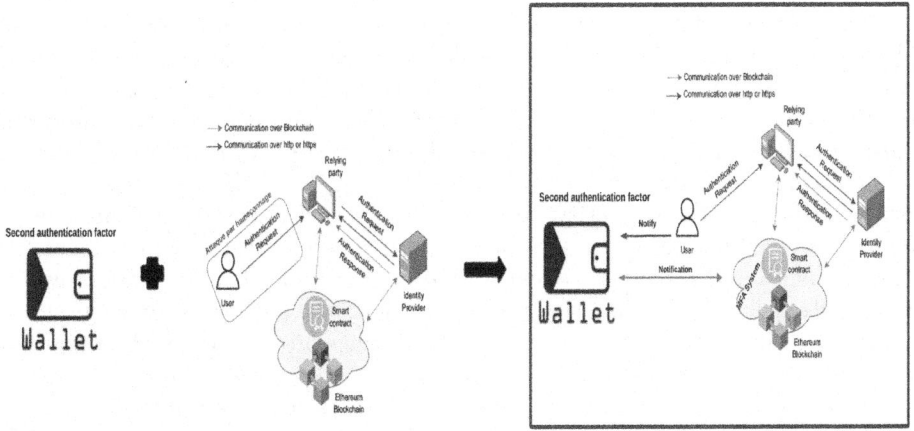

Fig. 2. Integration of a decentralized multi-factor authentication mechanism into the reference model

4.3 Proposed Model

In this subsection, we propose our model depicted in Fig. 3. Our approach involves three main actors:

- **the User**: the person who wishes to access an application or service and whose identity needs to be authenticated,
- **the Identity Provider (IdP)**: the entity that verifies the user's identity and issues authentication tokens and profile information to the Relying Party,
- **the Relying Party (RP)**: the application or service that requests and uses the user's identity information provided by the Identity Provider to grant access to its resources.

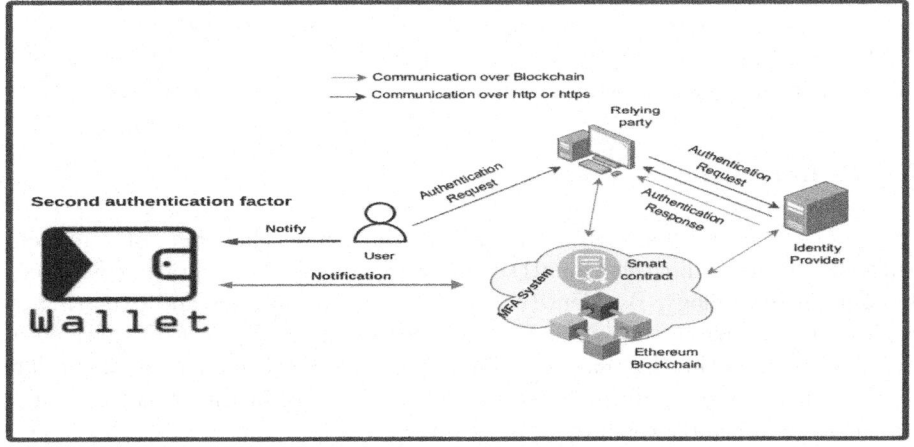

Fig. 3. Description of our methodological approach

Each of these actors assumes a dual role as an Ethereum node within the blockchain network. Specifically, the identity provider is responsible for managing the smart contract that generates non-fungible tokens (NFTs). When a user attempts to access a protected resource from the service provider requiring authentication, the process is triggered. The service provider (RP) initiates an authentication request with its identity provider (IdP), seeking the user's authorization to access their identity information stored with their IdP. This request is made by redirecting the user's browser to their identity provider, an entity that manages and provides credential information to authenticate users within a computer system. The identity provider reviews the authorization request and performs verification of the legitimacy of the service provider using the Ethereum blockchain-based smart contract technology.

If everything is verified, it prompts the user to log in to prove their identity using their credential data as the first factor of authentication. Next, the second factor of authentication comes into play, wherein the identity provider calls the smart contract on the Ethereum blockchain to verify the user's identity. The smart contract generates a specific transaction, which is then sent to the wallet for signing. At this point, a pop-up window appears, prompting the user to confirm the transaction by signing it using their private key. The smart contract then performs a verification using the public key associated with the user's Ethereum address to validate the signature provided by the wallet. If the signature is deemed valid, the contract is then authorized to perform the requested action. This process serves as the second factor of authentication, complementing the user's credential information, conclusively demonstrating that they are the authorized person to access the account.

This dual authentication enhances the security of the process because even if an attacker obtains the user's credential information, they cannot authenticate without confirming the wallet transaction. Once authenticated, the user is prompted to give consent to share the necessary information with the service provider. The identity provider creates tokens and calls on the smart contract to generate corresponding non-fungible tokens (NFTs) for each token. These NFTs are securely transmitted on the Ethereum blockchain to the recipient entity. An NFT is a form of unique digital token that represents ownership or proof of authenticity of a specific asset.

5 Conclusion

In this article, we have undertaken the persistent challenge of enhancing authentication within the OpenID Connect protocol by integrating Ethereum blockchain technology. By identifying existing vulnerabilities and exploring the limitations of current authentication systems, we have devised a robust multi-factor authentication mechanism using Ethereum blockchain technology. This mechanism adds an additional layer of protection within the OpenID Connect protocol, significantly reinforcing its security.

References

1. Ali, S.T.: MO-Auth: a novel approach for authentication in modern applications. Int. J. Adv. Res. Ideas Innov. Technol. **9**(2) (2023). www.IJARIIT.com
2. Mittal, N., Misbahuddin, M., Mustafa, A.S.: Enabling trust in single sign-on using DNS based authentication of named entities. Int. J. Microw. Wirel. Technol. **1**(1), 41–53 (2022). https://doi.org/10.5815/ijwmt.2022.01.05. http://www.mecs-press.org/ijwmt/ijwmt-v12-n1/v12n1-5.html
3. Ghasemisharif, M., Kanich, C., Polakis, J.: Towards automated auditing for account and session management flaws in single sign-on deployments. In: 2022 IEEE Symposium on Security and Privacy (SP), pp. 1774–1790. IEEE (2022). https://doi.org/10.1109/SP46214.2022.9833753. https://ieeexplore.ieee.org/abstract/document/9833753/
4. Sharif, M.H.U.: Web attacks analysis and mitigation techniques. Int. J. Eng. Res. Technol. 10–12 (2022). https://www.academia.edu/download/80622531/Web_Attacks_Analysis_and_Mitigation_Techniques.pdf
5. Xu, R., Yang, S., Zhang, F., Fang, Z.: MISO: legacy-compatible privacy-preserving single sign-on using trusted execution environments. In: 2023 IEEE 8th European Symposium on Security and Privacy (EuroS&P), pp. 352–372. IEEE (2023). https://ieeexplore.ieee.org/abstract/document/10190538/
6. Joseph, J., Bhadauria, S.: Cookie based protocol to defend malicious browser extensions. In: 2019 International Carnahan Conference on Security Technology (ICCST), pp. 1–6. IEEE (2019). https://doi.org/10.1109/CCST.2019.8888425. https://ieeexplore.ieee.org/document/8888425/
7. Zhong, L.: A Survey of Prevent and Detect Access Control Vulnerabilities. arXiv preprint arXiv:2304.10600 (2023). https://arxiv.org/abs/2304.10600
8. Ghasemisharif, M., Ramesh, A., Checkoway, S., Kanich, C., Polakis, J.: O single sign-off, where art thou? An empirical analysis of single sign-on account hijacking and session management on the web. In: 27th USENIX Security Symposium (USENIX Security 2018), pp. 1475–1492 (2018). https://www.usenix.org/conference/usenixsecurity18/presentation/ghasemisharif
9. Singh, T., Meenakshi: Prevention of session hijacking using token and session id reset approach. Int. J. Inf. Technol. **12**, 781–788 (2020). https://doi.org/10.1007/s41870-020-00486-w
10. Fett, D., Küsters, R., Schmitz, G.: A comprehensive formal security analysis of OAuth 2.0. In: Proceedings of the 2016 ACM SIGSAC Conference on Computer and Communications Security, pp. 1204–1215 (2016). https://dl.acm.org/doi/abs/10.1145/2976749.2978385
11. Zhang, Z., Król, M., Sonnino, A., Zhang, L., Rivière, E.: El passo: privacy-preserving, asynchronous single sign-on. arXiv preprint arXiv:2002.10289 (2020). https://arxiv.org/abs/2002.10289
12. Yousra, B., Yassine, S., Yassine, M., Said, S., Lo'ai, T., Salah, K.: A novel secure and privacy-preserving model for OpenID connect based on blockchain. IEEE Access (2023). https://doi.org/10.1109/ACCESS.2023.3292143. https://ieeexplore.ieee.org/abstract/document/10172179/
13. Ezawa, Y., et al.: Designing authentication and authorization system with blockchain. In: 2019 14th Asia Joint Conference on Information Security (AsiaJCIS), pp. 111–118. IEEE (2019). https://doi.org/10.1109/AsiaJCIS.2019.00006. https://ieeexplore.ieee.org/abstract/document/8826910/

14. Tanrıverdi, M.: Design and implementation of blockchain based single sign-on authentication system for web applications. Sakarya Univ. J. Comput. Inf. Sci. **3**(3), 343–354 (2020). https://doi.org/10.35377/saucis.03.03.757459. https://dergipark.org.tr/en/download/article-file/1167051
15. Shuhan, M.K.B., Hasnayeen, S.M., Das, T.K., Sakib, M.N., Ferdous, M.S.: Decentralised Identity Federations using Blockchain. arXiv e-prints, arXiv-2305 (2023). https://ui.adsabs.harvard.edu/abs/2023arXiv230500315K/abstract
16. Yawalkar, P.M., Paithankar, D.N., Pabale, A.R., Kolhe, R.V., William, P.: Integrated identity and auditing management using blockchain mechanism. Measur. Sens. **27**, 100732 (2023). https://doi.org/10.1016/j.measen.2023.100732. https://www.sciencedirect.com/science/article/pii/S2665917423000685
17. Fotiou, N., Pittaras, I., Siris, V.A., Voulgaris, S., Polyzos, G.C.: OAuth 2.0 authorization using blockchain-based tokens. arXiv preprint arXiv:2001.10461 (2020). https://arxiv.org/abs/2001.10461
18. Fugkeaw, S.: Achieving decentralized and dynamic SSO-identity access management system for multi-application outsourced in cloud. IEEE Access **11**, 25480–25491 (2023). https://doi.org/10.1109/ACCESS.2023.3255885. https://ieeexplore.ieee.org/abstract/document/10066292/
19. Naik, N., Jenkins, P.: Securing digital identities in the cloud by selecting an apposite federated identity management from SAML, OAuth and OpenID connect. In: 2017 11th International Conference on Research Challenges in Information Science (RCIS), pp. 163–174. IEEE (2017). https://ieeexplore.ieee.org/abstract/document/7956534/
20. Rémi, C.C., Olivier, L.: OpenID Connect: présentation du protocole et étude de l'attaque Broken End-User Authentication. J. MISC (2018). http://paperstreet.picty.org/yeye/2018/magazine-misc-CassamChenaiL18/
21. Bal, M., Ner, C.: NFTracer: a Non-Fungible token tracking proof-of-concept using Hyperledger Fabric. arXiv preprint arXiv:1905.04795 (2019). https://arxiv.org/abs/1905.04795
22. Regner, F., Urbach, N., Schweizer, A.: NFTs in practice-non-fungible tokens as core component of a blockchain-based event ticketing application (2019). https://www.fim-rc.de/Paperbibliothek/Veroeffentlicht/1045/wi-1045.pdf
23. Leech, O.: What Are NFTs and How Do They Work? (2023). https://www.coindesk.com/what-are-nfts
24. Leloup, L.: Blockchain: La révolution de la confiance. Publisher Editions Eyrolles (2017). https://www.amazon.com/Blockchain-r%C3%A9volution-confiance-Laurent-Leloup/dp/2212566654
25. Huang, C.Y., Ma, S.P., Chen, K.T.: Using one-time passwords to prevent password phishing attacks. J. Netw. Comput. Appl. **34**(4), 1292–1301 (2011). https://www.sciencedirect.com/science/article/pii/S1084804511000427
26. Lamport, L.: Password authentication with insecure communication. Commun. ACM **24**(11), 770–772 (1981). https://doi.org/10.1145/358527.358533. https://dl.acm.org/doi/abs/10.1145/358790.358797
27. Lu, Z., Yu, H.: One Time Password Generating Method and Apparatus. U.S. Patent No. 8,184,872. U.S. Patent and Trademark Office, Washington, DC (2012). https://patents.google.com/patent/US8184872B2/en
28. Suriadi, S., Foo, E., Jøsang, A.: A user-centric federated single sign-on system. J. Netw. Comput. Appl. **32**(2), 388–401 (2009). https://www.sciencedirect.com/science/article/pii/S1084804508000519

29. Almuairfi, S., Veeraraghavan, P., Chilamkurti, N.: A novel image-based implicit password authentication system (IPAS) for mobile and non-mobile devices. Math. Comput. Model. **58**(1-2), 108–116 (2013). https://www.sciencedirect.com/science/article/pii/S0895717712001719
30. Wang, D., Wang, P.: Two birds with one stone: two-factor authentication with security beyond conventional bound. IEEE Trans. Dependable Secure Comput. **15**(4), 708–722 (2016). https://ieeexplore.ieee.org/abstract/document/7558124/
31. Huang, B., Khan, M.K., Wu, L., Muhaya, F.T.B., He, D.: An efficient remote user authentication with key agreement scheme using elliptic curve cryptography. J. Wirel. Pers. Commun. **85**, 225–240 (2015). https://doi.org/10.1007/s11277-015-2864-5

An Experimental 5G Standalone Testbed for Rural Connectivity

Mahamadou Diawara[1,2(✉)] and Andre Faye[1,3]

[1] Gaston Berger University, Saint-Louis, Senegal
diawara.mahamadou@ugb.edu.sn
[2] UFR de Sciences Appliquées et Technologie, Dedougou, Burkina Faso
[3] Institut Polytechnique de Saint-Louis (IPSL), Saint-Louis, Senegal

Abstract. Digital transformation in service sectors like agriculture, education and healthcare has to be accelerated specifically in African countries to achieve the Sustainable Development Goals (SDG) in 2030. 5G technology allowing flexibility and scalability in networks service deployment is among the technologies that can help this acceleration but its deployment is expensive with proprietary and vendor specific hardware and software. Therefore, open-source implementation allowing low-cost system design gains importance mainly for rural areas where the duration of a return on investment is long or even not guaranteed for operators, thus promoting private initiatives. Even though non standalone 5G networks (5G NSA) deployment approach is seen as an economic way for 5G migration, it is not suitable in contexts where 4G LTE is barely deployed or for private networks. This is the case for most Sub-Saharan countries where 4G LTE coverage is foreseen to be lower than 30% in 2025. We deployed a low cost standalone 5G network (5G SA) using the open source OpenAirInterface (OAI) and commercial-off-the-shelf (COTS) equipment to leverage 5G technology. This testbed helps to test and validate 5G services with private networks affordable to low budget laboratories for digital transformation in rural zones. Two types of experiments were conducted to validate the platform: (1) to assess enhanced mobile broadband (eMBB), massive machine-type communications (mMTC), and ultra-reliable low latency (URLLC) capabilities, (2) to assess common users needs by implementing and testing Voice over New Radio (VoNR).

Keywords: 5G · Standalone · OpenAirInterface · VoNR

1 Introduction

The question of the optimal deployment mode for the transition from 4G to 5G is widely addressed in the literature and cost is often put forward to choose the NSA

Supported by WAEMU through Programme de Bourses d'excellence.

mode. 5G NSA constitutes the majority of the first deployments and relies on the existing 4G infrastructure to benefit from low-band coverage and connection to the 4G network's evolved packet core (EPC) to which the functionalities required to support the new 5G standard are added for more reliable connectivity with enhanced mobile broadband. However, such a choice requires an existing global 4G coverage but this is not the case in many African countries where the level of 4G coverage is low with disparities between urban and rural areas. The resulting digital divide is an obstacle to economic, health care, very high attendance social activities. The question arises for operators whether to invest in 4G infrastructure and deployment or to make the leap from 3G to 5G and adopt standalone migration to 5G despite the cost of investment. Bridging the digital divide is an urgent need if we want to achieve the SDGs in 2030 and long-term strategies cannot prosper and this favours private initiatives.

Actually, use cases where ultra-low latency and much higher capacity are required will only be feasible with 5G SA. Consequently, a different migration scheme not relying on 4G LTE infrastructure and able to provide full benefits of a 5G network would be more appropriate and beneficial. As such, directly implementing 5G SA, without going through 5G NSA, may be an appropriate choice. Besides offering greater possibilities to exploit new network use cases, 5G SA also makes it possible to overcome spectral and technological constraints for those who have not deployed 4G [1]. Liu et al. [2] analysed and compared new radio (NR) 5G SA and 5G NSA in terms of coverage, network capacity, interworking between 4G and 5G, complexity, deployment cost and the latest developments in the sector. While 5G NSA NR appears to outperform in terms of interworking in the initial phase, 5G SA NR outperforms in terms of network capacity, device performance, energy efficiency, simplicity of network deployment and cost-effectiveness [3]. Another advantage of 5G-SA is network slicing which gives the possibility to divide the network according to utilisation needs and perform network resources sharing. In addition, 5G represents a major turning point for Internet access at much higher speeds than 4G, African countries must adopt this technology, particularly to bridge the SDGs. Deploying 5G networks can help reduce the digital divide by improving Internet accessibility in rural and remote areas where fixed infrastructure is limited. It also can enable the rural communities to access connectivity based services such as distance education and remote medical care. Low cost private networks capable to deliver customised solutions can help to bridge the digital divide and 5G SA are great opportunity to exploit.

However, the cost of deploying 5G can be expensive. It is thus important to set up testbeds to deploy 5G SA networks to study and test use cases, particularly in the absence of a 4G LTE network. Network simulators are often used to this end but they are not always sufficient and a rigorous evaluation of the actual operating mode is required [4]. The option of carrying out real-life evaluations on testbeds using commercial 5G equipment is a scenario with many restrictions related to the constraints on deployment and configuration flexibility inherent to proprietary solutions. This is why the market for open-source solutions is booming in the telecoms sector, particularly in mobile networks. The traditional RAN has, for example, evolved into an open, flexible and virtualised network known as Open-RAN [5] which enables multi-vendor deployment to use interchangeable hardware and software with open interfaces. Thus, thanks to open-source implementations and SDN (Software Defined Networking) and NFV (Network Functions Virtualisation) technologies, we can deploy a 5G network in real mode and at low cost.

F. John et al. [6] and Y. Gao et al. [7] addressed OAI-based deployment of 5G SA networks and several others like F. M Tufeano et al. [8] used software-based deployment. A minimal deployment is presented in [6] while a minimal and basic deployments using virtual machines (VM) were considered in [7] and a comparison between the performance of minimal and basic deployments with the gnbsim software was established in [8]. Tufeano's results in [8] are based on simulations while emulation of real-mode operation is desirable with real equipment, particularly for 5G-SA. The VM used Gao in [7] are known to use far more resources than docker containers [8,9] and require powerful machines and constitute a major limitation for low budget designs considered in this work. Furthermore, although the unified data management (UDM) function is used in [7], as compared to [6], the authentication server function (AUSF) server and the unified data repository (UDR) are not included whereas AUSF is a complementary function to UDM necessary to provide a secure and consistent user experience in a 5G network [10].

The main contributions of this paper include (1) building a low cost 5G SA testbed with open-source solution, limited energy consumption and applicable in challenging environments and rural areas in the absence of 4G Telecommunication infrastructure preventing NSA migration. (2) Developing a testbed with eMBB, mMTC, and URLLC capabilities to enhance connectivity and digital services opportunities in rural zone to bridge the digital divide and promote 5G education, heath and intelligent agriculture uses cases to leverage 5G technology to achieve SDG. (3) Validating the testbed capability to cover users' common needs and support VoNR implementation.

This paper addresses the implementation and tests of an affordable basic 5G SA testbed using OAI open-source solutions, docker containers, Universal Software Radio Peripherals (USRP B210) and COST equipment. The affordable testbed is intended to build privates networks to set up 5G use cases to reduce the digital divide in rural and remote areas. The rest of the paper is organised as follows. Section 2 is devoted to the presentation of the 5G SA testbed. Section 3 gives the results of the assessment tests of the testbed along with experimental results on VoNR tests to validate the deployment. Section 4 draws concluding remarks and outline ongoing work.

2 The 5G SA Testbed

Our testbed is based on the open source OpenAirInterface (OAI) implementation [11] which enables to set up future open-source cellular networks by offering both core (5GC) and radio access (5G RAN) deployment possibilities with Docker containers to virtually create all the components and enhance resource usage. The OAI 5G RAN stack supports and emulates [12] the gNodeB and the user equipment (UE) and manages the interactions between them. The UE can be either a 5G phone or an OAI-UE. The OAI-5GC provides a 3GPP-compliant implementation and is easily adaptable to different 5G use cases [13]. The system is deployed on computers with the following specifications: Operating System: Linux Lowlatency kernel Ubuntu 20.04 LTS; Processors: Intel(R) Core (TM) i5-10210U CPU @ 1.60GHz 2.11 GHz; RAM: 8 GB; UHD Driver. Two USRP B210 SDRs are used in the setup, one acting as a radio access point at the gNB level and the other emulating a UE. We also used an Oppo 5G phone equipped with an Open cells SIM card. Each USRP is linked to a machine via an Universal Serial Bus (USB) 3.0 interface. The experimentation was performed in the n78 band (3300 MHz–3800 MHz) at a 3.6 GHz frequency and a 40 MHz bandwidth (106 PRB). The key physical layer parameters are gathered in Table 1. The architecture of the basic 5G SA with the network functions (NF) deployed are shown in Fig. 1.

Table 1. Key parameters of the physical layer.

Parameter	FR1
Access scheme	DL: CP-OFDM, UL: CP-OFDM
	14 Symbols: DL (6), UL (4) flexible (4)
carrier aggregation	1 carrier: 3.6 GHz
Bandwidth per carrier	40 MHz (106 PRB)
Subcarrier spacing	30 kHz
Number of subcarriers	1272
Modulation scheme	QPSK, 64 QAM
MIMO scheme	1x1
Duplex mode	TDD

The IP addresses of all the subsystems and NFs are grouped in Table 2. The NFs in the 5GC and the IMS are deployed in a docker container in the same computer as the gNB to reduce the latency.

The AMF (access and mobility function), UPF (user plane function), SMF, AUSF, UDM, UDR and NRF functions are deployed in the 5GC. The experimental platform is shown in Fig. 2, it features four subsystems: 1) the 5GC (core network), 2) the 5G-RAN (access network), 3) the OAI UE and 4) the oppo 5G phone.

2.1 OAI 5GC and 5G RAN Configurations

The OAI provides the image of each network core component in a Docker containers. After extraction, the *docker − compose.yaml* file must be mod-

Table 2. IP addresses.

Subsystem/NF	IP address	Subsystem/NF	IP address
5GC	192.168.70.0/24	OAI-EXT-DN	192.168.70.135
gNB	192.168.70.129	UDM	192.168.70.137
NRF	192.168.70.130	UDR	192.168.70.136
AMF	192.168.70.132	AUSF	192.168.70.138
SMF	192.168.70.133	IMS	192.168.70.139
UPF	192.168.70.134	UE	12.1.1.128/25

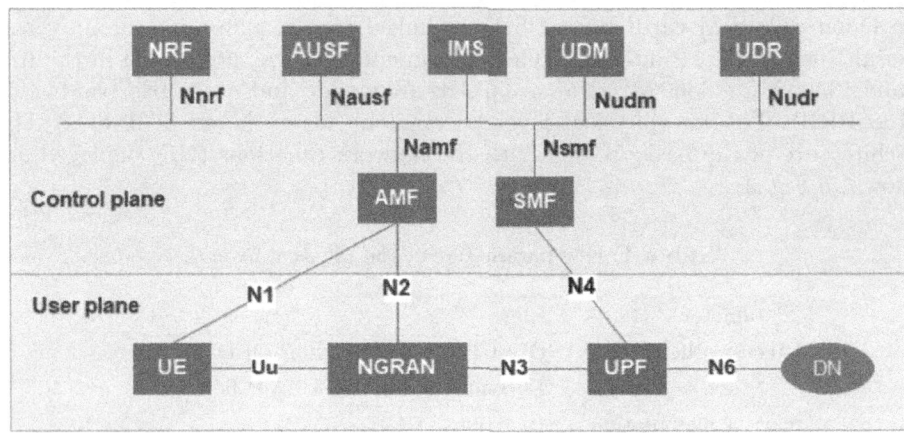

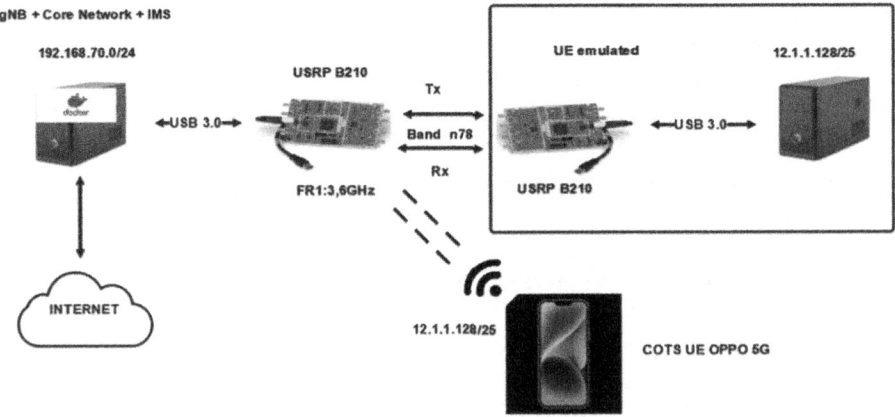

Fig. 1. The deployed basic 5G SA architecture with all the necessary NFs and used subsystems along with their IP addresses.

ified to achieve successful and stable communication between all components. As Docker container traffic is not forwarded to the outside world by default, IP forwarding must be enabled using the following Linux commands:

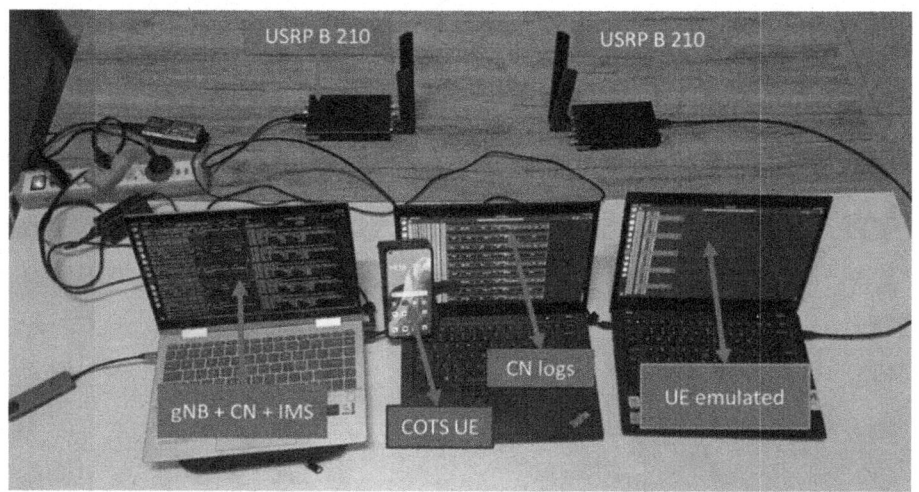

Fig. 2. The experimental 5G SA testbed.

$sudo\ sysctl\ net.ipv4.conf.all.forwarding = 1$ and $sudoiptables - PFORWARD\ ACCEPT$. Once the packet forwarding rules are defined, the Subscriber Identity Module (SIM) details for the OAI UE are added to the $oai\_db.sql2file$. The information added includes the user Identity (IMSI) and the corresponding key, so that the 5GC can identify and authenticate subscribers such as UEs. An interface called $demo - oai$ which contains all the network components and the static IP address configuration is created when the 5GC is launched. The $2024.w03$ branch is used to configure the access network for the gNodeB and the UE; it can handle up to 16 UEs. The same SIM details must be used in the gNodeB configuration file ($gnb.sa.band78.fr1.106PRB.usrpb210.conf$), as added to the 5GC. The same mobile country code (MCC) and mobile network code (MNC) as those used when defining the IMSI should be used. The UE information details are as follow: $uicc0 = \{imsi = $ "208950000000031"$; key = $ "0C0A3460 1D4F07677303652C0462535B"$; opc = $ "63bfa50ee6523365ff14c1f45f88737d"$; dnn = $ "oai"$; nssai\_sst = 1; nssai\_sd = 0xFFFFFF; \}$ where dnn is the domain name, OPC is the operator cipher key, nssai is the Network Slice Selection Assistance Information, sst is the slice/service type and sd is the slice differentiator. Deployment is for one slice.

2.2 5G SA Network Deployment Assessment

Successful deployment is assessed by verifying that (1) all NFs are well configured, healthy and registered with the NRF, (2) downlink and uplink synchronisation are performed, (3) the gNodeB is successfully linked to the AMF, (4) the UE is registered to the AMF and, IMSI, downlink and uplink IDs, PLMN, MNC and cell ID are specified, (5) the PDU session is established, and an IP address is assigned to the UE. The proofs of successful implementation of these steps are given in Fig. 3, 4, 5 and 6.

Fig. 3. Core network successfully deployed. All NFs are registered with the NRF.

Fig. 4. Downlink and uplink synchronisations procedure after 5G RAN and UE deployment and random access procedure execution with contention resolution (msg1, msg2, msg3, msg4). Shown in gNodeB-log file and UE-log file.

3 Experimentation and Validation

In this section we perform experiments to validate the performance of the testbed. Once the 5GC is successfully deployed with all the NFs well configured and healthy, synchronisation is successfully completed for downlink and uplink channels, the 5G SA network is ready for use. The UE communicates with the gNodeB which transmits information to the AMF in the 5GC. The

Fig. 5. gNodeB and UE registration shown in the AMF-log file, PLMN = 208, MNC = 95, IMSI = 200950000000031, downlink channel ID = 0, uplink channel ID = 1, cell ID = 14680064.

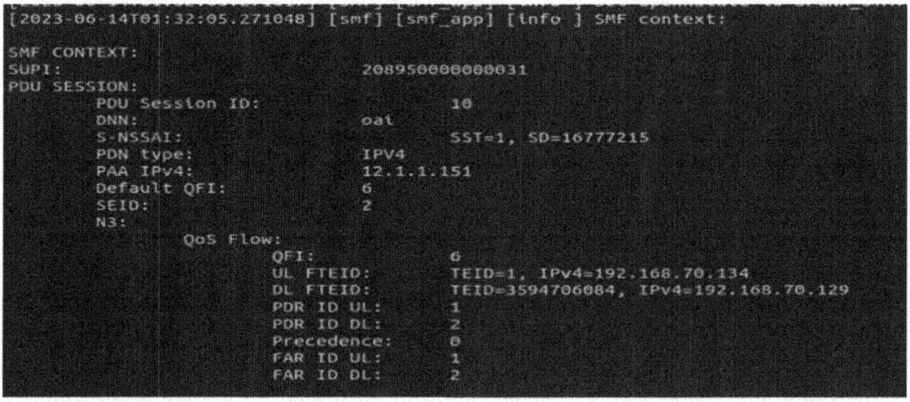

Fig. 6. An IP address = 12.1.1.151 assigned to the UE in the SMF-log file after PDU session establishment.

information is mainly transmitted using the next generation application protocol (NGAP) located on the N2 reference point between the gNodeB and the AMF and related to the authentication and configuration of radio communication established between the gNodeB and the UE.

The first experiment assessed the network capability of the testbed by evaluating (1) handshake validation, UE connection, and network traffic with Wireshark tool, (2) internet connectivity and network latency with the ping command and (3) jitter and throughput performances with the Iperf3 tool. VoNR is implemented in the second experiment and web browsing and video streaming are tested.

Experiment 1 Tests with an OAI-UE: The main goal of this experiment is to test and validate the functioning of the 5G SA testbed. As such, UE connection to the 5G deployed network, data traffic and low latency capabilities are tested to validate the deployment with an OAI-UE. The handshake and session establishment through the NGAP protocol which is used in the communication between the gNB and the AMF are shown on Fig. 7. The gNodeB (IP 192.168.70.129) first synchronises with the AMF (IP 192.168.70.132) and sends registration request to the AMF on behalf of the UE. The process for authentication and security for downlink (DL) and uplink (UL) resource reservation is then initiated along with overall initial UE context. Once radio communications are established, the core network components exchange messages using the HTTP protocol and check whether the UE's SIM information is correctly configured. The SMF (192.168.70.133) finally establishes the PDU session. The involved components are the gNodeB (IP 192.168.70.129), the AMF (IP 192.168.70.132) and the SMF (192.168.70.133) which finally establishes the PDU session after the UE registration.

Internet connectivity is tested by pinging the google's DNS server (8.8.8.8) with an average round-trip time (RTT) of 61.078 ms as shown in Fig. 8.

The Iperf3 tool is used to generate TCP/UDP data streams and measure the throughput, and the jitter. To this end, we started two Iperf processes in the UE and the external data network $oai-ext-dn$ (an Ubuntu Linux container with a WiFi Internet connection). For the downstream flow test, the UE/$oai-ext-dn$ is used as the server/client. For the upload test, the UE/$oai-ext-dn$ is used as the client/server. We measured the uplink and downlink throughputs with target throughput of 35 Mbits. The system achieved an average jitter of 0.7 ms and an average throughput of 30 Mbps on the uplink channel, as shown in Fig. 9 while an average jitter of 0.5 ms and a throughput of 35 Mbps were achieved on the downlink. Theory calculations, give a minimum throughput of 17.40/12.41 Mbit/s and a maximum throughput of 72.91/52 Mbit/s on the downlink and the uplink channels, respectively. The throughput values could appear somewhat low but this can be attributed to several factors including the performance of the computers and the bandwidth limitation of the USRP B210 devices with no amplification and MIMO. As for the jitter, the values are way below the cisco limit recommandation of 30 ms for VoIP.

For latency tests, we sent ping messages, consecutively within 10 s, between the $oai-ext-dn$ container on the 5G network core machine and the UE. We obtained a RTT in the interval [5.481,13.902] ms with an average value of 9.161 ms. These values are significantly lower than typical values in LTE networks at around 100 ms and can be lowered in subsequent system improvement.

Experiment 2 Web Browsing, Video Streaming and VoNR Tests with a Commercial 5G Phone: The goal of this experiment is to test the common user needs like web browsing and video streaming with the 5G SA testbed using a commercial UE, namely the oppo 5G phone. In addition VoNR is also implemented and tested.

Video Streaming: Similarly, we successfully implemented the video streaming application using the StreamLink Python library, as illustrated in Fig. 10. StreamLink is a command-line utility that enables users to access and stream

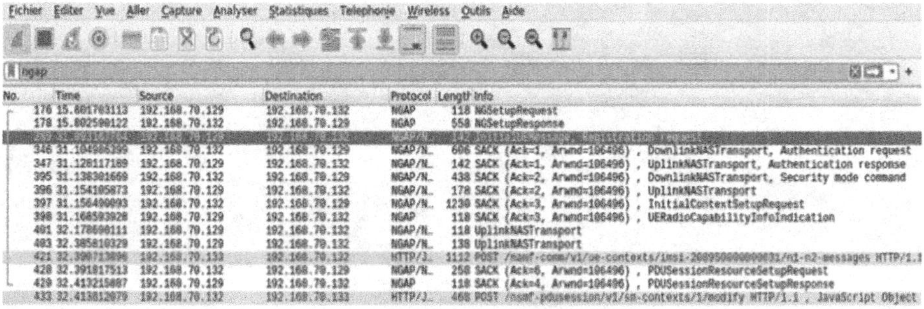

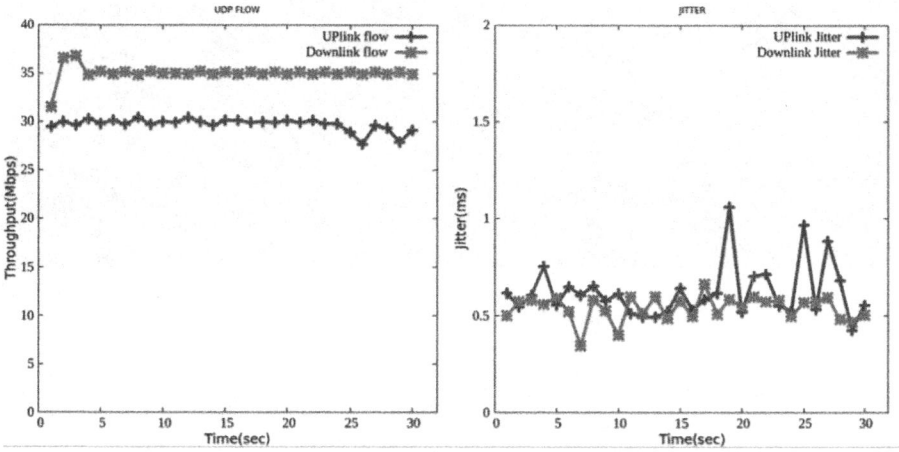

Fig. 7. NGAP messages between gNodeB and AMF for authentication, security and PDU establishment.

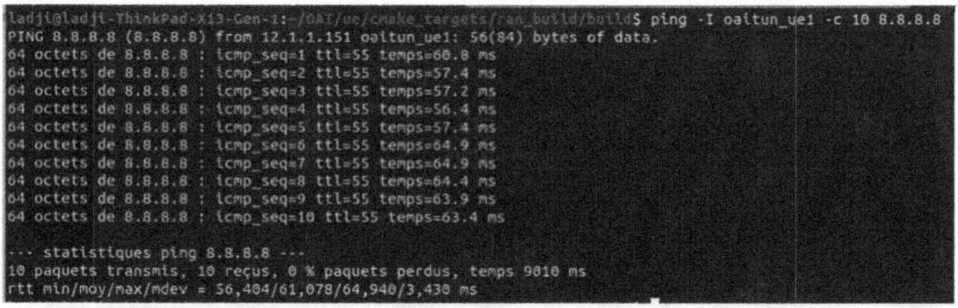

Fig. 8. Internet connectivity with an average RTT of 61.078 ms for google DNS ping.

Fig. 9. Downlink, uplink and jitter measurements with Iperf3.

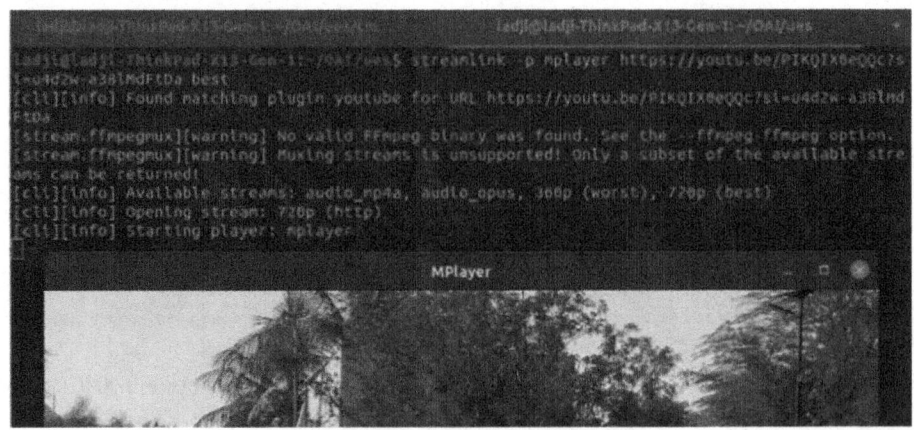

Fig. 10. Video streaming test.

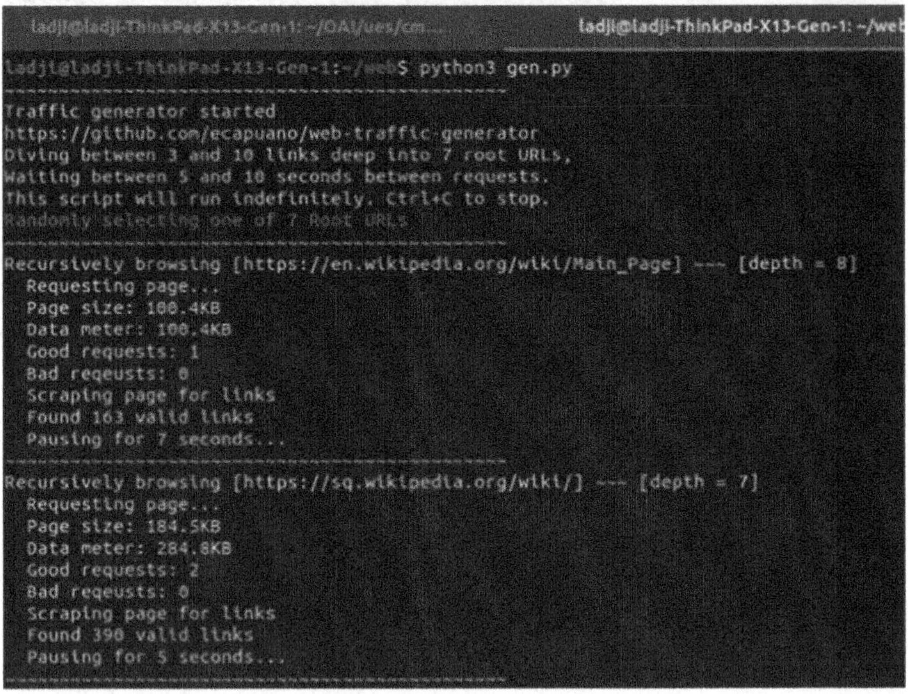

Fig. 11. Web browsing test.

video feeds from various streaming platforms through their preferred media player, rather than via a web browser. It supports various streaming services, including livestreams, Twitch, YouTube, and many others.

Web Browsing: To assess the web browsing capability with the OAI-UE, we used the web traffic generator module available in GitLab [14] which simulates real user navigation on the internet. Web browsing is illustrated in Fig. 11.

VoNR: When the network is deployed, the oppo 5G phone equipped with an open cell sim card configured to access the 5G network is used to test VoNR implementation. We set up an infrastructure using Asterisk software, hosted in a docker container, acting as an IP Multimedia Subsystem (IMS) server deployed with the 5G system in the same computer. Asterisk is a open source software providing the flexibility needed to develop business applications communication supporting text, voice and video. We established a duplex voice call between the OAI-UE and an oppo 5G phone. Each UE was identified by a distinct IP address after the PDU session establishment. The IP addresses 12.1.1.131, 12.1.1.130, 192.168.70.139 and 192.168.70.134 are assigned to the USRP emulated UE, the COTS phone, the IMS server and the UPF server, respectively. We monitored the traffic with Wireshark to capture the trace of packets exchanged. Figure 12 illustrates the graphical representation of the voice call trace and Fig. 13 shows the flow exchange graph between UEs, UPF, IMS. We conducted performance analysis at the end of the call, revealing an average jitter of 3.30 ms for the outbound voice stream and 3.83 ms for the inbound voice stream. Furthermore, out of the 6177 expected packets, no loss was observed. These results are illustrated in Fig. 14.

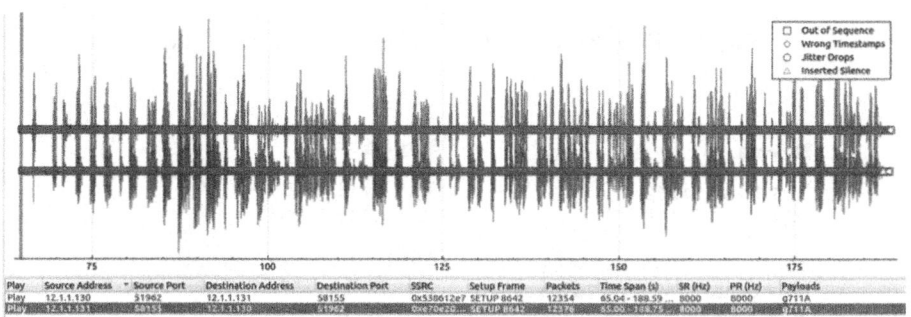

Fig. 12. Outbound and inbound voice signal traces

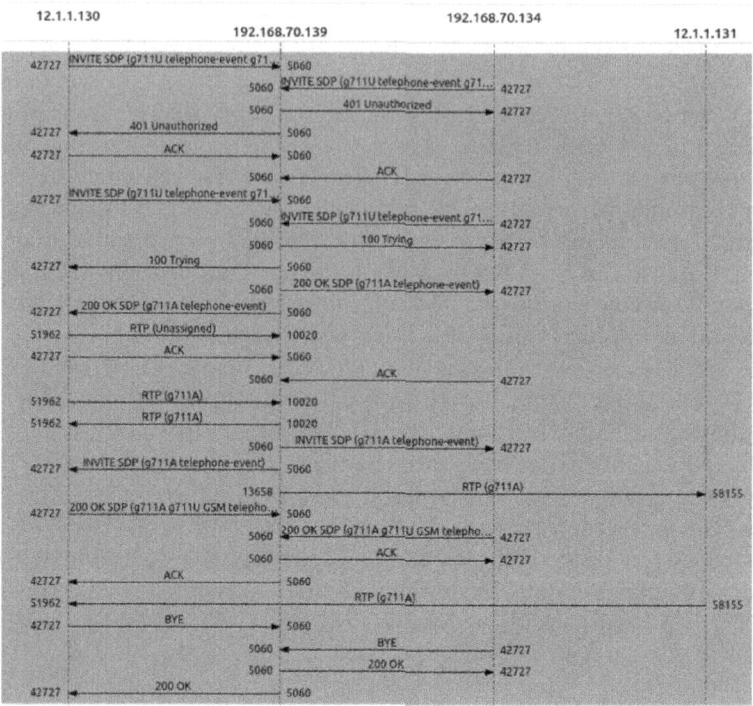

Fig. 13. Flow Exchange Graph between UEs, UPF, IMS

Stream		Stream	
12.1.1.130:51962 → 12.1.1.131:58155		12.1.1.131:58155 → 12.1.1.130:51962	
SSRC	0x538612e7	SSRC	0xe70e203d
Max Delta	69.559270 ms @ 8723	Max Delta	59.898544 ms @ 8683
Max Jitter	10.277530 ms	Max Jitter	9.314093 ms
Mean Jitter	3.303632 ms	Mean Jitter	3.830478 ms
Max Skew	-58.005626 ms	Max Skew	-40.079992 ms
RTP Packets	12354	RTP Packets	12376
Expected	6177	Expected	6188
Lost	-6177 (-100.00 %)	Lost	-6188 (-100.00 %)
Seq Errs	6177	Seq Errs	6188
Start at	65.037378 s @ 8660	Start at	65.003547 s @ 8644
Duration	123.55 s	Duration	123.74 s
Clock Drift	-36 ms	Clock Drift	-7 ms
Freq Drift	7995 Hz (-0.03 %)	Freq Drift	7999 Hz (-0.01 %)

Fig. 14. Performance analysis of the VoNR call.

4 Concluding Remarks

In this article, we deployed and tested a 5G SA network applicable in rural areas on an ongoing research to help attain the SDG by reducing the digital divide with 5G technology. We carried out a basic deployment of a standalone and low-cost 5G network using the OpenAirInterface open-source implementation and the USRP B210 SDR technology and a commercial 5G phone. In a first experiment we assessed the network performances and obtained satisfactorily results with respect to jitter and throughput. Though the throughput is limited by the characteristics of the used USRP B210, obtained values outperform the characteristics of the local 4G network. The round-trip time and jitters measurements give lower values than those experienced in 4G and required for common needs for digitised societies. In a second experiment we implemented VoNR over the 5G system and tested duplex calls with a commercial phone. Optimisation of the 5G SA testbed is underway for resource sharing and use cases implementation with network slicing, Multi-Access Edge Computing (MEC) for education, agriculture and rescue use cases.

References

1. Cox, C.: An Introduction to 5G: The New Radio, 5G Network and Beyond. Wiley (2020)
2. Liu, G., Huang, Y., Chen, Z., Liu, L., Wang, Q., Li, N.: 5G deployment: standalone vs. non-standalone from the operator perspective. IEEE Commun. Mag. **58**(11), 83–89 (2020)
3. Ericsson. https://www.ericsson.com/en/blog/2023/2/is-it-still-worth-to-invest-in-5g-in-a-flat-revenue-scenario. Accessed 22 July 2023
4. Judd, G., Steenkiste, P.: Using emulation to understand and improve wireless networks and applications. In: Proceedings of the 2nd Conference on Symposium on Networked Systems Design & Implementation, vol. 2, pp. 203–216 (2005)
5. Kempf, J., Yegani, P.: OpenRAN: a new architecture for mobile wireless internet radio access networks. IEEE Commun. Mag. **40**(5), 118–123 (2002). https://doi.org/10.1109/35.1000222
6. John, F., Schuljak, J., Vosteen, L. B., Sievers, B., Hanemann, A., Hellbrück, H.: A reference deployment of a minimal open-source private industry and campus 5G standalone (SA) system. In: 2022 IEEE 10th International Conference on Information, Communication and Networks (ICICN), pp. 1–9. IEEE (2022)
7. Gao, Y., Zhang, X., Yuan, H.: Integration and connection test for OpenAirInterface 5G standalone system. In: 2021 IEEE 3rd International Conference on Civil Aviation Safety and Information Technology (ICCASIT), pp. 1010–1014 (2021). https://doi.org/10.1109/ICCASIT53235.2021.9633433.
8. Tufeanu, L.-M., Martian, A., Vochin, M.-C., Paraschiv, C.-L., Li, F.-Y.: Building an open source containerized 5G SA network through docker and Kubernetes. In: 2022 25th International Symposium on Wireless Personal Multimedia Communications (WPMC), pp. 381–386. IEEE (2022)
9. Arora, S.: https://cloudacademy.com/blog/docker-vs-virtual-machines-differences-you-should-know. Accessed 31 July 2023

10. Rommer, S., Hedman, P., Olsson, M., Frid, L., Sultana, S., Mulligan, C.: Network functions and services, in 5G core networks, pp. 287–336. Elsevier (2020). https://doi.org/10.1016/B978-0-08-103009-7.00013-2
11. OpenAirInterface. https://openairinterface.org. Accessed 22 July 2023
12. 5G RAN OpenAirInterface. https://openairinterface.org/oai-5g-ran-project. Accessed 22 July 2023
13. 5G CORE NETWORK OpenAirInterface. https://openairinterface.org/oai-5g-core-network-project. Accessed 22 July 2023
14. Traffic generator. https://github.com/ReconInfoSec/web-traffic-generator. Accessed 31 Mar 2024

An Application of the Hough Transform and Convolutional Neural Networks to Detect Straight Lines

Moussa Bamogo[1](✉) and Abdoulaye Sere[2]

[1] ER-SIC, LAMDI, Universite Nazi BONI, Bobo Dioulasso, Burkina Faso
bmgm25@gmail.com
[2] Reseau des Enseignants Chercheurs et Chercheurs en Informatique du Faso (RECIF), Ouagadougou, Burkina Faso
abdoulaye.sere@recifaso.org
https://www.recifaso.org

Abstract. The topic addressed in this research study concerns the combination of the Hough Transform with convolutional neural networks to improve pattern recognition in a collection of images. We propose a neural network model that takes as input a collection of images. In order to be able to compare the results obtained, the collection is processed by the Extended Hough Transform on the one hand, and on the other hand, it has not undergone any processing by the Extended Standard Hough Transform. The model proposed in our approach is composed of a set of convolutional layers and a fully connected layer. For this study, we used a dataset containing a total of 10,200 images. The experimental results obtained with our model give an accuracy of 70.00% with the dataset treated with the Extended Hough Transform and 66.67% with the other dataset. It can also detect images containing lines. In view of the experiments carried out, we have seen that the size of the learning base and the material resources are key factors in obtaining better results. Hough Transforms help to improve the accuracy of the convolutional neural network.

Keywords: Convolutional Neural Networks · Hough Transform · Pattern Recognition

1 Introduction

The Hough Transform is an image processing technique that was initially developed to detect geometric shapes in an image, such as straight lines or circles. Over the years, it has been adapted to solve various computer vision problems. The Hough Transform enables the detection of lines and curves in an image by converting points in the image to a parametric representation in a voting space.

Nowadays, with the advent of big data, processing large volumes of data is essential. They are found in many fields, such as medical imaging, cartography, biomedical research, research laboratories, computer vision, and systems monitoring [26]. Serval research has been done on image processing, and different techniques have been implemented. Among these, we can cite Hough Transform and deep learning, which make it possible to recognize a shape in an image. Many efforts have been agreed upon in the literature with a view to optimize them. But building an automatic system that recognizes shapes in an image remains a challenge.

The problem addressed in this study is how to improve pattern recognition in image collections by combining the Hough Transform with convolutional neural networks (CNN). In other words, the study focuses on how to exploit the advantages of classical image processing techniques such as the Hough Transform by effectively integrating them with modern deep learning approaches like CNNs to obtain better results in terms of pattern recognition accuracy.

The central question we want to solve is, How can integrating the Hough Transform with convolutional neural networks improve the accuracy of pattern recognition in a collection of images?

The hypothesis we pose in this study is that Integration of the Hough Transform with convolutional neural networks will improve the accuracy of pattern recognition in a collection of images compared to the exclusive use of convolutional neural networks without this integration.

Learning is a field of artificial intelligence that attempts to mimic the neural functioning of the human brain through an artificial neural network. It appeared in 1980, following the work of Yann Lecun [1]. Together with two other computer scientists, they developed a particular type of algorithm called a convolutional neural network. The use of this algorithm has become widespread with the emergence of a new generation of graphics chips (GPU) capable of performing more than a trillion operations per second and with the availability of large amounts of computer data. Deep learning has caused a major upheaval in the field of artificial intelligence and its applications. He has also contributed to many applications, such as image recognition and classification [2] and automatic processing of natural languages [2]. This progress is explained by the availability of large amounts of learning data produced by sensors, surveys, social networks, and the Internet of Things in various types and formats. This massive amount of data of various types and formats is known as big data. This data allows artificial intelligence to understand and learn like humans think.

Convolutional neural networks (CNN) are a type of acyclic artificial neural network that can automatically extract features from input images while remaining invariant to slight image distortions. They also implement the notion of weight sharing, making it possible to considerably reduce the number of network parameters. This makes it possible to considerably count the local correlations contained in an image. These networks were inspired by the work of [7,8], and [9]. The weights are forced to be equal to detect lines, points, or corners at all possible locations in the image, effectively implementing the idea of weight sharing [10]. In these works [11], CNNs are used for handwritten character recognition. They are used in image and video recognition, recommendation systems, and natural language processing [11–13]. The more data a CNN receives, the more it learns and the more accurate it becomes. What about Hough's transformation? The Hough Transform, which is a technique for recognizing geometric shapes in a digital image, was introduced in the 1960s by Paul V.C. Hough [3] with the aim of detecting alignments (straight lines). This technique has been extended to the detection of other geometric shapes thanks to the work of Rosenfeld [4] and Duda et al. [5]. With [6,14–19], it was generalized to the detection of arbitrary and complex geometric shapes. The work [20–23] proposed several methods of applying pattern recognition by Hough Transform. The Extended Standard Hough Transform (ESHT) is a method introduced by SERE et al. [25] that can detect discrete straight lines that are seen as a sequence of pixels. For the reconstruction of a discrete line into a continuous line, two essential notions have been introduced: dual and preimage. Dual is an equivalent of the Hough Standard Transformation in ESHT. Algorithm 1 describes the sequence of discrete, naive, and standard straight-line recognition by the Extended Standard Hough Transform (ESHT).

Algorithm 1. Naive and standard discrete straight-line recognition

    data : A set S of n pixels $P_1; P_2; ...; P_n$
    Begin
    Preimage $\leftarrow$ Dual(P_1)
    $i \leftarrow 2$
    while Preimage $\neq \emptyset$ $eti \leq$ n **do**
      Preimage $\leftarrow$ Preimage $\cap$ Dual(P_i)
      $i \leftarrow i + 1$
    end while
    if Preimage $\neq \emptyset$ **then**
      S belongs to a line
    else
      S does not belong to a line
    end if
    End

In this paper, we are interested in pattern recognition in an image database using deep learning. This is for us to propose an algorithmic approach to processing a collection of images while combining the Hough Transform and convolutional neural networks. This document is organized as follows: in Sect. 2, method description; in Sect. 3, the experimental results; and in Sect. 4, the conclusion and perspectives.

2 Method Description

The objective of our study is to increase the prediction rate of a convolutional neural network while reducing the failure rate in a collection of images. To achieve this objective, we will use ESHT to preprocess the images and then pass them through a predictive model based on convolutional neural networks. In this section, we present our approach in the context of this study and the test data. Our model is made up of three convolution layers, a Max Pooling layer placed after each convolutional layer, and a fully connected layer. The model receives a collection of images as input. The images are fed into the first convolution layer, which is composed of filters of size 3×3, with a ReLU correction function applied to each layer. A matrix called a feature map is created at the output of this layer. We then pass this matrix through the pooling layer (Max Pooling) in order to reduce the size of this matrix and only keep the important information. The matrix obtained at the output is given as input to the second convolution layer, which has the same characteristics as the first. Indeed, it is composed of filters and implements a ReLU correction function. This is followed by a max-pooling layer. The same processing is followed as in the previous one. The third convolution layer is composed of filters of size 3×3 and implements a ReLU correction function. The values of the last obtained feature map are passed to the last Max Pooling layer. The values obtained by this last Max Pooling layer are concatenated into a single vector and transmitted to a fully connected layer. The input vector values are transformed to return a new output vector. This last vector contains as many elements as there are classes: each element of the vector indicates the probability for the image to belong to a class.

These probabilities are calculated by the fully connected layer, which uses a sigmoid function, in our case, as the activation function. A loss function, or cost function, is associated with the fully connected layer to measure the error between the network prediction and the actual data annotation. For updating the model in order to minimize the cost function and have better predictions, we chose Adam, which is an optimization algorithm. This choice is justified by a comparative study of the simulations extracted in [24]. Bringing together different methods shows that for the same optimization problem and the same learning rate, adam tends to make the error converge towards zero much more quickly. The Fig. 1, Algorithm 2 and Algorithm 3 illustrate our method.

Algorithm 2. How our method works

---
    données : dataset a collection of images $I = \{I_1; I_2; ...; P_N\}$
    Begin
    Function $modelCNN(dataset)$:
    for all $I_k \in dataset$ **do**
      ConvolutionRelu()
      MaxPooling()
      ConvolutionRelu()
      MaxPooling()
      ConvolutionRelu()
      MaxPooling()
      ConnectedLayer()
    end for
    Return Prediction()
    End

Algorithm 2 describes the process of our CNN model, which takes a set of images as input and then carries out processing return predictions.

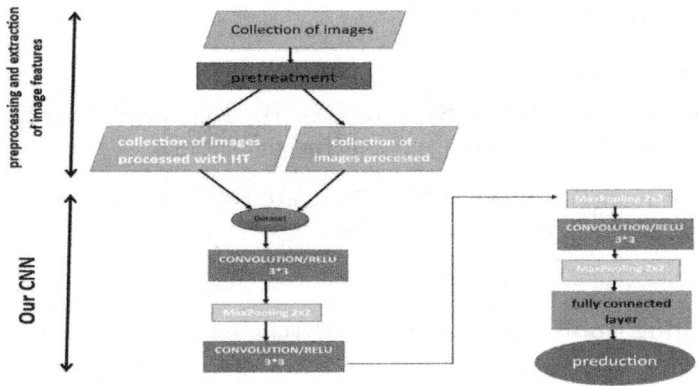

Fig. 1. Illustration of our method Hough Transform and CNN

Algorithm 3. Process of data preparation and processing with EHST

data : A collection of images $I = \{I_1; I_2; ...; P_N\}$
f : A file containing images
Begin
Function *collect(Collection I)* :Function saving images to a file
for all $I_k \in I$ **do**
  if I_k **then**
    CreateEmpty file f
    OpenFile(f) "in writing"
    AddInFile(f, I_k)
    CloseFile(f)
  end if
end for
Function *traitemenTH(f)* :Processing function with EHST
OpenFile(f) "read"
for all $I_k \in f$ **do**
  if I_k **then**
    FunctionEHST(I_k)
    CreateEmpty file $f2$
    OpenFile($f2$) "in writing"
    AddInFile($f2, I_k$)
    CloseFile($f2$)
  end if
end for
End

Algorithm 3 illustrates data preparations with the Extended Standard Hough Transform.

3 Experimental Results

3.1 Working Environment

Hardware and Operating System. An HP computer with the following specifications has been used to carry out the simulations:

- Processor: Intel(R) Core(TM) i5 CPU 2.56 GHz. Item RAM: 6 Go
- Operating system: Windows 10, 64 bits.

Programming Tools and Language. Python has been selected as the simulation's chosen software environment. For programming, graphical visualization, and numerical computation, Python is an effective tool. Being object-oriented and having dynamic semantics, it is a high-level interpreted programming language, meaning there is no compilation step. Developers and programmers in general have embraced Python worldwide. Code maintenance costs can be minimized due to the language's ease of learning and simplicity.

Open Source Computer Vision (Open CV) is a free library. Originally developed by Intel, specializing in real-time image processingreal. We used this tool in the data preprocessing phase. Shewas used to more precisely implement the techniques of image normalization, zooming, rotation, and translation. We used Keras for its power and efficiency. It is an open-source library that allows rapid experimentation with neural network models and is very simple to use. It is a Python library that encapsulates access to functions offered by several machine learning libraries, including Tensorflow. It was used to implement our learning model.

3.2 Dataset

We carried out our experiments on a data set that we created. This database contains images of size 32×32. These images belong to two classes, namely those containing straight lines and those not containing any. We drew these images ourselves. Data augmentation is a method used in deep learning to enlarge the size of data when the dataset is not consistent. This operation duplicates the data by applying certain geometric transformation operations in image processing in order to prevent the same data from being repeated in the data set. Since our dataset does not contain enough images, this operation is very important. In our context, it is based on image processing applications. The data processing consisted, first of all, of duplicating our dataset to have two batches. Then we proceeded to process the second batch with the Extended Hough Standard Transform. This made it possible to improve the images by clearly marking the presence of the straight lines. Figure 2 shows an image processed with the

Extended Hough Standard Transform (EHST) and another unprocessed. The organization of the data consisted of making a mixture of all the labels collected, namely the images containing straight lines and the images not containing any. The goal is to slice, then split, and define the data for training, testing, and validating the neural network model. Indeed, for training our model, we used a total of two hundred (100) simulated images in our dataset. Then, we applied deep learning data augmentation methods mentioned above to reach 10,200 images. After the augmentation technique, we divided this set into three subsets, including 70% of the data for training, 15% for testing, and 15% for model validation.

3.3 Evaluation Metrics

Metrics allow define indicators to evaluate the performance of a learning model. These are the confusion matrix, precision, recall and f-measure. To find out the type of errors made, we use the confusion matrix which is a summary of the prediction results on a classification problem. Correct and incorrect predictions are divided by class (Table 1):

Precision is the proportion of relevant elements among all the elements proposed. It is calculated using the formula $P = \frac{VP}{VP+FP}$ where VP is the number of true positives and FP that of false positives. The recall which represents the proportion of relevant elements proposed among all the relevant elements is cal-

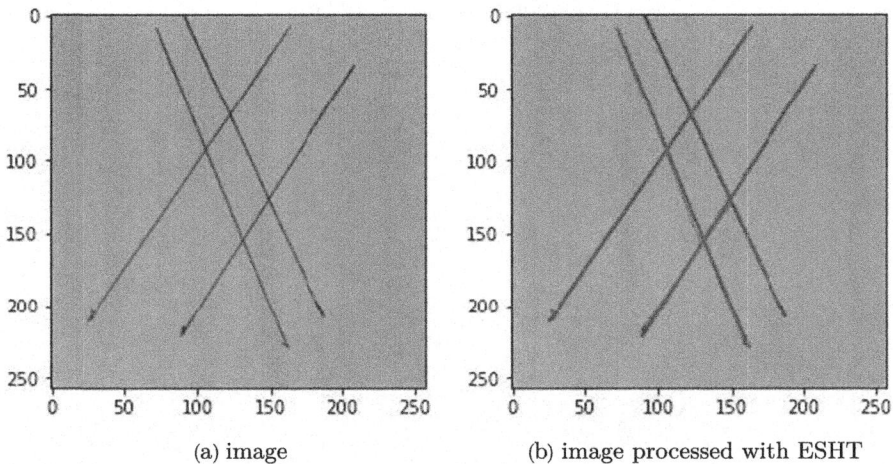

(a) image (b) image processed with ESHT

Fig. 2. Illustration of processing with Hough Transformation

Table 1. Confusion matrix

		Positive	Negative
Predicted Class	Positive	True Positive	False Positive
	Negative	False Negative	True Negative

culated with the formula $R = \frac{VP}{VP+FN}$, FN being the number of false negatives. The F-measure is a measure that combines precision and recall. This is their average. The formula is as follows

$$F - mesure = 2 * \frac{(Precision * Recall)}{(Precision + Recall)}$$

3.4 Results

The Table 2 below summarizes the overall results obtained with our model. There is an improvement in accuracy with the dataset that has been processed with Hough Transformation.

Figures 3 and 4 show the results of detecting lines with our method. The Fig. 3 shows the results of detecting lines.

Figure 4 shows a comparison of straight line detection with our method. The first Fig. 4a of the material illustrates the detection of lines without Hough Transform. Figure 4b shows the visual output with our method, we see more vertical and horizontal lines clearly detected.

Table 2. Summary table of the different results

	Without HT	with HT
Prediction	66.67%	70.00%
Loss	33,33 %	30,00 %

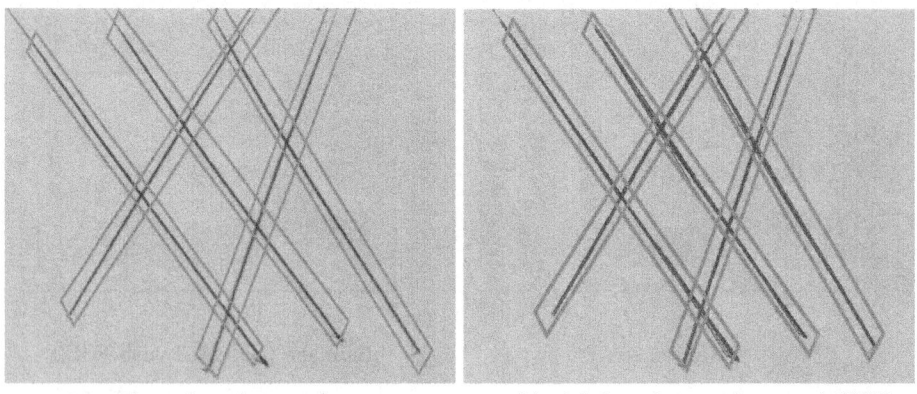

(a) without hough transform   (b) with hough transform and CNN

Fig. 3. Illustration of detection with hough transform and CNN

(a) without hough transform (b) with hough transform and CNN

Fig. 4. Illustration of detection with hough transform and CNN

3.5 Discussions

The results obtained after evaluation of classification model give an accuracy rate of 66.67% and 33.33% without processing with Extended Hough Standard Transform, compared to 70.00% and 30.00% with the dataset processed with Extended Hough Standard Transform. After an analysis of the confusion matrices, we found that the classifier of our model recognizes the images containing straight lines in the test data of the two batches of the dataset. Using the Hough Transform improves detection accuracy. The first difficulty lies in the availability of real data. We simulated and collected the images by taking photos with our smartphones, which undoubtedly affects the quality of the images. Added to this is the memory space capacity that we have. The difficulty is the low capacity of the memory space in our work environment. This is why we used images in 32×32 format. In fact, training a CNN model requires larger memory space.

4 Conclusion and Perspectives

In this paper, we propose a methodology for the recognition of shapes in an image by coupling the Hough transform and deep learning. A state-of-the art of previous works and methods on the Hough Transform and deep learning are reported. This guided us to make a goodchoice of a methodology adapted to the problem, as well as for the design of the recognition model. We have proposed a convolutional neural network that takes as input image data and preprocessed image data with theExtended Standard Hough Transform. These different technologies have a great ability to solve complex problems in the fields of computer vision and pattern recognition. However, their userequires a large amount of data and more powerful computing machines to perform and produce better results. In our model, the convolutional part was used to extract features from the images, and the fully connected layer part was used for prediction. For the evaluation of our approach, we used images that we have collected, and the experimental results obtained with the model have been illustrated. In fact, the accuracy of our model was 70.00% with the dataset that was processed with the Extended Standard Hough Transform and 66.67% with the other dataset that was not processed treated with the Extended Standard Hough Transform. The model is used to classify images containing lines. In perspective, we will extend our approach by diversifying the data sources, strengthening the model, proposing an application in transport.

References

1. LeCun, Y., Boser, B., Denker, J., Henderson, D., Howard, R., Hubbard, W., Jackel, L.: Handwritten digit recognition with a back propagation network. In: Advances in Neural Information Processing Systems 2, pp. 396–404, 219. Morgan Kaufmann, San Francisco (1990)
2. Zbontar, J., LeCun, Y.: Stereo matching by training a convolutional neural network to compare image patches. Mach. Learn. Res. 17–49 (2016)
3. Hough, P.V.C.: Method and means for recognazing complex patterns, US3283070A (1960)
4. Rosenfeld, A.: Progress in picture processing: 1969–71. ACM Comput. Surv. **5**, 81–108 (1973)
5. Duda, R.O., Hart, P.E.: Use of the hough transformation to detect lines and curves in pictures, W. Newman, University of Nevada (1972)
6. Ballard, D.H.: Generalizing the hough transform to detect arbitrary shapes. Pattern Recognit. **13**, 111–122 (1981)
7. Hubel, D.H., Wiesel, T.N.: Receptive fields, binocular interaction and functional architecture in the cat's visual cortex. J. Physiol. **160**, 106–154 (1962)
8. Fukushima, K.: Neocognitron: a self-organizing neural network model for a mechanism of pattern recognition unaffected by shift in position. Biol. Cybern. **36**, 193–202 (1980)
9. Fukushima, K.: A neural network model for selective attention in visual pattern recognition. Biol. Cybern. **55**, 5–15 (1986)
10. Rumelhart, D.E., McClelland, J.L.: Parallel Distributed Processing: Explorations in the Microstructure of Cognition: Foundations. The MIT Press (1986)
11. Denke, J.S., Henderson, D., Howard, R.E., Hubbard, W., Jackel, L.D., LeCun, Y., Boser, B.: Handwritten Digit Recognition with a Back-Propagation Network. BibSonomy. https://www.bibsonomy.org/bibtex/d0f161d61285aca3b30c3add9416921e
12. Collobert, R., Weston, J.: A unified architecture for natural language processing: deep neural networks with multitask learning, pp. 160–167. ACM Press (2008)
13. Sutskever, I., Hinton, G.E., Krizhevsky, A.: ImageNet Classification with Deep Convolutional Neural Networks, pp. 1097–1105. Curran Associates, Inc. (2012)
14. Maitre, H.: Un panorama de la transformation de Hough. Traitement du Signal **2** (1985)
15. Duda, R.O., Hart, P.E.: Use of the hough transformation to detect lines and curves in pictures. W. Newman (1972)
16. Merlin, P.M., Farber, D.J.: A parallel mechanism for detecting curves in pictures. IEEE Trans. Comput. **C-24**, 96–98 (1975)

17. Shapiro, S.D.: Feature space transforms for curve detection. Pattern Recognit. **10**, 129–143 (1978)
18. Shapiro, S.D.: Transform method of curve detection for textured image data. IEEE Trans. Comput. **C-27**, 254–255 (1978)
19. Shapiro, S.D.: Transformations for the computer detection of curves in noisy pictures. Comput. Graph. Image Process. **4**, 328–338 (1975)
20. Kälviäinen, H., Hirvonen, P., Xu, L., Oja, E.: Comparisons of probabilistic and non-probabilistic hough transforms, vol. 801, pp. 350–360. Springer, Heidelberg (1994)
21. Sere, A., Coulibali, L., Diarra, M., Sie, O., Ouedraogo, F.T.: An Application of the Triangular Hough Transform and the Rectangular Hough Transform in Noisy Analytical Straight Line Recognition. Africomm 2015 (2015)
22. Sere, A., Sie, O., Traore, S.: Extensions of standard hough transform based on object dual and application. J. Emerg. Trends Comput. Inf. Sci. **6** (2015)
23. Sere, A., Sie, O., Andres, E.: Extended standard hough transform for analytical line recognition. Int. J. Adv. Comput. Sci. Appl. **4** (2013)
24. Kingma, D.P., Ba, J.: Adam: a method for stochastic optimization. In: Conference paper at the 3rd International Conference for Learning Representations, San Diego (2014)
25. Sere, A., Sie, O., Andres, E.: Extended standard hough transform for analytical line recognition. In: 6th International Conference on Sciences of Electronics, Technologies of Information and Telecommunications (SETIT). IEEE Xplore (2012)
26. Dash, S., Shakyawar, S.K., Sharma, M., Kaushik, S.: Big data in healthcare: management, analysis and future prospects. J. Big Data **6** (2019)

A Slotted Random Access Algorithm for Efficient Transmission in White Area: Case of Artisanal Fishing in West Africa

Fatoumata Awa Yandé Diouf[1]($\boxtimes$), Madoune R. Seye[1], Moussa Diallo[1], and Bamba Gueye[2]

[1] Department of Computer Science, Polytechnic Institute (ESP), Cheikh Anta Diop University, Dakar, Senegal
{fatoumataawayandediouf,moussa.diallo}@esp.sn

[2] Department of Mathematics and Computer Science, Faculty of Science and Technology (FST), Cheikh Anta Diop University, Dakar, Senegal
http://per-edmi.ucad.sn/~moussadiallo/

Abstract. LORA technology is increasingly used for white zone communications. The access to the channel for the different nodes of the network is managed in various ways. We propose an algorithm based on a controlled sliding backoff for communication in a maritime environment: the case of Senegal. Indeed, fishing activities in Senegal are carried out in an offshore environment, without network coverage and therefore without means of communication in case of danger. We define different communication phases according to the type of information to be transmitted, and analyze the network behavior thanks to mathematical equations. Simulations are used to set parameters and determine the duration of each communication phase.

Keywords: Ad hoc Network · Artisanal fishing · Communication · Localization · LoRa

1 Introduction

The access of several devices to a shared bandwidth is always controlled to avoid or minimize possible collisions. An access control algorithm is used to enable different devices to use a resource simultaneously. These algorithms can be divided into two groups:

– The first group concerns the algorithms that operate in a predetermined way such as time division multiple access (TDMA), frequency division multiple access (FDMA), code division multiple access (CDMA), orthogonal frequency division multiple access (OFDMA) or single carrier frequency division multiple access (SC-FDMA). Each device knows exactly how to access the resource without any possible collision. These techniques are often used in radio access

network (RAN) of mobile telecommunications systems like Long Term Evolution (LTE) or 5G for example.
- The second group concerns the random access based algorithms. When traffic or the number of devices is low, users can randomly access the entire bandwidth and transmit data at any time. However, in case of high traffic or high device density, collisions become important. In this case, several algorithms can be used to optimize the success rate, such as ALOHA, slotted ALOHA or carrier sense multiple access (CSMA).

In our work, we are interested in artisanal fishing in the west african coasts, especially in Senegal. The artisanal fishers have to go far from the coast, sometimes even beyond 20 km, to find fish because of the effects of climate change. As a result, artisanal fishing is carried out in white spot areas where no operator has deployed its mobile and/or internet network. Fishers have no means of communication or alert in case of distress (MAYDAY). The social and human conditions are difficult, including safety problems (nearly 100 deaths per year). Our goal is to set up a very long range "ad hoc" network to interconnect embedded devices on fishers canoes, based on LoRa technology. It is important to note that conventional centralized marine positioning systems (VMS or AIS) are not used for financial reasons. Indeed, the purchasing power of fishers does not allow them to buy this type of system. Since there is no network infrastructure at sea, we focus on random access techniques.

Different types of information are sent by fishermen, and transmissions must meet a certain quality of service. The access technique used in Lora networks is Aloha, but it is subject to interference with a success rate of 18.4% [6]. This is insufficient to ensure safety at sea. In this paper, we propose an algorithm based on slotted aloha, but which differs from it in certain functional aspects. This is a controlled sliding backoff algorithm, adapted to our study context, to enable the sharing of information between canoes at sea with a high success rate. The objective is to size the duration of the different transmission phases according to the number of users and the required success rate.

The rest of the paper is organized as follows: Sect. 2 describes the related works on random channel access techniques, Sect. 3 analyzes the communication system, in Sect. 4 the performance analysis of slotted ALOHA algorithm is made, Sect. 5 deals with the proposed algorithm, Sect. 6 discusses the obtained results and Sect. 7 concludes our work.

2 Related Work

In this section, we review some random channel access techniques. LoRa is a technology using the chirp spread spectrum (CSS) modulation. It is more and more used in the deployment of ad hoc communication systems in white areas [1,2,5,8–10]. In a Lora network, access to the transmission channel must be managed. LoRaWAN is a MAC layer standard which coordinates the medium and adopts pure Aloha [1]. Aloha is a medium access control (MAC) protocol for transmission of data via a shared network channel. In pure aloha, each station transmits when data is available without checking whether the channel is free or not. Thus, collisions can occur and the data frame can be lost. In Pure Aloha, maximum efficiency is 18.4% [6]. Many techniques such as slotted Aloha, CSMA or other random access solutions are exploited as an alternative to Pure Aloha [6].

Slotted aloha does not allow the transmission of data whenever the station wants to send it. In slotted Aloha, the shared channel is divided into fixed time intervals called slots. Thus, if a station wants to send a frame in a shared channel, the frame can only be sent at the beginning of the slot, and only one frame is allowed to be sent to each slot. If the station has failed to send the data, it has to wait until the next slot. The maximum success rate in slotted aloha networks is 37% [7].

The purpose of CSMA is to check the state of the medium before transmission. If it is busy, the transmitter waits until it is idle before starting to transmit. This effectively minimizes the risk of collision and allows more efficient use of the medium. This variant of CSMA is also known as persistent CSMA. Another variant of CSMA is non-persistent CSMA. The main difference between persistent CSMA and non-persistent CSMA is that a non-persistent CSMA node does not continuously listen to the channel to determine when it becomes free. When a non-persistent CSMA terminal detects that the transmission channel is busy, it waits a random amount of time before detecting the channel again. This improves channel utilization compared with persistent CSMA. The maximum success rate in CSMA persistent is 52.9% and for CSMA non-persistent it is 81.5% [7].

Aloha and Slotted Aloha techniques have low transmission success rates and do not provide the level of security required for offshore fishing. For CSMA techniques, the time taken to listen to the medium before sending could be problematic if it is long and if there are many nodes. We will take advantage of the slotted aloha technique, and adapt it to our context through our Mac Access algorithm.

The communication system is discussed in the Sect. 2.

3 Communication System and Goals

3.1 The Different Components of the System

In order to allow communication in maritime area, we propose a communication system illustrated in Fig. 1.

- A communication device, named mobile relay, is embedded in each pirogue (canoe). The mobile relay has two communication interfaces. A WLAN (Wireless Local Area Network) interface that enables interconnection with the fishermen's smartphones and a LPWAN (Low Power Wide Area Network) interface for long range communications with other canoes and/or base stations on the mainland.
- A mobile application developed as part of this work is installed on the fishers' smartphones. This application enables to retrieve the time, the location of

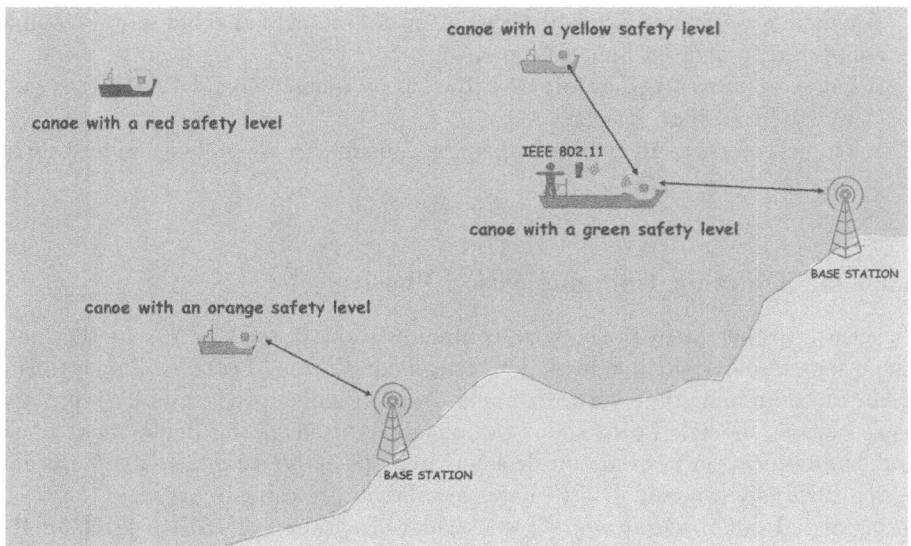

Fig. 1. Communication system

the canoe and the alerts sent in case of distress. Indeed, the mobile interface enables to send a distress message by turning on the "MAYDAY" button. The application also enables to visualize on a map the positions received from other canoes, the level of security (we will come back to this in the following) and the messages from the base stations.
- Base stations with two communication interfaces are deployed on mainland. The LPWAN (Low Power Wide Area Network) interface enables long range communications with canoe. The base station are also connected to internet (3G and/or 4G). On the one hand, in the sea-land direction, the base stations can receive the information sent by the canoe. This information will be transferred via internet to the servers of the Senegalese national navy. The navy can have a map of the canoe at sea but also alerts in case of "MAYDAY" with the position of the concerned canoe. On the other hand, information about weather warnings from the Senegalese National Agency for Civil Aviation and Meteorology (ANACIM) can reach the canoe via the land-sea link.

3.2 The Different Safely Levels

Fig. 1 depicts the different situation of connectivity according to our cases studies. This is an "ad hoc" network where the nodes are transceivers. Therefore, a canoe can be in four different states called safety level:

- A canoe is on **green safely level** when its embedded relay mobile is both connected to at least another canoe and a base station.

- A canoe is on **yellow safely level** when its embedded relay mobile is only connected to at least another canoe.
- A canoe is on **orange safely level** when its embedded relay mobile is only connected to a base station.
- A canoe is on **red safely level** when its embedded relay mobile can't establish any connection.

3.3 The Different Communication Phases

To ensure proper operation of our communication system, access to the long-range communication link must be controlled. We use LoRa technology as a mean of communication between mobile relays and between mobile relay and base station. Indeed, LoRa radio technology is used in the deployment of ad hoc communication systems, in disaster areas [8,9], white areas [1,2,5,10] and agricultural environment [12] to have very large and robust coverage. Coverage tests carried out in rural white areas achieved a range of 16 Km [2,5]. In the context of a maritime area, on the other hand, the tests carried out in Senegal and Finland made it possible to reach a range of more than 20 Km [1,10]. We have previously worked on an algorithm for location updates in deep-sea communications [13].

In addition to the access control problem, it is mandatory to define a communication strategy according to the type of information but also the appropriate time of their transmissions. The communication strategy we propose is shown in the Fig. 2.

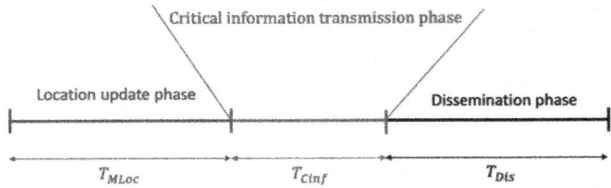

Fig. 2. The different communication phases

We propose three different phases of communication that are repeated periodically over time. It is important to note that the synchronization between the different mobile relays is possible via the time recovered from the smartphones.

The cycle begins with the location phase. Each mobile relay must update its location before sending it through its LoRa interface. During this phase, the base stations must also send their beacon to indicate their presence. At the end of this phase, each mobile relay or base station has a map of its neighbors. The safety levels are then visible on the smartphones' interfaces according to what the relay has received or not.

After that, the critical information transmission phase will begin. During that phase, information about weather warnings have to be sent by the different base stations. As previously explained, fishermen can turn on the "MAYDAY" button at any time. However, a mobile relay receiving a "MAYDAY" from the smartphones of its local network (WLAN) must wait for the arrival of this phase to broadcast the alert.

The last phase is called dissemination phase. During this phase, any mobile relay that received an alert message during the previous phase must broadcast it.

The access control to the long-range communication link during these phases and the probability of non-collision (success rate) are studied in the following sections.

4 Performance Analysis of Slotted ALOHA Algorithm

In this section, we mathematically analyze the behavior of a network using the slotted ALOHA access technique. To do this, we are interested in the ratio between the traffic successfully transmitted $A_{Success}$ (without collision) and the total traffic A_{Total} (all transmission attempts of all devices). These two traffic are defined by the following Eq. 1 and 2.

$$A_{Total} = \lambda_{Total} * \tau_{slot}, \tag{1}$$

where λ_{Total} is the frequency of transmission and τ_{slot} is the time slot duration.

$$A_{Success} = \lambda_{Success} * \tau_{slot}, \tag{2}$$

where $\lambda_{Success}$ is the frequency of transmission.

Denoting the probability of non-collision by $P_{Success}$, $A_{Success}$ can be written as:

$$A_{Success} = P_{Success} * A_{Total}. \tag{3}$$

In random access context, each device transmits with probability p independently of the other devices on the shared bandwidth. In that context, the commonly used model is the discrete time Poisson process [18]. Thus, the probability that k devices generate a frame during the same time slot is given by the Poisson distribution formula:

$$P(k) = \frac{(\lambda_{Total} * \tau_{slot})^k * e^{-\lambda_{Total} * \tau_{slot}}}{k!} \tag{4}$$

When a device generates a frame, it is now possible to determinate the probability of non-collision $P_{Success}$ which is the probability that no other device generates a frame during the same time slot:

$$P_{Success} = P(0) = \frac{(A_{Total})^0 * e^{-A_{Total}}}{0!} = e^{-A_{Total}} \tag{5}$$

4.1 Discussion

On the one hand, the use of slotted ALOHA as an access control technique is coherent in our study context, since all the device can be synchronized thanks to the clock available in the fishermen's smartphone (see Sect. 3.1).

On the other hand, in the considered communication system, the information that each device have to send is available at the beginning of each of the three communication phases (see Sect. 3.3). The data to be sent by each device during each communication phase is not important. Devices only send respectively location, "MAYDAY" and weather warnings during phases 1,2 and 3. One frame per device is largely sufficient per communication phase.

Based on this last remark, the frequency of transmission per device for each communication phase can be set to 1. Then, instead of the commonly considered discrete time Poisson process, we can propose a specific model.

5 Mac Access Algorithm

5.1 Random Access by Drawing Slots in a Sliding Time Window

The principle of our algorithm is shown in Fig. 3. The idea is to divide the time into several time slots of fixed size, each slot corresponding to a number. As shown in the diagram, we have for example 2 transmission phases of 7 and 6 time slots. The principle is to allow each node to choose a number between 1 and the number of slots at random, and send to the corresponding slot number.

Each node sends once per transmission phase.

When 2 nodes choose the same number, they send to the same slot and a collision occurs (as in slot 4 of phase 1, device 2 and 4 collide).

Phase duration is not fixed and varies according to the number of users accessing the network. If the number of users increases, the number of time slots increases. If the number of users decreases, the number of time slots also decreases. Hence the name: Random access by drawing slots in a sliding time window.

We first deal with the case of the first phase of communication. We will then extend it to the other phases by analogy.

– The first step is to divide T_{MLoc} (Location phase duration) into $N_{slot} = \frac{T_{MLoc}}{\tau_{slot}}$ time slot. N_{slot} is the number of time slot. Note that the time slot duration τ_{slot} must be set to a value that allows to send a full frame.
– At the second step, each device randomly chooses a value between 1 and N_{slot}. This backoff strategy is used to avoid collisions.
– At the last step, each device transmit its frame during the chosen time slot number.

We will then determine the duration of each communication phase: T_{MLoc} (the location phase duration), T_{Cinf} (the critical information transmission phase duration) and T_{Dis} (the dissemination phase duration).

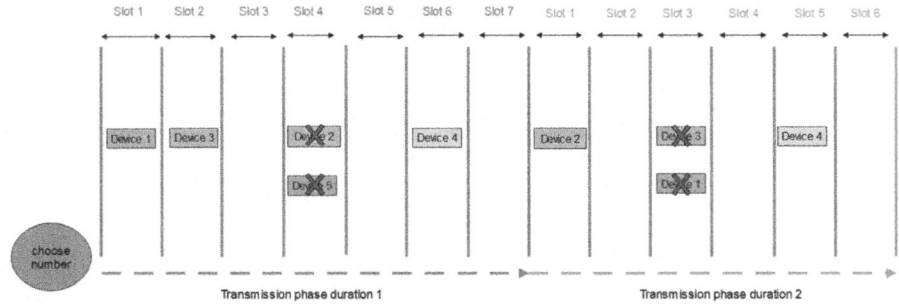

Fig. 3. Mac Access SAFE

5.2 Performance Analysis

Since each device randomly selects a time slot, the probability that the i-th device selects the j-th time slot is:

$$P_i(j) = \frac{1}{N_{slot}}, \; 1 \leq j \leq N_{slot} \tag{6}$$

Then, the probability of non-collision (success rate) denoted by $P_{Success}$ becomes:

$$P_{Success} = \sum_{j=1}^{N_{slot}} P_i(j)[1 - P_i(j)]^{N-1} = (1 - \frac{1}{N_{slot}})^{N-1}, \tag{7}$$

where N is the number of device that have to send a frame.

By analogy, the Eq. 7 is the same for all three phases of communication. However, the parameters N and N_{slot} will vary from one phase to another. We consider the following notations:

- N^1, N^2 and N^3 as the number of device that have to send a frame for respectively the communication phase 1,2 and 3.
- N_{slot}^1, N_{slot}^2 and N_{slot}^3 as the number of time slot in respectively the communication phase 1,2 and 3.

6 Evaluation

We carry out a series of simulations in order to analyze the performance of the proposed random access technique, in terms of probability of non-collision (success rate), under low, medium and high load conditions. We have to determine the optimal value of N_{slot}^1, N_{slot}^2 and N_{slot}^3.

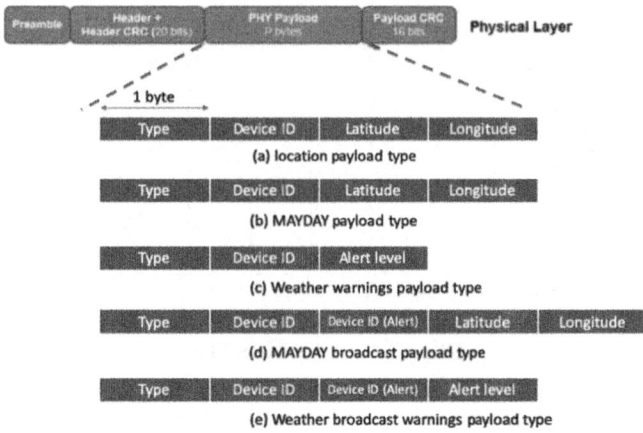

Fig. 4. The five different types of payloads

6.1 Simulation Settings

LoRa Interface Configuration. There are several transmission modes in LoRa technology and each mode is a combination of three parameters: bandwidth (BW), coding rate (CR) and spreading factor (SF). In the simulations, we consider the same parameters that we used in our radio coverage tests at sea [1] which were: $BW = 125$ KHz, $CR = 4/5$ and $SF = 12$. This LoRa mode, called Mode 1, allows to reach the maximum range with a sensitivity of -134 dBm. However, the time to transmit a packet, called time-on-air, is the longest. In Senegal, we use LoRa devices operating on the ISM EU868 band. The maximum payload size, in this context, for the Mode 1 is 51 bytes [19]. As explained in Sect. 4.1, the data to be sent by each device during each communication phase is not important in terms of size. We propose, in our context, five types of payloads (see Fig. 4), however we can divide them into 3 groups:

- the location type payload which have to be used in the communication phase 1. Four bytes are enough (1 for the type, 1 for the device ID, 1 for the latitude and the last one for the longitude).
- the "MAYDAY" and weather warnings types which have to be used in the critical information transmission phase 2. Four bytes are enough for the "MAYDAY" (1 for the type, 1 for the device ID,Data types used in the dissemination phase 3 by mobile relay to broadcast the received "MAYDAY" and weather warnings during the phase 2. 1 for the latitude and the last one for the longitude) and three for the weather warnings(1 for the type, 1 for the base station ID and the last one for the alert level).
- Broadcast types used in the dissemination phase 3 by mobile relay to broadcast the received "MAYDAY" and weather warnings during the phase 2. Five bytes are enough to broadcast a "MAYDAY" (1 for the type, 1 for the device ID, 1 for ID of the alerting device, 1 for the latitude and the last one for the

longitude) and four for the weather warnings(1 for the type, 1 for the device ID, 1 for base station ID and the last one for the alert level).

Therefore, only five bytes are enough to handle all the type of information to be sent.

As previously fixed, only 5 bytes preamble are enough. The corresponding time-on-air value is 1318.9 ms [19]. Based on this, we fix the time slot to $\tau_{slot} = 1.5$ s.

6.2 Simulation Results

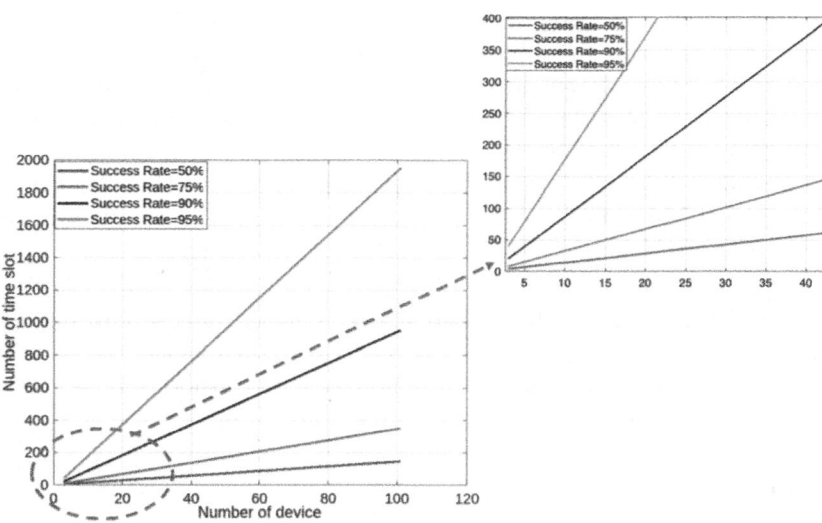

Fig. 5. The number of time slot as a function of devices number for predefined probability of non-collision (success rate)

The Fig. 5 shows the number of time slots required for different non-collision probabilities (Success rate) and different numbers of device. We based on Eq. 7. The idea is to fix a transmission success rate according to the concerned phase, then choose the number of devices that can be supported and deduce the number of time slots required. We use Matlab platform for the simulation.

The first observation is that, no matter the number of considered device we can have, the higher the fixed success rate, the higher the number of time slots required is. Remember that the duration of each of the three communication phases, we are trying to size, is linked to the number of slots required. ($T_{MLoc} = \tau_{slot} * N^1_{slot}$, $T_{Cinf} = \tau_{slot} * N^2_{slot}$ and $T_{Dis} = \tau_{slot} * N^3_{slot}$).

Sizing of the Critical Information Transmission Phase Duration

- On the one hand, only the base stations that broadcast weather warnings and the canoes in distress ("MAYDAY") have to transmit during that phase. The number of devices that have to randomly access the shared bandwidth is very small.
- On the other hand, the information transmitted during this phase is of great importance. thus, the success rate have to be set at a very high threshold.

Therefore, we propose to set the success rate equal to 95% and to also consider that the maximum number of canoes in distress does not exceed 10. The required number of slots is equal to 200 and then $T_{Cinf} = \tau_{slot} * N_{slot}^2 = 1.5 * 200 = 5$ mn.

Sizing of the Dissemination Phase Duration. During phase 3, the equipment that received alerts in phase 2 are the ones that transmit. They disseminate the same information to spread alerts. In this case, we don't need a very high success rate since a single frame sent successfully is enough to reach the canoes over a radius of several kilometers.

We consider a success rate of 50% and a phase duration of 2 mn and 30 s which represent 100 time slot. We can have up to 70 devices disseminating alerts with 50% success rate.

Sizing of the Location Phase Duration. This phase allows to update the previously (Sect. 3.2) defined security levels. Up to 100 devices will be able to share their location with a success rate of 50% if we consider a phase duration of 3 mn and 45 s (150 time slot).

7 Conclusion

Safety at sea has become a real concern for Senegalese fishers over the past two decades. Artisanal fishing is carried out on the deep sea in the absence of communication networks. Fishers have no means of sharing location, alerts or information in case of danger. For financial reasons, they can't afford conventional centralized marine positioning systems.

We have therefore proposed an ad hoc communication system based on lora technology. It is necessary to manage access to the transmission channel for the various nodes in the network. Aloha, the access technique used in lora networks, does not allow efficient use of the channel. We proposed a controlled sliding backoff algorithm to size the transmission phases and achieve a high success rate. The results show that the network is adaptive. In fact, depending on parameters such as the number of users, the target success rate and the number of time slots, we obtain different duration of the transmission phases. Our solution is intended for delay-tolerant networks and can be an important support for security issues in maritime areas, especially in Senegal.

In a future work we plan to implement a version of this model in our mobile relays in order to have empirical tests.

References

1. Seye, M.R., Ngom, B., Diallo, M., Gueye, B.: Work in progress: a low cost geographical localization system for a more secure coastal artisanal fishery in Senegal. In: 2019 International Conference on Information and Communication Technologies for Disaster Management (ICT-DM), pp. 1–4 (2019). https://doi.org/10.1109/ICT-DM47966.2019.9032947
2. Seye, M.R., Diallo, M., Gueye, B., Cambier, C.: An Ad Hoc communication system for an efficient milk collection within white areas. In: 2019 15th International Wireless Communications & Mobile Computing Conference (IWCMC), pp. 1828–1832 (2019). https://doi.org/10.1109/IWCMC.2019.8766524
3. Sénégal : Pêche industrielle et pêche artisanale, l'impossible cohabitation?https://www.greenpeace.org/africa/fr/les-blogs/13337/senegal-peche-industrielle-et-peche-artisanale-limpossible-cohabitation/
4. Publication des données du secteur des pêches au Sénégal: une bataille sans merci https://cenozo.org/publication-des-donnees-du-secteur-des-peches-au-senegal-une-bataille-sans-merci/
5. Seye, M.R., Diallo, M., Gueye, B., Cambier, C.: COWShED: communication within white spots for breeders. In: 2019 22nd Conference on Innovation in Clouds, Internet and Networks and Workshops (ICIN), pp. 236–238 (2019). https://doi.org/10.1109/ICIN.2019.8685838
6. Beltramelli, L., Mahmood, A., Österberg, P., Gidlund, M.: LoRa beyond ALOHA: an investigation of alternative random access protocols. IEEE Trans. Ind. Inf. **17**(5), 3544–3554 (2020). https://doi.org/10.1109/TII.2020.2977046
7. Kleinrock, L., Tobagi, F.: Packet switching in radio channels: part I-carrier sense multiple-access modes and their throughput-delay characteristics. IEEE Trans. Commun. **23**(12), 1400–1416 (1975)
8. Baumgartner, L., Lieser, P., Zobel, J., Bloessl, B., Steinmetz, R., Mezini, M.: LoRAgent: a DTN-based location-aware communication system using LoRa. In: IEEE Global Humanitarian Technology Conference (GHTC) 2020, pp. 1–8 (2020). https://doi.org/10.1109/GHTC46280.2020.9342886
9. Gao, P., Li, Z., Li, F., Li, H., Yang, Z., Zhou, W.: Design of distributed three component seismic data acquisition system based on LoRa wireless communication technology. In: 2018 37th Chinese Control Conference (CCC), pp. 10285–10288 (2018). https://doi.org/10.23919/ChiCC.2018.8483229
10. Petajajarvi, J., Mikhaylov, K., Roivainen, A., Hanninen, T.: On the coverage of LPWANs: range evaluation and channel attenuation model for LoRa technology. In: 14th International Conference on ITS Telecommunications (ITST) (2015)
11. Ertürk, M.A., Aydın, M.A., Büyükakkaslarand, M.T., Evirgen, H.: A survey on LoRaWAN architecture, protocol and technologies (2019)
12. Wang, Z., Jiang, Z., Hu, J., Song, T., Cao, Z.: Research on agricultural environment information collection system based on LoRa. In: 2018 IEEE 4th International Conference on Computer and Communications (ICCC), pp. 2441–2445 (2018). https://doi.org/10.1109/CompComm.2018.8780762
13. Diouf, F.A.Y., Seye, M.R., Diallo, M., Gueye, B.: SAFeComNet: safer artisanal fishing intEgrating a COMmunity NETwork. In: Eighth International Congress on Information and Communication Technology (ICICT 2023), pp. 281–292 (2023). https://doi.org/10.1007/978-981-99-3236-8_22
14. Vangelista, L., Zanella, A., Zorzi, M.: Long-range IoT technologies: the dawn of LoRa^{TM}. In: Atanasovski, V., Leon-Garcia, A. (eds.) FABULOUS 2015. LNICST,

vol. 159, pp. 51–58. Springer, Cham (2015). https://doi.org/10.1007/978-3-319-27072-2_7
15. Georgiou, O., Raza, U.: Low power wide area network analysis: can LoRa scale? IEEE Wirel. Commun. Lett. **6**(2), 162–165 (2017). https://doi.org/10.1109/LWC.2016.2647247
16. Polonelli, T., Brunelli, D., Benini, L.: Slotted ALOHA overlay on LoRaWAN - a distributed synchronization approach. In: 2018 IEEE 16th International Conference on Embedded and Ubiquitous Computing (EUC), Bucharest (2018)
17. Xanthopoulos, A., Valkanis, A., Beletsioti, G., Papadimitriou, G.I., Nicopolitidis, P.: On the use of backoff algorithms in slotted ALOHA LoRaWAN networks. In: 2020 International Conference on Computer, Information and Telecommunication Systems (CITS), pp. 1–4 (2020). https://doi.org/10.1109/CITS49457.2020.9232577
18. Stamatiou, K., Haenggi, M.: Random-access poisson networks: stability and delay. IEEE Commun. Lett. **14**(11), 1035–1037 (2010). https://doi.org/10.1109/LCOMM.2010.100810.100762
19. The Things Network, LoRa Alliance Member. LoRaWAN airtime calculator. https://www.thethingsnetwork.org/airtime-calculator/

A New Delay History Predictor for Multi-skill Call Center

Mamadou Thiongane[✉], Mohamed M. Ould Deye, Modou Gueye, and Mbaye Séne

Department of Mathematics and Computer Science, University Cheikh Anta Diop, Dakar, Senegal
{mamadou.thiongane,mohamed.oulddeye,modou2.gueye,mbaye.sene}@ucad.edu.sn

Abstract. We are interesting in methods for predicting the time that a customer must wait at this arrival in multi-skilled call centers. We propose a free-parameters delay history predictor that can be used in multi-skilled contexts. It only uses the waiting times of previous customers in the same class who found the same length of queue when they joined the system, and computes a weighted average of this past delays. In our numerical experiments with simulation models and real multi-skill call center, this new predictor is very competitive with existing delay history predictors. It gives often better results than other delay history predictors, and it is also very easy to implement in practice. This delay predictors can also be used in other service systems such as medical clinic, bank or emergency service.

Keywords: Delay History Predictor · Real Data · Call Center

1 Introduction

In service systems like emergency services, banks queueing services, call centers, and so on, announcing the estimated waiting time to new customers at their arrival can greatly increase customers satisfaction and experience at service providers. It can also help to improve the global system performance. By way of example, many hospitals in the USA and Canada periodically calculate the average waiting time for patients in their emergency rooms, and the results are published online or displayed on digital dashboard. This information can help to reduce emergency rooms saturation by encouraging new patients to go to a less crowded hospital. In call center, the queue is generally invisible to a calling customer, contrary to a physical queue in bank, supermarket or department store. The customer can only rely on the information provided by the call system. Providing delay announcements to customers, in addition to increasing customer's satisfaction, can significantly reduce the number of abandonments, and increases the overall system service rate. A growing number of call centers now provide delay announcement to their customers when they arrive in queue. Once the customer hears the estimated delay, she or he can choose to leave the queue, wait in the queue until receiving service or request to be recalled later if this option is available [2].

The related work on delay estimation can be classified in two categories. Some studies, like ours, focus solely on delay prediction without announcement to customers, whereas other studies integrate the impacts of the announcement of delays on the attitudes of the customers into their estimation models.

Most of the studies on delay prediction has been conducted for single queue systems. These works can be divided into two categories: *"Queue-Length"* (QL) delay estimators and *"Delay-History"* (DH) estimators. In QL delay estimators, the length of the queue and the parameters of the system as the number of used servers, and their service rate are used to predict the waiting delay, while the DH estimators use just the past customers delay time to predict the waiting time of a new customer in the system. The *"Last-to-Enter-Service"* (LES) predictor, which predict the waiting time of a new arrival customer by the wait time of the last customer who began his service, is the most popular DH predictor. DH predictors are much less accurate than QL predictors, however the latter are not applicable in a multi-skilled call centers. In modern call centers, which are multi-skill system, customers are classified by call type, and agents are grouped according to their skills. An agent can only serve a customer if she/he has the skills required for that call type. In Gan et al. [4] a well-detailed description of all the operational aspects of modern call centers has been done. In this work, the words "customer" and "call" are used interchangeably, as well as "server" and "agent".

Very few delay estimators have been done for multi-queue and multi-server systems, such as modern call centers. Senderovich et al. [11] have proposed predictors for a multi-skill system with only one agent group and many call type. Thiongane et al. [13,15,16] study more general method of delay estimation which can be applied in multi-skill systems. This work uses machine learning algorithms (Artificial Neural Networks (ANNs), Regression Smoothing Splines (RS)) and data collected on the system to learn a prediction function. The machine learning methods give good performance in multi-skill context but one drawbacks of them is they need many data and computational time to train model. The machine learning methods are also not easy to apply in practice, and one would have to rely on the simpler DH predictors.

In this paper, we propose a new DH delay predictor which predicts the customer waiting delay by an exponential smoothing weight average of the wait time of the past customers that have found the same queue length in the system at their arrival's. We call this predictor the *Weigth Exponential Smoothing Average Conditional LES* (WAvgC-LES). This predictor, like most DH predictors, are attractive in practice, because it requires no parameter estimation, and no optimization. We are studying these delay predictors in call centers context, but they could also be used in many other kinds of service systems.

In this work, we do not look at the influence of delay notification on the customer's waiting time. In practice, we often find the *LES* or *average LES* (Avg-LES). Thiongane et al. [14] propose AvgC-LES which is more accurate than LES and Avg-LES but the latter need to store too many data to give good prediction unlike WAvgC-LES which stores only little data. In our numerical experiments with real and simulated data, we observe that WAvgC-LES is often more accurate than AvgC-LES.

The rest of this document is organised as follows. In Sect. 2, we present work that are done on delay estimation for service systems. In Sect. 3, we describe the general structure of modern multiskill call center models and present three examples of model which are used to evaluate the efficiency of predictors. In Sect. 4, we introduce the new delay predictor and also present other delay predictors that will be used to compare their performance with that of the new one. This comparison is made in Sect. 5. In Sect. 6, we conclude this work.

2 Review of the Literature

Most of work for delay estimation method has been done for single queue system for which customers are served in FCFS order. In that system a new arrival customer does not affect the waiting of customers that are already in queue. Assume a new customer who enters in a queue in which there are K customers already waiting. Let W denote the random variable representing the customer waiting time. A naturel and good predictor of W is the QL predictor, which predicts its expectation conditional on K. For the GI/M/c queue in which we have c servers, arrivals follow a general distribution, service times follow an exponential distribution with mean μ^{-1}, and customers have infinite patience (no abandonment) then the conditional expectation of W is given by $\mathbb{E}[W \mid K] = (K+1)/(c\mu)$ [17]. In a GI/M/s+M queue, where customers have exponential patience time with rate ν. The virtual expected delay, conditional on K, is predicted by $\mathbb{E}[W \mid K] = \sum_{k=0}^{K} 1/(c\mu + k\nu)$.

It is often very difficult to develop QL predictors for multi-skilled systems. For these system, we have multiple queues, agents have limited skills (i.e. each agent has a subset of customer types that he can serve), and agents often assign different priorities to different customer types. For the special case where each server can serve all customer types with the same order of priority, Senderovich [12] propose QL formulas for the special case that give upper and lower bounds on the expected delay time. Ibrahim et al. [7,9] propose DH predictors for single-queue systems. However, it should be noted that these predictors can be used in multi-skilled systems. These predictors use the waiting times of the past customers to predict the waiting time of a new customer. They include "last-to-enter-service" (LES) customer, "head-of-line" (HOL) customer, "last-to-complete-service" (LCS) customer, or the most "recent-arrival-to-complete-service" (RCS). The authors show that LES and HOL give more accurate prediction than RCS and LCS. Thiongane et al. [14] propose two DH predictors. The first is called E-LES. It estimates the waiting time of a new customer by extrapolating the waiting history of customers in the queue, and returns a weighted average of the extrapolated waits. The second, called AvgC-LES, predicts the waiting time of a new customer by averaging the waiting times of customers of the same type (class) already served and having observed the same queue length on arrival.

Another class of predictors (usable in multi-skill context) which use machine learning algorithms (e.g., decision trees, splines regressions, and artificial neural networks) are proposed in recent years. The reader can see for example [1, 10, 12, 13, 15, 16] for more information on their implementation. These algorithms use data collected on system to learn the delay predictors. They give predictions that are better than those of DH. Their disadvantage is that they are complex to implement in practice. A large amount of data is required, and learning step times can often be too long. This is why simpler methods continue to attract interest.

3 The Model of Call Center

Here, we consider multi-skilled call center models. In these call center customers are classified according to the type of service they require. Agents are also divided into groups and the agents in the same group have the same skills. Call center opening hours are divided into periods of equal length. Customers arrival rate vary throughout the day. The distribution of the arrivals, the service time and the patience times can be very general. In the numericals examples with simulation models, we assume that arrivals of call type k at period p follow a Poisson process with rate $\lambda_{k,p}$ which is constant in period $p \in P$, service time are exponentials with rate μ_k and patience times also exponentials with rate ν_k. A customer leaves the queue when his waiting time exceeds his patience time. We define by $s_g = (s_{g,1}, \ldots, s_{g,P})$ the staffing vector of agents in group g, where $s_{g,p}$ is the number of agents of group g at period p. We use one queue per service type and customers in the same queue are served with "first-come, first-served" (FCFS) rule. If a call of type k arrives and there are no agents available with the skills to serve it, it will be placed in the k queue. Calls will be assigned according to the routing policy used in the examples.

Figure 1 shows three of the canonical models of multi-skilled call centers [5]. The first is the "V-model" with two types of calls and one agents group that handle the both types of calls. The second is the "N-model" with two type of call and two agent groups, where the group 1 have the skill sets to serve call type 1 et the group 2 can serve both call type. The third is the "W-model" with three calls types and two agents groups. The group 1 have the skill to serve call type 1 and 2, and the group 2 have the skill to serve the call type 2 and 3.

4 The Predictors of Delay

We start this section by presenting the DH predictor used in this study, and we finish by presenting our new DH predictor. For comparison, in our numerical experiment, we use a machine learning delay predictor (ANN) that is the better in multi-skill settings. It should be noted that, even though the ANN perform much better, these predictors have other drawbacks, as mentioned above. The

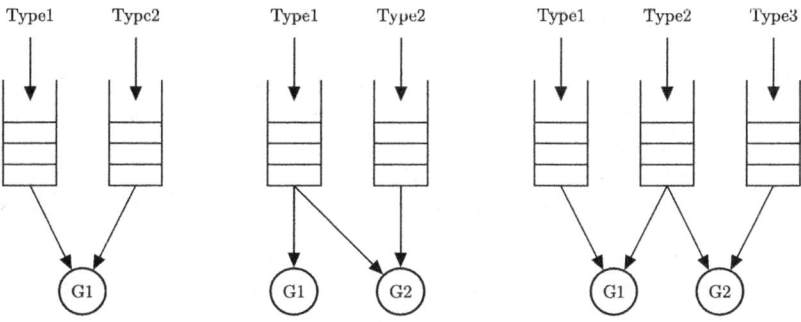

Fig. 1. The V, N, and W multi-skill models.

DH predictors use only the past customers delays of the same type to predict the waiting time of a new arrival customer in a queue. So, for each method considered, there is a different predictor for each call type class k, even if we don't always index it explicitly by j.

4.1 Last-to-Enter-Service (LES)

The predicted waiting time for a new customer is the wait time experienced by the last customer of the same type who was begin his service [8]. It is the most used DH predictor in practice.

4.2 Average-LES (Avg-LES)

This predictor is a version of LES that returns the average of several LES prediction. It predicts the waiting time of a new customer by averaging the waiting times of the N(A constant integer number) last customers of the same type who entered service. As LES, It is often used in practice [3]. Like LES, it is also widely used in practice.

4.3 Proportional-Queue-LES (P-LES)

The P-LES predictor is a predictor that takes into account the variation in queue length [6]. It uses the queue length Q at the arrival of the new customer, the queue length at the LES customer's arrival QL_{LES} and its waiting time x, and predict the new customer's waiting time D by the ratio Q/Q_{LES}. The predictor actually used is :

$$D = x \frac{Q+1}{Q_{\text{LES}}+1}.$$

It solves the case where the last customer to enter service is to find an empty queue ($Q_{\text{LES}} = 0$).

4.4 Extrapolated-LES (E-LES)

To predict customers waiting time, the E-LES predictor uses information on the waiting delays of customers actually in the queue. The final waiting times of these customers (which are unknown) are obtained by extrapolating the times that they have already elapsed. E-LES returns the weighted average of the extrapolated waiting times as the prediction of the new customer's waiting time [14].

4.5 Average-LES-Conditional-on-Queue-Length (AvgC-LES)

This predictor, introduced by Thiongane et al. [14], predicts the waiting time of a new customer by averaging the waiting times of customers already served who have observed the same queue length on arrival as the new customer. The authors have shown in some simulated systems and in some real call centers data that this predictor is better than LES, Avg-LES, P-LES, and other DH predictors [15]. For each queue j, we store for each queue length $q \in \{1, \ldots, Q\}$, the waiting times of the last N_q (a fixed integer greater than 0) customers that observe a queue equal to q at their arrival. So for a new customer of type j who observes a queue length q, the average of these N_q waiting times will be the prediction of his waiting time.

Unlike Avg-LES, here a predictor for which N_q is large performs better than a predictor with $N_q = 1$. For AvgC-LES to be efficient, N_q must be large, and for this a lot of memory is needed to store the N_q delay for all $q \in \{1, \ldots, Q\}$. However in most call center software, there is not enough memory to store all this information. This is the main drawback of this predictor and this is one of the reasons why we propose a new version that uses less memory and gives even better performance measures.

4.6 Weighted-Average-LES-Conditional-on-Queue-Length (WAvgC-LES)

To solve the need for a large quantity of memory with AvgC-LES, we propose a new predictor which is an "average versions" of AvgC-LES, which replace the ordinary average of the N_q wait times for class j and queue size q by a "weighted average". In this work, we use exponential decreasing weighting. To ensure that each new observation (each waiting time) makes a relatively small contribution, we have chosen small α smoothing factors (e.g., 0.2 or smaller). With exponential smoothing, we no longer need to store any individual information on customer waiting times. In our numerical experiments, WAvgC-LES gave better or similar results than AvgC-LES in terms of prediction error.

Here we describe how to predict the delay for a new arrival customer in system who find q customer in queue. When the arrival customer is the first one who observe this queue length (so we have $S_q = -1$), so his wait time is predicted by LES, otherwise his wait time is predicted by S_q value.

Now we describe how to update S_q. When a customer, who have found q customers in queue at its arrival and after waited a delay W, exits the queue to receive service, the value of S_q is update by

$$S_q = W \tag{1}$$

if its value is minus one, else it is updated by an exponential smoothing average

$$S_q = \alpha \cdot W + (1 - \alpha) \cdot S_q \tag{2}$$

where α is the smoothing factor, and $0 < \alpha \leq 1$.

Based in our numerical experiment, we observe that in system with time varying arrival process and time varying servers as the modern call centers, a small value for the smoothing factor give better predictions than large value. This mean that it is better to give small weight to new LES and large weight to the old LES values for this system. We recommend $\alpha = 0.2$. We observe also that in single queue system with long run simulation, the precision of WAvgC-LES is very similar to that of QL. This can be explained by the fact that WAvgC-LES has gathered sufficient data to calculate a good expected waiting time conditional on queue length.

5 Numerical Model Results

In this section, we present the numerical results of experiments with simulated models, as well as the numerical results of experiments with a real multiskill call center. We compare the precision of the predictors on all the models studied. We start with the M/M/s+M model, for which we have an analytical formula for calculating the expectation of waiting time conditional on queue length. This example is studied in order to check the accuracy of our predictions in relation to the actual value. Our second example is an N (multi-skilled) model (see Fig. 1). It has two types of customer and two groups of agents. Agents in group 1 have the skill to serve only type 1 customers, and agents in group 2 can serve any type of customer. Our third and final example is an actual multi-skilled call center. It has several call types (27 in all) and several agent groups.

5.1 Measure of the Prediction Errors

To measure the accuracy of our delay predictors, we use the *"Mean Squared Error"* (MSE). Let D be the predicted waiting time of a customer and W the actual waiting time. The MSE is given by

$$\text{MSE} = \mathbb{E}\left[(W - D)^2\right].$$

In practice, we use its empirical version, called the *"Average Squared Error"* (ASE), The ASE is given by

$$\text{ASE} = \frac{1}{N} \sum_{n=1}^{N} (W_n - D_n)^2,$$

where D_n, W_n, and N are respectively the predicted waiting time, the real waiting, and the total number of served customers. The normalized version of the ASE called *"Root Relative Average Squared Error"* (RRASE) is reported in numerical results.

$$\text{RRASE} = \frac{\sqrt{\text{ASE}}}{\sum_{n=1}^{N} W_n/N} \times 100.$$

5.2 An M/M/s+M Model Queue System

We compare the accuracy of the predictors in an M/M/s+M model. We consider that the arrival rate varies over the day. The day is divided into 20 periods of 1 h each, and in each period p arrivals follow a Poisson process of constant rate λ_p. Service time follow an exponential distribution with rate 1. The distribution of patience times is also exponential with rate 0.5. We take $s = 20$ for the whole day, $\lambda_p = 25$ for even-numbered periods, and $\lambda_p = 20$ for odd-numbered periods. We run 100 independent simulations and estimated the accuracy of the delay predictors. We observe that the average waiting time is equals to 20 min, the average queue length is 8 customers, the probability of a customer waiting is around 92%, and the probability that a customer leave the queue without served is 15.8. For this model, it is well known that QL is an optimal predictor of waiting time expectation conditional on queue length. Our objective is to compare the performance of the other predictors with QL predictor to see how they score against the optimum.

Table 1 shows the RRASE values for the different predictors. Here are the predictors parameters used to compute the RRASE. $N_j = 2$, $N_{j,k} = 100$, and $\delta = 0.1$ respectively for Avg-LES, AvgC-LES, and WAvgC-LES. QL gives the best performance, which is no surprise. It's closely followed by AvgC-LES and WAvgC-LES, which give roughly the same result. The other methods perform much less well. They give much larger RRASEs. It should be noted that Avg-LES ($N_j \geq 2$), which is often used in practice, performs less well than LES ($N_j = 1$). Ibrahim et al. [6] found comparable results. P-LES is the worst predictor.

Table 1. The RRASE result for the M/M/20+M simulated example.

	LES	Avg-LES	P-LES	E-LES	AvgC-LES	WAvgC-LES	QL
RRASE	46.9	49.4	59.2	43.6	32.9	32.8	32.1

5.3 The N-Model Example

An N-model is illustrated in Fig. 1 by the middle image. The routing policy used is as follows. Calls are served according to their order of arrival in each queue (FCFS order). Agents of group 2 give priority to calls type 2. They serve calls type 1 only if there are no type 2 calls waiting. If a call type 1 arrives, an agent of group 1 who has been idle for the longest time is preferred. If no agent of group 1 is free, the call is routed to the Group 2 agent who has been inactive the longest. If all agents in group 2 are busy, the call is placed in queue 1.

We divide the day into 10 periods of 1hour, and for each period arrival follow a Poisson process with constant rate. The service times and patience times are exponential with constant rates over the day. The parameters for model simulation are $\lambda_1 = (25, 34, 43, 48, 51, 57, 42, 34, 22, 18)$ per hour, the vector of arrival for type 1, $\lambda_2 = (26, 40, 47, 59, 68, 59, 48, 43, 39, 29)$ the vector of arrival rate for call type 2. The mean service time for call type 1 is $\mu_1^{-1} = 21$ minutes and their mean patience is $\nu_1^{-1} = 46.7$ minutes. For call type 2, the mean service time is $\mu_2^{-1} = 11$, and mean patience time is $\nu_2^{-1} = 30$. The staffing vectors are $s_1 = (4, 6, 9, 10, 9, 9, 9, 8, 5, 5)$ for group 1 and $s_2 = (4, 7, 9, 10, 9, 8, 7, 8, 6, 5)$ for group 2. We run 100 independent simulation of days. We observe that only 22% of calls type 2 are served by group 2, and the 88% by group 1. The probability of delay is 94.0 % for call type 1, and 97% for call type 2. The ratio of abandonment is 33% and 23% for call type 1 and call type 2 respectively. The average queue length is 9.7 for type 1 and 5.5 for type2. The average waiting for call type 1 is 938 s and 426 s for call type 2.

Table 2 shows the RRASE for both types of call, for different predictors. We use $N_j = 7$, $N_{j,k} = 100$, and $\delta = 0.2$ for Avg-LES, AvgC-LES, and WAvgC-LES respectively. The QL predictor is not usable in a multi-skill context, so here we use ANN predictor, which is known to perform best in a multi-skill context [13]. Unsurprisingly, ANN, which needs a learning steep, a lot of data, and difficult to implement in practice, gives the best results. After the ANN, WAvgC-LES is DH predictors who gives the best result. P-LES, as in the other examples, still gives the worst performance. LES, Avg-LES and E-LES gives close results.

Table 2. The RRASE of the N-model.

Call Type	LES	Avg-LES	P-LES	E-LES	AvgC-LES	WAvgC-LES	ANN
T1	49.5	51.8	70.4	46.8	37.5	36.4	32.4
T2	62.1	66.7	94.3	61.4	47.8	44.3	41.2

5.4 The Real System Example

The real system studied in this work is a multi-skilled call center situated in the Netherlands. There are two datasets collected during the year 2014. The first dataset concerns call information logs and the second is a dataset on the different activities of agents during the day at the call center. The call log data set contains information on arrival time of call, the begin and the end service time of a call, the type of service asked by a caller, information that identify the agent, etc. The activity data contains the identity of the activity, the begin and end time of an activity, etc.

The call center is open 12 h a day. It opens at 8 a.m. and closes at 8 p.m. Monday to Friday. There are 27 possible types of service, and 312 separate agents worked over the year. An analysis of the data showed 56% of calls are answered immediately with no waiting time, 38% of callers had to wait in a queue before receiving service, and around 6% of customers leave queue before receiving service. In this work, we report only the results of the 5 call types (T1, T2, T3, T4, and T5) that received nearly 90% of call volume (Table 3).

Table 3. Some statistical summary over the year for the real system.

	T1	T2	T3	T4	T5
Total number calls	568 554	270 675	311 523	112 711	25 839
Served, no wait	61%	52%	55%	45%	34%
Served, waited	35%	40%	40%	46%	54%
Abandon	4%	7%	5%	8%	12%
Avg wait time (sec)	77	91	83	85	110
Avg service time (sec)	350	308	281	411	311
Avg queue length	8.2	3.3	4.4	4.3	0.9

Table 4 shows the RRASEs for different predictors in the real system for the five that have received bigger call type volume. We use $N_j = 10$, $N_{j,k} = 100$, and $\delta = 0.2$ for Avg-LES, AvgC-LES, and WAvgC-LES respectively. As in the previous example, we compare DH predictors with ANN predictor from Thiongane et al. [13,15]. ANN predictors are more efficient, but they require a very costly learning phase and involve many parameters. In this example also we also observe that our new WAvgC-LES predictor is the better DH predictor, far behind ANN. WAvgC-LES is shortly followed by AvgC-LES. As observed in Ibrahim et al. [3] LES is better than Avg-LES. As in two other example, we notice that the performance of P-LES is always bad.

Table 4. RRASE for the five call types of real system.

Call Types	Delay Predictors						
	P-LES	Avg-LES	LES	E-LES	AvgC-LES	WAvgC-LES	ANN
T1	81.75	76.28	58.66	68.59	56.97	56.62	42.24
T2	98.01	74.09	61.02	56.27	60.87	58.49	44.18
T3	94.87	82.19	62.43	67.86	63.68	62.44	48.32
T4	92.96	82.22	63.53	69.68	63.12	62.17	50.25
T5	92.44	70.87	53.47	53.54	53.20	51.28	39.47

6 Conclusion

In this work, we develop and compare a delay history predictor for multi-skill call centers. The new delay history predictor compute an exponential smoothing average of wait times of the past customer who observe the same queue length at their arrival. We find that our new DH predictor performs much better than other DH predictors. The ANN predictor, which is difficult to implement in practice, is better than the WAvgC-LES, but the latter is easy to use in practice and also gives fairly accurate performance. In this work, the predictions are point estimate of the waiting time. The prediction is an estimate of the expected waiting time conditional on the queue length and other system parameters when the customer enters the queue. As part of our ongoing work, we aim to develop efficient methods for predicting and announcing the expected waiting time and its variance that are conditional on the system state when a customer enters in queue.

Acknowledgements. Thanks to Ger Koole (VU Amsterdam) for the data provided.

References

1. Ang, E., Kwasnick, S., Bayati, M., Plambeck, E., Aratow, M.: Accurate emergency department wait time prediction. Manuf. Serv. Oper. Manag. **18**(1), 141–156 (2016)
2. Armony, M., Shimkin, N., Whitt, W.: The impact of delay announcements in many-server queues with abandonments. Oper. Res. **57**, 66–81 (2009)
3. Dong, J., Yom Tov, E., Yom Tov, G.: The impact of delay announcements on hospital network coordination and waiting times (2016)
4. Gans, N., Koole, G., Mandelbaum, A.: Telephone call centers: tutorial, review, and research prospects. Manuf. Serv. Oper. Manag. **5**, 79–141 (2003)
5. Garnett, O., Mandelbaum, A., Reiman, M.: Designing a call center with impatient customers. Manuf. Serv. Oper. Manag. **4**(3), 208–227 (2002)
6. Ibrahim, R., Armony, M., Bassamboo, A.: Does the past predict the future? The case of delay announcements in service systems. Manag. Sci. (2016)
7. Ibrahim, R., Whitt, W.: Real-time delay estimation based on delay history. Manuf. Serv. Oper. Manag. **11**, 397–415 (2009)
8. Ibrahim, R., Whitt, W.: Real-time delay estimation in overloaded multiserver queues with abandonments. Manage. Sci. **55**(10), 1729–1742 (2009)
9. Ibrahim, R., Whitt, W.: Real-time delay estimation based on delay history in many-server service systems with time-varying arrivals. Prod. Oper. Manag. **20**(5), 654–667 (2011)
10. Senderovich, A., Weidlich, M., Gal, A., Mandelbaum, A.: Queue mining – predicting delays in service processes. In: Jarke, M., Mylopoulos, J., Quix, C., Rolland, C., Manolopoulos, Y., Mouratidis, H., Horkoff, J. (eds.) CAiSE 2014. LNCS, vol. 8484, pp. 42–57. Springer, Cham (2014). https://doi.org/10.1007/978-3-319-07881-6_4
11. Senderovich, A., Weidlich, M., Gal, A., Mandelbaum, A.: Queue mining for delay prediction in multi-class service processes. Inf. Syst. **53**, 278–295 (2015). http://dx.doi.org/10.1016/j.is.2015.03.010

12. Senderovich, A., Weidlich, M., Gal, A., Mandelbaum, A.: Queue mining for delay prediction in multi-class service processes. Inf. Syst. **53**, 278–295 (2015)
13. Thiongane, M., Chan, W., L'Ecuyer, P.: Waiting time predictors for multiskill call centers. In: Proceedings of the 2015 Winter Simulation Conference, pp. 3073–3084. IEEE Press (2015)
14. Thiongane, M., Chan, W., L'Ecuyer, P.: New history-based delay predictors for service systems. In: Proceedings of the 2016 Winter Simulation Conference, pp. 425–436. IEEE Press (2016)
15. Thiongane, M., Chan, W., L'Ecuyer, P.: Delay predictors in multi-skill call centers: An empirical comparison with real data. In: Proceedings of the International Conference on Operations Research and Enterprise Systems (ICORES), pp. 100–108. SciTePress (2020)
16. Thiongane, M., Chan, W., L'Ecuyer, P.: Learning-based prediction of conditional wait time distributions in multiskill call centers. In: Parlier, G.H., Liberatore, F., Demange, M. (eds.) Operations Research and Enterprise Systems, pp. 83–106. Springer, Cham (2022). https://doi.org/10.1007/978-3-031-10725-2_5
17. Whitt, W.: Predicting queueing delays. Manag. Sci. **45**(6), 870–888 (1999)

Retrieving Data from Social Network Platforms: A State-of-Art Review

Harriet Sibitenda[1](✉)[iD], Awa Diattara[1][iD], Assitan Traore[2], and B. A. Cheikh[1][iD]

[1] Laboratoire d'Analyse Numerique et Informatique, University of Gaston Berger, Saint-Louis, Senegal
{harriet.sibitenda,awa.diattara,cheikh2.ba}@ugb.edu.sn
[2] Business and Decision, Grenoble, France
assitan.traore@free.fr

Abstract. Analyzing public concerns gives feedback to organizations about goods and services. The means of collecting social concerns differ for each social media platform. There is a need to explore the literature about automated tools applied by researchers to collect social issues. The goal of this paper is to provide an overview of data collection methods from social media platforms. This is to guide the collection of public concerns through machine learning approaches. Following the preferred reporting items for systematic reviews and meta-analyses standards, we collected 2180 articles from the Google Scholar database based on keywords. We screened the reviews for relevancy based on abstract and title. Considering the exclusion criteria, we removed all full articles not related to social media platforms. We manually analyzed only 298 articles to identify classifications within methods of data collection. From the reviews, we retrieved five categories of data collection. These include; manual observations, self-report surveys, public repositories, existing licensed tools, public application programming interfaces, and web crawlers or scrapers. Considering sample networks of Facebook, Twitter, and YouTube, we explored the trends of tools. And we stated the pros and cons. In conclusion, to collect social concerns at no cost and in large amounts, we recommend using open libraries of public application programming interfaces and web scrapers. In the future, we plan to extract public data using the recommended trendy automated tools for each category and sample social networks.

Keywords: Data collection · social networks · social concerns

1 Introduction

In society, individuals usually experience challenges and hardships that hinder their daily effort at work and ways of living [1]. We call these personal troubles

---

PASET-RSIF, UGB.

© ICST Institute for Computer Sciences, Social Informatics and Telecommunications Engineering 2025
Published by Springer Nature Switzerland AG 2025. All Rights Reserved
K. Cheikh M. F. Kebe et al. (Eds.): InterSol 2024, LNICST 610, pp. 151–166, 2025.
https://doi.org/10.1007/978-3-031-86493-3_13

or problems. The occurrence of similar challenges to a large group of people within the same society implies the emergence of social issues. There is a need for an urgent response to reduce the magnitude of the issue's damage and spread. Consistent social issues affect the development of societies [2]. The collection of many social issues triggers the emergence of another. Social concerns have a historical cycle to their occurrence.

A study, by [3] highlights the occurrence of concerns in society. Initially, the occurrence of specific problems to many people creates common issues. People report their concerns to authorities like police, media platforms, government activists, and more. This stage is called legislation for action. After the legislative stage, the authorities develop laws and regulations to handle the situation. There is a probability that different sectors recover from the common social problem or adopt change. Finally, there is a need to assess the transformation action plan to preserve society for sustainable development and public governance [4].

There are four major methods of *Understanding social concerns* [5]. These include; (i) Surveys that gather data from a sample study population using questions that respondents interact by mobile phone, web, and face-to-face tools like paper. (ii) Experiments that are conducted in the natural and physical sciences based on cause-and-effect relationships. (iii) Observations that are field research sessions that involve watching the situation on participants to make reports. (iv) Existing dataset is data that someone else has already gathered and used in another study, for example, data from the US Census Bureau. Globally, the *Statista report 2020* highlights that the use of SNPs is increasing, and Facebook leads other networks like YouTube and WhatsApp [6]. Communication over SNPs involves user perceptions, posts, comments, reactions, emotions, and many more [7]. The social comments form big unstructured data, and this includes text, images, audio, and video clips. The big data attracts researchers to apply Artificial Intelligence (AI) tools to explore hidden knowledge insights. In Africa, social media usage penetration is growing higher with the Northern region at 45%, Southern 41%, western 16%, Eastern 10%, and Central 8%. [8]. We will focus on common SNPs like Facebook, Twitter, and YouTube to explore the methods of data collection for social issues reported on these networks.

The goal of this study is to give a global overview of methods of data collection from SNPs to identify public concerns using Machine Learning (ML) approaches. To attain the goal, we consider the following specific objectives: (i) To review the existing literature about collecting data from social networks. (ii) To explore Machine Learning (ML) tools to extract the social comments. (iii) To propose suggestions of trends for data collection from sample social media platforms.

This study includes three sections: The first section introduces the need for social feedback to policy-makers from comments reported on the SNPs. The second section describes findings from the State-of-art review with subsections like related literature, the methodology to use, exploration of the data types of comments, and the methods of collection used in reviews. Finally, the third section summarizes the findings of the study, discusses its limitations, and recommends future research directions.

2 State-of-Art Review for Data Collection from SNPs

2.1 Related Literature

Authors in [9] conduct a systematic review of ML text mining techniques on previous research from Twitter. They explored trends of topics between the years of 2006 to 2019. Collected data (18,000 articles) from IEEE, the Web of Science, and EBSCO. They used search keywords of "Twitter AND Survey" and "Twitter AND Review". The research displays a high-level analysis of topics from articles. The study has a limit of eliminating the study of subcategories from the full review of the papers. We note to use an index database and search keywords to collect review papers relevant to a study's purpose.

The study in [10] involved a systematic review of the use of Twitter for higher professional education. They used keyword search strings like "Twitter in higher education", and "higher education academics", to collect 615 paper reviews from databases like Scopus, and Google Scholar. Authors repeatedly collected some articles using Google Scholar and Scopus, and this increased the time for screening. They also used the snowball method to add some articles in the references to reviews and manually analyzed 28 reviews to classify the content. The authors excluded many articles to consider only articles of interest. This narrowed their findings to the themes, ethical issues, and theoretical methodologies used. We note to identify exclusion criteria to obtain relevant findings from full articles.

The authors in [11] explored challenges for data discovery, collection, preparation, and analysis on social media. They collected 260 papers using keyword search strings and databases like ACM, AIS, IEE, and Science Direct. They conducted a backward search using citations in the references to create a citation network of relevant papers. With Text mining techniques, they also extracted themes, opinions, and sentiments based on the text of titles and abstracts. The authors identified challenges for each stage and proposed solutions from reviews. We note that they didn't explore deeper subcategories for solutions. Analysis of each stage from a broader perspective would give profound findings about challenges, solutions, and methods used.

A study by [12] explored how digital technologies support urban and regional Agro-food purchasing and its characteristics. They used Scopus and Web of Science to collect 370 and 398 articles, respectively. Using the PRISMA (Preferred reporting items for systematic reviews and meta-analyses) protocol guidelines. The PRISMA guide protocol used was logical for the exclusion of articles. They manually analyzed inclusion articles and represented the findings of classification using graphs. This aided the understanding of the findings. We note the usefulness of the PRISMA protocol to select papers for inclusion.

Therefore, this study proposes to collect previous literature related to data collection on social media for a period of years, from 2018 to 2022. To attain this purpose, we explore three questions: (i) What is the type of data from social comments? (ii) What are the ML methods applied in reviews to collect the data, and how do they work? (iii) What are the trends, strengths, and limitations of ML methods for data collection? In this study, we adopted the use of one index database named Google Scholar to reduce duplication of articles. We searched for articles using keywords. The PRISMA protocol was a guide for the exclusion and inclusion of articles. We manually analyzed inclusion articles to discover subcategories within methods of data collection for sample networks. Thus, our study adds an exploration of the state-of-art review about data collection and the classification of subcategories needed by researchers to select methods to extract social comments from SNPs.

2.2 Methodology

To begin with, we followed the PRISMA protocol guidelines suggested by [13] to construct a protocol to use in this study. The PRISMA standard for systematic review includes four major steps: identification of papers, screening, setting eligibility criteria, and selecting inclusion articles. We adopted the steps as shown in Fig. 1. Using the "Publish and Perish" open software, we selected the Google Scholar index database to collect articles for review. With the Google Scholar search, we entered keyword strings like "data collection and social networks", "data collection and Twitter", and "data collection and Facebook", for a specified period from 2018 to 2022. As a result, we collected 2180 articles and saved a copy of the output as "csv" and "ris" files. The csv file included the citation index details for each article. The ris file included referencing details for articles stored by reference software like Mendeley.

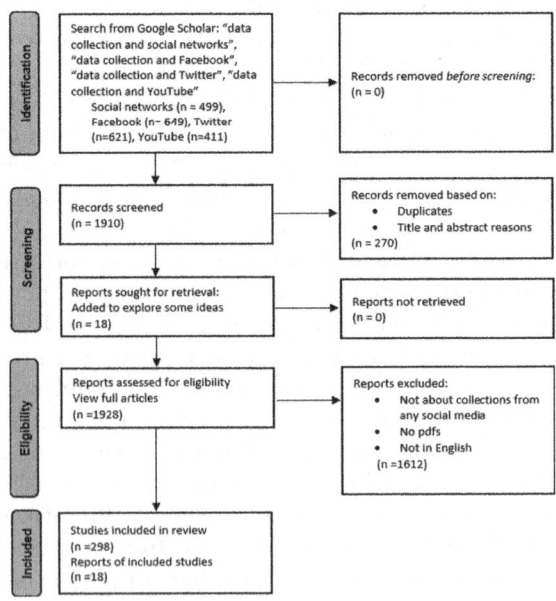

Fig. 1. The PRISMA flow protocol we adopted from Moher et al., 2009

After obtaining the articles, we began the screening process. We removed 270 irrelevant articles based on duplicates, the title, and the abstract. Using an eligibility criterion, we excluded 1612 articles. The criteria for exclusion and inclusion involved reading full articles. The csv file included a column of links to access the available full articles for each record of review. We eliminated records of articles without full PDFs, missing collections from any social media, and written in languages other than English. Finally, we had a csv file including 298 articles to consider for manual analysis. We added 18 papers to describe specific terms and ideas revealed from the reviews using the snowball method. We stored all these files in the Mendeley reference software to enable easy citation of articles.

Exploration of Papers Collected

Considering the csv dataset, the data contains data types such as text (with columns like Authors, Title, Type of document, Abstract, Age of paper). Number (with columns like Cites, GSrank, CitesPerYear, CitesPerAuthor). Date (with columns like Year, QueryDate). And links (with columns like ArticleURL, FullTextURL, CitesURL). The articles collected included years from 2018 to 2022. We collected articles in totals of 403, 355, 440, 382, and 380, from years, 2018, 2019, 2020, 2021, and 2022, respectively. After the screening and exclusion processes, we analyzed only 78, 38, 76, 56, and 45 inclusion articles respectively to the sequence of years.

2.3 Data Types of Social Comments from Reviews

Our first research question requires identifying types of data collected from social comments. From the reviews, researchers collected comments with data types like; text, URL links, images, video clips of ads, and stories. Text stores any kind of text data. It can contain both single-byte and multibyte characters. A URL (Uniform Resource Locator) is "a unique identifier used to locate a resource on the Internet". The video data type is "a type of file format for storing digital video data on a computer system". Image data type stores or references any type of image files in binary format like jpg, BMP, png, and more. From the reviews, the common data collected from SNPs is of text data type. The text was collected from sources like posts or comments, groups and pages, participant responses from surveys, news articles, publication papers, video comments and captions, and image text. Some reviews extract text from the metadata of images and transcribed text or captions from videos.

2.4 Methods of Data Collection

The second research question requires analyzing the ML methods used for data collection on SNPs. From the findings, we have retrieved five methods of data collection over the sequential years of 2018 to 2022. These included 23 articles for manual observations, 24 for self-reports, 15 for public repositories, 35 for existing licensed tools, 190 for public APIs, and 23 for web scrapers or crawlers. The use of public APIs was most common. We also note that manual observations are still in use. We further explored each method of data collection to identify the pros and cons to suggest trends of adoption for sample social networks.

Data Collection by Manual Observations

Manual observation involves the visual analysis of data and writing findings by oneself. This is the manual coding of findings. Manual observation requires the user to navigate the website using keywords/hashtags and URL links. From our reviews, some researchers used manual observation to record findings. One pro of using manual observations is the ability to collect data from private accounts without sending notifications to owners [14]. The cons include: (i) More than one person may be required to collect data to quicken the process, [15]. (ii) They collect a small portion of results to generalize findings [15]. (iii) Inability to collect some meta-data features like subscriptions, and links to other websites [16]. After exploring these suggestions, we ignored the use of manual methods. We opt to recommend the use of automatic methods that use open-source tools to collect usage data.

Data Collection by Self-report Surveys

Self-reports give responses about a discussion. A self-report is a test or survey that relies on one's own interest/response. To do this, we use tools like questionnaires, interviews, and observations. Questionnaires involve questions with a choice to answer. Interviews involve structured conversation where one participant responds to asked questions by the other party. From the reviews, we analyzed three methods of self-reports, these include traditional, online, and mixed surveys.

Traditional surveys: These involve physical interaction with tools like questionnaires, and observations. The pros of using traditional surveys include; no requirement for technical and programming skills, and provide user interests and emotions. Some cons include: (i) Required participant compensation fees. (ii) Extra expenses to distribute user interaction tools like questionnaires. (iii) Biased responses like time spent on social media [17]. (iv) A need to automate the collection of responses from participants [18]. We note that traditional surveys use manual means of data collection.

Online Surveys: This involves sending electronic responses on the internet [19]. The collection of data is automatic or by manual observations. The tools used with online surveys include questionnaires, interviews, and observation. Most reviews about online surveys used questionnaires sent to participants over online platforms like Google Forms, phone apps, web portals, SurveyMonkey, and video ads. The interviews from online surveys involved videos and audio clips. Observation of responses on an online platform was also used to collect data. The pros of using online surveys include; the conduction of surveys at any preferable time, anywhere, and providing user interests and emotions. The cons include: (i) Some online platforms are non-user-friendly to participants [20]. (ii)

Inability to keep track of changes of content after closing the survey [21]. (iii) It is time-consuming for participants to use interfaces like ads. We thus disregard the use of online surveys because of increased expenses on the many participants.

Mixed surveys: These combine data from self-reports and usage data from the websites. The usage data is a collection of a visitor's actions on a website. The common sources of usage data reviewed include keywords, hashtags, and URL links. A keyword is a word or concept to identify digital content on a specific topic. A hashtag is a keyword preceded by the # symbol, thus we refer to keywords and hashtags interchangeably in our study. This mixed survey method requires participants to give responses online, and then collect usage data about user profile details on the social media account. From the reviews, the common tools used with the mixed method include questionnaires, interviews, and user usage data about profile accounts. The pros of using mixed surveys include the ability to gain depth in research findings [22]. And an increased number of participants [23]. The cons include: (i) Inability to restrict responses from non-target participants [23]. (ii) Requires the consent of participants to share their data about the account profile, [14,20]. (iii) A need to offer incentives to participants [24]. We thus recommend the use of mixed surveys for cases of combining user interests or emotions with usage data but at minimum or no participant compensation fees. Table 1 shows the pros and cons of self-report surveys.

Table 1. Comparing the methods of self-report surveys

Method	Pros	Cons
Traditional survey	- Do not require programming skills	- Require participant compensation fees
	- Provide user interests and emotions	- Extra expenses to distribute user interaction tools like questionnaires
		- Biased responses like time spent on social media
		- Need to automate collection of responses from participants
Online Survey	- Conducted at any time and anywhere	- Some online platforms are not user-friendly to submit responses
	- Provide user interests and emotions	- Inability to keep track of changes for new content after the survey
		- It is time-consuming for participants to use interfaces like ads
Mixed methods	- The ability to gain in-depth findings	- It is easy for non-target participants to give responses
	- Increases number of participants	- Requires consent of participants to share their account profile data
	- Provide user interests and emotions	- Complex method of data collection
		- Need to offer incentives to participants

Data Collection by Public Repositories

Public repositories are accessible to everyone on the internet to collect existing datasets from both self-report and usage data. Downloading the datasets from public repositories may require using keywords related to a topic or a link to the repository. From the reviews, we also observed that previous studies provide public existing datasets on organizations or individual websites. Table 2 shows samples of existing datasets from studies of other authors and organizations.

Table 2. Public repositories with existing datasets

Source	Public repository	Description of dataset
Other authors	Ramos et al., 2018	Has demographics from 1,000 Facebook status updates
	Wang et al. 2016	About influenza study with Geo-Tagged Twitter data
	Basu et al. 2019	Containing tweet IDs about Nepal and Italy earthquakes
	Dimitrov, D., et al. 2020	Containing Tweets about the COVID-19 Pandemic
	Kaczmirek et al., 2014	About German Bundestag elections 2013 for Facebook and Twitter
Organizations	Georgia State Uni. Lab	Can only provide tweet IDs
	Kaggle	Provide Covid-19 Tweets for late April Tweets using hashtags
		Spam detection comments from Twitter and Email
	British Geological Survey	Has tweets related to landslide events
	National Science Foundation	Has posts about spam detection from Facebook
	Our World in Data	Provides daily world statistics about Covid-19
	US state-level health data	Provide details for America's Health Rankings Annual Report
	Honeypot	useful for studying spam activity on Twitter

The pros of using existing datasets include (i) The ability to download data, including worldwide posts in different languages [25]. (ii) Some public repositories enable the use of keywords to return datasets relevant to a specific topic [26]. The cons of using public existing datasets include: (i) Inability to track continuous changes in comments after the occurrence of the event, [27]. We ignore the use of public repositories.

Data Collection by Existing Licensed Tools

An existing licensed tool is software that provides legally binding guidelines for data collection and requires a fee after the trial period. From the reviews, some existing licensed tools include Net viz, Netlytic, Gnip, NVivo, Sifter, SocialBlade, Brandwatch, Tuber, and more. The pros of using existing licensed tools include; (i) They provide other functionalities, such as text analysis and visualization [28]. (ii) The ability to access public APIs to extract meta-data in real-time and past historical times, [29,30]. (iii) Offer trial periods and basic packages at no cost [24]. Some cons for using the existing licensed tools include (i) Searching one hashtag per request is time-consuming [28]. (ii) A need to filter columns with irrelevant features for a goal of study [31]. (iii) The use of search keywords eliminates relevant related data without the key terms [31]. (iv) A need to consider words based on the user sentiment found in the data traffic at a specific time [32]. (v) The basic versions usually have limitations to data volume [33]. We ignore using this method and explore other means that support free collections of data.

Data Collection by Public APIs

An Application Programming Interface (API) is a set of functions and procedures followed to create applications needed to access data from the network operating system. Open/Public APIs refer to APIs made publicly available to software developers. Public APIs require one to apply for developer access authentication rights to extract social network usage data without violating the public privacy laws of users. Users interact with comments/posts of text, audio, videos, and images. From the reviews, the common sources of usage data include hashtags/keywords, IDs or URL links, and user logs.

To begin with, Facebook Graph API "is an HTTP-based API that allows developers to extract data from the Facebook platform". Marketing API is "an HTTP-based API used to query data, create and manage ads, and perform a wide variety of other tasks". Marketing APIs are a collection of Graph API endpoints used to advertise on Facebook. There are open libraries used to call the Facebook Graph API like Facepager and CrowdTangle. Facepager "is for fetching public available data from YouTube, Twitter and other websites using APIs and web scraping". CrowdTangle uses its API to provide access to Facebook Graph API to collect posts from public groups and pages. CrowdTangle is most commonly used over sequential years.

For Twitter, the standard level of developers provides three APIs. These include streaming, search, and sampling APIs. From the reviews, we retrieved two commonly used Public APIs, namely; Streaming and Search APIs. Twitter API allows you to stream public Tweets from the platform in real-time. Streaming API has a limit of 15 tweets per request. The Twitter Search API "is an HTTP-based RESTful API that returns responses encoded in JSON format". Twitter's REST (Representational States Transfer) API "allows you to search terms based on specific parameters". The Search API includes a limit of 500 tweets per request in the past seven days. The Sampling API "delivers a random sample of publicly available Tweets in real-time, but supports selecting which fields return in the payload" [34]. Some reviews used enterprise-level Twitter APIs like; Power Track API [35], Historical PowerTrack API [36], and GetOldTweets API [37]. Commonly used open libraries for Twitter APIs, include; Tweepy, Twitter 4J, TwitterMySQL, Apache, Crowdbreaks, Rtweet, and Twarc. We also identified the Botometer API and Wayback Machine API. The Botometer API "checks the activity of a Twitter account and gives it a score based on the extent to which it matches accounts that use automation". The Wayback Machine API "is a historical database that captures web pages using the internet archive". This API attains web data from different social media with some missing features.

For YouTube, the YouTube API was used to collect data. YouTube "provides the ability to retrieve feeds related to videos, users, and playlists". The YouTube Data tools library was commonly used to access data via the YouTube API. Table 3 demonstrates the use of these public APIs over the sequential years.

Table 3. Use of trending Public APIs over sequential years

Social Platform	Year	Public API(No. of papers)- Added packages
YouTube	2018	YouTube AP(I4)- YouTube Data Tool
	2019	YouTube API(1)
	2020	YouTube API(1)- YouTube Data Tool
	2021	YouTube API(4)- YouTube Data Tool
	2022	YouTube API(8)- YouTube Data Tool
Facebook	2018	Facebook Graph API(5)
	2019	Facebook Graph API (4)- pySocialWatcher, Facebook Marketing API(2)- pySocialWatcher
	2020	Facebook Graph API (8)- Facepager, CrowdTangle
	2021	Facebook Graph API (5)- CrowdTangle, Facebook Marketing API (1)- Facebook ads manager
	2022	Facebook Graph API (5)- CrowdTangle, Facebook Marketing API(1)
Twitter	2018	1. Streaming API (26)- Tweepy, Twitter4j, Apache, TwitterMySQL
		2. Search API (11)- Twiter4j, Historical PowerTrack API (2), Botometer API (2)
	2019	1. Streaming API (17)- Tweepy, Apache
		2. Search API (3)- Rtweet, Botometer API (2)
	2020	1. Streaming API (13)- Tweepy, Apache
		2. Search API (3)- Rtweet
	2021	1. Streaming API (13)- Tweepy, twitteR, Crowdbreaks
		2. Search API (6)- Rtweet, Twarc, Twitter4J, Sampling API(1)
	2022	1. Streaming API (9)- Tweepy, TwitterMySQL
		2. Search API (7)- Rtweet, Twarc, Sampling API (1), Botometer API (1)

Sample Trends of Public APIs Used

We identified four trendy open libraries used with the Twitter API. These include Tweepy, Twitter4J, Rtweet, and Twarc. Tweepy is a Python-based package that gives one access to Twitter Streaming and Search APIs [38]. Tweepy has a limit of providing fewer streams of data (1% of total tweets) and has a bias in returning most tweets in the English language. Twiter4J is an open-source Java library, which provides access to both Twitter Streaming and Searching APIs [39]. Twitter4J has a limit to access private accounts. Rtweet is the "R package that provides users a range of functions designed to extract data from Twitter REST/Search and streaming APIs" [40]. Rtweet has a limit on the use of R programming skills. Twarc "is a command-line tool and Python library for collecting and archiving Twitter JSON data via the Twitter API". This Python library allows the use of a premium version of Search API at a fee [41]. Twarc gives an entire conversation, including its direct replies and nested replies. Using Twarc has a limit of the restrictive 7-day window of data collection by Search API.

For Facebook, we explored that the most commonly used open library is CrowdTangle. CrowdTangle uses its API to access Facebook Graph API to retrieve posts from public groups and pages. It provides historical data on posts shared by public pages or groups, and the user can add new account IDs to collect posts. Some limitations of CrowdTangle include: (i) the inability to track every public account, private profile, and group, [42]. (ii) Some public pages have removed content [43]. (iii) And it ignores public pages whose likes and followers are more than 25K [25].

We observed that the reviews commonly used YouTube API with the open library of YouTube Data tools. Some pros of using YouTube Data tools include: (i) Provides access to modules like video list info and video network [44]. (ii) It enables the retrieving of new channels that satisfy a search query [45]. The cons include: (i) Some feature variables of meta-data were missing, like watch time [44]. (ii) Some captions of transcribed text were missing [46]. (iii) It has a limit to access 1000 requests per day.

Data Collection by Web Crawlers or Scrappers

From a general perspective, [47] explains that we use the terms "web scraping" and "web crawling" interchangeably to imply data extraction from web pages. Web scraping is "a procedure of automatic extraction of data from websites using software". Web crawling is "about finding or discovering URLs or links on the web". For this study, we refer to these two terms to mean the same. Web scrapers access public data without the limitations that exist with APIs. The user searches the web pages of interest using tools like hashtags, and IDs/URL links. And thereafter analyses the HTML/XML inspect elements (CSS or XPath selectors) [48]. The CSS Selector "combines an element selector and a selector value to identify particular elements on a web page". XPath is "used to navigate through elements and attributes in an XML document". Collecting a list of web CSS or XPath elements requires web crawlers that use coding languages such as Python and R [49]. We have three modes for scraping or crawling data [50]. These include web extensions, existing licensed software, and open-source tools. A web browser extension is "a small software application that adds a capacity or functionality to a web browser". Table 4 demonstrates the modes of web crawlers/scrapers used in the reviews.

Table 4. Modes of web crawlers or scrapers

Mode	Functionality	Crawler or Scraper	Social platform
Open software	Require user guidelines to create new codes	Scrapy	Twitter, YouTube, Facebook
		Selenium and Beautifulsoup	YouTube
		IMcrawler	Facebook
		TwitterScraper	Twitter
		Twint	Twitter
		Snscrape	Twitter
Licensed software	Private and public existing tools that require a fee	Octoparse scraper	Twitter
		OpinionScraper	News sites
Web extensions	Public web extensions that run on a browser	WebDataRA	Twitter
		Ncapture	Twitter, YouTube

The web extensions used in reviews include WebDataRA and NCapture. These extensions have some limitations. (i) Some web extensions are free, but others require a fee. (ii) The user may not access all the features that APIs offer. We ignore the use of web extensions because of the manual methods involved in accessing data. Existing licensed software is "proprietary software distributed under a licensed agreement to enable users to access data". These tools have terms of service required to follow. And after the trial period, one requires payment fees for premium packages. We retrieved some common licensed tools used, such as Octoparse scraper [51] and OpinionScraper [52]. These tools are public or private. The public ones like Octoparse provide both standard and premium packages to extract data from different websites. Existing licensed tools have a limit on costs incurred to access large amounts of data. The open-source tools are freely available to extract data without a commercial license or paying for standard packages in particular. Most open-source tools available require programming skills to follow user guidelines set to extract the data. The open software tools from reviews include Scrapy, Selenium, Beautifulsoup, IMcrawler, TwitterScraper, Twint, and Snscrape. We will further explore the pros and cons of top open software tools.

Trends of Scrapers and Crawlers for Sample Tools

We reviewed four common open-source tools for web scraping or crawling. The tools include Scrapy, TwitterScraper, Twint, and Beautifulsoup. Scrapy is "a free and open-source web crawling framework written in Python". Networks like Facebook, Twitter, and YouTube. Some pros of using Scrapy include; (i) The ability to attain historical data [53]. (ii) Provides some features of meta-data that public APIs omit, such as subscribers and thumbnails from YouTube [54]. The cons of using Scrapy include: (i) Requires the consent of user login credentials to access data from a website. (ii) And the user has to disable pop requests that would discontinue the crawling process [55]. TwitterScraper is for Twitter only. It is "a simple script to scrape Tweets into JSON raw format, using the Python package requests [56]". TwitterScrapper overpasses limitations of public APIs such as the length of tweets and the style of posts, [47]. TwitterScraper has a limit of internet speed/bandwidth, and how many instances started at each request [47]. Twint is another trending scraping method used for Twitter. Twint "is a scraping tool developed in Python to extract and scrape tweets from specific users and tweets on specific topics". Twint is most reliable when a list of users of interest is to be extracted [57]. Because of the depreciation of the developer support end, Twint has a limit on the probability of reduced functions. Selenium is "an open-source tool that is used for automating the tests carried out on web browsers". Beautiful Soup "is a Python library for pulling data out of HTML and XML files". At first, Selenium allows access to a website (different websites), and then Beautifulsoup crawls the data into a list of data represented in JSON format or csv and more. Using Selenium and Beautifulsoup provides the ability to collect more features as viewed on the screen, [54]. Selenium requires automatic scroll through all files to capture as much data as possible, [58]. From the reviews, researchers rarely used web scrapers. They applied them to specific objectives, such as volume of data increase, and access to features that are not offered by the Public APIs.

3 Conclusion

3.1 Discussion of Findings

This study aims to provide solutions to three research objectives. First, we reviewed existing literature about methods of data collection from social networks. Using the Google Scholar database and search keywords, we collected previous articles from 2018 to 2022. Second, we explored the kinds of ML methods used for data collection. We reviewed five general methods, these are; self-report surveys, Public APIs, Web crawlers or scrapers, public repositories, and manual observations. We explored the pros and cons of each method. Finally, we identified trends in ML methods to collect data for sample networks like Facebook, Twitter, and YouTube. Table 5 demonstrates a summary of a comparison of the methods of data collection.

Table 5. A summary of comparison for methods of data collection

Method	Pros.	Cons.
Manual observations	Ability to record all data displayed on screen	Tiresome, and requires another software to record data
Traditional surveys	The ability to collect user interests and emotions	Requires participants compensation expenses
Online surveys	Timely collection of user interests and emotions	Require participant fees and training before use
Mixed surveys	Increased access to user interests, emotions, and profiles	Requires participant compensation fees and their consent
Public repositories	Provide already compiled datasets with easy access	Inflexibility to adjust contents with trends in comments
Existing Licensed tools	Offer more functionalities like analysis of data	Requires a fee after the trial period
Public APIs	Provide access to most features of meta-data	Limited streaming and historical data
Crawlers or Scrapers	Provide increased volume of data and missing features	Require advanced programming skills

The limitations of our study include; having fewer reviews for some categories of methods used for data collection. Most reviews did not highlight the challenges faced during the data collection step. The different sample social networks have different methods of data collection, there was a need to review each separately to attain better perceptions.

3.2 Recommendation and Future Work

This study provided answers to all our research questions ((i) What is the type of data from social comments? (ii) What are the ML methods applied in reviews to collect the data, and how do they work? (iii) What are the trends, strengths, and limitations of the ML methods of data collection?). Based on the findings, to collect data at no cost and in large amounts, we recommend using open-source tools that support using ML algorithms. These are public APIs and web scrapers. In the future, we plan to extract public data using the recommended trendy ML tools for sample social networks.

References

1. Stepney, P.: Social Work in the 21st Century. Int. Soc. Work. **41**(3), 394–396 (1998)
2. Hart, H.: What is a social problem? Am. J. Sociol. **29**(3), 345–352 (1923)
3. Geels, F.W., Penna, C.: Societal problems and industry reorientation: elaborating the Dialectic Issue LifeCycle (DILC) model and a case study of car safety in the USA (1900–1995). Res. Policy **44**(1), 67–82 (2015)
4. Anthikad, J.: Social problems. In: Sociology for Graduate Nurses, p. 156 (2014)
5. Martin, B.: Sociological research methods, pp. 36–67 (2017)
6. Statcounter. Social Media Stats Africa—StatCounter Global Stats (2021)
7. Hartmann, J., Huppertz, J., Schamp, C., Heitmann, M.: Comparing automated text classification methods. Int. J. Res. Mark. **36**(1), 20–38 (2019)
8. Ortiz-Ospina, E.: The rise of social media - Our World in Data (2019)
9. Karami, A., Lundy, M., Webb, F., Dwivedi, Y.K.: Twitter and research: a systematic literature review through text mining. IEEE Access **8**, 67698–67717 (2020)
10. Singh, L.: A systematic review of higher education academics' use of microblogging for professional development: case of twitter. Open Educ. Stud. **2**(1), 66–81 (2020)
11. Stieglitz, S., Mirbabaie, M., Ross, B., Neuberger, C.: Social media analytics–Challenges in topic discovery, data collection, and data preparation. Int. J. Inf. Manag. **39**, 156–168 (2018)
12. Samoggia, A., Monticone, F., Bertazzoli, A.: Innovative digital technologies for purchasing and consumption in urban and regional agro-food systems: a systematic review. Foods **10**(2), 208 (2021)
13. Moher, S., Liberatl, A., Tetzlaff, J., Alttman, D.H., Parisma Group: So schaffst du deine Ausbildung. Ausbildungsbegleitende Hilfen (abH) **151**(4), 264–269 (2009)
14. Stellefson, M., Paige, S., Apperson, A., Spratt, S.: Social media content analysis of public diabetes facebook groups. J. Diab. Sci. Technol. **13**(3), 428–438 (2019)
15. Livas, C., Delli, K., Pandis, N.: "My Invisalign experience;;: content, metrics and comment sentiment analysis of the most popular patient testimonials on YouTube. Prog. Orthodont. **19**, 1–8 (2018)
16. Lenczowski, E., Dahiya, M.: Psoriasis and the digital landscape: YouTube as an information source for patients and medical professionals. J. Clin. Aesthet. Dermatol. **11**(3), 36–38 (2018)
17. Seabrook, E.M., Kern, M.L., Fulcher, B.D., Rickard, N.S.: Predicting depression from language-based emotion dynamics: longitudinal analysis of Facebook and Twitter status updates. J. Med. Internet Res. **20**(5), e168 (2018)
18. Busam, B., Solomon-Moore, E.: Public understanding of childhood obesity: qualitative analysis of news articles and comments on facebook. Health Commun. **00**(00), 1–14 (2021)
19. Eysenbach, G.: Improving the quality of web surveys: the checklist for reporting results of internet E-surveys (CHERRIES). J. Med. Internet Res. **6**(3), 1–6 (2004)
20. Nova, F.F., et al.: "Facebook promotes more harassment": social media ecosystem, skill and marginalized hijra identity in Bangladesh. In: Proceedings of the ACM on Human-Computer Interaction, vol. 5, no. CSCW1, pp. 1–35 (2021)

21. Docimo, S., Jacob, B., Seras, K., Ghanem, O.: Closed Facebook groups and COVID-19: an evaluation of utilization prior to and during the pandemic. Surg. Endosc. **35**(9), 4986–4990 (2021)
22. Spiliotopoulos, T., Oakley, I.: Post or tweet: lessons from a study of facebook and twitter usage. In: Following User Pathways: Using Cross Platform and Mixed Methods Analysis in Social Media Studies Workshop at ACM CHI 2016 (2016)
23. Pötzschke, S., Weiß, B.: Realizing a global survey of emigrants through facebook and instagram (2021)
24. Gündüzalp, S., Şener, G.: The analysis of opinions about teaching profession on twitter through text mining. Res. Educ. Media **12**(1), 3–12 (2020)
25. Etta, G., et al.: COVID-19 infodemic on Facebook and containment measures in Italy, United Kingdom and New Zealand. PLoS ONE **17**(5 May), 1–14 (2022)
26. Inuwa-Dutse, I., Liptrott, M., Korkontzelos, I.: Detection of spam-posting accounts on Twitter. Neurocomputing **315**, 496–511 (2018)
27. Lyu, J.C., Luli, G.K.: Understanding the public discussion about the centers for disease control and prevention during the COVID-19 pandemic using twitter data: text mining analysis study. J. Med. Internet Res. **23**(2), e25108 (2021)
28. Anderson, M.: Social media and COVID-19 : Characterizing anti-quarantine comments on Twitter, pp. 2–5 (2020)
29. Al-Ramahi, M., Elnoshokaty, A., El-Gayar, O., Nasralah, T., Wahbeh, A.: Public discourse against masks in the COVID-19 Era: infodemiology study of twitter data. JMIR Public Health Surveill. **7**(4), 1–12 (2021)
30. Dashtian, H., Murthy, D.: Cml-Covid: a large-scale covid-19 twitter dataset with latent topics, sentiment and location information. Academia Lett. **1**, 1–6 (2021)
31. Karami, A., et al.: 2020 U.S. presidential election in swing states: gender differences in Twitter conversations. Int. J. Inf. Manag. Data Insights **2**(2) (2022)
32. Fahey, R.A., Boo, J., Ueda, M.: Covariance in diurnal patterns of suicide-related expressions on Twitter and recorded suicide deaths. Soc. Sci. Med. **253**(March), 112960 (2020)
33. Park, H.W., Park, S., Chong, M.: Conversations and medical news frames on twitter: infodemiological study on COVID-19 in South Korea. J. Med. Internet Res. **22**(5), e18897 (2020)
34. Mahaini, M.I., Li, S.: Detecting cyber security related Twitter accounts and different sub-groups: a multi-classifier approach. In: Proceedings of the 2021 IEEE/ACM International Conference on Advances in Social Networks Analysis and Mining, ASONAM 2021, pp. 599–606 (2021)
35. Mohammadi, E., Thelwall, M., Kwasny, M., Holmes, K.L.: Academic information on twitter: a user survey. PLoS ONE **13**(5), 1–18 (2018)
36. Kim, Y., Emery, S.L., Vera, L., David, B., Huang, J.: At the speed of Juul: measuring the twitter conversation related to ENDS and Juul across space and time (2017–2018). Tob. Control **30**(2), 137–146 (2021)
37. Dev, J.: Spring 2020 discussing privacy and surveillance on twitter: a case study of COVID-19 Jayati Dev, pp. 1–10 (2020)
38. Reuter, K., et al.: Monitoring Twitter conversations for targeted recruitment in cancer trials in Los Angeles county: protocol for a mixed-methods pilot study. JMIR Res. Protoc. **7**(9), 1–17 (2018)
39. Abdulsattar, G., Alkubaisi, A.J., Kamaruddin, S.S., Husni, H.: Conceptual framework for stock market classification model using sentiment analysis on twitter based on Hybrid Naïve Bayes Classifiers. Int. J. Eng. Technol. (UAE) **7**(2), 57–61 (2018)

40. Rahman, M.M., Ali, G.G.M.N., Li, X.J., Paul, K.C., Chong, P.H.J.: Twitter and census data analytics to explore socioeconomic factors for post-COVID-19 reopening sentiment. medRxiv (2020)
41. Graham, T., Bruns, A., Angus, D., Hurcombe, E., Hames, S.: #IStandWithDan versus #DictatorDan: the polarised dynamics of Twitter discussions about Victoria's COVID-19 restrictions. Media Int. Aust. **179**(1), 127–148 (2021)
42. Celestini, A., Di Giovanni, M., Guarino, S., Pierri, F.: Information disorders on Italian Facebook during COVID-19 infodemic, pp. 1–16 (2020)
43. Broniatowski, D.A., et al.: Facebook pages, the "disneyland" measles outbreak, and promotion of vaccine refusal as a civil right, 2009–2019. Am. J. Public Health **110**, S312–S318 (2020)
44. Rieder, B., Matamoros-Fernández, A., Coromina, Ò.: From ranking algorithms to 'ranking cultures': investigating the modulation of visibility in YouTube search results. Convergence **24**(1), 50–68 (2018)
45. Vargas Meza, X., Yamanaka, T.: Food communication and its related sentiment in local and organic food videos on YouTube. J. Med. Internet Res. **22**(8), e16761 (2020)
46. Kim, T., Jo, H., Yhee, Y., Koo, C.: Robots, artificial intelligence, and service automation (RAISA) in hospitality: sentiment analysis of YouTube streaming data. Electron. Mark. **32**(1), 259–275 (2022)
47. Permatasari, R., Rakhmawati, N.A.: Features selection for entity resolution in prostitution on twitter. Int. J. Adv. Data Inf. Syst. **2**(1), 53–61 (2021)
48. Gunawan, R., Rahmatulloh, A., Darmawan, I., Firdaus, F.: Comparison of web scraping techniques: regular expression, HTML DOM and Xpath. In: IcoIESE 2018, vol. 2, pp. 283–287 (2019)
49. Krotov, V., Silva, L.: Legality and ethics of web scraping. In: Americas Conference on Information Systems 2018: Digital Disruption, AMCIS 2018 (2018)
50. Diouf, R., Sarr, E.N., Sall, O., Birregah, B., Bousso, M., Mbaye, S.N.: Web scraping: state-of-the-art and areas of application. In: Proceedings - 2019 IEEE International Conference on Big Data, Big Data 2019, pp. 6040–6042 (2019)
51. Mittelmeier, J., Cockayne, H.: Global representations of international students in a time of crisis: a qualitative analysis of Twitter data during COVID-19. In: International Studies in Sociology of Education, pp. 1–18 (2022)
52. Faty, L., Ndiaye, M., Sarr, E.N., Sall, O.: OpinionScraper: a news comments extraction tool for opinion mining. In: 2020 7th International Conference on Social Network Analysis, Management and Security, SNAMS 2020, pp. 4–8 (2020)
53. Hinduja, S., Afrin, M., Mistry, S., Krishna, A.: Machine learning-based proactive social-sensor service for mental health monitoring using twitter data. Int. J. Inf. Manag. Data Insights **2**(2), 100113 (2022)
54. Anand, V., Shukla, R., Gupta, A., Kumar, A.: Customized video filtering on YouTube, pp. 1–13 (2019)
55. Gray, L.: Gender Bias Detection Using Facebook Reactions (2020)
56. Franco-Riquelme, J.N., Bello-Garcia, A., Ordieres-Meré, J.: Indicator Proposal for measuring regional political support for the electoral process on twitter: the case of Spain's 2015 and 2016 general elections. IEEE Access **7**, 62545–62560 (2019)
57. Gutierrez, C.G., et al.: Analyzing and visualizing twitter conversations. In: Proceedings of the 31st Annual International Conference on Computer Science and Software Engineering, pp. 4–13 (2021)
58. Jin, J., Lam, S., Savas, O., McCulloh, I.: Approaches for quantifying video prominence, narratives, discussion: engagement on COVID-19 related youtube videos. In: Proceedings of the 2020 IEEE/ACM International Conference on Advances in Social Networks Analysis and Mining, ASONAM 2020, pp. 811–818 (2020)

Strabismus Diagnosis and Angular Deviation Calculation Based on Artificial Intelligence Approaches: A Review

Madior Gueye[1,2,3,4(✉)], Ousmane Khoum[5,6], Mandicou Ba[1,2,3,4], Idy Diop[1,2,3,4], Alassane Bah[1,2,3,4], Doudou Dione[1,2,3,4], Regina Esi Turkson[7], and Aly Mb Kâ[8]

[1] Cheikh Anta Diop University (UCAD), Dakar, Senegal
{madior1.gueye,doudou2.dione}@ucad.edu.sn, {mandicou.ba, idy.diop,alassane.bah}@esp.sn
[2] Department of Computer Science, Polytechnic Institute (ESP), Dakar, Senegal
[3] Laboratoire d'Imagerie Médicale et de bio-Informatique (LIMBI), Dakar, Senegal
[4] UMI UMMISCO UCAD, Dakar, Senegal
[5] Amadou Mahtar Mbow University (UAM), Diamniadio, Senegal
ousmane.khouma@uam.edu.sn
[6] Sciences and Engineering Techniques Institute (ESTI), Dakar, Senegal
[7] University of Cape Coast, Coast, Ghana
rturkson@ucc.edu.gh
[8] Ophthalmology Department, Abass Ndao Hospital, Dakar, Senegal

Abstract. In Senegal, there is 1 ophthalmologist per 507,000 inhabitants whereas the World Health Organization (WHO) standard is 1 ophthalmologist per 250,000 inhabitants. In addition, out of the country's 14 regions, 6 regions have no ophthalmologist. 84% of ophthalmologists are stationed in the capital, Dakar. Rural areas lack qualified human resources. WHO estimates that 88.4 million people worldwide are visually impaired as a result of uncorrected refractive errors such as amblyopia (irreversible visual impairment). It is a cause of children dropping from school. One of the causes of amblyopia is strabismus. Strabismus is a defect in the parallelism of the eyes. WHO estimates the worldwide prevalence rate of strabismus at 2 to 5% in Caucasians and 0.37 to 1.5% in African melanoderma. It is important to diagnose children at an early age so that they can be treated quickly. The objective is to spare them a visual handicap in the future. To assist ophthalmologists, automatic diagnostic methods for strabismus based on artificial intelligence approaches have been proposed in the literature. In this article, we provide an overview of projects that involve the use of image processing basic techniques, machine learning and deep learning approaches for strabismus diagnosis and angular deviation calculation.

Keywords: Strabismus · Amblyopia · Angular Deviation · Artificial Intelligence · Hirschberg Test

1 Introduction

World Health Organization estimates that more than 2.2 billion people are affected by visual impairment or blindness, 5.9 million people in Africa [1]. The prevalence rate has exceeded the 2% in some sahelian countries [2]. In Senegal, the prevalence rate of blindness is 1 to 1.5% [3]. The loss of productivity due to visual impairment is estimated at USD 411 billion in the world [4]. In sub-Saharan Africa, it is estimated that 0.5% of GDP will be lost annually in the absence of intervention [5]. Among the causes of the visual impairment, there is the uncorrected refractive errors (88.4 million) [4]. One cause of uncorrected refractive errors is strabismus. This disease is an eye misalignment. This deviation can lead to diplopia (double vision) in adults or amblyopia (irreversible decrease in visual acuity) in children [6]. It is a cause of children dropping out from school. Deploying Artificial Intelligence (AI) in this branch appears to be a viable and long-term solution. Machine Learning and Deep Learning algorithms have recently demons-trated exceptional performance on a variety of tasks, particularly the diagnosis of ophthalmology diseases such as strabismus.

This research critically examines current method for automatic diagnosis of strabismus based on artificial intelligence. Following that, we will identify the limitations of existing solutions and potential challenges that will allow to improve the disease management.

After the introduction, Sect. 2 delves into the landscape of ophthalmology in Senegal. Section 3 is dedicated to exploring the application of AI in ophthalmology. Section 4 outlines automatic diagnosis techniques for strabismus, while Sect. 5 delves into the various methods of automatic diagnosis employed. Finally, Sect. 6 synthesizes the findings and draws conclusions.

2 Ophthalmology in Senegal

According to the Senegalese Medical Association, there are 35 ophthalmologists in the public health service and 40 ophthalmologists in the private health service for 17 738 795 residents in 2022 [7, 8] (Fig. 1).

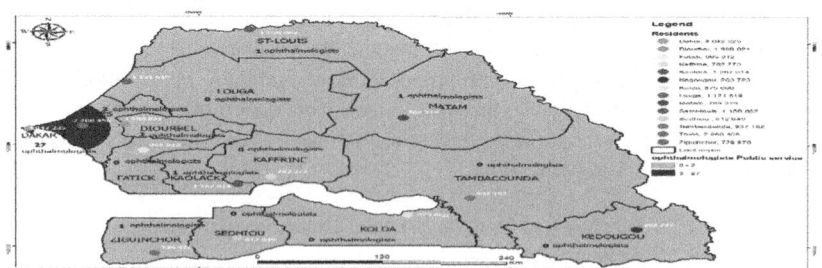

Fig. 1. Number of ophthalmologists in public service by region

Many regions such as Louga, Tambacounda, Kaffrine, Kedougou, Sedhiou, Fatick and Kolda do not have an ophthalmologist [7]. So, the patients travel miles to have a consultation in ophthalmology. Sometimes, without money, the patients stay at home without diagnosis and treatment. This situation can have serious consequences on people's health (visual impairment and blindness). In addition, the public health clinic of ophthalmology have no enough equipment to properly support the patients. It is therefore essential to find solutions to this lack of staff and equipment. One cause of visual impairment (amblyopia) is the strabismus. It is important to diagnose children at an early age so that they can be cared for at an early stage, in order to spare them a visual handicap in the future. The artificial intelligence could provide solutions for the early diagnosis of eye diseases.

3 Artificial Intelligence in Ophthalmology

Medical diagnosis assisted by AI using images are evolving rapidly. In Ophthalmology, deep learning techniques can be applied to diagnose in order to predict variations in the visual prognosis of patients. Intelligent systems are an important means of revolutionizing eye care [9–11]. As a result, the costs associated with eye care could be reduced [4, 5]. Supervised learning is the most widely used in AI applications. This methodology is used to classify, segment images and predict scenarios for diagnosing ophthalmic diseases such as Diabetic Retinopathy, Glaucoma, and Age-Related Macular Degeneration etc.

3.1 State of Art of Detection and Classification Algorithms for Ophthalmic Diseases

Some eye diseases such as Diabetic Retinopathy (DR), Age-Related Macular Degeneration (AMD) and Glaucoma (GLC) can be diagnosed using artificial intelligence.

IDx-DR is the first algorithm used to diagnose the Diabetic Retinopathy (DR) and approved by the FDA (Food and Drug Administration) in USA [9]. It applies a set of CNN-based detectors to analyze the retinal images in order to detect the signs of the DR. The accuracy and the specificity are under 90%. Google DeepMind has developed an algorithm to diagnose the DR with 96.1% of sensibility and 93.9% of specificity. The neural network used is the Inception-v3 architecture [10]. P Saranya and al. Have proposed an automatic method to detect DR [11]. Advanced Convolutional Layer Architecture in U-Net was used to support pixel-level class labeling. The images obtained was used as input to feed the CNN to train and classify the type of DR depending on severity. This techniques have an accuracy, a specificity and sensitivity of 94%, 93.8% and 92.3% respectively. Neil Vaughan and al. Have reviewed the various moderns techniques using smartphone to detect the DR [12]. Smartphone funduscopy devices are comprised of lens devices connecting with smartphones. Software applications integrated in the smartphone analyze the mobile retinal image captured to diagnose DR. These devices are a modern diagnostic tools and help ophthalmologist for diagnosing and monitoring of disease.

The diagnosis of the Age-Related Macular Degeneration (AMD) know progress.

with AI. Nakhim Chea and al. Have developed a method to detect Diabetic Retinopathy (DR), Glaucoma (GLC) and Age-related Macular Degeneration (AMD). This methods have an accuracy rate of 85.79% and a specificity of 99.63%, 99.82%, and 91.90%, res-pectively for GLC, AMD and DR [13]. He and al. Have proposed a deep learning model using OCT images to detect AMD (neovascular and non-neovascular) with a sensitivity of 95% and a specificity of 95%, [14]. In the same way, Lee and al. Have used an architecture VGG-16 of CNN model to classify the OCT images between AMD and healthy. This method has an accuracy rate of 87.6% [15].

For diagnosing Glaucoma, Chi Li and al. Proposed a machine learning (ML) method. This study has used two OCT images datasets (Asian and Caucasians datasets). For the Asian dataset, the model has an accuracy rate of 92%. However, in the Caucasian dataset, the model trained with compensated data has an accuracy rate of 84%. This poor reproducibility of the ML model is due to the difference between the ocular characteristics of Asian test dataset and the Caucasian test dataset [16]. With 99% of accuracy rate, Qaisar Abbas had developed a deep learning model to detect the glaucoma using retinal fundus images [17]. In this method, a CNN unsupervised architecture, the deep-belief network (DBN) model and softmax linear classifier were used to differentiate between glaucoma and non-glaucoma retinal fundus image.

In brief, deep learning and machine learning algorithms have always helped ophthalmologists to automatically diagnose the retinal disease such as diabetic retinopathy, AMD and Glaucoma using retinal images (Table 1).

Table 1. Some examples of methods based on Deep Learning and Machine Learning Approaches for diagnosing DR, AMD and GL

References	Disease prediction	Accuracy	Architectures	Disease retinal image / OCT image
[11] 2023	Diabetic Retinopathy	94%	U-NET + CNN	
[14] 2022	Age-Related Macular Degenerative	sensitivity of 95.0% and specificity of 95.0%,	CNN	
[16] 2023	Glaucoma	92%	ML model	

Such as retinal diseases, AI algorithms can help ophthalmologists for diagnosing strabismus early.

3.2 Strabismus

Strabismus is a defect in the parallelism of the eye [6]. In adults, the disease is manifested by a diplopia (double vision). For children, this diplopia can be inhibited by the phenomenon of suppression. Indeed, the child has the ability to neutralize the image of the eye whose vision is abnormal and promote normal eye. Over time, the abnormal eye becomes weak and creates what we call amblyopia. The latter is defined as a unilateral or bilateral, functional or organic reduction of certain visual functions, mainly the discrimination of forms [6]. The tests used for diagnosis include the Hirschberg test. The test, as illustrated in Fig. 2, is performed as follows:

- The examiner projects a light 20 cm from the eyes;
- He analyzes the position of the corneal white reflection in relation to the center of the cornea.

The diagnosis will be positive if the two centers do not coincide or the angular deviation is higher than 5DP (Prismatic Diopter).

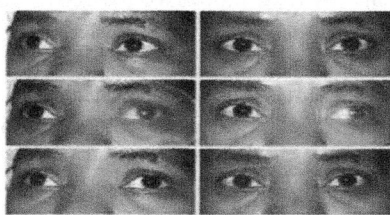

Fig. 2. Clinical diagnosis of strabismus

There are many causes of strabismus. It can be a neurological problem [early strabismus (convergent or divergent)], an ametropia (accommodative strabismus) or a partial or permanent paralysis of an oculomotor muscle (intermittent divergent strabismus) [18]. The treatment of strabismus depends on the cause. It can range from a simple optical correction to surgery to straighten the eye [18]. However, to diagnose, monitor and surgically treat the deviation, the ophthalmologist needs to know the angular devia-tion. In hospitals, the angular deviation calculation requires patient's cooperation, an experienced examiner, use of prisms and requires lots of time. Artificial intelligence (AI) offers intelligent solutions to these problems (Fig. 3).

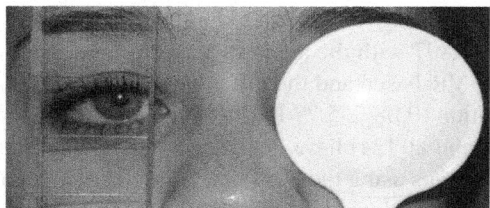

Fig. 3. Objective method for measuring angular deviation with the prism

4 Strabismus and Automatic Diagnosis Techniques

4.1 Detection of Strabismus Using Image Processing Approaches

Oren Yehezkel and al. [19] proposed an automatic system for diagnosing strabismus and calculating angular deviation. They used a system named EyeSwift System created by the company NovaSight Ltd based in Israel. It is an eye tracking system and a near infrared illumination for detecting corneal reflection and the pupil center. An infrared camera detects the angle between the cornea and the pupil reflection. An image processing algorithm is used to estimate the position of the eye and the point gaze. The correlation coefficient between this method and manual calculation was 0.9 ($P < 0.001$) for the horizontal deviation, 0.91 ($P < 0.001$) for the vertical deviation, with 100% correct for diagnosing the type of the strabismus. The system developed by Yang Zheng and al. [20] based on the cover test to diagnose the strabismus has 91% accuracy rate. They created a video database using a recording device. The video is fed into the proposed algorithm that consists of six stages: (1) eye region extraction, (2) iris boundary detection, (3) key frame detection, (4) pupil localization, (5) deviation calculation, and (6) evaluation of strabismus. It is a complex method which requires the patient's pre-sence and an electronic data collection device. Valente and al. [21] proposed an eye tracking system using image processing algorithm for diagnosing strabismus. This method has 93.33% accuracy rate to diagnose the patients with exotropia. But, this technique has globally 87% accuracy rate to diagnose the other types of strabismus and does not calculate the angular deviation. Xilang Huang and al. [22] have proposed a pre-trained convolutional neural network-based face-detection model. Then, they used a detector for 68 facial landmarks to extract the eye region for a frontal facial image. Otsu's binarization and the HSV color model are applied to the image to eliminate the influence of eyelashes and canthi. The aim is to calculate the distance between the pupil center and canthi using the least square method to obtain the coordinate of the pupil center. The sample mean and sample standard deviation of the positional similarity of the normal and strabismus images were 1.073 ± 0.014 and 0.039, as well as 1.924 ± 0.169 and 0.472, respectively. This method seems very interesting in diagnosis strabismus. However, it does not calculate the angular deviation. Po-Han Yeh and al. [23] also proposed a method using an eye-tracking virtual reality (VR). This method have an interclass correlation coefficient of 0.897 with the alternative prism cover test (APCT). This system is a commercial-grade VR-based and the difference between VR and the APCT reveals a large standard deviation (0.88 ± 5.77 PD) which is not negligible.

Shrinivas Pundlik and al. [24] have developed an application integrated in a smartphone to detect a strabismus using the Hirschberg test. This application named EyeTurn App, used image processing algorithms to automatically measure the distance between the corneal reflection position and the eye center. For the latent and manifest deviation, the application measurements were coherent with the comparator clinical methods.

Shorav Singh Suriyal has presented a thesis entitled: Quantitative analysis of strabismus using image processing [25]. He has used the basic techniques of image processing. It is an interesting method that did not use AI for the automatic detection. Dmitri Model and Moshe Eizenman have developed an automatic Hirschberg test for infants [26]. The system requires two cameras and a computer with an integrated calculation system. The method is used to estimate the Hirschberg Ratio (HR) and the angle Kappa (the angle between the visual and optical axis) for each infant. The objective is to calculate the angle of eye misalignment. The results of the test with five infants show that the 95% limits of agreement between repeated measurements of angle Kappa are ± 0.61°. The maximum error in the estimation of eye alignment in orthotropic infants was 0.9° with 95% limits of agreement between repeated measurements of 0.75°. The method is interesting but the number of tests is small. N. Bushuieva and D. Romanenko have developed a method using a software to assess the angular deviation and the oblique muscle function in strabismus patients [27]. They analyzed the two-dimensional eye globe in diagnostic gaze positions of healthy patients and strabismus patients. The results obtained show that the correlation coefficient between angular deviation measured with the method and Hirschberg test is 0.797, mean difference measurements was 1.1°. The correlation coefficient between angular deviation with the method and Fresnel prim test was O.881, mean difference between measurements was 3.8 PD. This method has 80% of correlation with conventional scale in the analysis of oblique muscle function. The Table 2 offers an overview of solutions based on image processing approaches.

4.2 Strabismus and Machine Learning Approaches

The method proposed by Mengash and Mahmoud has 95.9% of accuracy rate [28]. A set of training video was used to create a data set. The data set includes videos for eye region before and after cover test for the two eyes. Then, a decision tree (ID3) is built using labeled cases from actual strabismus diagnosis. The model are extracted from the corresponding videos of patients, and an association between the extracted features and actual diagnoses is established. This method require a bigger volume of videos, the cooperation of the patient and a recording device when the patient do the cover test. Rohismadi and al. [28] have proposed a system which has 91.8% of accuracy rate for strabismus detection using a case-based reasoning algorithm. It is a good method to classify strabismus. System developed by Alla Daher and al. [29] has 98.5% accuracy rate for diagnosing strabismus. This method used the electro-oculography (EOG) signal to analyze eye muscle irregularities. They used K-Nearest Neighbors (KNN) and wavelet decomposition method to extract and to classify the features from EOG signal. EOG is an examination that records the position and movements of the eye.

The Table 3 shows an overview of solutions based on machine learning approaches.

4.3 Strabismus and Deep Learning Approaches

A system developed by Jiewei Lu and al. [30] has 96.1% accuracy rate for diagnosing the strabismus. R-FCN (Region based Fully Convolutional Networks) is used to extract the eye of the image facial and a pre-entrained convolutional neural network (CNN) classifies the features. The angular deviation is not calculate. Zengai Chen and al. [31] have also proposed an automatic method for diagnosing the strabismus. This method has 95.2% accuracy arte. They used an eye tracker to record a subject's eye movements. A gaze deviation (GaDe) image is then proposed to characterize the subject's eye-tracking data according to the accuracies of gaze points. The GaDe image is fed to a pre-trained convolutional neural network (CNN) and SVM algorithm is used to classify the features

Table 2. Overview of solutions based on Image Processing Approaches

References	Materials	Dataset	Methods	Results	Advantage (A), Limitation (L)
[19] 2019	Eye tracker device, infrared light	69 children	EyeSwift System	Accuracy: 90\% for the horizontal deviation, 91\% for the vertical deviation and 100\% for diagnosis strabismus	A: High accuracy for strabismus diagnosis L: system not adapted to muscle paralysis or patient with nystagmus; The 95% limits of agreement is not negligible (±11,4 DP)
[20] 2019	Electronic data collection device	undefined	Images processing basic techniques	Accuracy: 91% in horizontal direction (error of 8 diopters) and 86% in vertical direction (error of 6 diopters)	A: allow an intelligent evaluation of strabismus L: significant error; Accuracy in vertical direction under 90%
[21] 2017	Recording Camera	undefined	Eye-tracking system + image processing basic technique	Accuracy: 93.33% for the exotropia, 87% for diagnosis strabismus	A: high accuracy for exotropia L: doesn't calculate angular deviation
[22] 2021	undefined	iBUG 300-W	CNN + Detector for 68 facial landmarks + Otsu's binarization + HSV color model	Normal eye: $1,073 \pm 0,014$ Strabismic eye: $1,924 \pm 0,169$	A: automatic diagnosis of strabismus L: doesn't calculate angular deviation

(*continued*)

Table 2. (*continued*)

References	Materials	Dataset	Methods	Results	Advantage (A), Limitation (L)
[23] 2021	Eye-tracking virtual reality (VR) device	38 strabismus patients	The system eye-tracking virtual reality headset simulate the APCT (Alternative prism Cover Test)	Mean difference between VR and APCT is $0{,}88 \pm 5{,}77$ PD ($p = 0{,}352$) ICC comparing VR and APCT is $0{,}897$ ($p < 0{,}001$)	A: calculate deviation without prism or occlude L: system do not correct patient's refractive error; eyeglasses increase measurement error
[24] 2019	smartphone	undefined	EyeTurn Application	Phoria measurements with the app were consistent with MT (slope $= 0.94$, $R2 = 0.97$, $P < 0.001$, RMSE $= 1.7\Delta$). Measurements with the app were higher than with Synoptophore (slope $= 1.15$, $R2 = 0.91$, $P < 0.001$), but consistent with CTPN (slope $= 0.95$, $R2 = 0.95$, $P < 0.001$)	A: automatic horizontal strabismus diagnosis L: Method used only horizontal direction, not evaluate the effect of glasses

(*continued*)

Table 2. (*continued*)

References	Materials	Dataset	Methods	Results	Advantage (A), Limitation (L)
[25] 2018	undefined	28 images 100 images	Basic technique of image processing Logistic regression model for training	Accuracy: 78% Accuracy: 93%	A: High accuracy with Logistic regression model L: method using image processing
[26] 2011	computer, two camera	06 children	Eye-tracking technique	The average difference between two independent measurements of eye misalignment was − 0.27∘ ± 0.38∘ and the 95% limits of agreement for repeated measurements were ± 0.75∘	A: simulate the Hirschberg test L: the number of test is small
[27] 2015	undefined	140 normal patients 148 strabismus patients	Program calculate pupil center shift relative to pupil center position in primary gaze	Accuracy: 80%	A: simplified method L: accuracy under 90%

(strabismus or normal). This technique is used to diagnose only the strabismus but not to calculate the angular deviation. Moreover, it used a complex system. The system proposed by Keli Mao and al. [32] used deep learning for diagnosing strabismus. Indeed, Inception ResNetV2 architecture of CNN is used to locate the pupil center in order to know the position of the eye (strabismus or normal). The accuracy rate is 94.17% using the digital images. However, this method only treats horizontal strabismus (esotropia, exotropia). In addition, their photos were obtained from an Asian population. These studies need to be extended to other ethnic groups. Another system developed by Thayane de Oliveira Simoes and al. [33] has 96.6% accuracy rate for diagnosing strabismus. They calculate the distance between the center of the limb and the point between the corners of the eyes. They used U-NET architectures to segment the image and extract features,

Table 3. Overview of solutions based on Machine Learning Methods

References	Methods	Accuracy	Features extracted	Advantages (A), Limitation (L)
[28] 2021	G-Transform model + Decision Tree (ID3)	95.9%	Distance between the center of iris and the right, left boundaries respectively	A: High accuracy L: require a bigger volume of videos, presence and cooperation of patient, videos recording system
[28] 2023	Case-based reasoning algorithm	91.8%	unknown	A: good for diagnosing strabismus L: did not calculate angular deviation
[29] 2023	KNN + wavelet decomposition tree method	98.5%	Electro-oculography (EOG) signal	A: High level of accuracy. Further research is necessary to explore the potential of these methods

and ResNet to classify them. Laura Alves de Figueiredo and al. [34] proposed a software which has 42% to 92% accuracy rate for diagnosing strabismus by analyzing the 9 eye gaze positions. Their method used ResNet 50 to eva-luate ocular motility but requires further research. Method proposed by Haider Shamil Hamid and al. [35] has 95.62% accuracy rate to diagnose strabismus. They used Viola-Jones algorithm to detect eye region and deep learning algorithm to detect and classify strabismus in normal, exotropia and esotropia. But it does not evaluate the vertical deviation. Sukru Karaaslan and al. [36] proposed a method using deep learning and image processing to detect strabismus. Their method has 90% to 91% accuracy rate. It is a good method but can be improved. The Table 4 offers an overview of solutions based on deep learning approaches.

5 Discussion and Potential Challenges

This survey reviews various approaches using eye-tracking system associated with basic techniques of image processing, various machine learning techniques and several deep learning algorithms. These approaches are differentiated by their accuracy, time and complexity. Indeed, the proposed methodologies share steps such as image acquisition or video, image preparation, eye region detection, image segmentation to extract the features, model classification that uses the extracted features and predicts the di-sease and model evaluation. But, there are some differences between machine learning, deep learning and image processing approaches. In machine learning approaches, features

Table 4. Overview of solutions based on Deep Learning Approaches

References	Datasets	Architecture and Feature extracted	Accuracy	Advantages (A), Limitation (L)
[30] 2018	5685 images including 3409 training dataset (701 strabismus images, 2708 normal images and 2276 testing dataset (470 strabismus images, 1806 normal images)	R-FCN + CNN R-FCN for eye region extraction and CNN for classifying	96.1%	A: high level accuracy L: doesn't calculate angular deviation
[31] 2018	undefined	CNN + SVM classifier Color image feature and bright point of GaDe image (Gaze Deviation image)	95.2%	A: automatic diagnosis strabismus with good accuracy L: not calculate angular deviation and use some equipment that is not accessible to everyone
[32] 2020	5,595 images divided into training (70%), validation (15%) and retrospective test sets (15%)	CNN architecture InceptionResNet V2 Feature extracted: unknown	Retrospective testing: 99.0% Prospective testing: 97.2%	A: high accuracy L: method only treats horizontal strabismus (exotropia, exotropia). In addition, their photos were obtained from an asian population. These studies need to be extended to other ethnic groups
[33] 2019	undefined	U-Net + ResNet Networks	96.6%	A: high accuracy L: did not calculate angular deviation

(continued)

Table 4. (*continued*)

References	Datasets	Architecture and Feature extracted	Accuracy	Advantages (A), Limitation (L)
[34] 2020	110 strabismus patients	ResNet 50 Networks	42% to 92% according to the eye gaze position (1 to 9)	A: allows the evaluation of ocular motility L: variable accuracy, further exploratory research and validations are required
[35] 2022	285 facial images	Viola-Jones algorithm + CNN algorithm	95.62%	A: High accuracy L: did not calculate angular deviation
[36] 2023	88 strabismic patients	Deep learning algorithm + image processing	90% to 91%	A: good accuracy but can be improved

extraction is the input and the objects classes as output while the deep learning algorithm use the image to classify the objects. The image processing approaches use the image to locate the eye region, extract eye and classify the objet using basic techniques of image processing. Another difference is noted in the image acquisition. Eye-tracking system requires some material to record image facial with their complexity. It requires the cooperation of the patient. In addition, image processing technique requires a good command of eye location techniques, filter and others. Machine learning.

methods requires a deep knowledge in image processing domain for extracting features. It is done manually. While in deep learning algorithm, the features extraction is done automatically. In terms of accuracy, machine learning approaches and deep learning approaches offer greater precision to diagnose strabismus than image processing approaches. Machine learning methods and deep learning techniques are roughly equivalent in terms of accuracy. Some machine learning and deep learning techniques detect automatically the strabismus without calculating the angular deviation. These methods are interesting for diagnosing the disease but limited. Indeed, the angular deviation calculation is an additional step that allows the ophthalmologist to confirm the diagnosis, to monitor the disease and to use this value in the event of surgery. These automatic diagnosis methods can be used in African hospital particularly in Senegal. In collaboration with Abass Ndao hospital in Dakar, we plan to create a database of facial images (strabismus patients with angular deviation, normal patients). Then we will create an artificial intelligence model for diagnosing strabismus and angular deviation calculation in order to use it in ophthalmology department especially in remote areas.

6 Conclusion and Future Works

Currently, amblyopia continues to be one of the causes of school drop-out among children. Early diagnosis of strabismus is becoming a key factor in the fight against visual impairment. Artificial Intelligence offers solutions for diagnosing strabismus early.

In this study, we analysed various automatic diagnostic techniques of strabismus such as image processing approaches, machine learning methods and deep learning techniques. All these methods are interesting. However, in Africa, particularly in Senegal, some of the devices used are not available in our hospital unlike the developed countries. The Challenge is to boost the use of artificial intelligence in our hospital. The aim is to help the specialist for early diagnosing and monitoring of the disease. As future works, we plan to collect data at the Abass Ndao hospital in Dakar. We will combine a deep learning model and a classifier prediction model with the value of the angular deviation as input for diagnosing strabismus automatically.

References

1. Rapport Mondiale sur la Vision. ISBN 978-92-4-000297-5 (version électronique), ISBN 978-92-4-000298-2 (version imprimée). Publié le 08 Octobre 2019
2. OMS: Eye Health. https://www.afro.who.int/health-topics/eye-health. Accessed on 16 Nov 2023
3. Mémoire de Master de Madior Gueye : Evaluation des effectifs et des dotations du matériel d'Ophtalmologie au Sénégal à la lumière des normes nationales et de l'OMS. Soutenu le 19/12/2020 à l'Université Polytechnique de l'Ouest Africain (UPOA), Dakar, Sénégal
4. OMS : Cécité et déficience visuelle. https://ww.who.int/fr/news-room/fact-sheets/detail/blindness-and-visual-impairment. Accessed on 10 Oct 2023
5. Frick, K.D., Foster, A.: The magnitude and the cost of global blindness: an increasing problem that can be alleviated. Am. J. Ophthalmol. **135**(4), 471–47 (2003)
6. Prince Kwalu Akowuah and al.: Strabismus and amblyopia in Africa – A systematic review and meta-analysis (2022). https://doi.org/10.1080/09273972.2022.2157023
7. Tableau de l'ordre national des médecins du Sénégal (2022). https://www.ordremedecins.sn/
8. Rapport annuel sur la Population du Sénégal en 2022. https://www.ansd.sn/. Accessed on 16 Nov 2023
9. Abràmoff, M.D., et al.: Improved automated detection of diabetic retinopathy on a publicly available dataset through integration of deep learning (2016). Investigative Ophthalmology & Visual Science October 2016, vol.57, pp. 5200–5206. https://doi.org/10.1167/iovs.16-19964
10. Gulshan V., Peng L., Coram M., et al.: Development and validation of a deep learning algorithm for detection of diabetic retinopathy in retinal fundus photographs (2016). JAMA **316**(22), 2402–2410. https://doi.org/10.1001/jama.2016.17216
11. Saranya, P., et al.: Detection and classification of red lesions from retinal images for diabetic retinopathy detection using deep learning models (2023). https://doi.org/10.1007/s11042-023-15045-1
12. Vaughan, N., et al.: Review of smartphone funduscopy for diabetic retinopathy screening (2023). https://doi.org/10.1016/j.survophthal.2023.10.006
13. Chea, N., et al.: Classification of Fundus Images Based on Deep Learning for Detecting Eye Diseases (2021). https://doi.org/10.32604/cmc.2021.013390
14. He, T., et al.: Automatic detection of age-related macular degeneration based on deep learning and local outlier factor algorithm. Diagnostics (Basel) (2022). https://doi.org/10.3390/diagnostics12020

15. Lee, C.S., et al.: Deep learning is effective for the classification of OCT images of normal versus age-related macular degeneration. Ophthal. Retina (2017). https://doi.org/10.1016/j.oret.2016.12.009
16. Li, C., et al.: Assessing the external validity of machine learning-based detection of glaucoma (2023). https://doi.org/10.1038/s41598-023-27783-1
17. Abbas, Q.: Detection of Glaucoma Eye Disease on Retinal Fundus Images using Deep Learning (2017). (IJACSA) Int. J. Adv. Comput. Sci. Appl. **8**(6) (2017)
18. Loba, P., et al.: Guidelines for the management of strabismus in children (2022). 3/2022, vol. 124, pp.127–130. https://doi.org/10.5114/ko.2022.118848
19. Yehezkel, O., et al.: Automated diagnosis and measurement of strabismus in children (2019). Am. J. Ophthalmol. **213**, 226–234 (2019). https://doi.org/10.1016/j.ajo.2019.12.018
20. Zheng, Y., et al.: Intelligent evaluation of strabismus in videos based on an automated cover test. Appl. Sci. **9**, 731 (2019). https://doi.org/10.3390/app9040731
21. Valente, T.L.A., et al.: Automatic diagnosis of strabismus in digital videos through cover test (2017). Comput. Methods Programs Biomed. **140**, 295–305 (2017). https://doi.org/10.1016/j.cmpb.2017.01.002
22. Huang, X., et al.: An automatic screening method for strabismus detection based on image processing (2021). https://doi.org/10.1371/journal.pone.0255643
23. Yeh, P.-H., et al.: To measure the amount of ocular deviation in strabismus patients with an eye-tracking virtual reality headset (2021). BMC Ophthalmol. **21**, Article number 246
24. Pundlik, S., et al.: Development and Preliminary Evaluation of a Smartphone App for Measuring Eye Alignment (2019). https://doi.org/10.1167/tvst.8.1.19
25. Suriyal, S.S.: Quantitative analysis of strabismus using image processing (2018). A thesis, presented to the Department of Electrical Engineering California State University, Long Beach, August 2018
26. Dmitri Model and Moshe Eizenman: An Automated Hirschberg Test for Infants (2011). IEEE Trans. Biomed. Eng. **58**(1) (2011). https://doi.org/10.1109/TBME.2010.2085000
27. Bushuyeva, N., Romanenko, D.: Assessment of deviation angle and oblique muscle function in strabismus patients using analysis of two-dimensional eye globe pictures in diagnostic gaze positions (2015). https://doi.org/10.1111/j.1755-3768.2015.0446
28. Amirul, M., et al.: An automated strabismus classification using machine learning algorithm for binocular vision management system (2023). https://doi.org/10.1109/ICSECS58457.2023.10256291
29. Daher, A., et al.: Artificial Intelligence Powered System for Detecting, Diagnosing and Rehabiliting Strabismus Disorder (2023). 10.1109/ICABME59496.2023.10293014
30. Lua, J., et al.: Automated Strabismus Detection for Telemedicine Applications (2018). https://www.researchgate.net/publication/327571320
31. Chen, Z., et al.: Strabismus recognition Using Eye-Tracking Data and Convolutional Neural Networks (2018). Hindawi, J. Healthcare Eng. Article ID 7692198, 9 p. https://doi.org/10.1155/2018/7692198
32. Mao, K., et al.: An artificial intelligence platform for the diagnosis and surgical planning of strabismus using corneal light-reflection photos (2020). Submitted Jul 22, 2020. Accepted for publication Dec 18, 2020. https://doi.org/10.21037/atm-20-5442
33. Simoes, T.O., et al.: Automatic ocular alignment evaluation for strabismus detection using U-NET and ResNet networks (2019). 8th Brazilian Conference on Intelligent Systems, Salvador, Brazil, pp. 239–244 (2019)
34. Alves de Figueiredo, L., et al.: Strabismus and Artificial Intelligence App: Optimizing Diagnostic and Accuracy (2020). https://doi.org/10.1167/tvst.10.7.22

35. Hamad, H.S., et al.: An Intelligent Strabismus detection method based on convolution neural networks (2022). https://doi.org/10.12928/TELKOMNIKA.v20i6.24232
36. Karaaslan, S., et al.: A new method based on deep learning and image processing for detection of strabismus with Hirschberg test (2023). 10.1016/j.pdpdt.2023.103805

Towards the Implementation of a Dynamic IDS for IoT: Anomaly Detection in MQTT Traffic

Abdoulaye Diallo[1(✉)], Lionel Affognon[2], Chérif Diallo[1], and Eugène C. Ezin[2,3]

[1] Department of Informatique, UFR des Sciences Appliquées et de Technologies, Université Gaston Berger, Saint-Louis, Senegal
{diallo.abdoulaye8,cherif.diallo}@ugb.edu.sn
[2] Institut de Mathématiques et de Sciences Physiques (IMSP), Université D'Abomey-Calavi, Dangbo, Benin
lionel.affognon@imsp-uac.org, eugene.ezin@uac.bj
[3] Institut de Formation et de Recherche en Informatique, University d'Abomey-Calavi, Abomey-Calavi, Benin

Abstract. The proliferation of IoT is evident in numerous domains today. Its applications are expanding rapidly, offering significant benefits. Nonetheless, it is plagued by numerous security flaws that can hinder its adoption in critical areas. This paper addresses the development of an intrusion detection system (IDS) for IoT networks. Specifically, we implement an autoencoder, an unsupervised deep learning model frequently employed in anomaly detection. The model is trained using the MQTTSet dataset, which contains both normal MQTT traffic and attack data. Training focused exclusively on legitimate data. Testing was conducted on both benign and malicious data to assess the model's effectiveness. The results indicate detection rates of 99.86% and 98.56% for normal and attack data, respectively.

Keywords: Internet of things · intrusion detection system · anomaly detection · deep learning · autoencoder

1 Introduction

The Internet of Things (IoT) represents a major technological advancement, connecting the physical and digital worlds. IoT devices collect, exchange, and analyze data to automate and improve processes in sectors such as healthcare, industry, agriculture, and smart cities, enhancing operational efficiency and enabling real-time, data-driven decision-making [1].

IoT devices use various sensors and communication technologies (e.g., Wi-Fi, Bluetooth, Zigbee) to monitor and interact with their environment. They transmit data to servers for real-time analysis and alerts. IoT's potential lies in transforming raw data into actionable insights, applicable in supply chain management, remote health monitoring, industrial automation, energy management, and smart home [2].

Despite benefits, increased interconnectivity presents significant security challenges. IoT devices are vulnerable to threats like data theft and service disruption due to the lack of unified security standards and diverse Technologies [3]. Data privacy is a major concern, as IoT devices often collect sensitive information. Inadequate security practices, like default passwords, exacerbate these risks.

These vulnerabilities stem from neglecting security during IoT device design. Many devices are sold with exploitable default settings. Manufacturers must adopt secure design practices to minimize vulnerabilities. However, IoT devices' limited computing and storage capacities make embedding sophisticated security mechanisms challenging. Innovative security solutions, like AI-based technologies (machine learning and deep learning), offer advanced capabilities to detect and respond to sophisticated attacks by analyzing network traffic for anomalies [4].

Anomaly detection in IoT networks is crucial for ensuring system integrity. Researchers are developing intrusion detection systems using machine learning and deep learning. Classical algorithms (e.g., SVM, KNN) are less effective with large data volumes typical of IoT. Deep learning models are more suitable for massive data volumes. Supervised learning models are precise in detecting known intrusions but fail against "zero-day attacks." Unsupervised learning models are more effective in detecting new attacks.

Message Queuing Telemetry Transport (MQTT), an OASIS standard for IoT messaging, is a lightweight publish/subscribe protocol designed for efficiently connecting remote devices with minimal code and network bandwidth [5, 6]. In this paper, we propose an anomaly detection method in MQTT-based IoT network using autoencoders, unsupervised deep learning models. This approach characterizes normal system functioning, with deviations considered anomalies, for anomaly detection in IoT networks.

The remainder of this paper is structured as follows: Sect. 2 reviews relevant literature, Sect. 3 outlines the methodology, including the deep learning model and dataset, Sect. 4 discusses the results and evaluates the model's performance, and Sect. 5 concludes the paper.

2 Related Works

Numerous researchers are investigating IDS for IoT networks [7], with increasing focus on machine learning and deep learning approaches. Traditional machine learning algorithms like Support Vector Machine (SVM) and K-Nearest Neighbor (KNN) are effective with smaller datasets but struggle with larger volumes typical in IoT. Deep learning models, however, improve with more data, making them suitable for IoT applications. Deep learning models can be categorized into supervised and unsupervised learning. Supervised models excel in detecting known intrusions and are widely used for traffic classification to identify attacks.

For instance, a study by authors [8] implemented a Deep Neural Network (DNN) for MQTT-based intrusion detection, trained and tested on MQTT-IoT-IDS2020 dataset. They achieved high accuracy in detecting various attacks. Another study by E. Ciklabakkal et al. [9] used the PyOD library to implement several machine learning models for anomaly-based IDS, focusing on MQTT attacks. The OCSVM model performed best for normal data, while K-Means and Random Forest excelled with attack data.

N. Elsayed et al. [10] proposed a smart home IDS using a hybrid deep learning model combining BiLSTM and CNN, demonstrating effective detection of network anomalies. Unsupervised learning models, such as autoencoders, are particularly adept at detecting new, unknown attacks, which prompted our focus on these models.

In this context, [11] implemented an autoencoder for anomaly detection in a smart home system. A. Legrand et al. [12] compared convolutional and recurrent autoencoders for anomaly detection in connected buildings, finding recurrent autoencoders to be more effective. A. Dawood et al. [13] conducted a comparative study between autoencoders and Restricted Boltzmann Machines (RBM) for anomaly detection, concluding that autoencoders performed better. I. Apostol et al. [14] proposed an unsupervised deep learning approach using autoencoders to detect IoT botnet activities, demonstrating the model's effectiveness under various conditions.

3 Methodology

Autoencoders, when used for anomaly detection, are trained on normal system patterns. Initially, we segregated normal traffic data from abnormal traffic and trained the autoencoder exclusively on normal data, allowing it to reconstruct normal patterns with minimal error. Anomalies result in higher reconstruction errors, exceeding a predefined threshold.

3.1 Dataset

We utilized the MQTTSet dataset [15], comprising IoT traffic data primarily using the MQTT protocol. This dataset was chosen for its inclusion of common IoT attacks like DoS and brute force, and its manageable number of features. The MQTT protocol is widely adopted for sensor or event data communication. MQTTSet captures traffic during various attack scenarios, making it suitable for our study. MQTT is a widely used publish–subscribe-based protocol for the communication of sensor or event data.

The scenario is assimilated to a smart home environment composed by 8 sensors such as temperature, light intensity, humidity, CO-Gas, motion, smoke, motion sensors and fan speed controller.

The traffic is captured from the broker. During the attack phases, the malicious node is directly connected to the broker in order to execute the cyber-attacks. The following picture show sensors' location (Fig. 1).

MQTTset includes the following types of attacks: DoS, MQTT Publish flood, SlowITe, malformed data, and brute force authentication. The following figure presents the taxonomy of MQTTSet attacks (Fig. 2).

The dataset contains over 12 million records. Benign data represents 98% of the dataset. As we can see MQTTSet dataset is strongly unbalanced. But it is very suitable for our use case.

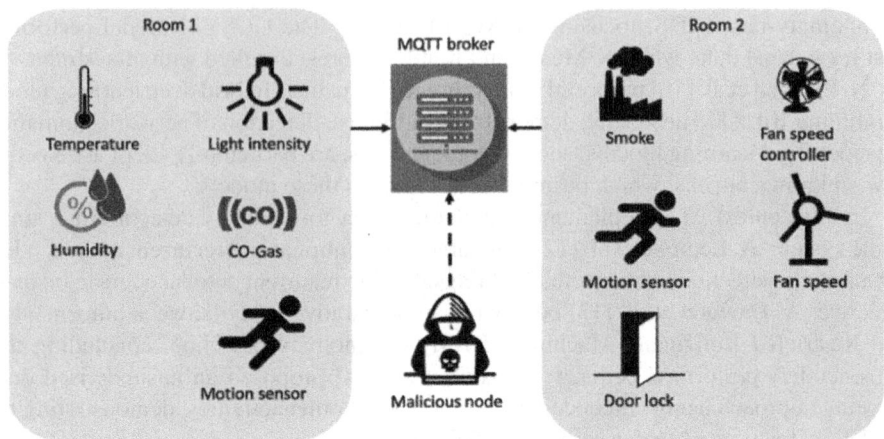

Fig. 1. The scenario considered in MQTTset [15]

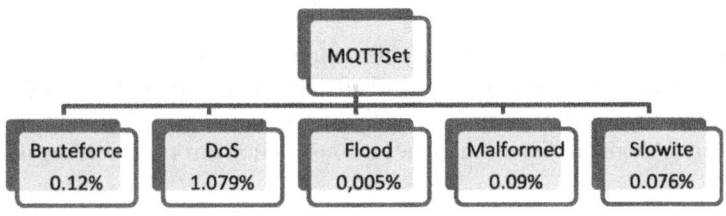

Fig. 2. MQTTSet attacks taxonomy

3.2 Autoencoder and Anomaly Detection

Autoencoders [17], a type of artificial neural network, are frequently employed in anomaly detection due to their ability to learn compact data representations and accurately reconstruct inputs similar to the ones they have been trained on. Typically, autoencoders are trained on data deemed normal, which represents typical or healthy behavior within a system. Their advantage lies in their capacity to learn meaningful data representations without explicit supervision for anomalies. The model inherently learns to compactly represent normal data in the latent space, making anomalies easier to detect due to their deviation from this learned representation (Fig. 3).

The model reconstructs the input ($\mathcal{X}$) into its output ($\mathcal{X}\prime$). Thus, the model is trained by minimizing reconstruction errors, which are defined as a loss ($\mathcal{L}oss$) function as follows:

$$\mathcal{L}oss(\mathcal{X}, \mathcal{X}\prime) = \|\mathcal{X} - \mathcal{X}\prime\|^2 \tag{1}$$

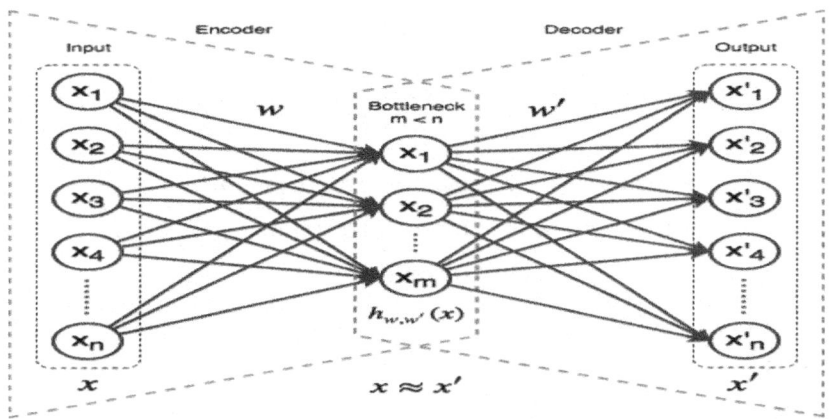

Fig. 3. Autoencoder architecture, image source [18]

During training, autoencoders minimize a loss function that measures the difference between the input and the model's reconstruction. Once trained, these autoencoders can be used to reconstruct new inputs and evaluate the quality of the reconstruction by calculating an error measure, typically based on the distance or divergence between the original inputs and their reconstructions. To determine whether an input is normal or abnormal, an error threshold is often established. Inputs with reconstruction errors exceeding this threshold are classified as abnormal, whereas those with errors below the threshold are considered normal.

The following equations demonstrates how the autoencoder model predicts the nature of an input:

$$x_{error} = \mathcal{L}oss(\mathcal{X}, \mathcal{X}\prime) \tag{2}$$

$$predictor(x) = \begin{cases} Normal, x_{error} < Threshold \\ Anomaly, x_{error} \geq Threshold \end{cases} \tag{3}$$

The following algorithm gives more details on anomaly prediction by autoencoders.

Algorithm 1: Anomaly detection by autoencoder

```
1: Function predictor(x,threshold,autoencoder):
2:     x' ← AE.predict(x)
3:     x_error ← calculate_error(x, x')
4:     if x_error < threshold then
5:             return "Normal"
6:     else
7:             return "Anomaly"
8: end

1: Function calculate_error(x, x'):
2:     x_error ← ||x - x'||^2
3:             return x_error
4: end
```

Choosing the appropriate error threshold is crucial and can be influenced by various factors, such as the specific nature of the anomaly detection problem, the data distribution, and the requirements for performance and tolerance to false positives and false negatives. In practice, this anomaly detection approach with autoencoders can be effective in numerous fields, including cybersecurity, fraud detection, predictive maintenance, and industrial system monitoring. It is important to note that the success of anomaly detection using autoencoders depends on several factors, including the quality and representativeness of the training data, the appropriate choice of model architecture and hyperparameters, and the careful selection of the error threshold. Additionally, it is often necessary to periodically reevaluate and adjust these parameters to maintain the model's performance in dynamic environments or when facing sophisticated attacks.

3.3 Our Autoencoder Architecture

The process of constructing the autoencoder model was meticulous and strategic, involving several key steps to achieve an optimal configuration. Initially, we conducted an exhaustive search for the best hyperparameters for the loss function and optimizer. This initial phase was crucial in determining the fundamental parameters that directly influence the model's outcomes. For this search, we utilized GridSearchCV.

After identifying the Mean Squared Error (MSE) loss function and the Adam optimizer as the best choices, we proceeded to determine the optimal structure of the autoencoder. This phase involved exploring different configurations for the number of neurons in each layer of the autoencoder, as well as the bottleneck. Again, we used GridSearchCV to systematically explore various parameter combinations and identify the optimal configuration.

Upon analyzing the results of this comprehensive search, we identified an optimal autoencoder configuration with 128 neurons in the first and seventh hidden layers, 64 neurons in the second and sixth hidden layers, 32 neurons in the third and fifth hidden layers, and 16 neurons for the latent space or bottleneck. These parameters were selected considering the dataset's complexity and the model's generalization capability.

Finally, with the best hyperparameters identified, we proceeded to build the autoencoder model using the Keras library. Each layer was configured according to the number of neurons determined during the hyperparameter search, and the ReLU and sigmoid activation functions were chosen based on the nature of the data and modeling objectives. Compiled with the Adam optimizer and the MSE loss function, the model is now ready to be trained and tested.

$$MSE = \frac{1}{n} \cdot \sum_{i=1}^{n} (X_i - X\prime_i)^2 \tag{4}$$

X is a feature vector provided as input to the autoencoder, and $X\prime$ is the reconstructed output.

4 Results and Discussion

After the training phase, we performed two tests. The first test is done on normal data and we did the second test on attack data. We tested different thresholds but the best of them was obtained with the formula below:

$$Threshold = Mean(train\_loss) + Std(train\_loss) \tag{4}$$

The results are illustrated in the following figures. The abscissas represent the features and the ordinates are the values of the features.

The previous figures (Fig. 4a, Fig. 4b, Fig. 4c) present three examples of normal input data and their corresponding reconstructed output. They show the ability of the model to reconstruct normal data. The model achieves a perfect reconstruction of the normal data. The error rate at this level is very low. Its accuracy on detecting normal data is 99.86%.

On the other hand, the attack data is poorly reconstructed. The figures below show the behavior of the model on attack data (DoS, Bruteforce, Malformed, Slowite, Flood) (Figs. 5, 6, 7, 8 and 9).

By observing the previous figures which show the behavior of the model on attack data, we can see that the reconstruction error is very large. It exceeds the threshold that has been defined. Thus, there is a big difference between the reconstruction error of normal data and that of attack data. Therefore, these data are considered malicious. An alert can therefore be launched to report an intrusion. The detection rate of attack data is 98.56%

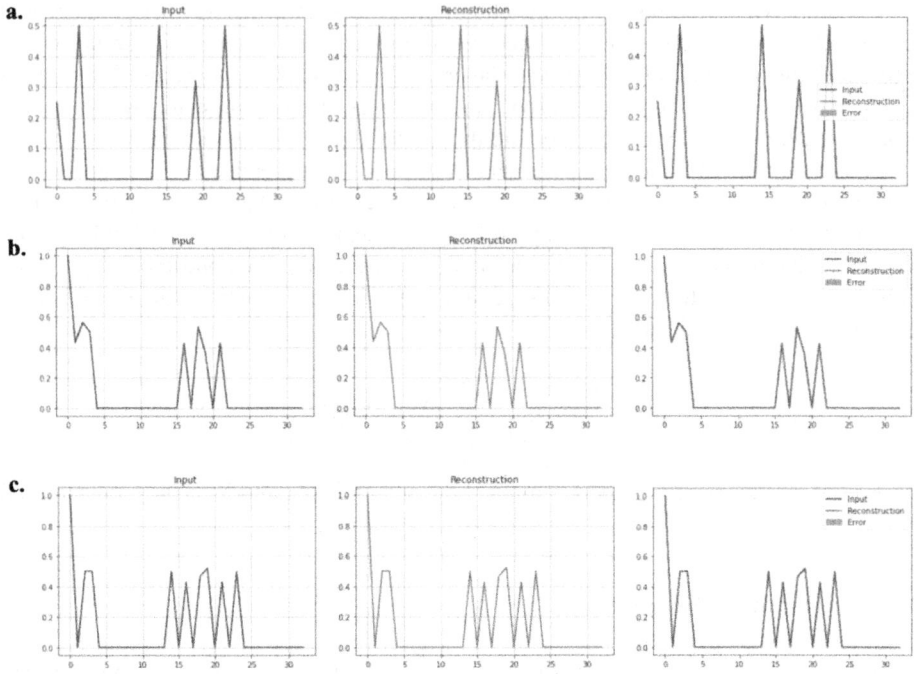

Fig. 4. a. Normal input and reconstructed output. **b.** Normal input and reconstructed output. **c.** Normal input and reconstructed output.

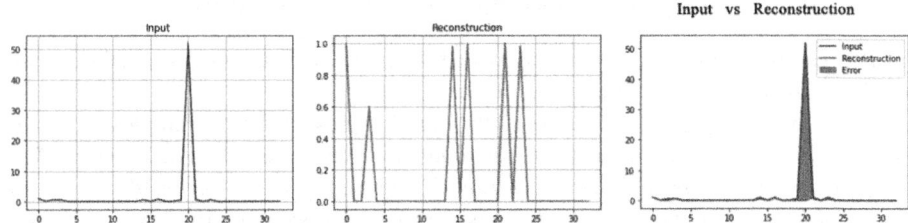

Fig. 5. Here the input is DoS attack data

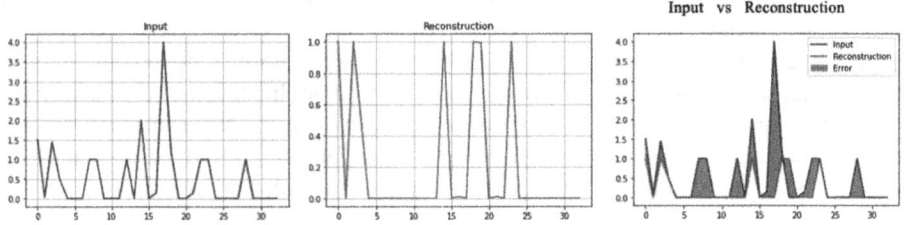

Fig. 6. When the model receives bruteforce attack data as input

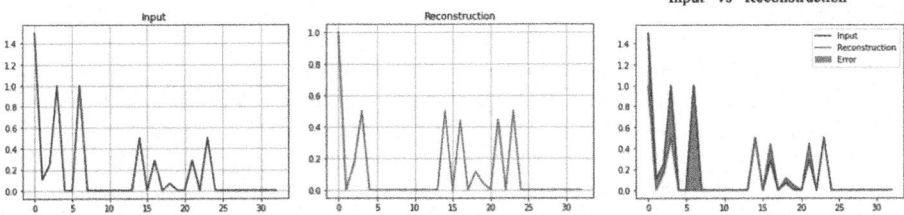

Fig. 7. When the input is malformed data

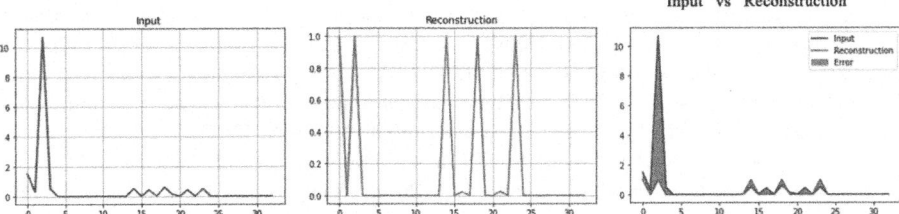

Fig. 8. The model receives Slowite attack data as input

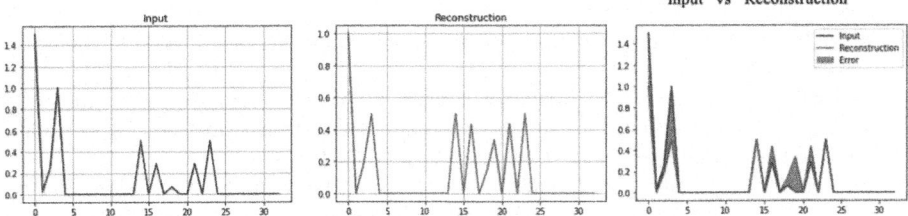

Fig. 9. This input is Flood attack data

5 Conclusion and Future Works

This paper presents an autoencoder-based IDS for IoT networks using MQTT protocol data, capable of detecting zero-day attacks. The model achieved high accuracy in distinguishing normal and malicious traffic. The model achieves an accuracy of 99.86% in recognizing normal traffic. It scores 98.56% in detecting malicious traffic. However, it must be said that autoencoders can have poor performance if the training data is not representative of normal system traffic. In our next work we intend to go further than in the detection of intrusions. Future work will focus on combining this model with others to not only detect but also identify specific intrusions.

Acknowledgments. This publication was made possible through the DSTN (Digital Science and Technology Network) supported by IRD (Institut de Recherche pour le Développement) and AFD (Agence Française de Développement).

References

1. Ramson, S.R.J., Vishnu, S., Shanmugam, M.: Applications of İnternet of Things (IoT)–an overview. In: 2020 5th İnternational Conference on Devices, Circuits and Systems (ICDCS). IEEE (2020)
2. Diallo, A., Diallo, C.: Human activity recognition in smart home using deep learning models. In: 2021 IEEE International Conference on Computational Science and Computational Intelligence (CSCI) – Las Vegas, USA. pp. 1721–1727 (2021). https://doi.org/10.1109/CSCI54926.2021.00326
3. OWASP IoT Top 10. https://owasp.org/www-chapter-toronto/assets/slides/2019-12-11-OWASP-IoT-Top-10---Introduction-and-Root-Causes.pdf
4. Hamed, T., Ernst, J.B., Kremer S.C.: A survey and taxonomy of classifiers of ıntrusion detection systems. Computer and Network Security Essentials (2018)
5. Nikolov, N.: Research of MQTT, CoAP, HTTP and XMPP IoT communication protocols for Embedded Systems. In: 2020 XXIX International Scientific Conference Electronics (ET), Sozopol, Bulgaria, pp. 1–4 (2020) https://doi.org/10.1109/ET50336.2020.9238208
6. Soni, D., Ashwin, M.: A survey on MQTT: a protocol of Internet of Things (IoT). In: International Conference on Telecommunication, Power Analysis and Computing Techniques (ICTPACT-2017) (2017)
7. Sekhar, C., Pavani, K., Rao, M.S.: Comparative analysis on ıntrusion detection system through ML and DL Techniques: Survey. In: 2021 International Conference on Computational Intelligence and Computing Applications (ICCICA), Nagpur, India, pp. 1–5 (2021). https://doi.org/10.1109/ICCICA524589697291
8. Khan, M.A., et al.: A deep learning-based intrusion detection system for MQTT enabled IoT. Sensors **21**(21), 7016 (2021)
9. Ciklabakkal, E., Donmez, A., Erdemir, M., Suren, E., Yilmaz, M.K., Angin, P.: Artemis: an intrusion detection system for mqtt attacks in İnternet of Things. In: 38th Symposium on Reliable Distributed Systems (SRDS), pp. 369–3692 (2019)
10. Elsayed, N., Zaghloul, Z.S., Azhuma, S.W., and Li, C.: Intrusion detection system in smart home network using bidirectional lstm and convolutional neural networks hybrid model. In: 2021 IEEE Interna- tional Midwest Symposium on Circuits and Systems (MWSCAS), pp. 55–58 (2021)
11. Cultice, T., Ionel, D., and Thapliyal, H.: Smart home sensor anomaly detection using convolutional autoencoder neural network. In: 2020 IEEE International Symposium on Smart Electronic Systems (iSES) (Formerly iNiS), pp. 67–70 (2020)
12. Legrand, A.,Niepceron, B., Cournier. A, Trannois, H.: Study of autoencoder neural networks for anomaly detection in connected buildings. In: 2018 IEEE Global Conference on Internet of Things (GCIoT), pp. 1–5 (2018). https://doi.org/10.1109/GCIoT.2018.8620158
13. Dawoud, A., Sianaki, O.A., Shahristani, S., Raun, C.: Internet of Things intrusion detection: a deep learning approach. In: 2020 IEEE Symposium Series on Computational Intelligence (SSCI), pp. 1516–1522 (2020)
14. Apostol, I., Preda, M., Nila, C., Bica, I.: IoT botnet anomaly detection using unsupervised deep learning. Electronics **10**(16), 1876 (2021)
15. Vaccari, I., Chiola, G., Aiello, M., Mongelli, M., Cambiaso, E.: MQTTset, a new dataset for machine learning techniques on MQTT. Sensors (2020)
16. Hindy, H., Bayne, E., Bures, M., Atkinson, R., Tachtatzis, C., Bellekens, X.: Machine Learning Based IoT Intrusion Detection System: An MQTT Case Study (MQTT-IoT-IDS2020 Dataset) (2021)
17. Sewak, M., Sahay, S.K., Rathore, H.: An overview of deep learning architecture of deep neural networks and autoencoders. J. Comput. Theor. Nanosci. **17**(1). American Scientific

Publisher, pp. A82–188 (2020). https://subscription.packtpub.com/book/python/9781789348460/6/ch06lvl1sec37/variational-autoencoders

18. Diallo,A., Affognon,L., Diallo, C., Ezin, E.C.: Deep learning based binary and multi-class classification for anomaly detection. In: 2022 International Conference on Engineering and Emerging Technologies ICEET, Kuala Lumpur, Malaysia, pp. 1–6 (2022)

ICT Enabler

Straight-Line Recognition in a Virtual Hexagonal Grid Using Hough Transform

Moïse Ouedraogo[✉] and Abdoulaye Sere

Equipe de Recherche Signal, Image et Communications (ER-SIC), Laboratoire d'Algèbre de Mathématiques Discrètes et Informatique (LAMDI), Université Nazi BONI (UNB), Bobo-Dioulasso, Burkina Faso
moisewedra@gmail.com, abdoulaye.sere@recifaso.org

Abstract. The Hough transform is a powerful mathematical tool designed for detecting geometric patterns, including straight lines, circles, and other shapes, within images. The fundamental idea behind this transformation is to represent the points of an image in a parameter space specific to the pattern one aims to detect. This paper focuses on analytical straight-line recognition, using standard Hough Transform in a virtual grid. Each cell in the virtual grid is hexagonal. The method consists of superimposing a virtual grid on the image and calculating the transformation of lit pixels in hexagonal cells where the rate of lit pixels exceeds a threshold. The voting threshold is a criterion that determines how many votes are required for a line to be considered detected. It is an important parameter that influences the quality and reliability of line detection in an image. A lower voting threshold includes noise and consequently degrades the detection quality. Our approach takes advantage of this limitation to optimize analytical straight-line recognition. The experimental results show an improvement in execution time compared with the standard Hough transform method.

Keywords: Hough Transform · Reconstruction · straight-line Recognition · Virtual Hexagonal Grid

1 Introduction

The Hough transform is a robust technique in computer vision, serving to identify shapes and patterns within images with remarkable accuracy. Its significance lies in its ability to transcend the confines of pixel-based analysis, delving instead into the realm of parameter space exploration. This approach was originally conceived by Paul Hough [3] in 1962, with the aim of detecting straight lines in noisy images. Since its inception, the Hough transform has evolved and generalized, making it adaptable to many applications. Notably, it has been extended to recognize arbitrary shapes [4,40,54], intricate ellipses [5], curves [41,45,47,53], circular formations [6,50], and analytically defined lines [7,44,55].

Over the years, the researchers have developed several variants [4,22–38] of Hough transform. It has been applied in different fields, including detecting roads in satellite images [8,9], managing traffic by determining road saturation in [10], lane tracking [51], agriculture [42,48,52], breeding [56],building [49], chirology [43], detecting lineaments in satellite images, autonomous vehicles [11,46,57], breast cancer detection screening [39], and localizing robots [12]. To improve computation time, Rectangular Hough Transform and Triangular Hough Transform were proposed by Traore [13] and Moïse Ouedraogo [14], respectively. These methods involve meshing the image with a rectangular or triangular grid and then applying the standard Hough transform.

Another technique to improve computation time is Parallel Hough Transform on a triangular grid by Abdoulaye Sere and al [15]. Sere and others in [16] proposed an Hough Transform method based on the map-reduce algorithm to perform speedily Big Data of images for pattern recognition. These works have been also extended by Mateus Coelho and others in [6] to propose circle recognition based on the map-reduce algorithm.

In this document, we focus on hexagonal image meshing. The use of a hexagonal grid offers significant advantages in the field of image processing. Drawing parallels with the biological domain, the complex hexagonal pattern observed in the retina of the human eye, as discussed in detail by Curcio et al. [17], testifies to the potential inherent in this geometric arrangement. This natural hexagonal arrangement of sensory cells aligns with the principles of efficiency and optimisation, inspiring its integration into image processing methodologies. The gains in efficiency brought about by the hexagonal grid go beyond the biological domain. Asharindavida et al. [18] claim that computational operations performed on images presented in a hexagonal format exhibit accelerated processing speeds. This unequivocally contributes to a notable enhancement in the overall efficiency of image processing tasks. The ramifications of this acceleration reverberate across diverse applications, ranging from cutting-edge deep learning techniques such as convolutional neural networks [19], to intricate geospatial computing endeavors [20], and even to foundational image pre-processing steps like edge detection [21]. The adoption of a hexagonal grid in image processing thus ushers in a new dimension of expedited operations and streamlined computational efforts. The implications are far-reaching, offering the potential to reshape the landscape of various domains reliant on efficient and rapid image analysis. As technological advancements continue to unfold, the hexagonal grid stands as a testament to the interplay between natural patterns and computational innovation, culminating in an augmented capacity to decipher the intricacies of visual data.

The central question underlying this study concerns the application of the Hough transform on a virtual hexagonal grid superimposed on an image. How can the Hough transform be adapted to ensure maximum accuracy and efficiency in the detection and recognition of straight lines using virtual hexagonal grids?

To meet this challenge, we need to explore the adjustments needed to optimise the exploitation of the geometric features inherent in the grid. This paves the way for significant progress in the detection of linear structures using virtual hexagonal grids.

The main objective of this study is to optimise the recognition of straight lines using the Hough transform technique by integrating a virtual hexagonal grid into the images. This objective encompasses several sub-objectives. Firstly, the research involves the design and superimposition of a virtual hexagonal grid on the image. Secondly, the study looks at the complex task of adapting the Hough transform in the specific context of a virtual hexagonal grid. By addressing these objectives, the research aims to advance the efficiency of straight line recognition in computer vision, providing valuable insights into the incorporation of virtual grids in digital image analysis.

This paper is organized as follows: Sect. 2 recalls basic definitions related to the analytical straight line and standard Hough transform to aid in understanding the following sections. Section 3 describes the method using various algorithms, while Sect. 4 presents experimental results of previous algorithms.

2 Preliminaries

A digital image is made up of a set of discrete elements, called pixels, arranged in a two-dimensional space. It can be considered as a discrete set in which the mathematical principles of discrete geometry can be applied.

Definition 1 (Analytical straight line) [1]. *Analytical straight line with parameters (a,b,μ) and thickness w is defined by the set of integer points (x,y) verifying:*

$$\mu \leq ax+by < \mu+w, \ (a,b,\mu,w) \in \mathbb{Z}^4, \ gcd(a,b) = 1 \tag{1}$$

Analytical straight line is:

- thin, if $w < \max(|a|,|b|)$
- naif, if $w = \max(|a|,|b|)$
- standard, if $w = (|a|+|b|)$
- thick, if $w > (|a|+|b|)$

Definition 2 (Standard Hough Transform (SHT)) [2]. *Let $\mathscr{I} \subset \mathbb{R}^2$ be an image space. Let l be the number of columns in an image. Let h be the number of rows in an image. Suppose that the point $(x,y) \in \mathscr{I}$. The dual of (x,y), denoted $S(x,y)$ is the Standard Hough Transform defined by the set of continuous points:*

$$\{(\theta,r) \in [0,\pi] \times [-\sqrt{l^2+h^2}, \sqrt{l^2+h^2}] \ / \ r = x\cos\theta + y\sin\theta\} \tag{2}$$

Definition 3 (Hexagon). *A hexagon is a six-sided polygon.*
γ define the size of hexagon.
AB, BC, CD, DE, EF and FA are the sides of hexagon illustrated in Fig. 1.

The hexagon is subdivided into three parts as illustrated in Fig. 1(a):

- the isosceles triangle ABF
- the rectangle BCEF
- the isosceles triangle BDE

Thales's theorem is used to browse pixels in the isosceles triangular area of each hexagon. The theorem is presented as follows:

Theorem 1 (Thales). *Let ABG be a right triangle. Let N and P be points on lines (AB) and (AG) respectively, with line NP parallel to line (BG). Then: $\frac{AP}{AG} = \frac{NP}{BG} = \frac{AN}{AB}$.*

Thales's theorem shows proportionality between parallel lines. For example, using the equation ($\frac{AP}{AG} = \frac{NP}{BG}$) from the theorem, we can find that $NP = \frac{AP \times BG}{AG}$. If $BG = AG = \gamma$, then $NP = AP$. Thus, $NP = PK$ because ABF is an isosceles triangle. Similarly, we have $MQ = QR = QD$ as shown in Fig. 1(b).

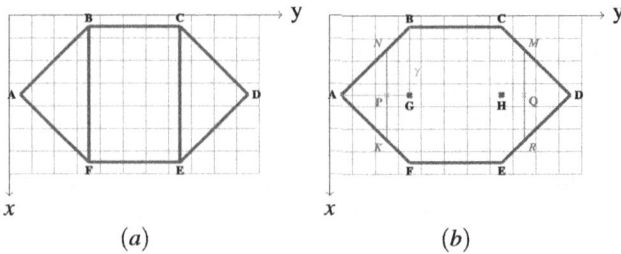

Fig. 1. Hexagon ABCDEF

3 Method Description

This section explains our method which involves placing a virtual hexagonal grid on the binary image and computing the rate of lit pixels in each cell. The dual of a hexagonal cell is computed when its lit pixel rate exceeds a reference rate. The hexagonal Hough transform method is applicable to binary images. Depending on the type of image (classique, multiband, RADAR), the corresponding pre-processing must be applied to obtain a binary image where the objects of interest are contrasted against the background.

3.1 Virtual Hexagonal Grid

Designing a virtual hexagonal grid using the image space mesh involves dividing an image into hexagonal cells and positioning these cells in such a way that they cover the image consistently. In this paper, the virtual hexagonal grid consists of hexagonal cells with the same characteristics. It is therefore a regular mesh(Illustrated in Fig. 2(a)).

```
Function mesh(image, γ : integer) : table of integer
    %γ is the size of hexagonal mesh;
    Variables: tab : table of 3 integers ;
    Output:    tab : table of 3 integers;
    Begin
        Nl ← the height of the image in pixels;
        Nc ← the width of the image in pixels ;
        tab[0] ← γ;
        tab[1] ← Nl mod(2γ−2);% residues on the height
        tab[2] ← Nc mod(4γ−2);% residues on the width
        Return: tab;
    end
end
```

Algorithm 1: Hexagonal mesh function

The Algorithm 1 is used for virtual hexagonal grid conception. With input parameters (γ and image) the Algorithm 1 returns an array of 3 integers. The first value in the array is γ expressed in pixels and noted px, the second and third values are the row residuals and column residuals, respectively.

3.2 Algorithm for Hexagonal Selection

The criteria for selecting a hexagon from the hexagon grid is the lit pixel rate in the hexagon. This rate is calculated with the Algorithm 4. It should be noted that for a

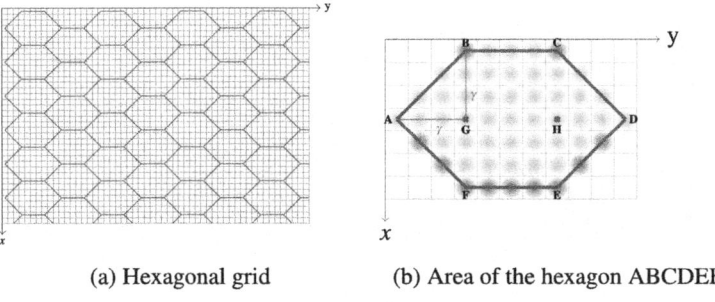

(a) Hexagonal grid   (b) Area of the hexagon ABCDEF

Fig. 2. Hexagonal mesh

given hexagon of the grid, all the pixels are not considered in the calculation of the rate. In Fig. 2(b) the pixels of green color are those considered in the computation. The others will be taken into account in the neighboring hexagons, as illustrated in Fig. 3. The exclusion of the red and magenta color pixels (with Algorithm 2) makes it possible not to consider twice the same pixel in two different hexagons.

```
Function Relate(A, B : tables of two integers) : list
    Variables: MAT : an integer couple list;
    Begin
        MAT ← points (pixels) coordinates
        between A and B, A and B excluded ;
        Return: MAT;
    end
end
```

Algorithm 2:   Relate pixels between A and B

3.3 Analytical Straight Line Recognition in a Virtual Hexagonal Mesh

The Algorithm 4, is the complete algorithm proposed for straight-line recognition in a hexagonal grid. Threshold, α, and γ are the input parameters of the Algorithm 4. The duals of the selected hexagons are computed with Algorithm 3 in the accumulator to determine the highest votes.

```
Procedure Acc_update(): void
    % Updating the accumulator
    if 0 ≤ i ≤ Nl and 0 ≤ j ≤ Nc then
        if img[i, j] ≠ 0 then
            for itheta between 0 and accum_row do
                theta ← itheta × dtheta;
                rho ← j × cos(theta) + i × sin(theta);
                irho ← int(rho);
                if irho > 0 and irho < accum_column then
                    | accum[itheta][irho] ← accum[itheta][irho] + 1
                end if
            end for
        end if
    end if
End
```

Algorithm 3:   Updating the accumulator data.

```
Function Hexagonal(imge,γ,α,threshold):table
    Pre-condition: 2 ≤ γ ≤ min(Nl+2/2 ; Nc+2/2), 0 ≤ α ≤ 1, 0<threshold
    Variables: tab : table of 6 integers ; A, B, C,D, E, F, G, H : tables of two integers;
    accum_ligne, accum_colon, irho, Nl, Nc : integers; accum : accumulator ; Seuil, α, dtheta, drho, rho,
    theta, DE : reels;
Begin
    Nl ← number of rows of image; Nc ← number of columns of image; % the dimensions of the image ;
    α = 0.8 % The rate of lit pixels from which the hexagon is selected ; threshold ← 150 % the minimum
    number of votes ;
    accum_row ← 180 ; accum_column ← E(√(Nc² + Nl²)); % the dimensions of the matrix ''accum'';
    γ ← 3; dtheta = π/180 ; tab ← mesh(image,γ) ; Ht ← Nl−tab[3]; La ← Nc−tab[4]; H1 ← Ht+2γ−2; L1 ← La+4γ−2;
    for  3γ−2 ≤ y ≤ L1 with the step of 4γ−2 do
        for  2γ−2 ≤ x ≤ H1 with the step of 2γ−2 do
            A[0] = x−tab[0]+1 ;  A[1] = y−3tab[0]+2 ;  B[0] = x−2tab[0]+2 ;  B[1] = y−2tab[0]+1 ;  C[0] = x−2tab[0]+2 ;
            C[1] = y−tab[0]+1 ;  D[0] = x−tab[0]+1 ;  D[1] = y ;  E[0] = x ;  E[1] = y−tab[0]+1 ;  F[0] = x ;
            F[1] = y−2tab[0]+1 ;  G[0] = x−tab[0]+1 ;  G[1] = y−2tab[0]+1 ;  H[0] = x−tab[0]+1 ;  H[1] = y−tab[0]+1 ;
            if count(img, A,B, D, E, F, G, H) ≥ α then
                MAT1 ← Relate(A,F); MAT2 ← Relate(F,E); MAT3 ← Relate(E,D);
                for  A[1] ≤ j ≤ D[1] do
                    if A[1] ≤ j ≤ G[1]−1 then
                        NP ← |j−A[1]|
                        for  A[0]−NP ≤ i ≤ A[0]+NP do
                            if (i,j) is an element of MAT1 then
                                do nothing;
                            else
                                Acc_update();
                            end if
                        end for
                    end if
                    if G[1] ≤ j ≤ H[1] then
                        for  B[0] ≤ i ≤ F[0] do
                            if (i,j)is an element of MAT2 then
                                do nothing;
                            else
                                Acc_update()
                            end if
                            ;
                        end for
                    end if
                    if H[1] ≤ j ≤ D[1] then
                        MQ ← |j−D[1]|
                        for  A[0]−MQ ≤ i ≤ A[0]+MQ do
                            if (i,j)is an element of MAT3 then
                                do nothing;
                            else
                                Acc_update()
                            end if
                            ;
                        end for
                    end if
                end for
            end if
        end for
    end for
    for  γ−1 ≤ y ≤ L1 with the step of 4γ−2 do
        for  γ−1 ≤ x ≤ H1 with the step of 2γ−2 do
            A[0] = x−tab[0]+1 ;  A[1] = y−3tab[0]+2 ;  B[0] = x−2tab[0]+2 ;  B[1] = y−2tab[0]+1 ;  C[0] = x−2tab[0]+2 ;
            C[1] = y−tab[0]+1 ;  D[0] = x−tab[0]+1 ;  D[1] = y ;  E[0] = x ;  E[1] = y−tab[0]+1 ;  F[0] = x ;
            F[1] = y−2tab[0]+1 ;  G[0] = x−tab[0]+1 ;  G[1] = y−2tab[0]+1 ;  H[0] = x−tab[0]+1 ;  H[1] = y−tab[0]+1 ;
            if count(img, A,B, C, D, E, F, G, H) ≥ α then
                MAT1 ← Relate(A,F); MAT2 ← Relate(F,E); MAT3 ← Relate(E,D);
                for  A[1] ≤ j ≤ D[1] do
                    if A[1] ≤ j ≤ G[1]−1 then
                        NP ← |j−A[1]|
                        for  A[0]−NP ≤ i ≤ A[0]+NP do
                            if (i,j) is an element of MAT1 then
                                do nothing;
                            else
                                Acc_update()
                            end if
                            ;
                        end for
                    end if
                    if G[1] ≤ j ≤ H[1] then
                        for  B[0] ≤ i ≤ F[0] do
                            if (i,j) is an element of MAT2 then
                                do nothing;
                            else
                                Acc_update();
                            end if
                        end for
                    end if
                    if H[1] ≤ j ≤ D[1] then
                        MQ ← |j−D[1]|
                        for  A[0]−MQ ≤ i ≤ A[0]+MQ do
                            if (i,j) is an element of MAT3 then
                                do nothing;
                            else
                                Acc_update()
                            end if
                            ;
                        end for
                    end if
                end for
            end if
        end for
    end for
    Search for maxima in the accumulator ;
    Line drawing ;
end
```

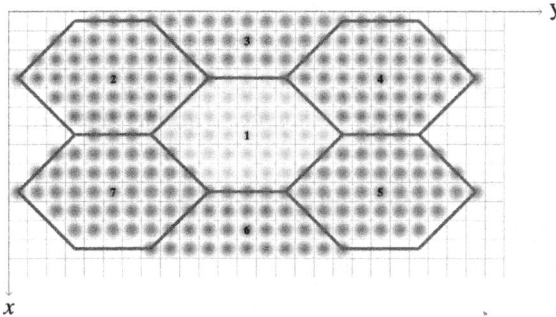

Fig. 3. A selection of hexagonal cells

3.4 Complexity

The Algorithm 4 for the hexagonal Hough transform calls several functions:

- the *mesh* function (Algorithm 1) with complexity $O(1)$.
- the *count* function (Algorithm 4) with complexity $O(S_H) = O(4(\gamma-1)(\gamma-\frac{1}{2})) = O(\gamma^2)$.
- the *Relate* function (Algorithm 2) with complexity $O(1)$.
- the *Acc_update* function (Algorithm 3) with complexity $O(1)$.

The Algorithm 4 of the Hexagonal Hough Transform begins with the initialization of variables and the array *tab*, as well as the calculation of the image and accumulator dimensions, all of which have a constant cost, hence $O(1)$. Then, it calls the *mesh* function whose complexity is $O(1)$.

Inside the main loops, there are two nested loops iterating over the points inside each hexagon, inside which are constant cost operations and the *Acc_update* function of complexity $O(1)$. The complexity of these loops is therefore $O(4(\gamma-1)(\gamma-\frac{1}{2})) = O(\gamma^2)$.

Thus, the cost of the two main nested loops traversing the hexagons of the grid, whose total number of iterations depends on the size of the image and the size of the hexagonal cells, containing a block of assignment operations of constant cost, a condition test on the *count_hex* function of complexity $O(\gamma^2)$, three assignments calling the *Rely* function of constant cost, the two nested loops of cost $4(\gamma-1)(\gamma-\frac{1}{2})$ traversing the pixels inside the hexagon, is $Nl/(4\gamma-2) \times Nc/(2\gamma-2) \times (1+4(\gamma-1)(\gamma-\frac{1}{2}) + 1 + 4(\gamma-1)(\gamma-\frac{1}{2}))$, therefore the complexity is $O(Nl/(4\gamma-2) \times Nc/(2\gamma-2) \times (1 + 4(\gamma-1)(\gamma-\frac{1}{2}) + 1 + 4(\gamma-1)(\gamma-\frac{1}{2}))) = O(Nl \times Nc)$.

Considering these points, the total complexity of the Hexagonal Hough Transform Algorithm 4 algorithm is $O(Nl \times Nc)$, where Nl and Nc are the image dimensions. This corresponds to the complexity of the standard Hough transform.

4 Simulation and Discussions

The Python programming language was utilized to implement the preceding algorithms. In order to carry out the simulation, a computer with the following specifications was used:

- Processor: Intel(R) Core(TM) i5 CPU M 480 @ 2.67 GHz 2.67 GHz
- Ram memory: 3.79 Go
- Operating System: kali linux, 64 bits.

Lemma 1. *Let γ be the size of an hexagon. The hexagon's surface S_H, represented by the green part of Fig. 2(b), is calculated using the following formula:*

$$S_H = 4(\gamma-1)(\gamma-\frac{1}{2}) \qquad (3)$$

Proof. (Lemma 1). Consider γ the size of the Hexagon.

- calculation of the surface S_r of the rectangle in which the hexagon is inscribed: $S_r = L \times l = (3\gamma-1)(2\gamma-1)$ where $L = (3\gamma-1)$ and $l = (2\gamma-1)$ represent, respectively the length and the width of the rectangle.
- calculation of the surface S_t of the four right-angled triangles (at the vertices of the rectangle): $S_t = 4(\frac{\gamma^2-\gamma}{2})$
- calculation of the surface S_e of the set of excluded pixels: $S_e = (\gamma-1) + 2 \times (\gamma-1) + 2 = 3\gamma - 1$ where $(\gamma-1)$ represents the number of red pixels at the bottom of the Hexagon, $2 \times (\gamma-1)$ represents the number of magenta color pixels on the left and right sides of the hexagon and end, 2 represents the two red pixels at the top of the Hexagon.
- calculation of the surface of the hexagon (only the green part of Fig. 2(right)): $S_H = S_r - (S_t + S_e)$.
  Which gives after simplification and factorization, $S_H = 4(\gamma-1)(\gamma-\frac{1}{2})$ □

For instance, for $\gamma = 4$, $S_H = 4(4-1)(4-\frac{1}{2}) = 4 \times 3 \times 3.5 = 42$ px^2 as shown in the Fig. 2(b). The unit of measurement for surface area is in pixels squared (px^2).

We simulated these algorithms on a building image presented in Fig. 5(a) and on a road image presented in Fig. 6(a). On this classique image, pre-processing was applied with the Canny filter (threshold between 500 and 200) to get edges. The resulting images on Fig. 5(b) and Fig. 6(b) are binaries. Algorithm 4, is applied to the resulting binary image to recognize straight lines. In all the following, the detected digital lines on images are highlighted in green.

4.1 The Case of a Building Image

We vary the surface of the grid hexagons as well as the rate of lit pixels in the hexagons.
The number of detected lines and the execution time of Algorithm 4, are summarized in the Table 3, in appendix.

Analysis of these results shows that if the hexagon surface is increasing, the execution time decreases in most of the cases, as illustrated on Fig. 4(right). Likewise, if the rate of light pixels is increasing, the execution time decreases in most cases, as illustrated on Fig. 4(left). As for the number of lines detected, it changes with the variation of the surface of the hexagon and decreases when the Rate α increases.

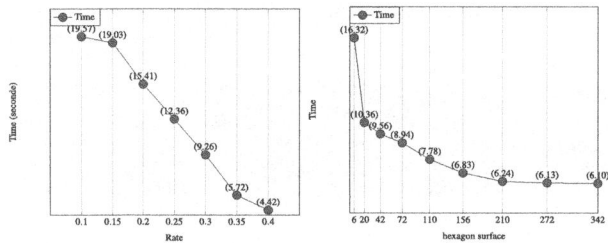

Fig. 4. Building's case: (left) execution time varies according to the rate and the parameters (threshold = 200, $\gamma = 4$); (right) Execution time varies according to the hexagon surface with the parameters (threshold = 200, $\alpha = 0.3$)

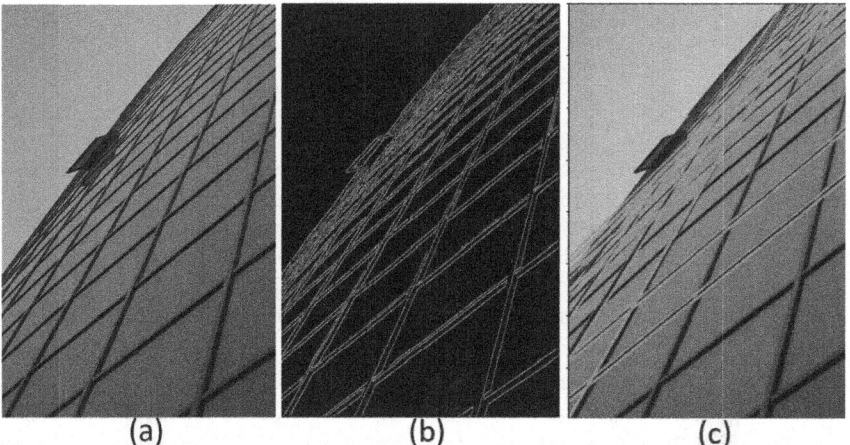

Fig. 5. Straight lines detected on the building with the parameters (threshold = 300, $\alpha = 0.2$, $\gamma = 2$)

4.2 The Case of a Road Image

The experimental results are summarized in the Table 4. The analysis of these results shows that the execution time decreases as the surface of the hexagon increases (we can see these results on Fig. 7(left)). Similarly, if the rate α increases, the execution time decreases (Fig. 7(right)), as well as the number of lines detected (Fig. 7(between)).

4.3 Comparison of Hexagonal Hough Transform and Standard Hough Transform

In order to accentuate the merits inherent in our approach as opposed to the conventional Hough transform, we will undertake a thorough comparative analysis. This involves leveraging a comprehensive evaluation to underscore the distinctive benefits of our method. To facilitate this, we will employ an image of a road (Fig. 6), strategically chosen to serve as a pertinent example for our investigation.

Fig. 6. Straight lines detected on road with the parameters (threshold = 100, $\alpha = 0.1$, $\gamma = 2$)

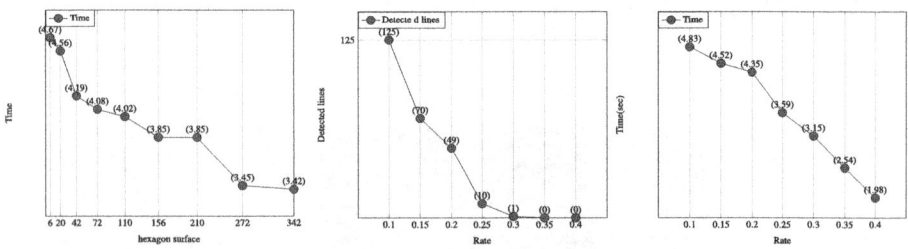

Fig. 7. The road image: (left) the execution time depending on hexagon surface with the parameters (threshold = 100, $\alpha = 0.1$); (between) detected lines depending on the rate with the parameters (threshold = 90, $\gamma = 4$); (right) execution time depending on rate with (threshold = 90, $\gamma = 4$)

The detection is accurate and reasonably fast when the threshold of standard Hough Transform is set high (greater than 100 votes). Table 1 displays the results of using a threshold of 100 votes, where 10 lines were detected in 1.2 s, or 0.12 s per line. On the other hand, the detection deteriorates for lower thresholds, as shown in Fig. 8(b). The latter (Fig. 8(b)) is the result of the standard Hough Transform algorithm with a threshold of 20 votes. With this threshold, 7581 lines were detected in 1.35 s, as illustrated in the first line of the Table 1.

One of the distinct advantages inherent to our proposed method resides in its remarkable flexibility, which can be attributed to the diverse range of input parameters it accommodates. In addition to the pivotal threshold parameter, we have ingeniously incorporated two supplementary parameters, denoted as α and γ. This astute inclusion further empowers users by granting them the ability to finely manipulate and calibrate the behavior of the method to suit specific contexts. The strategic utilization of these parameters presents a unique opportunity to enhance the outcomes delineated in the reference Table 1. By artfully adjusting the values of α and γ, a comprehensive spectrum of optimizations becomes attainable. This dynamic control over the input parameters not only refines the precision and efficacy of our method but also opens avenues for tailoring it to a multitude of scenarios, thereby bolstering its versatility.

In configuring the parameters to specific values (threshold = 50, $\gamma = 2$, $\alpha = 0.4$), our method detected 10 straight lines in an execution time of 0.84 s. This pivotal achievement is conspicuously showcased in Table 2. In stark comparison, the conventional algorithm took 1.2 s to achieve the same detection result. This substantial improvement is further quantified through the calculation of the acceleration factor denoted as A, where $A = \frac{T_s}{T_h} = \frac{1.2}{0.84} = 1.42$ (T_h represents the execution time of our method's algorithm, while T_s signifies the execution time of the standard algorithm). The fact that this acceleration factor surpasses 1 underscores a clear and tangible enhancement in the swiftness of straight-line detection. Notably, this accelerated performance isn't the sole advantage. The quality of detection is equally exceptional, as evidenced by the resultant Fig. 8(a). The lines demarcating the road's edges are impeccably detected and delineated. This visual validation harmoniously complements the quantitative results, corroborating the robustness and efficacy of our method. When we further lower the threshold to 20 votes, $\gamma = 3$ and $\alpha = 0.35$, 44 lines are detected in 0.53 s as illustrated in the Table 2.

Table 1. Results with Standard Hough Transform applied to a road image(time1 = time of all detected lines; time2 = single line detection time)

Threshold	number of detected lines	time1(sec)	time2(sec)
20	7581	1.35	0.00017
100	10	1.2	0.12

Table 2. Results with Hexagonal Hough Transform applied to a road image(time1 = time of all detected lines; time2 = single line detection time)

γ	$S_H(px^2)$	α	Threshold	number of detected lines	time1(sec)	time2(sec)
2	6	0.4	50	10	0.84	0.084
3	20	0.35	20	44	0.53	0.012

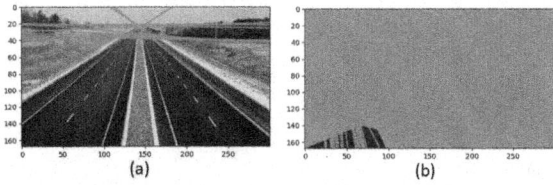

Fig. 8. (a) With Hexagonal Hough Transform (Threshold = 50, $\gamma = 2$, $\alpha = 0.4$); (b) With Standard Hough Transform (Threshold = 20)

The judicious selection of parameters ushered in a significant revolution in the detection process. The execution time was notably reduced, underscored by the acceleration factor, and the precision of detection, as exemplified in the visual output, stands as a testament to the prowess of our method in enhancing both speed and accuracy in line detection.

5 Conclusion and Perspectives

The method of straight-line recognition in an image by the Hough transform is simple and insensitive to noise. It is applicable to almost any type of image and allows you to vary many parameters.

In this paper, analytical straight-line recognition was treated using the Hough transform method on a virtual hexagonal mesh. We have seen that the hexagonal grid has several advantages in the field of image processing. Algorithms based on the standard Hough transform have been proposed to compute the duals of the selected hexagons in order to update the accumulator.

At the end of the analysis of the results of the simulations, there emerges a possibility of reducing the computation time.

Future works will center on enhancing these algorithms by concentrating on execution time refinement through the implementation of parallel programming. Also, we will study the possibility of extending this approach to other types of shapes or patterns beyond straight lines. Additionally, attention will be directed towards integrating Region Of Interest (ROI) practices within image processing to streamline performance. Furthermore, the introduction of artificial intelligence algorithms will be explored as a means to advance these methodologies.

6 Appendix

Table 3. (left) Results with Algorithm 4 applied to a building image, with the parameters (threshold = 200 and $\alpha = 0.3$); (right) Results with Algorithm 4 applied to a building image, with the parameters (threshold = 200 and $\gamma = 4$)

γ	$S_H(px^2)$	number of detected lines	time(sec)
2	6	135	16.32
3	20	27	10.36
4	42	46	9.56
5	72	52	8.94
6	110	34	7.78
7	156	44	6.83
8	210	27	6.24
9	272	38	6.13
10	342	17	6.10

α	number of detected lines	time(sec)
0.10	492	19.57
0.15	441	19.03
0.20	278	15.41
0.25	197	12.36
0.30	46	9.26
0.35	0	5.72
0.40	0	4.42

Table 4. (left) Results with Algorithm 4 applied to a road image, with the parameters (threshold = 100 and $\alpha = 0.1$); (right) Results with Algorithm 4 applied to a road image, with the parameters (threshold = 90 and $\gamma = 4$)

γ	$S_H(px^2)$	number of detected lines	time(sec)	α	number of detected lines	time(sec)
2	6	74	4.67	0.10	125	4.83
3	20	74	4.56	0.15	70	4.52
4	42	49	4.19	0.20	49	4.35
5	72	29	4.08	0.25	10	3.59
6	110	29	4.02	0.30	1	3.15
7	156	28	3.85	0.35	0	2.54
8	210	37	3.85	0.40	0	1.98
9	272	15	3.45			
10	342	16	3.42			

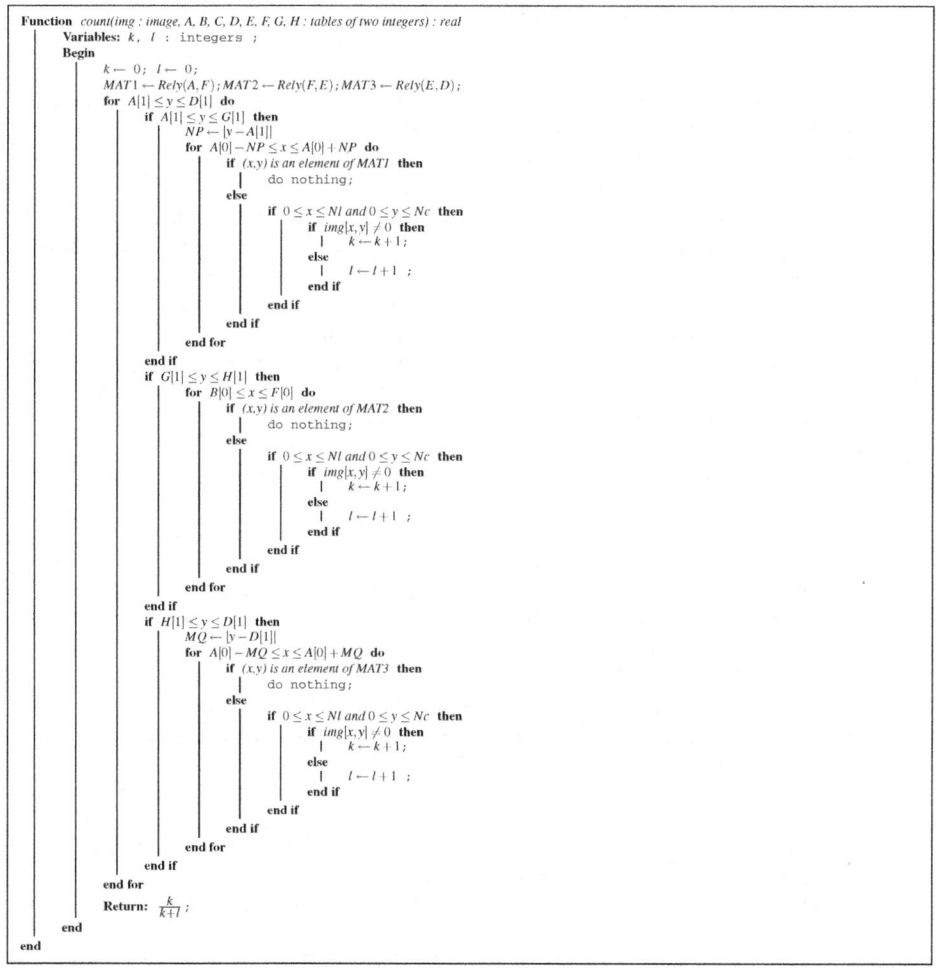

Algorithm 4: Computing the Rate for lit pixels

References

1. Reveilles, J.P.: Structures des droites discrètes. In Journées mathématique et informatique. Marseille-Luminy (1989)
2. Mejdani, S.E., Egli, R., Dubeau, F.: Champ de hauteurs de la transformée de Hough standard. Laboratoire MOIVRE, Département d'informatique, Faculté des sciences, Université de Sherbrooke, 2500, boul. de l'Université, J1K2R1, Sherbrooke (Québec), Canada (2005)
3. Hough, P.V.C.: Method and means for recognizing complex patterns. United States Pattent 3069654:47-64 (1962)
4. Duda, R.O., Hart, P.E.: Use of the hough transform to detect lines and curves in pictures. Commun. ACM **15**(1), 11–5 (1972)
5. Davies, E.R.: Finding ellipses using the generalized Hough transform. Pattern Recogn. Lett. **9**(2), 87–96 (1989). https://www.sciencedirect.com/science/article/pii/016786558990041X
6. Coelho, M., Sugimoto, D., Melo, G., Curtis, V., Bezerra, J.: A MapReduce based approach for circle detection. In: Proceedings of the 14th International Conference on Software Technologies - ICSOFT, pp. 454-459. INSTICC. SciTePress (2019)
7. Sere, A., Sie, O., Andres, E.: Extended standard hough transform for analytical line recognition. Int. J. Adv. Comput. Sci. Appl. (IJACSA) **4**(3), 256–266 (2013)
8. Geman, D., Jedynak, B.: An active testing model for tracking roads in satellite images. IEEE Trans. Pattern Anal. Mach. Intell. **18**(8), 1–14 (1996)
9. Benkouider, F., Hamami, L., Abdellaoui, A., Salmon, M.: Extraction de routes par classification supervisée et par réseaux de neurones artificiels á partir d'image spot : cas d'une ville oasienne (ALGÉRIE). Teledetection, Editions des Archives Contemporaines/Editions scientifiques GB/Gordon and Breach Scientific (2015). https://halshs.archives-ouvertes.fr/halshs-01133603
10. Sere, A., Traore, C., Traore, Y., Sie, O.: Towards traffic saturation detection based on the hough transform method. In: Arai, K., Kapoor, S., Bhatia, R. (eds.) FTC 2020. AISC, vol. 1289, pp. 263–270. Springer, Cham (2021). https://doi.org/10.1007/978-3-030-63089-8_16
11. Poncelet, N., Cornet, Y.: Transformée de Hough et détection de linéaments sur images satéllitaires et modèles numériques sur terrain. Unité de Géomatique, Département de Géographie, Université de Liège, Liège, Belgique. **54**, 145–56 (2010)
12. Hoppenot, P., Colle, E., Barat, C.: Off line localisation of a mobile robot using ultrasonic measures. Robotica **18**(8), 315–23 (2000)
13. Traore, C.A.D.G.: Application de la transformée de Hough rectangulaire à la détection de droites discrètes. Université Nazi BONI (2019)
14. Ouedraogo, M., Sere, A., Some, B.M.J., Traore, C.A.G.D.: Straight-line recognition using a triangular grid. In: Arai, K. (eds.) Advances in Information and Communication FICC 2022 Lecture Notes in Networks and Systems, vol. 438. Springer, Cham (2022). https://doi.org/10.1007/978-3-030-98012-2_45
15. Sere, A., Ouedraogo, M., Atiampo, A.L.: Parallel hough transform based on object dual and pymp library. Int. J. Adv. Comput. Sci. Appl. **13**(10) (2022). https://doi.org/10.14569/IJACSA.2022.0131084
16. Sere, A., Colazzo, D., Sie, O.: A hough transform based on a map-reduce algorithm. Int. J. Eng. Res. Appl. **6**(8), 7–15 (2016)
17. Curcio, C.A., Pohakr Sloan Jr, K.R.: Distribution of cones in human and monkey retina: individual variability and radial asymmetry (1987)
18. Asharindavida, F., Hundewale, N., Aljahdali, S.H.: Study on Hexagonal Grid in Image Processing (2012)
19. Middleton, L., Sivaswamy, J.: Edge detection in a hexagonal-image processing framework. Image Vision Comput. **19**(14), 1071–1081 (2001). https://www.sciencedirect.com/science/article/pii/S0262885601000671

20. Sahr, K.: Hexagonal discrete global grid systems for geospatial computing. Arch. Photogram. **22**, 363–376 (2011)
21. Varghese, P., Saroja, G.: Edge detection image operators in hexagonal pixel framework. Int. J. Adv. Res. Eng. Technol. **12**, 242–255 (2021)
22. Cha, J., Cofer, R.H., Kozaitis, S.P.: Extended Hough transform for linear feature detection. Pattern Recogn. **39**(5), 1034–1043 (2006)
23. Galambosy, C., Matas, J., Kittler, J.: Progressive probabilistic Hough transform Progressive probabilistic Hough transform for line detection. In: IEEE Computer Society Conference on Computer Vision and Pattern Recognition, vol. 1 (1999)
24. Ballard, D.: Hierarchical generalized Hough transform and line segment based generalized Hough transforms. Pattern Recogn. **15**, 277–285 (1982)
25. Kiryati, N., Eldar, Y., Bruckstein, A.M.: A probabilistic hough transform. Pattern Recogn. **24**(4), 303–316 (1991)
26. Luo, D., He, X., Teng, Q., Tao, Q.: Triplet circular Hough transform for circle detection. J. Electron. (China) **19**(4), 356–362 (2002)
27. Chia, A., Leung, M., Eng, H., Rahardja, S.: Ellipse detection with hough transform in one dimensional parametric space. In: IEEE International Conference on ICIP, vol. 5, pp. 333–336 (2007)
28. Lu, W., Tan, J.: Detection of incomplete ellipse in images with strong noise by iterative randomized Hough transform (IRHT). Pattern Recogn. **41**(4), 1268–1279 (2008)
29. Huang, C.L.: Elliptical feature extraction via an improved hough transform. Pattern Recogn. Lett. **10**(2), 93–100 (1989)
30. Daul, C., Graebling, P., Hirsch, E.: From the hough transform to a new approach for the detection and approximation of elliptical arcs. In: Computer Vision and Image Understanding, vol. 72, no. 3, pp. 215–236 (1998)
31. Kalviainen, H., Hirvonen, P., Xu, L., Oja, E.: Probabilistic and non-probabilistic Hough transforms: overview and comparisons. In: Image and Vision Computing, vol. 13, no. 4, pp. 239–252 (1995)
32. Khoshelham, K.: Extending generalized hough transform to detect 3D objects in laser range data. In: ISPRS Workshop on Laser Scanning 2007 and SilviLaser 2007, Espoo, finland, pp. 12–14 (2007)
33. Lopez-Krahe, J., Alamo-Cantarero, T., Davila-Gonzalez, E.: Discrete hough transform applied to small size pattern recognition. éditeur Télécom (1994)
34. Rhody, H., Carlson, C.F.: Hough Circle Transform, Center for Imaging Science, Rochester Institute of Technology (2005)
35. Svalbe, I.D.: Natural representations for straight lines and the Hough transform on discrete arrays. IEEE Trans. Pattern Anal. Mach. Intell. **11**(9), 941–950 (1989)
36. Maji, S., Malik, J.: Object detection using a max-margin Hough transform. In: CVPR 2009, pp. 1038–1045 (2009)
37. Pousset, P., Lopez-kraze, J., Cofer, R.H.: Transformée de hough discrète et bornée, application à la détection de droites parallèles et du réseau routier. Colloque TIPI, 5-N°4, 1988. éditeur Gretsi, Saint Martin d'Hères, France (1988)
38. Ballard, D.H.: Generalizing the Hough transform to detect arbitrary shapes. Pattern Recogn. **13**(2), 111–122 (1981)
39. Vijayarajeswari, R., Parthasarathy, P., Vivekanandan, S., Alavudeen Basha, A.: Classification of mammogram for early detection of breast cancer using SVM classifier and Hough transform. Measurement **146**, 800–805 (2019). ISSN 0263-2241. https://doi.org/10.1016/j.measurement.2019.05.083. https://www.sciencedirect.com/science/article/pii/S0263224119305275

40. Sere, A., Ouedraogo, F.T., Zerbo, B.: An improvement of the standard hough transform method based on geometric shapes. In: Arai, K., Kapoor, S., Bhatia, R. (eds.) FICC 2018. AISC, vol. 887, pp. 369–384. Springer, Cham (2019). https://doi.org/10.1007/978-3-030-03405-4_25
41. Bailey, D., Chang, Y., Le Moan, S.: Analysing arbitrary curves from the line hough transform. J. Imaging **6**, 26 (2020). https://doi.org/10.3390/jimaging6040026
42. Lin, G., Tang, Y., Zou, X., et al.: Fruit detection in natural environment using partial shape matching and probabilistic Hough transform. Precis. Agric. **21**, 160–177 (2020). https://doi.org/10.1007/s11119-019-09662-w
43. Liao, B., Li, J., Ju, Z., Ouyang, G.: Hand gesture recognition with generalized hough transform and DC-CNN using realsense. In: 2018 Eighth International Conference on Information Science and Technology (ICIST), Cordoba, Granada, and Seville, Spain, p. 84–90 (2018). https://doi.org/10.1109/ICIST.2018.8426125.
44. Zhao, K., Han, Q., Zhang, C.-B., Xu, J., Cheng, M.-M.: Deep hough transform for semantic line detection. IEEE Trans. Pattern Anal. Mach. Intell. **44**(9), 4793–4806 (2022). https://doi.org/10.1109/TPAMI.2021.3077129
45. Torrente, M.L., Biasotti, S., Falcidieno, B.: Recognition of feature curves on 3D shapes using an algebraic approach to Hough transforms. Pattern Recogn. **73**, 111–130 (2018). ISSN 0031-3203. https://doi.org/10.1016/j.patcog.2017.08.008. https://www.sciencedirect.com/science/article/pii/S0031320317303096
46. Zhang, C., Wang, F., Zou, Y., Dimyadi, J., Guo, B.H.W., Hou, L.: Automated UAV image-to-BIM registration for building façade inspection using improved generalised Hough transform, Autom. Construct. **153**, 104957 (2023). ISSN 0926-5805. https://doi.org/10.1016/j.autcon.2023.104957. https://www.sciencedirect.com/science/article/pii/S0926580523002170
47. Conti, C., Romani, L., Schenone, D.: Semi-automatic spline fitting of planar curvilinear profiles in digital images using the Hough transform. Pattern Recogn. **74**, 64–76 (2018). ISSN 0031-3203. https://doi.org/10.1016/j.patcog.2017.09.017. https://www.sciencedirect.com/science/article/pii/S0031320317303692
48. Soares, G.A., Abdala, D.D., Escarpinati, M.C.: Plantation rows identification by means of image tiling and hough transform. In: VISIGRAPP, vol. 4. VISAPP (2018)
49. Widyaningrum, E., Gorte, B., Lindenbergh, R.: Automatic building outline extraction from ALS point clouds by ordered points aided hough transform. Remote Sens. **11**(14), 1727 (2019). https://doi.org/10.3390/rs11141727
50. Liang, Q., et al.: Angle aided circle detection based on randomized Hough transform and its application in welding spots detection. Math. Biosci. Eng. **16**(3), 1244–1257 (2019)
51. Marzougui, M., Alasiry, A., Kortli, Y., Baili, J.: A lane tracking method based on progressive probabilistic hough transform. IEEE Access **8**, 84893–84905 (2020). https://doi.org/10.1109/ACCESS.2020.2991930
52. Winterhalter, W., Fleckenstein, F.V., Dornhege, C., Burgard, W.: Crop row detection on tiny plants with the pattern hough transform. IEEE Rob. Autom. Lett. **3**(4), 3394–3401 (2018). https://doi.org/10.1109/LRA.2018.2852841
53. Romanengo, C., Falcidieno, B., Biasotti, S.: Hough transform based recognition of space curves. J. Comput. Appl. Math. **415**, 114504 (2022). ISSN 0377-0427. https://doi.org/10.1016/j.cam.2022.114504. https://www.sciencedirect.com/science/article/pii/S0377042722002448
54. Yang, W., Li, Y., Hu, T., Fuchikami, R., Ikenaga, T.: Relative vectors clustering and temporal constraint based generalized Hough transform for high frame rate and ultra-low delay arbitrary shape detection. In: Proceedings of SPIE 12590, Third International Conference on Computer Vision and Information Technology (CVIT 2022), p. 1259002 (2023). https://doi.org/10.1117/12.2670011

55. Gabrielli, A., Alfonsi, F., Del Corso, F.: Simulated hough transform model optimized for straight-line recognition using frontier FPGA devices. Electronics **11**(4), 517 (2022). https://doi.org/10.3390/electronics11040517
56. Yang, C., Collins, J.: Improvement of honey bee tracking on 2D video with hough transform and kalman filter. J. Sign. Process. Syst. **90**, 1639–1650 (2018). https://doi.org/10.1007/s11265-017-1307-x
57. Freeman, A., Shi, W., Hwang, B.: Enhancing surveillance camera FOV quality via semantic line detection and classification with deep hough transform. In: Proceedings of the IEEE/CVF Winter Conference on Applications of Computer Vision (WACV) Workshops, January 2024, pp. 374–380 (2024)

Predicting the Rate of Aflatoxin Contamination in the White Corn Value Chain

Mahugnon Géraud Azehoun Pazou[✉], Julian Adjibi,
Régis Donald Hontinfinde, Elognissè Erasme Guérin Agossadou,
Vidédji Naéssé Adjahossou, Christian Djidjoho Akowanou,
and Macaire B. Agbomahena

National University of Science, Technology, Engineering and Mathematics
(UNSTIM), Abomey, Benin
geraud.pazou@unstim.bj
https://unstim.bj

Abstract. With the digital revolution, computer data is a resource of inestimable value. Businesses use them to understand consumer behavior, make informed decisions, and anticipate market trends. Governments rely on data to develop effective policies, monitor public health and manage resources. In this work, digital data collected in the agriculture sector allowed us to compare different machine learning models to predict aflatoxin infection levels in white corn crops. To do so, we use some qualitative and quantitative variables collected on the field, during a previous work. The compared methods are linear regression, random forests, artificial neural networks and support vector regression. The results of the analysis indicate that the random forest regression model stood out as the most effective in predicting aflatoxin infection levels. It posted an RMSE of 0.14 on the training set and 0.29 on the test set, accompanied by a coefficient of determination of 0.81, demonstrating its robustness on both data sets. This performance can be attributed to the ability of random forests to capture the complex and non-linear relationships between maize traits and aflatoxin levels. Evaluating the models on a separate test set confirmed their generalizability, that is, their ability to maintain accuracy with new data. This result constitutes a promising tool for actors in the agricultural sector, providing valuable information for risk management and strategic decision-making aimed at reducing consumer exposure to aflatoxin, thus contributing to the improvement of food safety and public health.

Keywords: machine learning · prediction models · random forest · aflatoxin contamination · white maize

---

Supported by UNSTIM.

1 Introduction

Given the escalating digital revolution, the importance of leveraging data has become paramount. Just as businesses use data for consumer insight and decision-making, governments use it to develop policies and monitor vital aspects such as public health and resource allocation. Maize (Zea mays L.) is the most produced cereal in the world, with a harvest of nearly 1,100 million tonnes in 2018/2019, followed by wheat (734 million tonnes) and rice (495 million tonnes) [16]. Africa consumes 30. 0% of the global production of maize, and sub-Saharan Africa accounts for 21. 0% of the consumption. About 14 countries in Africa consume between 85.0 and 95.0% maize as their staple food and are more inclined to consume white maize, with a consumption share of around 90.0%. [1].

Maize faces various diseases, such as corn rust (Puccinia sorghi), Corn downy mildew (Peronosclerospora sorghi), Corn bunt (Ustilago maydis), Corn cyst nematodes (Heterodera zeae), corn spots of maize disease (Cercospora zeae-maydis), as well as mycotoxin infections [19]. Some mycotoxins present in foods pose a serious threat to health. Among the most toxic are aflatoxins, produced by molds that grow in soil, rotting vegetation, and cereals, especially maize. These substances can have serious acute effects after ingestion, up to acute intoxication, and can be life-threatening by damaging the liver. Aflatoxins are also genotoxic, meaning that they can damage DNA and promote the development of cancer. They can also be found in the milk of animals fed with contaminated food [17]. Faced with the major health risks posed by mycotoxins, particularly aflatoxins, monitoring and controlling their presence in foods is of paramount importance.

The contamination of maize by aflatoxins is a global issue that has sparked numerous scientific investigations. Multiple studies have been conducted to better understand the factors that contribute to this contamination and to find potential solutions. For example, Wu et al. [18] demonstrated that natural contamination by aflatoxins has serious implications for both international trade and public health. They noted that more than 100 countries have implemented regulations on aflatoxins, although this also results in economic losses for exporting countries. The authors also note that even in regulated countries, many people consume uninspected maize, contributing to the adverse effects of aflatoxins on global trade and health.

Lauren et al. [9] studied a large outbreak of aflatoxicosis in rural Kenya in 2004, resulting in 317 cases and 125 deaths. They conducted a cross-sectional survey to assess maize contamination in markets and its link to this epidemic. Their results showed that 55% of the maize samples exceeded the Kenyan regulatory limit of 20 ppb of aflatoxin, with 35% at more than 100 ppb and 7% at over 1,000 ppb. They also observed that maize coming from affected areas was more likely to be contaminated, thus entering the distribution system and contributing to the widespread contamination of corn in markets.

Kamika et al. [8] studied the ubiquitous presence of aflatoxins in maize in the Democratic Republic of Congo, a problem that is both economic and public health. Their results showed that 32% of the maize samples collected were contaminated, with levels up to 103.89 μg/kg for total aflatoxins. This contamination was worsening throughout the supply chain, with 100% of the market samples showing levels up to 500 times higher than the maximum limit of 10 μg/kg established by the WHO. This significant increase ($p < 0.01$) between harvest and market distribution highlights the urgency of implementing strategies to control the proliferation of aflatoxins in corn.

Muga et al. [12] studied the impact of temperature, relative humidity, and moisture content on aflatoxin contamination of maize kernels. Their results showed that temperature and relative humidity had a significant effect, while moisture content did not. The contamination was higher at 30°C than at 20°C, and a relative humidity of 90% resulted in much higher aflatoxin levels than at 60%. They therefore concluded that maintaining a relative humidity below 60% makes it possible to significantly limit the contamination of corn grains by aflatoxins, thus ensuring their safety for consumption.

Kachapulula et al. [6] quantified aflatoxins in maize and peanuts in the three agroecologies of Zambia. Their results show that 17% of the market harvests exceeded the allowed limits, with higher contamination in the hottest agroecology (38%) than in the coldest and most humid (8%). They also observed that improper storage could increase contamination by more than 1000 times and that the structure of the fungal community influenced this increase. Their work highlights the need for aflatoxin management in Zambia, particularly through the use of atoxigenic biocontrol agents.

Hannah et al. [7] sought to determine the influence of post-harvest practices and storage conditions on the contamination of corn with aflatoxin in two specific countries. Their results showed that Makueni County had the highest positive sample rate, attributed to prolonged storage under poor conditions. In contrast, Baringo County showed less contamination, related to the harvest period. The authors observed that the storage type had a significant impact, explaining 11% of the variation, with burlap bags being the most contaminated. They concluded that proper drying of maize and its storage in airtight structures would reduce cases of aflatoxin contamination.

Various studies have also adopted the machine learning approach to address the challenges faced in the field of agriculture. Among these, we find that carried out by GENSERBE et al. [2] which focuses on the use of machine learning for mapping agropastoral resources in the Fitri region, northern Chad, using MSI Sentinel-2A images.

Hanadé et al. [3] proposed a modeling approach based on the assessment of drought vulnerability of agrosystems in the central Sahel, using machine learning techniques to analyze the extent of changes.

Recently, Makowski et al. [10] explored the application of supervised learning to simulate the impacts of climate change on agricultural yields, thus offering crucial perspectives for anticipating and mitigating these effects.

In this study, we attempt to automatically predict the occurrence of aflatoxin infection and the associated contamination level. To do this, we opted for an approach based on machine learning. We used data collected by Mugure et al. [7], who examined the impact of various factors such as temperature, relative humidity and moisture content on the contamination of maize. After carrying out a statistical analysis of these data to identify the main factors influencing aflatoxin contamination, we selected, implemented and compared four prediction models.

The paper proceeds as follows: Sect.2 outlines the materials and methods employed. Section3 presents and discusses the obtained results, leading to the conclusion in Sect. 4.

2 Material and Methods

2.1 Dataset

The data used in our study comes from the work of Mugure et al. [7] carried out on storage conditions and post-harvest practices affecting aflatoxin infection in the counties of Makueni and Baringo in Kenya. These data were obtained through surveys carried out by authors on farms in these regions, covering various aspects such as agricultural practices, storage methods, environmental conditions and other relevant factors.

The field surveys were designed to collect detailed information on farmers' agricultural practices, including cultivation methods, types of seeds used, pesticides applied, and harvesting practices. Additionally, data was collected on maize storage methods after harvest, such as the type of silos or bags used, temperature and humidity conditions, and duration of storage. These information were essential to assess potential risk factors for aflatoxin infection throughout the supply chain.

Alongside the field surveys, maize samples were taken from different farms for laboratory analyses. These analyzes included aflatoxin contamination tests, which were carried out to measure contamination levels in the corn samples collected. The data obtained from these analyzes were crucial to assess the presence and level of aflatoxin in the corn samples, thus forming the target variable of our study.

Among the variables in our dataset, we included information on the type of storage (in metal bins, open storage, plastic bags) which indicates the different types of containers used to store maize. In addition, we also took into account variables such as drying of the maize, and its conservation (poorly dried, wet, or poorly preserved).

Other important variables include information on storage practices, such as "Store bags on the ground," Dry grains on a tarpaulin, and "Dry grains on bare earth roofs," which describe methods of storage. In addition, we also included variables such as $Quality grains_{yes}$ and "Store bags on $wooden pallets_{yes}$ which provide information on the quality of the grains and the storage methods used.

Using these variables, we were able to characterize in detail the storage conditions and post-harvest practices associated with the maize studied. This characterization allowed us to explore the factors that influence aflatoxin levels in maize and develop accurate prediction models to identify potential risks of aflatoxin infection (Table 1).

Table 1. Variables and Types

Qualitative Variables	Quantitative Variables
Aflatoxin Level (ppb)	Type of Storage
Day - Positivity	Poorly Dried or Wet Corn
	Improper Storage of Corn
	Drying of Corn on the Ground
	Shelling of Wet Corn
	Processing Method
	Drying
	Shelling
	Canvas Bags
	Photo Bags
	Thatch from the Attic
	Attic Sheet Steel
	Waterproof Bins
	Airtight Storage
	Method of Conservation
	Store the Bags on the Ground
	Dry the Grains on a Tarpaulin
	Dry Grains on a Bare Earthen Roof
	Grain Quality
	Store Bags on Wooden Pallets

Table 2 presents descriptive statistics for two variables: aflatoxin level (in parts per billion, ppb) and number of days.

For the aflatoxin level, we can observe an average of 35.19 ppb, with a fairly high standard deviation of 50.55 ppb, indicating significant variability in the measurements. The minimum value is 0.23 ppb and the maximum value reaches 174.99 ppb. The 25%, 50% and 75% quartiles are 4.85 ppb, 6.19 ppb and 52.03 ppb respectively.

Concerning the number of days, the average is 107.7 days, with a standard deviation of 75.22 days. The minimum value is 30 days and the maximum value is 180 days, probably corresponding to the total duration of the study.

Table 2. Statistics for Aflatoxin Level (ppb) and Days variables

	Aflatoxin Level (ppb)	Days
count	139.000000	139.000000
mean	35.185633	107.697842
std	50.545483	75.222535
min	0.230000	30.000000
25%	4.850000	30.000000
50%	6.190000	180.000000
75%	52.030000	180.000000
max	174.990000	180.000000

2.2 Data Loading and Preprocessing

During the exploratory phase of the data, we carried out an in-depth visual analysis to better understand the characteristics of the target variable, namely the aflatoxin level (Fig. 1).

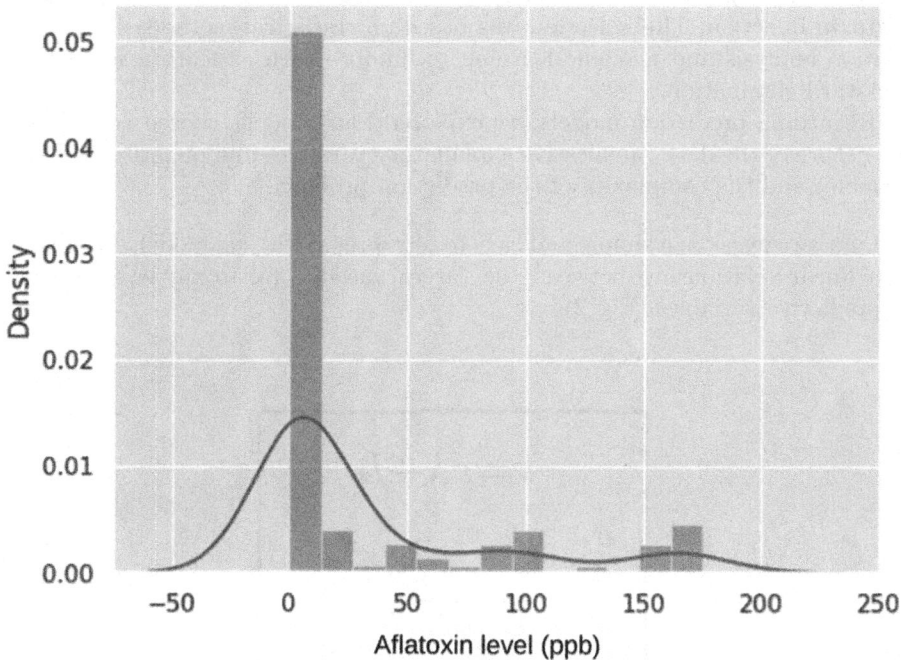

Fig. 1. Aflatoxin Level Histogram

Examination of the histogram of this variable revealed that it does not follow a normal distribution, which led us to reject traditional statistical methods for analyzing the effect of explanatory variables.

We then used box and whisker plots to visualize the impact of each of our explanatory variables on the target variable. This step allowed us to identify the most relevant variables to be included in the dataset used to train our predictive models. In addition, establishing a correlation matrix helped us to better understand the relationships between the different variables.

Once this initial exploration was completed, we proceeded to encode and standardize our variables using the One Hot Encoder library. Finally, we split our dataset into a training set (70%) and a testing set (30%), so that we can train our selected models on the training data. Data normalization was also performed to put all features on the same scale, which allowed us to avoid certain features dominating others in the model training process.

2.3 Data Exploration and Predictive Modeling

After data preprocessing, we conducted data analysis and modeling to develop prediction models for aflatoxin infection in maize. This step includes several sub-processes, including feature selection, model choice, model training and validation.

Data analysis consisted of selecting the most relevant features for predicting aflatoxin infection. This selection was based on statistical methods such as correlation analysis and machine learning techniques such as feature selection by backward elimination.

Regarding prediction models, we explored four models, chosen according to the nature of the data (qualitative explanatory variables and quantitative target variable) and the complexity of the prediction problem:

- Linear regression, a simple and easy to interpret statistical model, establishing a linear relationship between the target variable (aflatoxin level) and the predictive variables (Fig. 2).

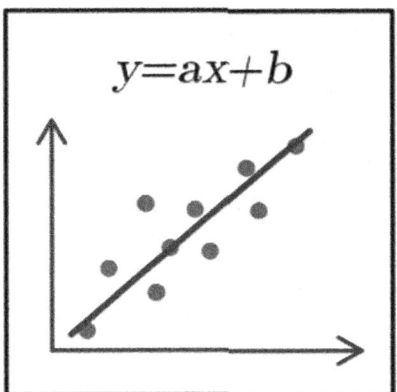

Fig. 2. Graphical representation of a linear regression [11]

- Random forests, a set of decision tree models providing a robust and efficient approach to managing complex datasets and capturing non-linear relationships (Fig. 3).

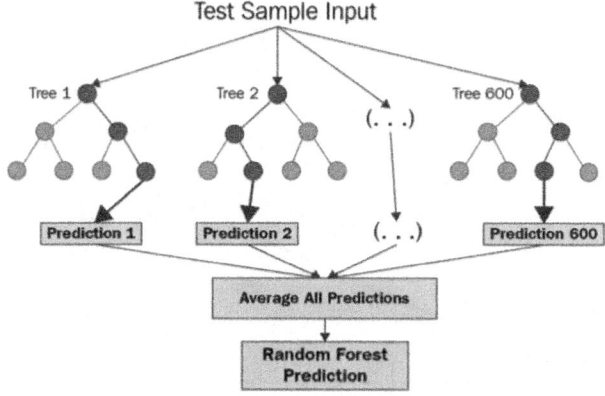

Fig. 3. Diagram above shows the structure of a Random Forest [13]

- Artificial neural networks (ANN), models inspired by the functioning of the human brain, capable of capturing complex and non-linear patterns from large data (Fig. 4).

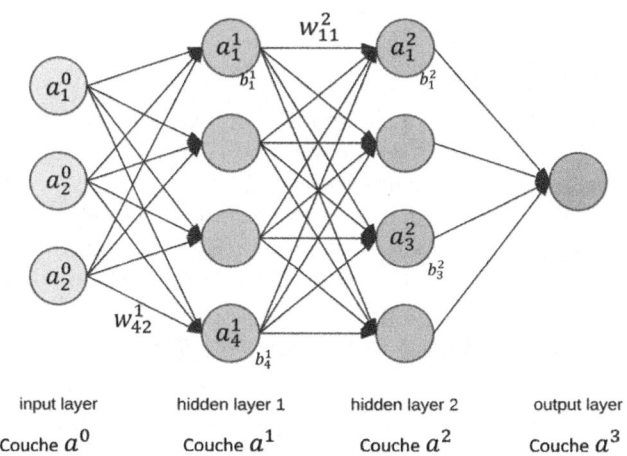

Fig. 4. Architecture of a multi-layer perceptron [14]

- Support vector regression (SVR), a machine learning method suitable for regression problems, particularly effective for dealing with non-linear data (Fig. 5).

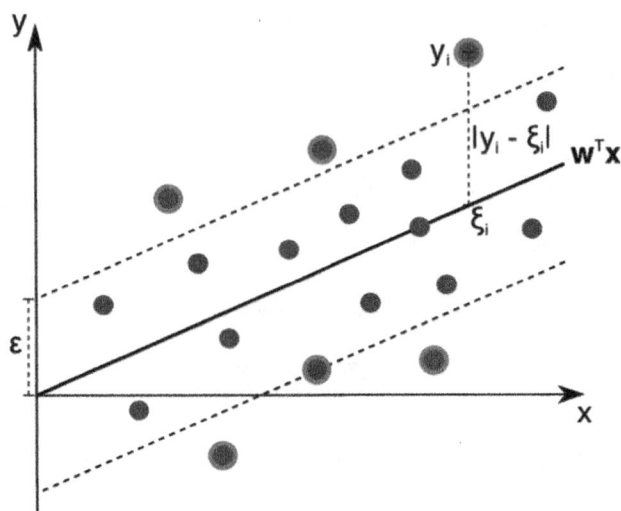

Fig. 5. Illustration of an SVR regression function [15]

We trained the models on the training dataset, using different optimization and hyperparameter tuning techniques to improve their performance.

2.4 Comparison Metric

We evaluated the performance of the models on a validation dataset to estimate their generalization capacity. We used metrics such as root mean square error (RMSE) and coefficient of determination (R^2).

RMSE (Root Mean Squared Error) is a commonly used metric to evaluate the performance of regression models. It measures the average difference between the values predicted by the model and the actual observed values. The lower the RMSE value is, the more accurate the model is in its predictions.

Mathematically, the RMSE is calculated as follows:

$$\text{RMSE} = \sqrt{\frac{\sum_{i=1}^{n}(y_i - \hat{y}_i)^2}{n}} \qquad (1)$$

where:

- $y_1, y_2, \ldots, y_n$ are the observed values
- $\hat{y}_1, \hat{y}_2, \ldots, \hat{y}_n$ are the predicted values
- n is the number of observations

The RMSE has the advantage of being in the same unit as the target variable, which facilitates the interpretation of the results. It further penalizes large prediction errors, making it a particularly suitable metric to evaluate the accuracy of the aflatoxin level prediction models in our study.

The coefficient of determination R^2 is a commonly used metric to evaluate the goodness of fit of a regression model. It measures the proportion of variance in the dependent variable (here, aflatoxin level) that is explained by the model. Mathematically, the R^2 is calculated as follows:

$$R^2 = \frac{\sum_{i=1}^{T}(y_i - \bar{y})^2}{\sum_{i=1}^{T}(y_i - \hat{y})^2} \qquad (2)$$

where:

- y_i are the observed values
- $\bar{y}$ is the average of the observed values
- $\hat{y}$ are the predicted values
- T is the total number of observations

The coefficient of determination R^2 varies between 0 and 1. A value of R^2 close to 1 indicates that the model explains a large part of the variance of the dependent variable, and therefore that the model has good predictive power. Conversely, a value close to 0 means that the model explains very little of the observed variance.

This metric will therefore be particularly useful to assess the overall quality of our aflatoxin level prediction models in the context of this study.

The in-depth analysis of performance metrics allowed us to objectively compare the models and select the one that offers the best predictions for our problem. This selected model will then constitute the basis of our final mathematical solution to estimate the aflatoxin level in corn.

2.5 Used Software and Tools

We implemented our models and metrics using the Python programming language, drawing on several key libraries. Pandas was used for manipulation and exploration of tabular data, while NumPy was employed for numerical calculations and processing data in the form of multidimensional arrays. Scikit-learn has played a crucial role in the application of machine learning algorithms such as linear regression, random forests, and neural networks, among others. For data visualization and graph creation to facilitate exploratory analysis, we used Matplotlib and Seaborn. The integration of these different Python libraries allowed us to efficiently carry out the different stages of developing our predictive models, ranging from data preprocessing to evaluating model performance.

3 Results and Discussion

3.1 Presentation of the Prediction Models Used

The analysis of the results made it possible to conclude that the random forest regression model (Random Forest Regressor) offers the best performance for predicting aflatoxin levels in maize. Indeed, this model obtained the lowest RMSE

(Root Mean Squared Error) value on the test set, indicating that it produces the most accurate predictions (see Table 3). Figure 6 presents the prediction accuracy of the different models.

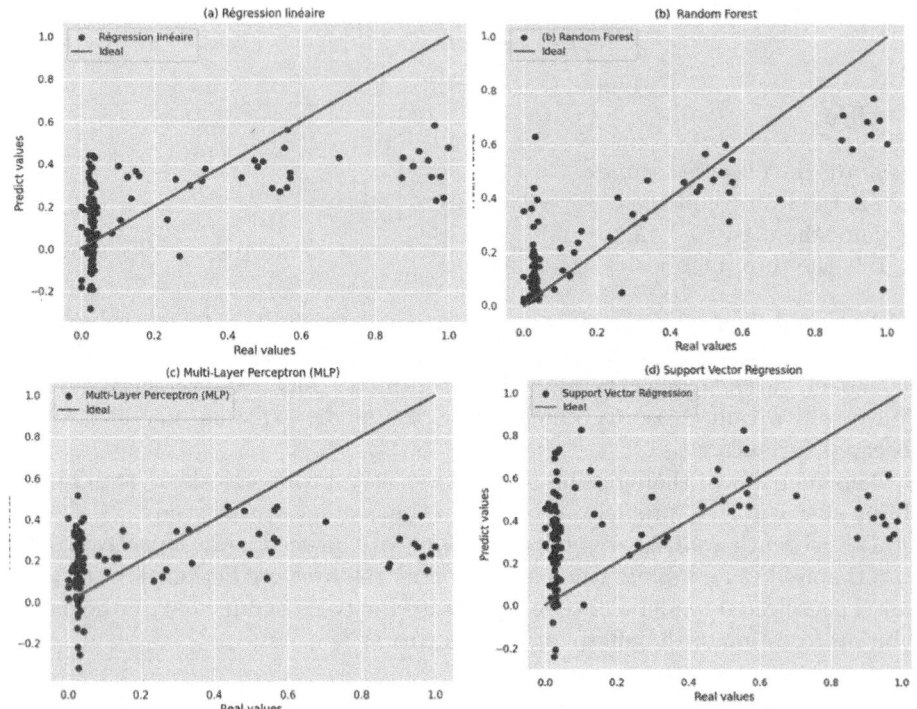

Fig. 6. Models Prediction accuracy: (a) Support Vector Regression (b) RandomForest Regression (c) Multi Layer Perceptron (d) Linear Regression.

Table 3. Metrics values for the different models

Models	Training		Test	
	R2	RMSE	R2	RMSE
Linear Regression	0.007	0.24	0.026	0.27
Random Forest Regressor	**0.81**	**0.14**	**0.81**	**0.29**
Support Vector Regression (SVR)	0.01	0.31	0.04	0.26
MLP Neural Network	4.63e−05	1.44	0.015	1.63

Several aspects deserve to be highlighted and interpreted in the results of this study:

The superiority of random forests can be attributed to their ability to capture the complex and nonlinear relationships between maize traits and aflatoxin levels. Random forests are robust to noisy data and can handle a large number of explanatory variables, making them a particularly suitable choice for this prediction problem.

Evaluating the performance of the models on a separate test set confirmed their generalization capacity, that is, their ability to maintain their accuracy when confronted with new data. This step is crucial to guarantee the robustness and reliability of the models developed in real conditions.

Finally, it should be emphasized that the validity of the results obtained is reinforced by their consistency with previous knowledge, in particular previous studies by MUGURE et al. [7] on storage conditions and practices post-harvest affecting aflatoxin infection in maize. This convergence between our results and existing research constitutes an additional confirmation factor of the relevance of our methodological approach and the reliability of our conclusions.

3.2 Pratical Implications for Farmers

Based on this study, farmers can reduce aflatoxin exposure by ensuring thorough drying of maize before storage, using airtight containers, maintaining clean and well-ventilated storage areas with low humidity, storing bags on wooden pallets instead of the ground, regularly inspecting stored maize, minimizing storage duration, and avoiding the shelling of wet maize. These practices, informed by our findings on the factors influencing aflatoxin levels, can significantly mitigate contamination risks, protecting both farmer livelihoods and consumer health.

4 Conclusion

In this study, we sought to use machine learning methods to predict aflatoxin levels in maize, which represents a major challenge for food security in the region. We explored several regression models, including linear regression, random forests, and neural networks, to evaluate their ability to accurately predict aflatoxin levels. Our results showed that random forest regression outperformed other models in terms of predictive performance, highlighting the importance of variables such as storage type and post-harvest practices in determining aflatoxin levels. This methodological approach constitutes a promising tool for actors in the agricultural sector, providing valuable information for risk management and strategic decision-making aimed at reducing consumer exposure to aflatoxins, and thus contributing to improving food safety and public health in the region.

References

1. Analyse de la taille et de la part du marché de la production de maïs en Afrique - Tendances et prévisions de croissance (2024–2029). https://www.mordorintelligence.com/fr/industry-reports/african-maize-market

2. Genserbe, B.M., Assoma, V.T., Kouame, K., N'guessan, B.V.H.: Machine learning appliquée aux images MSI Sentinel-2A pour la cartographie des ressources agropastorales dans le Fitri au nord du Tchad. Sciences Appliquées et de l'Ingénieur **5**(1), 57–64 (2023). issn: 2630-1164. http://publication.lecames.org/index.php/ing/article/view/29869
3. Hanadé Houmma, I., et al.: Drought vulnerability of central sahel agrosystems: a modelling-approach based on magnitudes of changes and machine learning techniques. Int. J. Remote Sens. **44**(14), 4262–4300 (2023). https://doi.org/10.1080/01431161.2023.2234094
4. Gouvernement du Bénin. Stratégie nationale pour l'e-Agriculture au Bénin 2020–2024. French (2020). https://faolex.fao.org/docs/pdf/ben210399.pdf
5. International Fund for Agricultural Development. International Fund for Agricultural Development. https://www.ifad.org/fr/web/operations/w/pays/benin
6. Kachapulula, P.W., et al.: Aflatoxin contamination of groundnut and maize in Zambia: observed and potential concentrations. J. Appl. Microbiol. **122**(6), 1471–1482 (2017). issn: 1364-5072. https://doi.org/10.1111/jam.13448. https://academic.oup.com/jambio/article-pdf/122/6/1471/47332725/jambio1471.pdf
7. Kamano, H.M., et al.: Storage conditions and postharvest practices lead to aflatoxin contamination in maize in two counties (Makueni and Baringo) in Kenya. Open Agric. **7**(1), 910–919 (2022). https://doi.org/10.1515/opag-2021-0054
8. Kamika, I., Ngbolua, H.N., Tekere, M.: Occurrence of aflatoxin contamination in maize throughout the supply chain in the Democratic Republic of Congo. Food Control **69**, 292–296 (2016). issn: 0956-7135. https://doi.org/10.1016/j.foodcont.2016.05.014. https://www.sciencedirect.com/science/article/pii/S0956713516302481
9. Lewis, L., et al.: Aflatoxin contamination of commercial maize products during an outbreak of acute aflatoxicosis in Eastern and Central Kenya. Environ. Health Perspect. **113**(12), 1763–1767 (2005). https://doi.org/10.1289/ehp.7998. https://ehp.niehs.nih.gov/doi/pdf/10.1289/ehp.7998
10. Makowski, D., Chen, M.: Apprentissage supervisé pour simuler l'effet du changement climatique sur les rendements agricoles. In: INRAE, AgroParisTech, Université Paris-Saclay, France (2024)
11. Module Régression Linéaire. Consulté le 11 avril 2024. https://www.privateteacher.ch/Module-Regression-Lineaire
12. Muga, F.C., Marenya, M.O., Workneh, T.S.: Effect of temperature, relative humidity and moisture on aflatoxin contamination of stored maize kernels. Bulgarian J. Agric. Sci. **25**(2), 271–277 (2019)
13. Random Forest Regression. Consulté le 11 avril 2024. https://levelup.gitconnected.com/random-forest-regression-209c0f354c84
14. Réseau de neurones : on va essayer de démystifier un peu tout ça. Consulté le 11 avril 2024. https://www.aspexit.com/reseau-de-neurones-onva-essayer-de-demystifier-un-peu-tout-ca-1/
15. Support Vector Regression (SVR): Illustration of an SVR regression function. Consulté le 11 avril 2024. https://www.researchgate.net/figure/Support-vector-regression-SVR-Illustration-of-an-SVR-regressionfunction-represented_fig12_248396465
16. Toutes les données sur la production céréalière. https://www.mccormick.it/fr/toutes-les-donnees-sur-la-production-cerealiere/
17. World Health Organization. Mycotoxines. https://www.who.int/news-room/fact-sheets/detail/mycotoxins

18. Wu, F.: Global impacts of aflatoxin in maize: trade and human health. World Mycotoxin J. **8**(2), 137–142 (2015). https://doi.org/10.3920/WMJ2014.1737. https://doi.org/10.3920/WMJ2014.1737
19. Yallou, C.G.: Le maïs au Bénin: atouts et perspectives. In: Direction de la recherche agronomique. https://www.fao.org/3/X5158F/x5158f0g.htm

The Impact of Agents Heterogeneous in Call Center Performance Measures

Mamadou Thiongane[✉], Mohamed M. Ould Deye, Modou Gueye, and Ndiouma Bame

Department of Mathematics and Computer Science, University Cheikh Anta Diop, Dakar, Senegal
{mamadou.thiongane,mohamed.oulddeye,modou2.gueye, ndiouma.bame}@ucad.edu.sn

Abstract. Modern call centers are highly complex queuing systems, in which there are several possible call types, and many agents groups. Due to this complexity, simulators are now preferred for their management than standard Erlang queuing models. Several studies have shown through data analysis that agents often have quite different speeds for processing a call type. However, this agent heterogeneity is often neglected, which is why most simulators have not been designed to use heterogeneous agents to process a service. In this work, we use simulation to study the impact of agent heterogeneity on the performance of call centers. We developed and integrated a module into the call center simulator, *ContactCenter*, which allows the use of heterogeneous agents to process a service. We have analyzed data collected from a real call center and have shown that agents have different processing speeds for handling a call type. We have modeled the distribution of arrivals, service times and patience times that will enable us to simulate this call center. Simulation result show that call center performance on a given day depends largely on the agents chosen to answer the calls.

Keywords: Agents Heterogeneous · Call Center · Real Data

1 Introduction

A call center is a set of resources for communication between an organization and its customers over the phone. Today, we also refer to them as *contact centers*, because agents can use other mediums of communication, such as post, e-mail, online chat, etc. Call center is widely used in various service and manufacturing industries. Effective call center management is a difficult task because of the considerable sources of uncertainty; these include call arrival rates, which typically vary over time and are stochastic, service times, which are random and whose distribution may depend on the type of call and the agent handling it, as well as agents who may be absent or may not follow their planned schedules [3,6,7,10,11,14]. Given to the complexity of modern call centers, simulators are much more widely used for call center management than standard Erlang models.

In this paper, we focus on the impact of agent heterogeneity on call center performance measures. We analyze data gathered at the call center of an information technology (IT) company in the Netherlands. This real call center setting is complex, consisting of many heterogeneous agents and multiple distinct call types. The data show that service times differ greatly across such agents. However, in call center management, this heterogeneity is often neglected, and it is often assumed that the distribution of call duration depends only on the type of call but not on the agent handling the call. That's why most of the simulators tools, such as *ContactCenters* [5], are not designed to take into account agent heterogeneity. They only allow the use of a single distribution of service time for a call type. To be more precise, the same distribution is used to generate service time for all agents that can serve a call type.

In this work, we will develop and add a module in *ContactCenters* that allows the specification of a distribution of service times for each pair (agent, call type). *ContactCenters* is a call center simulator developed with Java by the Stochastic Simulation Laboratory at the University of Montreal (Canada). It is also used by some companies to manage their call centers. We use this new version of the simulator and show that a simulation model that takes into account agent heterogeneity predicts call center performance better than a simulation model that ignores agent heterogeneity. However, before conducting the simulations, as a first step we will search through real data the distributions that best fit arrivals, service times, and patience times.

The remainder of this paper is structured as follows. Section 2 presents a literature review on agent heterogeneity in service systems, in particular for call centers. In Sect. 3, we describe and do a preliminary analysis of the data set that motivated this research. Section 4 present our call center modeling parameters, and the simulation experiments we conduct to show the impact of agent heterogeneity on call center performance. The conclusion is given in Sect. 5.

2 Litterature Review

To analyze call center operations, standard Erlang queueing models have been widely used. In these models, arrival are modeled as Poisson process, agent service times are modeled as independent, identically distributed exponential random variables with a constant mean. However, many studies have shown that the lognormal distribution is a remarkably good fit for the service-time distribution than the exponential distribution [4,7,11,15]. This is inevitably affecting call center performances. In queueing models, customer heterogeneity has received ample attention in both practice and theory. In contrast, server heterogeneity has received relatively scarce attention. There are not much research addressed on the statistical and practical implications of service time heterogeneity among agents. Some works on routing policies, which studied queueing models with heterogeneous servers, try to route incoming calls to minimize a performance measure, such as the average waiting time. Most of them try to find the optimal routing policies in large-scale systems under heavy-traffic conditions [1,2,8,9].

In general, these papers show that control decisions can actually benefit from agent heterogeneity, e.g., routing incoming calls to the fastest idle agents reduces customer waiting. Mehrotra et al. [13] do a numerical study to characterize overall performance in terms of customer waiting time and overall resolution rate. Wang et al. [16] study scheduling and routing strategies of heterogeneous agents in call centers. They construct an integer linear programming of the scheduling problem for call centers with agent heterogeneity, and combine the use of a discrete-event simulation model with an artificial bee colony algorithm to solve the model.

There is very little empirical research supporting that theoretical work. Gans et al. [7] analyze call-center data and identified both short-term and long-term factors associated with agent heterogeneity in practice. Ibrahim et al. [11] use mean service time from real data and propose a method to predict the variance of service times. Assuming that service times follow a lognormal distribution (that uses the mean and the predicted variance), they show through small simulation models that agents heterogeneity can have an impact on call center performance measures.

In this paper, we extend the theoretical research mentioned above with empirical work. We have analyzed data and shown that service times differ greatly across agents. We show through our data that the log-normal distribution fits service durations better than the exponential distribution, the call arrival follow a non-homogeneous Poisson process, and customers patience follow an exponential distribution. We will show through simulation that call center performance measures could be much closer to real performance when the agents heterogeneity is taken into account. Thus, we take a step forward to fill this gap in the literature.

3 Data and Analysis

In this section, we will describe the two datasets collected in the call center studied, and we will also perform an in-depth analysis of these data.

3.1 Datasets Description

In this work, we use two dataset collected by VANAD Laboratories located in Rotterdam, in The Netherlands. They were collected over the span of one year, ranging from January 1, 2014 to December 31, 2014. This center operates from 8 a.m to 8 p.m from Monday to Friday. Unlike most call center data, which are only aggregated data (that are not always complete to extract a day's parameters and performance measures), here we have call-by-call log data and agents activities data. In our data set, there are 27 call types. We call them T1, T2, $\cdots$, T27 from the one with the highest call volume to the one with the lowest. They are handled by a group of 312 agents. This includes part-time agents, full-time agents, agents that worked only for a few months and agents that worked in every month of the year. Each agent has a skill set, which consists of at least one skill. Not every agent has all the skills. In total, there are 2,983 distinct agent/call type combinations, where each combination corresponds to an agent handling a particular call type. Our data contains a total of 1,543,164 call logs and 1,639,770 activities logs.

The call-by-call data contains on each received call the following information: the call type, the arrival time, the date of the day, the desired service, the Voice Response Unit (VRU) entry and exit time. For the calls that have to wait, the data contains the queue entry time and the queue exit time. For each received call, we know whether it has been served or abandoned. When a call is abandoned, the time of abandonment is also known. Finally, for a served call, we have the started service time, the ended service time, and the ID of the agent who serve the call.

Activity data contains information on the activities carried out by an agent during a working day at the call center. This information includes the activity ID, the activity start time, the activity end time, and the agent ID.

3.2 Data Analysis

To sketch a temporal distribution of the workforce, we plot in Fig. 1 the average number of agents answering calls per weekday, with 95% confidence bands. We see that the number of agents is highly variable on Mondays, and that Fridays have the least number of agents, on average. In Fig. 2, we plot the total average call volume per weekday, including all call types. Consistent with Fig. 1, Fig. 2 shows that call volumes on Mondays exhibit the highest variance, and that call volumes on Fridays are lowest on average.

Figure 3 gives a scatter plot of the empirical means versus variances of service times for different call types in our data. Each point in the plot corresponds to a given (mean, variance) pair, corresponding to a given call type. Figure 3 shows that there are significant differences in means and variances across different call types. As expected, Fig. 3 shows that call types with longer durations generally exhibit higher variances.

Service time distributions for the same call type vary considerably depending on the agent. In Figs. 4 and 5, we illustrate this agent heterogeneity. We plot average service times for two call types: $T1$, which is handled by 286 agents, and $T2$, which is handled by 191 agents, as a function of the total number of calls answered (over the one-year period covered by our data) by each agent.

The horizontal line in each figure indicates the overall average service time across all agents, for each call type. Figures 4 and 5 show that there is significant variability in service times across all agents. Figures 4 and 5 also show that there are clearly clusters of agents who seem to perform in a roughly similar manner (having either shorter or longer than average service times). In general, agents who have handled many calls during the year are much faster on average than those who have handled few calls. The latter are either agents who have handled very few calls in general, or ones who have mostly handled calls of other types. To illustrate this, in Fig. 6, we plot the average service time of each months of some experienced agents and some new agents. As one can see from Fig. 6(a) the average service time of each experienced agents is different; furthermore, in Fig. 6(b), the average service time of new agents all exhibit a declining trend, which suggests that new agents learn over time, and their average service time decrease as they learn.

In Figs. 7 and 8, we plot the variances of service times for all agents handling call type $T1$ and $T2$, respectively, as a function of the total number of calls of that type answered by the agent. It appears that agents who have handled more calls tend to exhibit less variance in their service times. In other words, the larger dispersion is mainly exhibited by less experienced agents (those answering fewer calls). These Figures confirm that there are clear differences in variance of service times across agents.

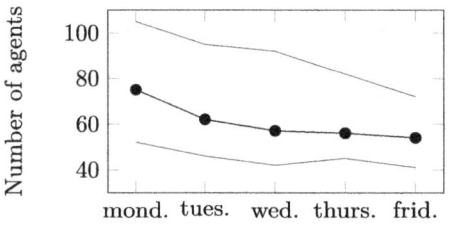

Fig. 1. Average number of agents per weekday and corresponding 95% confidence bands.

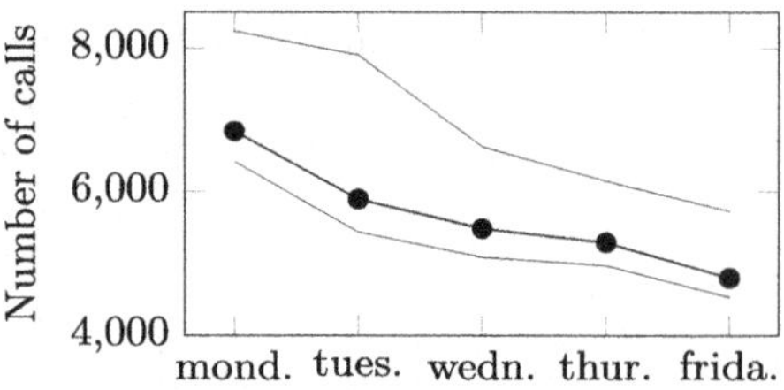

Fig. 2. Average number of calls per weekday and corresponding 95% confidence bands.

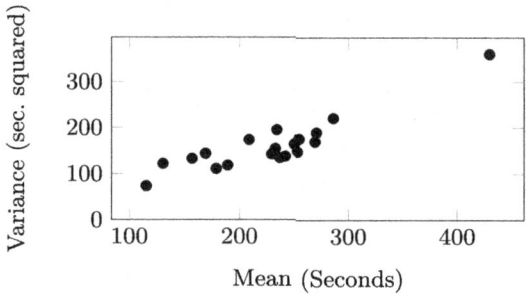

Fig. 3. Each point corresponds to a (mean, variance) pair for a given call type.

4 Call Center Modeling and Simulation Experiments

In this section, we present the call center parameters modeling, and we describe the simulation experiments that we conduct to evaluate the impact of agent heterogeneity on call center performances measures.

4.1 Call Center Modeling

As we said earlier, the call center studied in this work have $K = 27$ different call types. There is one waiting queue per call type. In this section, we describe how

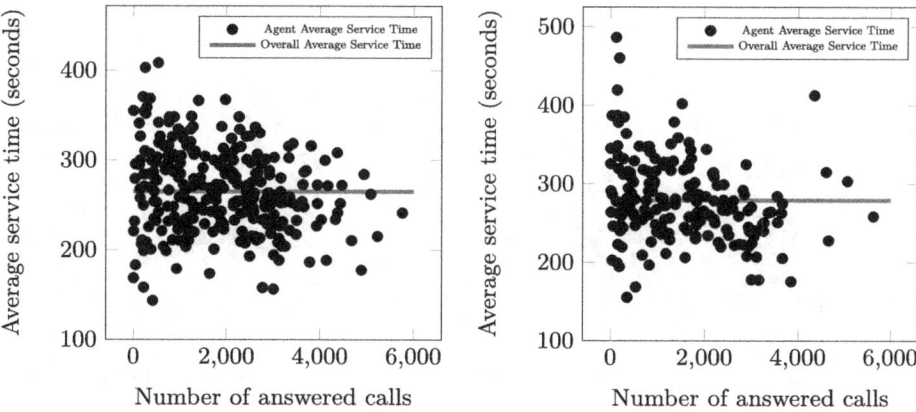

Fig. 4. Average service times for different agents handling type $T1$ calls as a function of the total number of calls answered per year.

Fig. 5. Average service times for different agents handling type $T2$ calls as a function of the total number of calls answered per year.

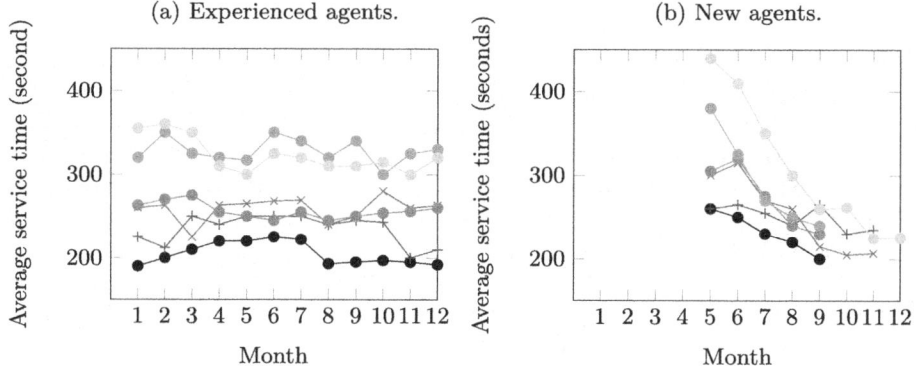

Fig. 6. Average service time per month of some agents.

we model call arrivals, service times, and patience times for use in a call center simulation. Note that in this section, we will report the results of modeling of one or two call types. However, it should be noted that the results are similar for all call types. It should also be noted that, prior to modeling, we removed the bad days from our dataset, i.e. holiday days and very special days. There are 21 such days in the year.

Arrival Process: Figure 9 and 10 shows the annual mean of arrival counts per period of 30 min and per weekday for call type T1 and call type T2, respectivrly. We see from these figures that the arrival behavior for Monday differs significantly from that of the other days and the arrival rate varies considerably during the day. Figure 11 shows the fit of call type T1 inter-arrival data with an exponential distribution. We observe that the exponential distribution fits the

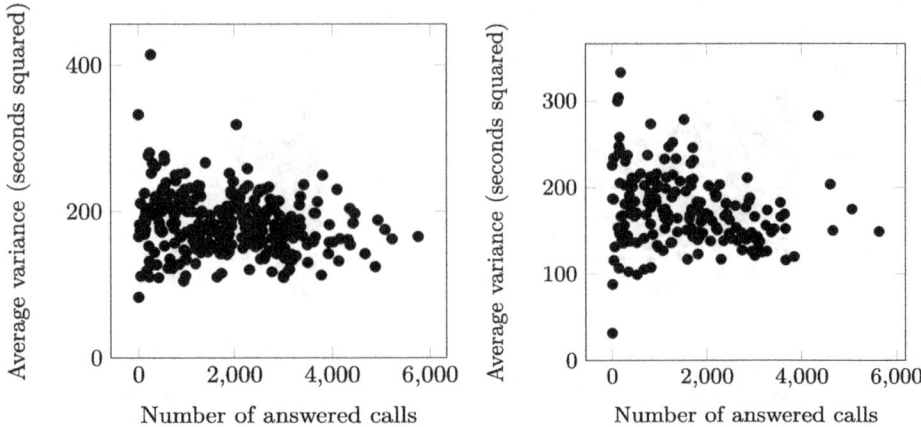

Fig. 7. Average variances of service times for agents handling type T1 calls as a function of the total number of calls answered per year.

Fig. 8. Average variances of service times for agents handling type T2 calls as a function of the total number of calls answered per year.

inter-arrival well, so we can deduce that arrivals follow a Poisson process. The result observed with Fig. 9 and Fig. 11 combined shows that the arrivals follow a non-stationary Poisson process. To take this into account in the simulation, we have divided the opening hours of the call center into $P = 24$ time periods of 30 min. So, for a call type k, the arrival process is a Poisson process with a constant rate $\lambda_{k,p}$ over each period p, so the vector of arrival rates over the P periods is $\lambda_k = (\lambda_{k,1}, \ldots, \lambda_{k,P})$.

Service Time: A service time often consists of a first part handled by an interactive voice response (IVR) system, and a second part where the call is handled by an agent. Since we are interested in service times from the viewpoint of agents, we do not consider the IVR part because agents are not involved for that part. From the viewpoint of an agent, an individual service time is the sum of: (i) the time spent actually talking to the customer (call time), and (ii) the post-call time spent by the agent to wrap up issues related to the call, during which s/he remains unavailable.

Figure 12 shows the fit of call type T1 service time data with an exponential and lognormal distribution. We observe that the lognormal fit better than the exponential distribution. In our simulation, for type k, the service times distribution are modeled by a lognormal distribution with mean μ_k and variance σ_k^2. Notice that to take into account the heterogeneity of agents we specify a distribution of service times for each pair (agent, call type).

Patience Time: The patience time represent the time a customer is willing to wait for service. A customer abandons the queue once her waiting time exceeds her patience time. Figure 13 shows the fit of call type T1 patience time data with the exponential distribution. We observe that the exponential distribution fits the patience time well. In simulation, the patience times for a call type k are exponential with mean $1/\nu_k$.

The Staffing: For each working day agents are divided into G groups. An agent of group $g \in \{1, \ldots, G\}$ has the skill set $\mathcal{S}_g \subseteq \{1, \ldots, K\}$ which defines the set of call types she can serve. Let $s_g = (s_{g,1}, \ldots, s_{g,P})$ be the staffing vector of group g, where $s_{g,p}$ is the number of agents from that group working in period p. For each working day, G the number of group, and s_g the staffing vector of group g can be calculated from the log activity data.

Routing Policy: The routing mechanism works as follows. When a customer calls, she will interact with the IVR by making use of her key pad to choose the call type k. If there is any agent available with the skill to handle that type of calls, then she is routed to the longest idle agent of those available agents; otherwise, she will wait in an invisible queue. The calls in this queue are served in the FCFS (first come first served) order.

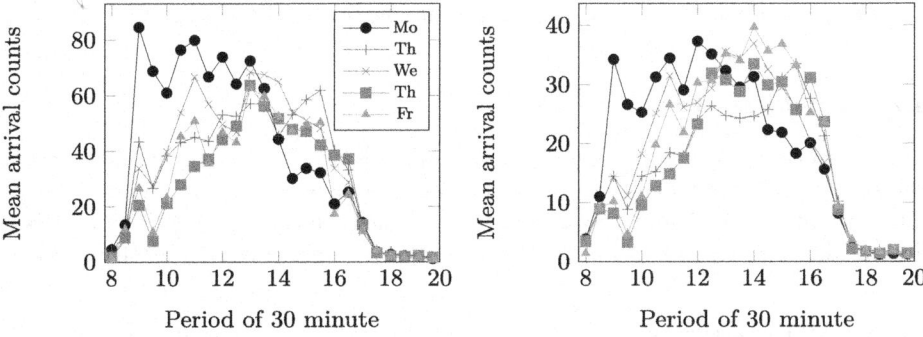

Fig. 9. Annual mean of arrival counts per 30 min and per weekday for call type T1

Fig. 10. Annual mean of arrival counts per 30 min and per weekday for call type T2.

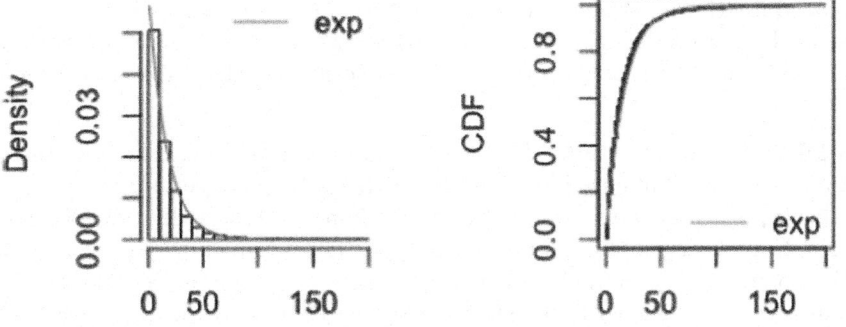

Fig. 11. Fit inter arrival with Exponential distribution for call type T1.

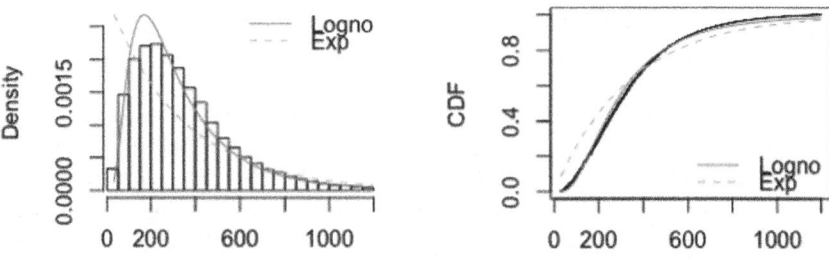

Fig. 12. Fit service time distribution for agent $a1$ for type T1 with Exponential and Lognormal.

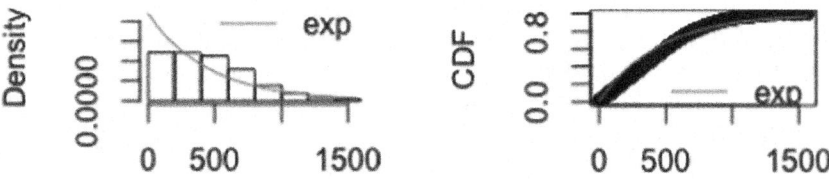

Fig. 13. Fit patience time with Exponential distribution for call type T1.

4.2 Simulation Experiments

In this section, we compare the performance of two simulation models of the call center with actual call center performance. This comparison is made on two different days, Day 1 and Day 2 chosen at random in our dataset. The first is a day in May and the second a day in July. Here's a description of each model.

Model 1: the arrival process is a piecewise constant Poisson process for each call type k. The vector λ_k that represent the arrival rate over all period and $1/\nu_k$ the mean patience time for call type k are calculated from the real data of the simulate day; The used agents are those who worked on the simulated day. Indeed, the number of group G, and the staffing vector s_g for each group g are calculated from the data; the service time distribution is lognormal and we take into account the heterogeneity of the agents. Thus for each pair (agent a, call type k) the parameters $(\mu_{a,k}, \sigma_{a,k})$ of lognormal distribution are also calculated from the data; The routing policy is that described in the previous section.

Model 2: It is similar to Model 1 except on service time distribution. Here, we assume that all agents are identical, so the distribution of service times depends on the type of call and not on the agent handling the call. Here we have a distribution of service times for each call type. The parameters of the distribution of the service times for each call type are calculated using data. The mean (the variance) is average of the mean (the variance) service time of all agents who have the skill to handle that call type.

The performances we consider are the average waiting time (AWT) of calls and the service level (SL(s)), defined as the percentage of calls whose waiting times are less than s seconds (here we fixed $s = 60$). We are only interested in the performance of the 8 call types that receive more than 99% of call volume.

The system we simulate is non-stationary. Consequently, the SL and AWT results are different for each simulation. Given this variability, we repeat the simulation $n = 10,000$ times. Therefore, for each model and for each day, there are 10,000 simulation results and one realization. To measure the difference between simulated and actual results, we use WAE (weighted absolute errors).

$$\text{WAE}_X = \frac{\sum_{i=1}^{n} A_i \mid E\hat{X}_i^{sim} - X_i^{act} \mid}{\sum_{i=1}^{n} A_i},$$

where $\hat{X}_i^{sim}$ is the simulated result of day i, and X_i^{act} is the actual result of day i, and A_i is the number of arrivals in day i. We compute the WAE of SL and AWT, which is WAE_{SL}, WAE_{AWT}, respectively.

WAE measures the difference between the simulation results and the actuals. If WAE is equals to 0 this means that the simulation model has produced a result that is equal to the actuals. In other words, the model is a perfect representation of the system to be simulated. However, this ideal does not exist in stochastic modeling, and WAE are always positive. One part of the WAE comes from the variability in SL, and AWT; for exemple the SL is different per simulation. The other part of WAE comes from the model; for example, if one simulates a model which does not describe the reality well, then there is a big difference between the simulation results and the actuals.

4.3 Results and Discussion

In Fig. 14(a) and Fig. 14(b), we plot the WAE_{AWT} values for Model 1 and 2 as function of the call type, for Day 1 and Day 2, respectively. We observe that the Model 1, which takes into account agent heterogeneity, have a WAE_{AWT} that is around 20 seconds less than that of the Model 2, which assumes that all agents are identical, for all call types. This means that Model 1 predicts the average waiting time better than Model 2. Figure 14(c) and Fig. 14(d) plot the WAE_{SL} for Model 1 and 2 as function of the call type, for Day 1 and Day 2, respectively. We can see that the Model 1 have a WAE_{SL} that is around 1.5% less than that of the Model 2. This means that Model 1 predicts the service level better than Model 2. With these results, we can conclude that Model 1 models the call center better than Model 2.

The difference in performance between the two models may appear minimal at first glance, however they could lead to significant cost savings in practice. ACS Wireless found that by reducing AWT by just 0.6 s will save $8 million a year [7,12]. In addition, small percentage differences in SL can make the difference between compliance and breach of service level agreements, which can lead to heavy penalties for the call center [7,11].

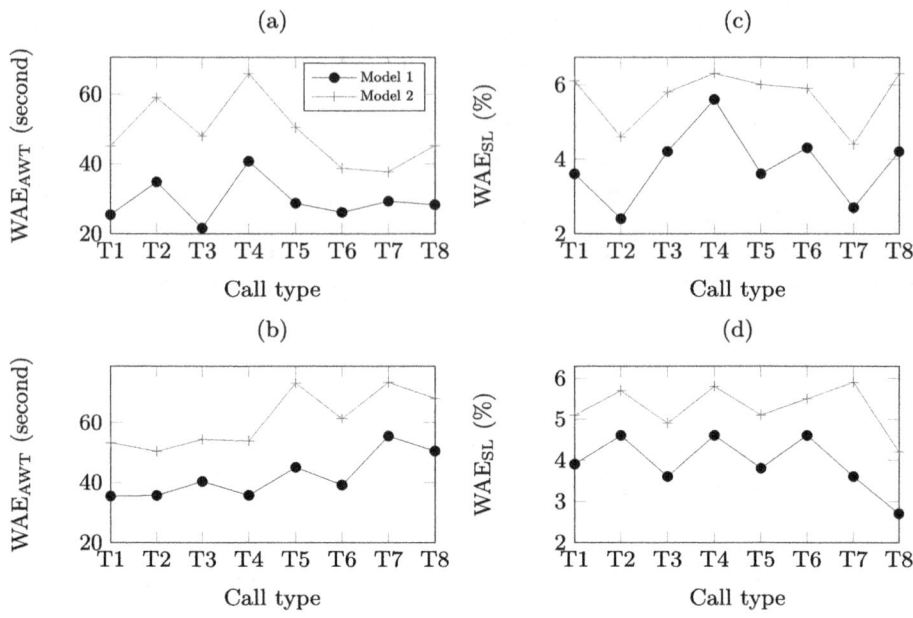

Fig. 14. WAE for Model 1, and Model 2 on Day 1 and Day 2

5 Conclusion

In this work, we looked at the impact of agent heterogeneity on the performance measures of a call center in which we have detailed data. We have reviewed the literature on agent heterogeneity in call centers. We analyzed real data and showed that agent service times vary considerably depending on the agent for a given service. A module for simulating a call center with heterogeneous agents was developed and added to the *ContactCenter* simulator. Modeling and parameter estimation with real data for the distribution of arrivals, service times, and patience times was done to enable us to simulate the call center. By simulating two call center models on two separate days, we have shown that taking into account agent heterogeneity leads to better predictions of call center performance. In future work, we plan to study the impact of unplanned breaks and correlation on the service times of call types handled by the same agent.

Acknowledgements. We thank Ger Koole, from VU Amsterdam, who provided the data.

References

1. Armony, M.: Dynamic routing in large-scale service systems with heterogeneous servers. Queue. Syst. **51**(3–4), 287–329 (2005)
2. Armony, M., Ward, A.R.: Fair dynamic routing in large-scale heterogeneous-server systems. Oper. Res. **58**(3), 624–637 (2010)
3. Avramidis, A.N., Deslauriers, A., L'Ecuyer, P.: Modeling daily arrivals to a telephone call center. Manag. Sci. **50**(7), 896–908 (2004)
4. Brown, L., et al.: Statistical analysis of a telephone call center: a queueing-science perspective. J. Am. Stat. Assoc. **100**, 36–50 (2005)
5. Buist, E., L'Ecuyer, P.: A Java library for simulating contact centers. In: Kuhl, M.E., Steiger, N.M., Armstrong, F.B., Joines, J.A. (eds.) Proceedings of the 2005 Winter Simulation Conference, pp. 556–565. IEEE Press (2005)
6. Gans, N., Koole, G., Mandelbaum, A.: Telephone call centers: tutorial, review, and research prospects. Manuf. Serv. Oper. Manag. **5**, 79–141 (2003)
7. Gans, N., Liu, N., Mandelbaum, A., Shen, H., Ye, H.: Service times in call centers: agent heterogeneity and learning with some operational consequences. In: Berger, J., Cai, T., Johnstone, I. (eds.) Borrowing Strength: Theory Powering Applications – A Festschrift for Lawrence D. Brown, vol. 6, pp. 99–123. Institute of Mathematical Statistics (2010)
8. Gurvich, I., Armony, M., Mandelbaum, A.: Service-level differentiation in call centers with fully flexible servers. Manag. Sci. **54**(2), 279–294 (2008)
9. Gurvich, I., Whitt, W.: Queue-and-idleness-ratio controls in many-server service systems. Math. Oper. Res. **34**(2), 363–396 (2009)
10. Ibrahim, R., L'Ecuyer, P., Régnard, N., Shen, H.: Modeling and prediction of service times in call centers (2013)
11. Ibrahim, R., L'Ecuyer, P., Shen, H., Thiongane, M.: Inter-dependent, heterogeneous, and time-varying service-time distributions in call centers. Eur. J. Oper. Res. **250**, 480–492 (2016)
12. J, H.: How the right headset affects call center productivity and the bottom line (2014). http://telecom.hellodirect.com/docs/tutorials/productivity.1.080701.asp. Accessed July 2015
13. Mehrotra, V., Ross, K., Ryder, G., Zhou, Y.P.: Routing to manage resolution and waiting time in call centers with heterogeneous servers. Manuf. Serv. Oper. Manag. **14**(1), 66–88 (2012)
14. Oreshkin, B., Régnard, N., L'Ecuyer, P.: Rate-based daily arrival process models with application to call centers. Oper. Res. **64**(2), 510–527 (2016)
15. Pichitlamken, J., Deslauriers, A., L'Ecuyer, P., Avramidis, A.N.: Modeling and simulation of a telephone call center. In: Proceedings of the 2003 Winter Simulation Conference, pp. 1805–1812. IEEE Press (2003)
16. Wang, M., Wang, X.: Study on the workforce scheduling and routing strategies of heterogeneous agents in call centers. In: Fifth International Conference on Economic and Business Management, vol. 159, pp. 577–583 (2020)

Towards a Mobile, Intelligent, Personalized and Adaptive E-learning System Considering Learners' Context in Semi-nomadic and Conflict Zones

Alhoudourou Almaimoune Maiga[1]($\boxtimes$), Richard Hotte[2], Gaoussou Camara[1], Mariem Abid[2], and Anis Masmoudi[2]

[1] Université Alioune Diop, Bambey, Sénégal
alhoudouroumali@gmail.com, gaoussou.camara@uadb.edu.sn
[2] Institut d'intelligence artificielle appliquée, UniversitéTELUQ, Québec, Canada
{richard.hotte,mariem.abid,anis.masmoudi}@teluq.ca

Abstract. According to the UNESCO (2023), the sub-Saharan Africa has the highest rate of out-of-school children for economic, cultural, socio-political and geopolitical reasons. Improving school attendance rates in such areas requires a preliminary study to understand the local realities and meet the expectations of learners and, above all, their parents, who have the power to decide whether or not to send them to school. In this paper, we study and design mobile-based, intelligent, personalized and adaptive e-learning solution in semi-nomadic and conflict zones. This solution is part of the AMI (Intelligence-Mediated Learning) project which aims to design, develop, and implement a mobile learning system made up of educational applications accessible from micro terminals (such as smartphones, tablets, and other devices). To properly assess the learning needs in such context, four field surveys were carried out in Kalani, a community in northern Mali, located in a conflict zone with a high rate of non-schooling and out-of-school children, where both sedentary and nomadic families live. These surveys made it possible to collect, analyze and process data of 100 Kalani children aged between 6 and 11, to build up a model that guide the implementation of our proposed educational solution. The data analysis revealed a strong link between the learners' interests and the needs expressed by the community.

Keywords: Education · sub-Saharan Africa · children · conflict zones · multi-sectoral and interdisciplinary research · mobile learning system · pedagogical engineering · data science

1 Introduction

According to the UNESCO (2023), the number of out-of-school children has increased by 6 million since 2021 and now stands at 250 million, revealing that progress in education continues to stagnate worldwide. Sub-Saharan Africa hosts nearly 30% of the world's out-of-school children, with 1 in 5 African children not attending school (19.7%), according to UNESCO (2023).

The populations most affected include girls, people with disabilities, indigenous people, and children in conflict zones and areas disadvantaged by population mobility and difficult access to educational resources. The latter one is the target population of the AMI (Intelligence-Mediated Learning) research project, on which several researchers and PhD students have been working since 2020 to meet the learning needs of children in Kalani, in northern Mali, aged between 6 and 11, who are the most affected by this situation, for a variety of reasons: geopolitical (conflicts, class closures, etc.), economic (high cost of schooling, lack of means of transport, etc.), cultural (unsuitability of schooling to local contexts, local traditional cultures, negative perception of western schooling, etc.). To meet these multiple challenges with a focus on the local context, researchers in information technology and computer science, human and social sciences, along with a local team made up of sociologists, teachers, psycho-pedagogues and linguists are working within the AMI project to develop an intelligent, personalized adaptive mobile e-learning system. This system aims to provide educational access to all children who lack formal schooling due to conflict zones and areas with limited resources and population mobility. However, a prior study of educational needs is necessary to guarantee the adoption of future solutions to be proposed. That's why, in this paper, we have carried out a study among children aged 6 to 11 and their parents to find the most appropriate pedagogical and technological solution for the Kalani context, characteristic of semi-nomadic and conflict zones.

The first part of the article outlines the context of our research, including the geographical context that motivates the choice of Kalani, and the presentation of the AMI project. The subsequent part delves into the challenges related to cross-sector development: from the methodology to the presentation of results. Thirdly, we address the dual engineering aspects of the proposed solution, both educational and technological. Finally, we discuss the solution within a global, scientific approach.

2 Background

2.1 Presentation of the Geographical Context of the Study

The choice of Kalani was motivated by its status as an at-risk area, disadvantaged by climate, poor access to resources, poverty, the nomadic nature of its inhabitants' lifestyle, and its high level of militarization, as well as the conflict-ridden nature of the region in which it is located. It is a district with several islands. Kalani falls within the administrative jurisdiction of the Bourem commune, the capital of the Bourem cercle, in the Gao region, where the Songhay, Touareg, Arab, and Peulh communities live. Their main activities include farming, livestock breeding, commerce, and fishing. The Songhay community is the most represented and the Songhay language the most spoken. Kalani is a community living between nomadism and sedentarism, due to the islands and the economic life linked to livestock farming. Kalani is located in an area straddling the desert and the river, where the exclusion rates for school-age children are due to the absence of schools, the semi-nomadic and semi-sedentary way of life, the insecurity that has caused schools to close and teachers to flee, and the culture of the communities.

In addition, the learning ecosystem in Kalani is inherent to internal factors (the child himself) and external factors (his environment), both endogenous (local realities, values, etc.) and exogenous (the influence of systemic trends inherited from Western colonization and Arab Islamization (Sanogo 2002). There are also several other factors, linked to the family's economic and educational situation, the parents' vision and opinion of education, and the needs and interests of the community, starting with the family (Maiga, A.A. et Hotte, R. 2021).

All these factors constitute major barriers to the adoption of existing educational systems coming essentially from the West.

2.2 Presentation of the AMI Project Framework

The AMI project (Hotte, R., et al. 2023) stems from the research program of the UNESCO Chair in Global Smart Disruptive Learning (GSDL, 2019-2023), creating and implementing a mobile learning system that is adapted for individual self-learning and designed to meet the needs of all learners (children, youth and adults) who have been excluded from the existing formal and informal education system. AMI aims to develop learning units, adapted to the local context of Kalani and integrated into educational pathways, based on activities drawn from local practices and meeting the learning objectives of the target community. Themes include food, health, environmental protection, understanding mathematics in local languages, learning trades, learning foreign languages such as French and English, local stories and more. This curriculum should introduce the community to multiple forms of knowledge and allow expression of local cultural values through adapted pedagogical activities in local languages.

AMI is an educational technology (EdTech) solution which is at the crossroads of 2 research disciplines: the humanities and social sciences (ethnography, linguistics, and educational sciences) and the natural sciences and engineering (computer science, software engineering, and artificial intelligence). As a result, successful implementation required collaborations from diverse teams across these various disciplines.

The contribution of the local human and social sciences team has left its mark on the entire AMI system, by collecting community and learners' profiles. Based on these data, a monographic profile of a child in Gao was created (Maïga and Hotte 2021), for whom the AMI solution is designed, including identity, psycho-social profile, family, and community ties, living environment, preferences, educational profile, and interests. Community meetings and discussion groups fostered trust and adoption of the AMI solution. Beyond this ethnographic dimension, linguistics is also an integrating factor in the AMI system. All field exchanges occur in the local language, understood by the entire Kalani population (Songhay), regardless of their community (Songhay, Tuareg, Bozo, etc.). Responding to the demand from residents and experts, the use of the local language ensures its preservation against the influence of other languages. Additionally, it encourages French language learning for children who already have a grounding in the local language. AMI is actively translating learning units created during the project. This approach ensures that content is available in both French and the local language. Surveys are conducted by a researcher from the same community where they were born, grew up, and still have family ties.

The AMI project, focused on educational technology for disadvantaged children, integrates insights from educational sciences. Field surveys and discussions with children and the community led local experts to recommend an integrative pedagogical approach that combines different disciplinary contents. This interdisciplinary strategy promotes knowledge integration (Lenoir, Y. and Sauvé, L. 1998) and offers theoretical insights across various practical domains. By blending endogenous and exogenous knowledge, including local and foreign languages, the AMI solution aims to be inclusive and adapted to expressed needs while optimizing time spent on education.

Xavier Roegiers (2011) explains integrative pedagogy as a framework aligning educational system goals with everyday teaching practices on the other. However, field research has made it possible to question the aims of the education system in favor of the community expressed needs. In the AMI system, community priorities— shaped by parents, children, socio-cultural realities, and values—take precedence. This approach diverges from politically defined orientations Rogiers (2011), focusing on locally relevant training and its impact on children's development and autonomy in daily life. The contribution of arts and culture is crucial. To propose a solution aligned with community needs, we leverage images, sounds, and language variants. A multimedia team conducts a thorough study proposing a contextualized product that considers the learner's physical, social, linguistic, and cultural realities. This artistic endeavor aims to engage the community and foster playful motivation for children's learning. Ensuring that users feel comfortable and can sustainably utilize the product is essential.

The research team, comprising software engineers, graduate students, and data science experts, focused on structuring and preprocessing collected data. Their goal was to create an intelligent, personalized, and adaptive e-learning system that is sensitive to local context (Hotte, R, et al. 2002). The AMI solution emphasizes contextualized data interpretation and aims to provide relevant recommendations aligned with learners' interests and the local context.

3 Study of Inter-sectoral Educational Challenges in Semi-nomadic and Conflict Zones

The project is based on three field surveys carried out in Kalani. The fieldwork involved personalized interviews, community meetings, focus groups and periodic validation sessions following data processing.

3.1 Data Collection

Two field surveys directly involving 100 pre-selected children were carried out after obtaining a certificate of ethics and following a series of community meetings attended by their parents/guardians and local stakeholders. The first survey, held in the spring of 2022, was designed to build up a database that would enable a detailed profile of future AMI users to be drawn up. Among the variables used in the survey form were the child's identity, living context, link with school, competencies acquired and targeted, interests, etc. (see Table 1 presenting responses from two children A093 and A089). The second survey assessed each child's knowledge and interests. It aimed to validate their basic or threshold competencies which are crucial data for identifying and classifying typical profiles. These profiles serve as the foundation for the AMI system's adaptability, aligning with the learner's cognitive profile and adjusting pathways as needed during

Table 1. Overview of skills assessment results

Categories: 39 questions (Q)	A093	A089
Recognizing numbers and letters	A	D
Recognizing numbers and letters (Q1)	1	0
Recognizing numbers from 0 to 50 (Q2)	1	0
Order from smallest to largest from 1 to 9 (Q3)	1	0
Recognizing the signs	A	D
Recognize the sign of addition (Q4)	1	0
Recognizing the sign of subtraction (Q5)	1	0
Recognizing the sign of multiplication (Q6)	1	0
Performing operations	I	D
Add [less than or equal to 10] (Q7)	1	0
Add [less than or equal to 20] (Q8 et Q9)	1	0
Subtract [less than or equal to 10] (Q10 et Q11)	1	0
Subtract [less than or equal to 20] (Q12)	0	0
Multiply [less than or equal to 30] (Q13 et Q14)	1	0
Multiply [less than or equal to 70] (Q15)	0	0
Divide [less than or equal to 10] (Q16, Q17 et Q18)	0	0
Color recognition	I	D
Identify Red, Black, Blue, Yellow, Green (Q19 à Q23)	1	0
Categories: 39 questions (Q)	**A093**	**A089**
Differentiate between green and black; green and yellow; green and blue (Q24 à Q26)	1	0
Recognize the flag of Mali (green-gold-red) (Q27)	1	0
Recognizing colors in Malian cows (Q28)	0	0
Read color names (Q29 à Q32)	0	0
Recognizing geometric shapes	D	D
Identify rectangle (Q33)	0	0
Identify triangle (Q34)	0	0
Identify square (Q35)	0	0
Identify circle (Q36)	0	0
Identify straight line (Q37)	0	0
Identify broken line (Q38)	0	0
Identify curved line (Q39)	0	0

learning. The questions are designed to define learning programs based on the diagnosis made and the learner's profile. They focus particularly on reading, writing, numeracy and problem-solving skills, and on the child's interests. It was also an opportunity to validate with parents the information linked to the socio-cultural context and the values they hold dear, without discontinuity with the training needs already expressed during the preliminary surveys (between 2021 and 2022). We assume that the content to be developed will be contextualized, i.e. we want to focus on children's interests to arouse, preserve and maintain their motivation, anchored in community and parental interests. Not to mention that content inspired by the learner's life reality and interests would generate a playful interest and could enhance his or her motivation to learn.

To measure the knowledge levels of the children we interviewed and categorized them into beginner (D), intermediate (I) and advanced (A) levels according to criteria adapted to their realities. These criteria consider the following variables: school environment, level of schooling, level of literacy. However, many children are helped in the local language during the test, to take account of their poor access to quality education and the total absence of schooling (Paquette 2002b).

Thus, any child who has not attended school or who has dropped out is considered a beginner if he/she has obtained a positive score of less than half the questions per domain (50%). Schooled children can be considered beginners if they score none or only 1 positive mark for 3 questions. Schooled children are considered intermediate if they obtain a positive mark equal to or greater than half the questions per area and less than 80%, and if they obtain 2 positive marks for 3 questions only. Advanced children are in school and have obtained a positive score greater than or equal to 80% of the questions per domain, and 3 positive scores for 3 questions only. Context being at the heart of this research, interactions with children during the second survey are also considered as a subjective measure (Paquette 2002b). For example, some children were able to answer certain questions with the help of only one other child.

The data collected guides the design of the knowledge model for each learning path to be integrated into the AMI system, by the software and data engineering team. It feeds the recommendation system for selecting or modifying a typical pathway. This is a recommendation system based on a selection of algorithms, using artificial intelligence and machine learning techniques (Chen and Wang 2021; Jeevamol Joy and Renumol Vemballiveli Govinda Pillai 2022). The aim is to offer the most suitable and appropriate learning path for a given learner's profile.

3.2 Correlation Analysis of the Learners' Attributes

Skill Levels

5 skills areas were used in the field tests: identifying numbers and letters; differentiating mathematical signs; solving mathematical problems (addition, subtraction, multiplication, and division); identifying colors and being able to read color names; recognizing geometric shapes. These choices were inspired by Bloom's taxonomy as revised by Anderson et al. (2001): identify, recognize are among the verbs linked to the first level of skills (I know what I'm talking about), followed by a second level of understanding (I know how to talk about it) and a third level of application where the learner can, for example, solve a problem, and so on.

Figure 1 below shows that most future AMI learners (92%) have a beginner's level (zero skills) in the simplest mathematical operations tested in the field: addition, multiplication, and subtraction with digits and then with numbers and differentiating between digits and numbers. Only one child out of the 100 was able to perform the mathematical operations correctly, and 6 children were able to obtain a few correct answers.

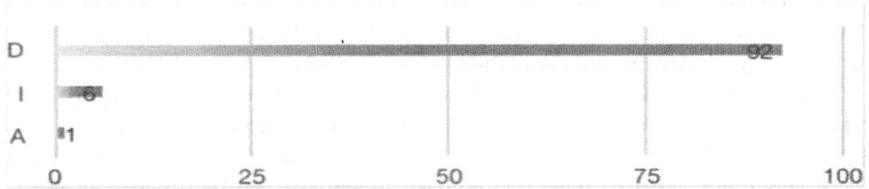

Fig. 1. Children's scores in mathematical operations test

Interests

Analyzing the fields of interest expressed by the children is crucial for designing effective learning paths and recommendation systems. There are three main categories of interest:

- **Community interest**: The community's expectations for the AMI system are multifaceted. They prioritize mobility, recognizing the population's diverse lifestyle—spanning both sedentary and nomadic contexts. Additionally, the system should be cost-effective, avoiding transportation expenses associated with conventional schooling in isolated areas. Internet access costs should also be minimal, considering the low-income levels. Furthermore, adherence to local traditions, language, and cultural values is crucial. The system's content must be tailored to meet the specific needs of the local population, emphasizing quality and practical relevance.
- **Playful interest** or entertainment value on the part of the personalized learner is expressed in the learner interest attribute. Expected values include cooking games, building houses out of banco, storytelling, drawing, playing with animals and other expressed needs such milking, counting, reading and writing; Interestingly, the cow emerges as a favorite animal among the children.
- **Pedagogical interest**: The local team, consisting of a psycho-pedagogue, linguist, sociologist, and teachers, emphasizes a pedagogical approach for the AMI system. This approach integrates diverse learning units into varied pathways, allowing learners to acquire multiple skills within short timeframes. Addressing the time challenge of keeping children in school, an integrative pedagogy strategy combines both local and external knowledge, emphasizing context and quality of education.

4 An Interdisciplinary Pedagogical and Engineering Solution in Semi-nomadic and Conflict Zones

4.1 Pedagogical Engineering Dimension

The AMI educational solution adapted to Kalani's needs can be framed around eight (8) courses according to expectations expressed in the survey data: an introductory course and seven (7) specific courses. These include courses on animal husbandry (knowing the different types of cows and how to market them, for example), food health (hygiene, cooking, the virtues and drawbacks of local fruit and vegetables), community life (respect, cultural values, living together), finance (arithmetic, currencies, business basics, customer loyalty tips), international languages (French, Arabic and English), animal health (animal symptoms, animal diseases transmissible to humans, animal nutrition) and the environment (protecting biodiversity, combating silting-up, among others). To design the prototype of the AMI educational system, the introductory course and a course integrating breeding and trade, entitled Discovering Malian cows, were chosen from among the 8 courses. These courses are therefore interrelated, and the choice of the following courses is justified by the results obtained.

Firstly, because these courses offer content linked to the interests expressed by the children during the field surveys: selling, counting, knowing about cows, being in the company of animals, among others, their interests are thus linked to areas related to trade and animal husbandry, two very frequent and useful areas of activity in Kalani's socio-economic life. Secondly, these courses consider the fundamental concerns of parents, namely respect for local socio-cultural values and the need for their children to receive training directly linked to their professional activities. Finally, it is an approach that responds adequately to the pedagogical approach proposed and discussed with local expertise, particularly the pedagogy of integration.

The pedagogical and media models will be inspired by these different aspects. While this approach gives the AMI education system an informal character, not based on conventional models, its relevance lies in its adaptability to a singular context. For example, the AMI system will offer a media environment similar that that in which the learner lives (river, bush, fields, island, Sahelian animals, wild date palms), in the local language and French to reinforce the skills of the targeted children. In this sense, a learning path that combines the children's interests and target skills with their sociocultural context is highly relevant. The choice of test courses and a story to support the course on the Malian cow are justified in the following Table 3.

Table 2 clearly shows that values such as storytelling, animal husbandry, trade, and arithmetic (calculating, counting) recur very frequently in the research results compiled in the AMI database. These values are associated with the children's interests and information obtained from other community members (parents/guardians, community leaders, local team) during the various phases of data collection. All these values are of the very frequent order in the database, i.e. they are expressed very frequently during the collection of information on the learner.

Table 2. Choice of test path

Selected values	The child's interests and target skills	Social, economic and cultural context
Arithmetic	How to count, calculate	Local market influenced by transactions/merchandising, children commissioned at the market, in the store, children keeping the parents' business and future heirs
Trade	Know how to sell, become a shopkeeper, help parent	Strengthening local trade for the community, reducing youth unemployment, making the project sustainable and anchoring it
Breeding	Know animals, know how to milk, be in the company of animals	Strengthening the local way of life (between nomadism and sedentarism), making the project sustainable and firmly rooted
Tale	Preference expressed by children	Moral to remember at the end of the tale, reality of life close by, oral civilization reinforced

4.2 Technology Engineering Dimension

This solution will be inspired by a domain model for a plural learner in a context of adaptation and socialization rooted in local socio-cultural values. The AMI domain model illustrates cross-sectoral work of the AMI project. The humanities and social sciences team brought their expertise to bear on the social, economic, cultural, community, educational and family aspects of the learner in this domain model. These aspects enriched the profile of the learner as an individual situated in a particular socio-cultural context and as a family (cousin, brother, sister, father, tutor, aunt, etc.). The team then provided the domain model of aspects related to the skill levels and interests of children and the community based on data from the field surveys. These data will be used to design the knowledge, pedagogical and media models on which the first prototype of the AMI system will be built. Supported by a visual arts and culture team, the team provides contextualized learning materials (text, audio, images, video).

The data collected during the requirements engineering phase will feed into the system implementation. Assuming that access to the internet or cloud computing will most likely be nonexistent or very limited, applications will be designed to operate entirely in an offline environment. The system will therefore be designed to be completely autonomous and independent of any network or network access. Access to the mobile learning system will be provided through mini terminals such as smartphones and tablets.

The team focused on the learning tool (i.e., the personalized adaptive systems) according to two dimensions: attributes of systems to support adaptive/personalized learning and the hardware where the system will be deployed (web-based application). Personalized adaptive e-learning recommender systems assist the learners by learning units' recommendation and adapts to the learning needs, interests, and performance of the learner (Raj, N.S. and Renumol, V.G. 2018; Xie, H., et al. 2019).

Meeting users' needs and interests is an ongoing challenge in developing personalized e-learning systems. The collected attributes to support personalized and adaptive learning are represented by six dimensions capable of accommodating most of the information describing the user, their interests, and skills, and as investigated in the literature (Hemmler, Y. M., et al. 2022). By leveraging artificial intelligence and natural language processing techniques, we can create intelligent algorithms that analyze the combination of the learner attributes, identify patterns and trends, and provide personalized recommendations and interventions. This would enable a more dynamic and tailored learning experience for everyone, addressing their unique needs and maximizing their learning outcomes.

In the AMI system, this dynamicity is embodied in two intelligent components: (1) an intelligent selection of one or more typical learning pathways, based on needs, on the economic, social, cultural, community, and academic profile and on the skills developed by the learner during his or her learning or, even, prior to that learning with family, friends, or community (2) updating the learning path according to the difficulties and progress of the learner in the current course (dynamic path in relation to the profile, difficulties, and level of advancement) (Hotte, R., et al. 2022).

The design of the mobile learning system (web-based application or portal) is based on the hybridization of educational and software engineering, to build an e-learning system to support personalized and adaptive learning. The user interfaces (UI) are designed to be user-friendly, intuitive, and functional, ensuring a seamless experience for all users (Hotte, R., et al. 2022). The software and data engineering team provides the domain model, the web-based application with its intelligent components.

5 Discussion

The field surveys revealed a close alignment between the community's expressed training needs and the interests of the interviewed children. Notably, there exists a significant disparity between these needs and the content typically taught in schools. The AMI system addresses this by prioritizing community concerns—such as respecting socio-cultural values and educational requirements—while tailoring content to children's interests. The AMI system is designed to be mobile, responding to the community's lifestyle (sedentary and nomadic) and given the widespread use of cell phones. This solution is locally supported by the expertise of the community and local players. The learning paths were proposed by the community. Drawing from local expertise, the pedagogical approach incorporates storytelling, the use of the local language alongside French, a virtual environment, and familiar characters. These elements enhance engagement and alignment with socio-cultural realities.

The AMI system offers contextualization tailored to each community's needs and socio-cultural realities. By prioritizing learners' interests, which closely align with community values, it becomes an adaptable and non-formal solution. As a result, children in Kalani—the target audience of this study—can thrive without assimilating into foreign cultures. They acquire practical skills relevant to local employment demands, reducing vulnerability to unemployment—a fertile ground for armed groups. Additionally, young girls can learn while remaining connected to their mothers and future husbands, potentially becoming vital supporters of education through their life experiences. For example, the AMI system may recommend courses in dietary health for a learner who wants to understand the virtues and evils of local fruits (wild dates, jujubes, etc.) to take good care of her future husband. Just as she may want to learn new skills in hygiene or fish sales to help her mother make a profit.

In the case of AMI, where learning is informal, it is taking into account the cultural context and locally expressed concerns that makes it relevant and sustainable: taking into account the local language, endogenous knowledge, the mobile nature of the lifestyle, the integrative approach in the design of models and the implementation of learning scenarios, the disconnected and simple nature proposed due to poor access to Internet and electricity, among others. This was not and will not be possible without the collaborative work of an AMI team made up of players from different disciplines. Interdisciplinary research is itself defined by the engineering of intersectorality, drawing on practices in engineering and the natural sciences on the one hand, and the humanities and social sciences on the other: software engineering, educational engineering and data engineering associated with artificial intelligence.

6 Conclusion

In this paper, we studied the multi-sectoral dimensions of the design, development and implementation of a learning tool for children in a community living in difficult and disadvantaged circumstances such as Gao, in northern Mali. According to the local realities and the trends emerging from data analysis, we need to innovate in terms of (1) pedagogical engineering, by designing adaptive and personalized content and pathways, and (2) technical engineering, by offering a mobile solution based on emerging technologies such as artificial intelligence.

Future work will involve the experimentation of our solution on the topics of interest identified in our study. The concrete usage of AI tools will also be explored and their added value assessed. A cloud-based architecture for hosting the system will be proposed and will strengthen accessibility and foster collaboration between the different stakeholders.

References

Anderson, L.W., Krathwohl, D.R., Bloom, B.S.: A Taxonomy for Learning, Teaching, and Assessing: A Revision of Bloom's Taxonomy of Educational Objectives: Allyn & Bacon (2001)

Chen, S.Y., Wang, J.-H.: Individual differences and personalized learning: a review and appraisal. Univ. Access Inf. Soc. **20**(4), 833–849 (2021). https://doi.org/10.1007/s10209-020-00753-4

Hemmler, Y.M., Ifenthaler, D.: Indicators of the learning context for supporting personalized and adaptive learning environments. In: 2022 International Conference on Advanced Learning Technologies (ICALT), pp. 61–65. IEEE (2022)

Hotte, R., Masmoudi A., Jaballah, A., Masmoudi, O., Maïga, A.A.: Work-in-progress about dynamicity as a foundation for AMI, a mobile intelligent and adaptive learning system. In:

Proceedings of the 14th International Conference on Interactive Mobile Communication Technologies and Learning (IMCL 2022). New Realities, Mobile Systems and Applications, vol. 411, pp. 111–119. Thessaloniki, Greece: Springer (2022)

Hotte, R., Maiga, A., Abid, M., Mimoudi, A.: IdO : une solution à l'éducation en zone défavorisée. Colloque international sur les objets et systèmes connectés COC 2023, juin 2023, Mahdia, Tunisie (2023)

Hotte, R., Pierre, S.: Leadership and conflict management support in a cooperative telelearning environment. Int. J. E-learn. **1**(2), 46–59 (2002). Association for the Advancement of Computing in Education (AACE).

Jeevamol, J., Renumol, V.G.P.: Review and classification of content recommenders in E-learning environment. J. King Saud Univ. – Comput. Inf. Sci. **34**(9), 7670–7685 (2022)

Maïga, A.A., Hotte, R.: Monographie de l'enfant de Gao: l'école en Afrique subsaharienne. Graph. Francophones **001**, 284–29 (2021)

Raj, N.S., Renumol, V.G.: Architecture of an adaptive personalized learning environment (APLE) for content recommendation. In: Proceedings of the 2nd International Conference on Digital Technology in Education, pp. 17–22 (2018)

Roegiers, X.: La Pédagogie de l'Intégration: ce qu'elle propose. Dans: Roegiers, X. Curricu-la et apprentissages au primaire et au secondaire : La Pédagogie de l'Intégration comme cadre de réflexion et d'action, pp. 55–74. Louvain-la-Neuve: De Boeck Supérieur (2011)

Sanogo, Y.: Valeurs et interventions éducatives : cas du développement rural en Afrique subsaharienne in Horizons philosophiques, **12** (2002)

UNESCO. Rapport mondial de suivi sur l'éducation (2023). https://unesdoc.unesco.org/ark:/48223/pf0000386147_fre

Xie, H., Chu, H.C., Hwang, G., Wang, C.C.: Trends and development in technology-enhanced adaptive/personalized learning: a systematic review of journal publications from 2007 to 2017. Comput. Educ. **140**, 103599 (2019)

Comparative Study of Machine Learning Models for the Detection of Abusive Messages: Case of Wolof-French Codes Mixing Data

Ibrahima Ndao[1(✉)], Khadim Dramé[1], Gorgoumack Sambe[1], and Gayo Diallo[2]

[1] Laboratoire d'Informatique et d'Ingénierie pour l'Innovation, Université Assane Seck de Ziguinchor, Diabir, Ziguinchor, Sénégal
`i.ndao20150570@zig.univ.sn`, `{khadim.drame,gsambe}@univ-zig.sn`
[2] AHead, Bordeaux Population Health - INSERM 1219 and LABRI, University, Bordeaux, France
`Gayo.Diallo@u-bordeaux.fr`

Abstract. This paper presents a comparative study of machine learning models for detecting abusive messages, focusing on code-mixed data in Wolof and French languages. With the increasing use of digital platforms, there has been a surge in derogatory comments, necessitating effective detection strategies. The study introduces a meticulously annotated dataset of 2022 Twitter tweets, manually classified as abusive or not. Extensive experiments are conducted with various machine learning algorithms, including deep learning, with a focus on comparing their performance on the test dataset.

Keywords: abusive messages · hate messages · code mixing · machine learning · deep learning · language models · low-resource languages

1 Introduction

The number of digital platform users has significantly increased [1]. The exponential increase, combined with the unregulated nature of social media usage, has facilitated the widespread spread of abusive messages. Abusive language encompasses a range of expressions that include excessive, false, exaggerated, or attacking communications directed at individuals or groups based on attributes such as race, ethnicity, or sexual orientation [2]. The statement *"i aint never worried bout no nigga"* can be considered a racist expression. Categorizing messages into distinct forms of abuse presents a classification obstacle when it comes to identifying abusive language [3]. As a result, these discourses that promote antisocial behavior require substantial actions from governments, companies, and other organizations to develop efficient strategies to counteract them [4]. Several methods have been suggested to control such behaviors [5, 6]. Nevertheless, users are progressively utilizing evasion strategies such as message camouflage, abbreviations, phonetic input, and code mixing, which make manual analysis and moderation more challenging, especially considering the immense volume of information being shared on social media platforms. Therefore, there is a pressing need for the automated identification of offensive messages.

While there has been a significant amount of research conducted on this matter for languages that have abundant resources, such as English and French, there has been relatively little effort dedicated to languages that have limited resources. Furthermore, there has been a lack of focus on identifying abusive messages in code-mixed data.

In order to fill this gap, we introduce the first annotated collection of Wolof-French code-mixed texts, which has been specifically created for the purpose of identifying abusive messages. Following that, we proceed with a sequence of experiments utilizing various machine learning (ML), deep learning (DL), and language models. The results of these experiments provide insight into the most efficient models within this distinct linguistic and contextual environment.

The following sections of this paper are structured as follows: Sect. 2 explores previous research on identifying offensive messages. Section 3 offers a comprehensive understanding of the corpus's construction and annotation process. Section 4 provides a comprehensive account of the experiments carried out using different models on our annotated corpus and analyzes their outcomes.

2 Related Work

In this section, we present related work on the detection of abusive messages which can be classified into three approaches: linguistic approach, ML-based, and DL-based approaches. Additionally, research conducted on low-resource languages and code-mixing is discussed.

2.1 Linguistic Approach

Linguistic approaches exploit different manually defined features. These include word lexicons, dictionaries, and so one. These features can be related to the number of offensive words used, hashtags, personal pronouns used, word distance metrics. In [7], the authors focus on users who openly display their hateful emotions in tweets using the sentence structure: "I < intensity > < user's intention > < target of hate > ". In [8], the authors address the subjective aspect of tweets and construct a word lexicon to perform a classification of hate into three distinct categories (highly hateful, mildly hateful, or non-hateful).

Although the results of these methods are satisfactory, they faced with manual dependency (definitions from dictionaries, lexicons, etc.). In addition, their performance is limited when faced with low-quality texts, such as spelling mistakes, phonetic input, etc. [5]. Furthermore, the use of certain terms (e.g., "nigger") may not be racist, requiring a contextual analysis of the content. Research conducted using this approach has focused on a specific type of abusive speech (hate [7, 8], racism [5], Offensive [3], sexist [9], etc.), a specific platform (twitter [2], etc.), or a particular language (english [3], arabic [2], etc.) due to its inability to be generalized.

2.2 Machine Learning-Based Approach

Several machine learning algorithms were explored in order to classify abusive messages: Support Vector Machine (SVM), Naive Bayes (NB), Logistic Regression (LR), Random Forest (RF) and so one. These classifiers were used with various features: bag of words (BOW), word or character n-grams, TF-IDF, etc. In [5], for example, the authors trained NB classifier with BOW features to perform a binary classification (racist or non-racist). In [9], the authors focused on sexist messages using SVM to classify tweets as hostile, benevolent, or other. The detection of anti-migrant discourses was studied in [10], using different classifiers with various feature extractors. Their model using word n-grams achieved the highest score.

Hate speech has also been studied, particularly in [11], where hierarchical regression models are used. The authors determine the amount of hate speech associated with a person through personal characteristics such as party affiliation, gender, or ethnic origin. In [12], the authors used patterns and unigrams as input features with several classifiers (NB, KNN, SVM, RF) to perform binary and ternary classification on a test dataset of 2010 tweets. Their best model achieved an accuracy of 87.4% for binary classification (offensive or not) and an accuracy of 78.4% for ternary classification (hateful, offensive, or clean). In [13], the authors experimented several classifiers with different features such as 3 to 5-g, unigrams, bigrams, linguistic features (average word length, punctuation count, comment length, etc.), and syntactic features to identify online hate content. They showed that models using n-grams features yielded good results, but their combinations with text extensions were more performant.

These different propositions allowed improving classification performance of tweets across a wide range of abusive message types. The supervised approach focuses on a set of features that will be used by machine learning algorithms. However, the different types of abusive messages in tweets lack discriminative features. Even though these studies obtained promising results, we noted degradation of their performance in other cases of abusive remarks.

2.3 Deep Learning-Based Approach

The use of deep learning approaches is justified by their ability to learn new feature representations from input data. The input data can be raw data or feature embeddings. Thus, the different operations performed on the stacked layers of these deep neural networks allow the classification of tweets, and the results show that they are more effective for this task. Among the studies in this approach, Chiril [14] explored in his doctorate thesis deep learning models such as BERT, FlauBERT, CNN, and Bi-LSTM with attention in the automatic detection of abusive messages, particularly for sexism. In [15], the authors introduced the treatment of polysemy, syntax, semantics, out-of-vocabulary words, as well as sentiment information combined into an input vector to a neural model (Bi-LSTM) to detect hateful messages and abusive language on Twitter. The authors in [16] addressed the problem under a more general approach by proposing a unified method for classifying tweets into different categories (hate speech, sexism, racism, bullying, sarcasm). They proposed DL-based model that allowed the identification of these different categories of abusive messages without requiring model tuning for each case. In [4], the authors explored the use of lexical extensions (word2vec, GloVe, ELMo,) and graph extensions (neural networks) for the detection of abusive messages. The evaluation of their models showed a clear improvement of performance when combining lexical and graphical extensions.

Other works combined ML-based and DL-based models. In [17], a set of features were used with SVM, CNN, and Multi-layer Perceptron (MLP) to perform binary classification (hateful or non-hateful). The authors in [18] focused on the treatment of hateful metaphors as features to identify hate speech and their targets in Dutch comments on Facebook. Evaluation of SVM, BERT, and RoBERTa models shows that the features of hateful metaphors increase the classification performance of hate speech. In [19], the authors collected a set of 197,566 comments from different platforms (YouTube, Reddit, Wikipedia, Twitter) and used several feature extractors (BOW, TF-IDF, word2vec, BERT) with classifiers (LR, NB, SVM, XGBoost, NN) for hate detection. Text extensions provided by BERT had a greater effect on the classification of tweets. In addition, the XGBoost model achieved the best F-measure of 0.92.

DL-based approaches improved the performance of the state of art in detecting abusive messages. However, despite the diversity of abusive message cases (hate, offense, cyberbullying, trolling, misinformation, etc.), most of existing works focus on one case by conducting binary classification (e.g., hateful or non-hateful). Furthermore, the majority focus on one rich-resource language (English, Arabic). Thus, detecting abusive messages is challenging, particularly in low-resource languages.

2.4 Low-Resource Languages and Code Mixing

Over the past few decades, many studies have addressed the detection of hate speech in low-resource languages. These languages are characterized by a scarcity or limited availability of high-quality annotated dataset [20]. In certain languages, there is the practice of incorporating characters or words from Latin derivatives through borrowing. This phenomenon is called code mixing. Several works have addressed these languages and linguistic phenomena. In [21], the authors proposed new method for detecting hate messages in Hindi-English code-mixing data. Their method involves using word embeddings with FastText to feed SVM and radial basis function (RBF) models. Their results showed that FastText produces much better representations than word2vec and doc2vec. In [22], the authors reported a comparative study of different transformer architectures on Hindi-English code-mixed texts for sentiment analysis, emotion recognition, and hate speech identification. The results of code-mixed models (HingBERT, HingRoBERTa, HingRoBERTa-Mixed, mBERT) were compared to models without code mixing (ALBERT, BERT, and RoBERTa). This study revealed notable performances of the HingBERT model and very low performance of the BERT model.

Other works focused specifically on certain dialects or low-resource languages without studying code-mixing. In [23], the authors proposed DL-based approach for detecting hate speech in Algerian dialect written in Arabic. This study was conducted on a corpus of 135,000 tweets annotated into two classes (hateful and non-hateful). The authors in [24] studied hate speech against women on YouTube. A corpus annotated by three annotators is used to train CNN, LSTM, and Bi-LSTM models. The CNN model achieved the best F-measure of 0.86. In [25], the authors studied offensive and abusive speech in

Facebook comments written in Algerian dialect in Arabic. Bi-LSTM, CNN, FastText, SVM, and NB models were used on a corpus of 8,700 tweets annotated as normal, abusive, and offensive.

These studies represent major advancements for these languages. They have led to the creation of annotated corpora for hate speech detection and the proposal of models with promising performance. However, this aspect remains to be studied in many other low-resource languages. This is the case for Senegalese comments where code-mixing is prevalent (English/French + Wolof). To our knowledge, Wolof, which is spoken by nearly 90% of the population, does not have annotated textual data for abusive messages detection [26].

In the following section, we present a dataset of Wolof/French code-mixing collected from Twitter and the annotation process of this dataset.

3 Data Collection and Annotation

The construction of high-quality dataset is a challenging and time-consuming task, especially for the unofficial languages like Wolof. Most users of this language do not strictly follow spelling and grammatical rules. In addition, French-Wolof mixing codes is widely used in social medias. This makes the available texts very heterogeneous and difficult to exploit.

In this work, we used the twint[1], an advanced Python scraping library, to collect tweets from Twitter. Twint allows scraping tweets from Twitter without using the Twitter API, which has limitations (3200 tweets per request for example).

A collection of 144,225 tweets from January 1, 2021 to May 31, 2023 was extracted. The extraction of these tweets includes keywords (e.g. World Cup, racist, politician, etc.), location or proximity (e.g. Senegal, Qatar, Cameroon, Morocco, Ghana, Algeria, Tunisia, Africa; etc.), person (e.g. Aliou cisse, Macky Sall, Ousmane Sonko, etc.), language (e.g. French) and so on. The queries launched for data collection enable coverage of tweets related to various domains, people, localities and over a specific time period. They also help to resolve class imbalance issues. The raw data collected contains both monolingual and multilingual data. Identifying the language in the messages is an integral part of our annotation process. Thus, we only consider tweets with Wolof-French code mixes. Since, to our knowledge, there are no resources available for abusive message detection on Wolof-French code-mix data, we are striving to produce one of the first coarse-grained datasets for abusive speech in Wolof-French. The annotation process includes pre-processing steps, such as the removal of emojis, URLs, hashtags and so on. The deletion of these entities is actually due to their lack of relevance to the analysis of the code-mix aspect under study.

Due to the lack of human resources for annotation, we had to annotate the corpus ourselves. As we are native speakers of Wolof and have a background in French, we see ourselves as endowed with the ability to understand both languages. In addition to the subjectivity of abusive message detection, we drew on the definition in [3] "Abusive language includes all excessive, false or attacking communications towards a person

---

[1] https://github.com/twintproject/twint

or group of people on the basis of characteristics such as their race, ethnicity, sexual orientation, etc." to annotate the corpus.

Thus, we annotated 2022 tweets manually for the detection of abusive messages. The annotation concerns two (2) classes: class 0 for non-abusive messages and class 1 for abusive messages. The corpus consists of 1069 tweets from class 0 and 953 tweets from class 1. Table 1 shows examples of annotated messages from our Wolof-French code-mix corpus. Text highlighted in red corresponds to words in Wolof and text in blue corresponds to words in French.

Table 1. Examples of messages from the annotated corpus

Label	Tweets	Tweets translated into English
1	La manifestation de la société civile: « Sunuy milliards du reesss »	Civil society protest: "Our billions will not be tolerated".
0	Sinon concert casserole bi tay degouma dara deh wala sama site bokoul ci senegal	Otherwise I haven't heard anything today about the saucepan concert, or maybe my neighbourhood isn't part of Senegal.
1	Mon cerveau a bug en entendant cette phrase. Xamna daf am benen **Senegal** bou outek bini guiss. **Sacré keur**	My brain bugged when I heard this sentence. There is certainly another senegal different from the one we see in Sacré Keur.
0	**Maky** deh dafa yakar ni senegal new-york leu . Discours bi on dirait deuk bi lep **nice** alors que non	Macky thinks Senegal is like the United States. His speech sounds like everything is impeccable, but it's not.

This resulting annotated dataset is then used to conduct experiments with different ML, DL and language models.

4 Experiments

In this section, we present the evaluation of the different models on our annotated dataset and compare their results. The first subsection present experiments with ML algorithms while the second report experiments with DL algorithms. The last subsection provides the results obtained by different language models. In each of the experiments, 70% of the dataset is used for training and 30% for evaluating the models. Precision, Recall, and F-measure as well as accuracy are used as evaluation metrics.

Machine Learning (ML) Algorithms. Seven ML algorithms were used: SVM, KNN, Decision Tree (DT), NB, RF, LR, and the Multi-Layer Perceptron (MLP). In addition, we experimented five (5) boosting algorithms (Cat Boost, LigthGBM, XGBoost, AdaBoost and Gradient Booster) as well as three (3) voting ensemble models (hard vote, soft vote and weighted vote). In the different experiments, we used four vectorization tools: TF-IDF, BOW, 2-g and word2vec. Table 2 presents the results of the top five algorithms, ranked in order (based on their accuracy) with the previously mentioned vectorization tools.

Table 2. Results of the top five ML algorithms according to the vectorization

Evaluation Measures		Precision		Recall		F-measure		Accuracy
Feature Extractors	Algorithms	0	1	0	1	0	1	X
TF-IDF	Naive Bayes	0.68	0.72	0.79	0.59	0.73	0.65	0.70
	Logistic Regression	0.67	0.71	0.78	0.59	0.72	0.64	0.69
	SVM	0.68	0.68	0.74	0.62	0.71	0.65	0.68
	MLP	0.67	0.68	0.73	0.61	0.70	0.64	0.67
	Random Forest	0.65	0.70	0.78	0.54	0.71	0.61	0.67
Bag Of Words	MLP	0.68	0.73	0.80	0.59	0.74	0.66	0.70
	Naive Bayes	0.70	0.68	0.71	0.68	0.70	0.68	0.69
	SVM	0.67	0.71	0.78	0.58	0.72	0.64	0.69
	Logistic Regression	0.66	0.72	0.81	0.55	0.72	0.62	0.68
	Random Forest	0.65	0.75	0.85	0.49	0.73	0.60	0.68
Ngram 2	Logistic Regression	0.62	0.83	0.93	0.38	0.74	0.52	0.66
	Naive Bayes	0.64	0.68	0.78	0.52	0.70	0.59	0.65
	SVM	0.59	0.75	0.90	0.34	0.71	0.46	0.63
	MLP	0.59	0.74	0.90	0.31	0.71	0.44	0.62
	XGBoost	0.58	0.82	0.95	0.26	0.72	0.39	0.62
Word2vec	Naive Bayes	0.69	0.68	0.71	0.65	0.70	0.66	0.68
	Logistic Regression	0.66	0.72	0.81	0.54	0.73	0.62	0.68
	CatBoost	0.65	0.77	0.86	0.49	0.74	0.60	0.68
	SVM	0.65	0.69	0.76	0.56	0.70	0.62	0.67
	Random Forest	0.64	0.72	0.82	0.50	0.72	0.59	0.67

The top five models yielded good results with accuracies ranging from 0.63 to 0.70. The results obtained with TF-IDF, BOW, and Word2vec features are quite similar while with the 2-g feature (2 words) the results are much lower in accuracy but higher according to the precision. This can be explained by the fact that the words that determine the abuse are mostly represented in multiple words (bi-grams). Overall, the NB, LR, and SVM algorithms got the best performances with 0.70, 0.69, 0.65, and 0.68 for NB, 0.69, 0.68, 0.66, and 0.68 for LR, and 0.68, 0.69, 0.63, and 0.67 for SVM respectively with the TF-IDF, BOW, 2-g, and Word2vec feature extractors.

Deep Learning (DL) Algorithms. We present the results obtained on different combinations of DL algorithms with features extracted with TF-IDF. First, eight (8) combinations of DL algorithms were explored: CNN (Convolutional Neural Network), RNN (Recurrent Neural Network), GRU (Gated Recurrent Unit), Seq2seq, LSTM (Long Short-Term Memory) with 1 layer, LSTM with 1 layer + dropout, LSTM with 2 layers + dropout, and Bi-LSTM. Then, attention layers were added to these models. Table 3 presents the results obtained by the DL models.

Table 3. Results of DL models

Evaluation Measures		Precision		Recall		F-measure		Accuracy
Attention	Algorithms	0	1	0	1	0	1	X
Without attention	Bi-LSTM	0.68	0.70	0.75	0.62	0.71	0.66	0.69
	LSTM + dropout	0.67	0.71	0.78	0.57	0.72	0.63	0.68
	LSTM with 2 layers + dropout	0.67	0.68	0.74	0.60	0.71	0.64	0.68
	Seq2seq	0.68	0.67	0.72	0.62	0.70	0.65	0.67
	CNN	0.65	0.69	0.78	0.55	0.71	0.61	0.67
	GRU	0.66	0.64	0.69	0.61	0.67	0.63	0.65
	LSTM with 1 layer	0.61	0.59	0.55	0.63	0.57	0.60	0.60
	RNN	0.54	0.50	0.55	0.49	0.54	0.49	0.52
With attention	LSTM + dropout	0.69	0.73	0.79	0.61	0.74	0.66	0.70
	LSTM with 2 layers + dropout	0.63	0.70	0.81	0.49	0.71	0.58	0.66
	CNN	0.66	0.75	0.83	0.54	0.74	0.62	0.69
	GRU	0.68	0.72	0.78	0.60	0.73	0.60	0.69
	LSTM with 1 layer	0.65	0.68	0.76	0.56	0.70	0.61	0.66
	RNN	0.60	0.80	0.92	0.33	0.73	0.47	0.64

Experiments on deep learning algorithms showed that CNN (0.67) and seq2seq (0.67) algorithms outperform the RNN (0.52) algorithm as well as its variants GRU (0.65) and LSTM (0.60). However, adding a dropout layer (0.68) or an additional layer to the LSTM model allows to improve its performance (0.68) compared to CNN and Seq2seq models. The extension of LSTM, Bi-LSTM, achieved the best results (0.69 of accuracy).

Adding attention layers increases the performance of each model. Thus, the LSTM + dropout model gains 2 more points in accuracy, the CNN gains 3 more points, the GRU gains 4 more points, the single-layer LSTM gains 6 more points, and the RNN model gains 12 more points.

Language Models. A series of experiments were conducted on five families of language models: multilingual models, monolingual models for English, monolingual models for French, monolingual models for Wolof and a bilingual French-Wolof model. All these models are available on https://huggingface.co. Table 4 presents the results obtained by language models in each category.

Table 4. Results of language models

Evaluation Measures		Precision		Recall		F-measure		Accuracy
Characteristic categories	Algorithms	0	1	0	1	0	1	X
Multilingual	bert-base-multilingual-uncased	0.80	0.49	0.46	0.82	0.58	0.61	0.66
	bert-base-multilingual-cased	0.74	0.50	0.55	0.69	0.63	0.58	0.62
	xlnet-base-cased	0.65	0.63	0.91	0.25	0.76	0.35	0.65
	Distilbert-base-multilingue-cased	0.74	0.58	0.72	0.61	0.73	0.60	0.68
	xlm-roberta-base	0.73	0.53	0.65	0.63	0.69	0.58	0.64
	google/electra-small-discriminator	0.73	0.51	0.60	0.66	0.66	0.57	0.62
English monolingual	roberta-base	0.87	0.41	0.13	0.97	0.22	0.58	0.45
	bert-base-cased	0.71	0.53	0.69	0.56	0.70	0.54	0.64
	bert-base-uncased	0.79	0.51	0.53	0.78	0.65	0.62	0.63
	albert-base-v2	0.72	0.51	0.62	0.62	0.66	0.56	0.62
	vinai/bertweet-base	0.78	0.44	0.28	0.88	0.41	0.58	0.51
	flaubert/flaubert_base_cased	0.76	0.54	0.63	0.68	0.69	0.61	0.65
	flaubert/flaubert_base_uncased	0.64	0.40	0.43	0.66	0.48	0.50	0.49
French monolingual	dbmdz/bert-base-french-europeana-cased	0.75	0.57	0.70	0.63	0.72	0.60	0.67
	dbmdz/electra-base-french-europeana-cased-discriminator	0.76	0.50	0.52	074	0.62	0.59	0.65
	dbmdz/electra-base-french-europeana-cased-generator	0.69	0.55	0.75	0.48	0.72	0.51	0.62
	claudelkros/bert-base-french	0.72	0.48	0.53	0.67	0.61	0.56	0.59
	geotrend/bert-base-fr-cased	0.74	0.48	0.49	0.73	0.59	0.58	0.58
	camembert-base	0.79	0.53	0.57	0.76	0.66	0.62	0.65
	abhilash1910/french-roberta	0.61	0.39	0.72	0.29	0.66	0.33	0.55
Monolingual Wolof	davlan/bert-base- multilingual-cased- finetuned-wolof	0.75	0.55	0.67	0.65	0.71	0.60	0.66
	abdouaziiz/ bert-base- wolof	0.80	0.52	0.54	0.79	0.64	0.63	0.63
	abdouaziiz/so raberta	0.69	0.51	0.67	0.54	0.68	0.52	0.62
Bilingual (Wolof / French)		0.73	0.53	0.65	0.63	0.69	0.58	0.64

The results obtained for class 0 (non-abusive) are very good, while those for class 1 (abusive) are very poor. However, the "Distilbert-base-multilingual-cased" model (multilingual) obtained the best f-measurement, i.e. 0.68. It was closely followed by the "dbmdz/bert-base-french-europeana-cased" model (monolingual French) with a fmeasure of 0.67, then the "bert-base-multilingual-uncased" model (multilingual) and the "davlan/bert-base- multilingual-cased- finetuned-wolof" model (monolingual Wolof) with a f-measure of 0.66. While the best accuracies for class 1 (abusive) are obtained by multilingual models ("xlnet-base-cased" (0.63) and "Distilbert-basemultilingual-cased" (0.58)). Assuming that the results obtained are close and mixed as a function of the measures, we can note that multilingual models are more stable than other language models as a function of precision for class 1 and accuracy.

In summary, we noted that classical ML algorithms, such as NB, SVM and LR with TF-IDF or BOW features, achieve comparable results to certain DL models with attention (LSMT + dropout, CNN, GRU). However, their results remain significantly superior to other models, especially language models, particularly in class 1 (abusive). This can be explained by the fact that language models are trained on large quantities of data, which are mostly non-abusive. Whereas for deep learning algorithms, they require more data to learn more complex data representations.

5 Conclusion and Future Work

The need for effective automation in identifying abusive messages on social media requires a proactive strategy. This study examines the scope of social media abuse, including cyberbullying, offensive language, trolling, and hate speech, providing a summary of relevant research. We have created a carefully annotated dataset consisting of 2022 tweets, which have been categorized into two classes for the purpose of detecting abusive messages. By conducting numerous experiments using various models and feature extractors on our distinct mixed-code Wolof-French dataset, we have determined the most efficient methods within this particular context.

In the future, our efforts will focus on expanding the dataset and developing novel strategies to tackle an important question: When faced with limited resources and code mixing, it is crucial to prioritize specific aspects in order to effectively identify abusive messages. This ongoing investigation is positioned to not only improve our comprehension of identifying abusive content in various languages and limited-resource settings, but also to enhance the efficiency of automated systems in tackling this widespread societal problem.

References

1. Toujani, R.: Opinions Mining from Posters' Users in Social Networks (2021)
2. Mubarak, H., Darwish, K., et Magdy, W.: Abusive language detection on arabic social media. In: Proceedings of the First Workshop on Abusive Language Online, Vancouver, BC, Canada: Association for Computational Linguistics, août 2017, pp. 52–56 (2017). https://doi.org/10.18653/v1/W17-3008
3. Davidson, T., Warmsley, D., Macy, M., et Weber, I.: Automated Hate Speech Detection and the Problem of Offensive Language. arXiv, 11 mars 2017. Consulté le: 22 novembre 2022. [En ligne]. http://arxiv.org/abs/1703.04009
4. N. Cécillon, R. Dufour, et V. Labatut, « Approche multimodale par plongement de texte et de graphes pour la détection de messages abusifs », p. 26, 2021
5. Kwok, I., Wang, Y.: Locate the hate: detecting tweets against blacks. In: Proceedings of the AAAI Conference on Artificial Intelligence, vol. 27, no. 1, pp. 1621–1622 (2013). https://doi.org/10.1609/aaai.v27i1.8539

6. Das, A., Gambäck, B.: Code-Mixing in Social Media Text, p. 24 (2013)
7. Silva, L., Mondal, M., Correa, D., Benevenuto, F., Weber, I.: Analyzing the targets of hate in online social media. In: Proceedings of the International AAAI Conference on Web and Social Media, vol. 10, no. 1, pp. 687–690 (2021). https://doi.org/10.1609/icwsm.v10i1.14811
8. Gitari, N.D., Zuping, Z., Damien, H., Long, J.: A Lexicon-based approach for hate speech detection. Int. J. Multimed. Ubiquitous Eng. **10**(4), 215–230 (2015). https://doi.org/10.14257/ijmue.2015.10.4.21
9. Jha, A., Mamidi, R.: When does a compliment become sexist? Analysis and classification of ambivalent sexism using twitter data. In: Proceedings of the Second Workshop on NLP and Computational Social Science, Vancouver, Canada: Association for Computational Linguistics, pp. 7–16 (2017). https://doi.org/10.18653/v1/W17-2902
10. Pitropakis, N., Kokot, K., Gkatzia, D., Ludwiniak, R., Mylonas, A., Kandias, M.: Monitoring users' behavior: anti-immigration speech detection on Twitter. Mach. Learn. Knowl. Extr. **2**(3), 192–215 (2020). https://doi.org/10.3390/make2030011
11. Solovev, K., Pröllochs, N.: Hate speech in the political discourse on social media: disparities across parties, gender, and ethnicity. Undefined (2022). https://doi.org/10.1145/3485447.3512261
12. Swamy, M.K., Jyothi, U.P.: An effective approach to hate speech detection on social media, vol. 08, no. 07 (2021)
13. Nobata, C., Tetreault, J., Thomas, A., Mehdad, Y., Chang, Y.: Abusive language detection in online user content. In: Proceedings of the 25th International Conference on World Wide Web, Montréal Québec Canada: International World Wide Web Conferences Steering Committee, avr. 2016, pp. 145–153 (2016). https://doi.org/10.1145/2872427.2883062
14. Chiril, P.: Automatic Hate Speech Detection on Social Media. Université Toulouse 3 - Paul Sabatier, 2022. Consulté le: 9 janvier 2024. [En ligne]. Disponible sur: https://theses.hal.science/tel-03599458
15. Naseem, U., Razzak, I., Hameed, I.A.: Deep context-aware embedding for abusive and hate speech detection on Twitter, vol. 15, no. 4, p. 8 (2019)
16. Founta, A.M., Chatzakou, D., Kourtellis, N., Blackburn, J., Vakali, A., Leontiadis, I.: A unified deep learning architecture for abuse detection. In: Proceedings of the 10th ACM Conference on Web Science, in WebSci 2019. New York, NY, USA: Association for Computing Machinery, juin 2019, pp. 105–114 (2019). https://doi.org/10.1145/3292522.3326028
17. Amjad, M., Ansari, M.Z., Alam, N.: An MLP based approach of hate speech detection on Twitter. vol. 6, no. 3 (2018))
18. J. Lemmens, J., Markov, I., Daelemans, W.: Improving hate speech type and target detection with hateful metaphor features. In: Proceedings of the Fourth Workshop on NLP for Internet Freedom: Censorship, Disinformation, and Propaganda, Online: Association for Computational Linguistics, pp. 7–1 (2021). https://doi.org/10.18653/v1/2021.nlp4if-1.2
19. Salminen, J., Hopf, M., Chowdhury, S.A., Jung, S.G., Almerekhi, H., Jansen, B.J.: Developing an online hate classifier for multiple social media platforms. Hum.-Centric Comput. Inf. Sci. **10**(1), 1 (2020). https://doi.org/10.1186/s13673-019-0205-6
20. Muhammad, S.H., et al.: AfriSenti: a twitter sentiment analysis benchmark for African languages. arXiv, 4 novembre 2023. Consulté le: 18 décembre 2023. http://arxiv.org/abs/2302.08956
21. Sreelakshmi, K., Premjith, B., Soman, K.P.: Detection of hate speech text in Hindi-English code-mixed data. Procedia Comput. Sci. **171**, 737–744 (2020). https://doi.org/10.1016/j.procs.2020.04.080
22. Patil, A., Patwardhan, V., Phaltankar, A., Takawane, G., Joshi, R.: Comparative study of pre-trained BERT models for code-mixed Hindi-English data. In: 2023 IEEE 8th International Conference for Convergence in Technology (I2CT), avr. 2023, pp. 1–7 (2023). https://doi.org/10.1109/I2CT57861.2023.10126273

23. Lanasri, D., Olano, J., Klioui, S., Lee, S.L., Sekkai, L.: Hate speech detection in algerian dialect using deep learning. arXiv, 20 septembre 2023. http://arxiv.org/abs/2309.11611
24. Guellil, I., Adeel, A., Azouaou, F., Boubred, M., Houichi, Y., Moumna, A.A.: Ara-women-hate: an annotated corpus dedicated to hate speech detection against women in the Arabic community. In: Proceedings of the Workshop on Dataset Creation for Lower-Resourced Languages within the 13th Language Resources and Evaluation Conference, J. Sälevä et C. Lignos, Éd., Marseille, France: European Language Resources Association, juin 2022, pp. 6875 (2022)
25. O. Boucherit, O., Abainia, K.: Offensive language detection in under-resourced Algerian dialectal Arabic language. In: Big Data, Machine Learning, and Applications, vol. 1053, M. D. Borah, D. S. Laiphrakpam, N. Auluck, et V. E. Balas, Éd., in Lecture Notes in Electrical Engineering, vol. 1053, 2022, pp. 639–647 (2022). https://doi.org/10.1007/978-981-99-3481-2_49
26. Mbaye, D., Diallo, M., Diop, T.I.: Low-Resourced Machine Translation for Senegalese Wolof Language. (2023). https://doi.org/10.48550/ARXIV.2305.00606

Towards an Ontology-Based Platform for Integrating Infectious Disease Simulation Models

Papa Alioune Cisse[✉]

Assane Seck University of Ziguinchor (UASZ), BP 523, Ziguinchor, Senegal
papaaliounecisse@yahoo.fr

Abstract. The control of infectious diseases is a perpetual challenge in public health. The need to understand their complex dynamics and the imperative to develop epidemiological surveillance, control and mitigation strategies often require modeling and numerical simulation activities. However, it should be noted that modeling and simulation of such complex systems requires expert skills in modeling tools and simulation platforms. This is often a stumbling block for practitioners and beginners in the field. In addition, communication between modelers and domain experts can be complicated by differences in the languages and concepts used on both sides. In this paper, we present an ongoing project aimed at providing solutions to these complications in order to facilitate the infectious disease modeling exercise, simplify the model simulation process, foster collaboration between researchers (practitioners and "modelers") and enable reproducibility and reuse of models and model parts. To implement this project, we are setting up a web-based platform for the integration of infectious disease simulation models. The microservices architecture we have proposed for this platform includes a simulation model repository, an ontology for annotating these models, and a set of services enabling autonomous orchestration of simulations by ensuring the selection, comparison, possible composition, formulation and simulation of models in dedicated simulators.

Keywords: infectious diseases · modeling · numerical simulation · ontologies · epidemiological monitoring systems · ontology driven simulation (ODS) · computational epidemiology · microservices architecture (MSA)

1 Introduction

The spread of infectious diseases involves a very large number of entities (hosts, transmission vectors, pathogens, risk factors, etc.) whose interactions give rise to the emergence of epidemiological situations that can occur at different spatial (regional, continental, worldwide) and temporal (seasonal, for example) scales. These types of phenomena, with their evolutions and emergences resulting from the interactions of their component parts, are described as complex systems [1, 2]. To analyze the evolution and dynamics of such complex systems, it is often necessary to resort to systemic modeling [3], which consists in building a model that reproduces its behavior in a simulation.

However, modeling and simulating complex systems in general, and infectious diseases in particular, requires expert knowledge of modeling tools (mathematical and/or computer science) on the one hand, and simulation platforms on the other. This is sometimes a major obstacle for practitioners (epidemiologists, biologists, etc.).

On the other hand, to model a disease or part of a disease, the computer scientist or mathematician needs expert knowledge and consistent data on the disease. These data are sometimes very difficult to find among practitioners. Besides, even if data are available, communication between the modelers and the domain experts can sometimes be difficult, due to differences in the concepts, terms and tools used on both sides, and the lack of a common framework for sharing and exchange.

What's more, for a novice modeler, the exercise of learning and self-training about disease modeling can be complicated by a lack of references and examples of models to draw on.

Furthermore, in scientific publications, authors often make their models available to the community, sometimes even the source codes of these models and the data they use. However, it has been found that reproducing the results presented in the publications is difficult, if not impossible, because certain details relating to simulator versions and dependencies, required operating systems and computing environments are omitted [4, 5].

We have recently initiated a project to help solve these problems. In this project, we are implementing a platform for the integration of infectious disease simulation models and simulators. The platform includes a directory of simulation models and simulators of these models, an ontology for annotating models and simulators, and an autonomous simulation orchestration module for the selection, comparison, composition, formulation and simulation of models. In this article, we present the foundations of this ongoing project, the microservices architecture of the platform and its various services.

This document is divided into three sections. The first section presents a few definitions of essential concepts to facilitate the reading of the document, and a bibliographical review of works that have addressed the issues we raise. The second section presents the foundations of our project, its objectives and expected results. The third section discusses the microservices architecture and the various components of our platform.

2 Literature Review

2.1 Definitions of Essential Notions

Complex System. The global behavior of a system, made up of multiple and possibly heterogeneous entities, can be explained by the result of interactions between its constituent entities. It is the ability to determine the system's overall behavior that enables us to characterize it as simple, and if not, as complex [6]. A complex system does not reveal a latent determinism that can be calculated, but manifests a certain form of possible unpredictability and plausible emergence of the new [3]. Indeed, the entities that make up a complex system are endowed with behaviors and sometimes decision-making mechanisms that guide their behavior independently of the other entities. It is the interaction and dynamics of interaction between these entities that determine the overall behavior of the system. However, the unpredictability of complex systems does not rule out their intelligibility. Since it is impossible to represent them definitively, i.e., to produce finite representations that are statically ready for use, we can, at a given moment, make representations that are themselves complex, so as to enable reasoning [7]. This process of producing a simplified representation of a system to make it intelligible is called modeling, and its result is a model.

Modeling. Modeling is the activity of building models. Along with experimentation (or "simulation"), it is one of the two main components of the scientific approach [6]. Indeed, modeling and simulation are two activities that go hand in hand, and together form a fully-fledged scientific approach whose aim is to propose specific theories, tools and vocabularies in order to produce knowledge about natural and artificial phenomena [8]. Modeling consists in constructing an abstraction of the system or phenomenon under study (the model), which retains only the characteristic quantities (state variables) of the system deemed relevant by the modeler [9].

Model. In science, a model is a simplified representation of a portion of reality from a particular point of view or in response to a particular question. There are two families of models: "physical" models and "abstract" models. Physical models (including scale models and animal models) are physical devices designed for experimentation. The latter are models designed to be implemented and run/simulated on a computer [6]. It is this second category of models that interests us in the context of this work.

The main purpose of a model is to be more explicit, simpler and easier to manipulate than the reality it is supposed to represent. To this end, models ignore a large number of details about the reality they represent, in order to focus on data deemed more relevant to the problem under study. In this way, there is a homomorphism between the object of study and the model that represents it. This makes it possible to apply the results of the model to the object itself [7], as shown in the following Fig. 1.

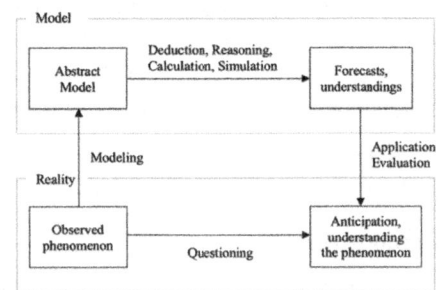

Fig. 1. Forecasting and understanding phenomena requires the development of models [7].

The observed phenomenon is translated into an abstraction (the model). This abstraction is then manipulated (by simulation, for example) to obtain results which can then be used to better understand or predict future situations of the observed phenomenon. Mechanisms of this kind can be used to predict the evolution of a disease in a given population, or to evaluate policies for controlling the spread of a disease or epidemic (vaccines, treatments, etc.).

Static vs. Dynamic Model. A model is called static when its purpose is to represent the structure of a reference system photographed at a given moment, without any reference to its evolution over time. Conversely, a model will be called dynamic when it includes in its representation assumptions or rules concerning the evolution over time of the reference system [6]. It should therefore be remembered that only dynamic models can be subjected to a process of experimentation or simulation. A static model, by definition, cannot be simulated.

Simulation. Simulation is the activity by which, according to precise objectives, and with the help of a computerized experimental device (called a simulator), a dynamic model is disturbed according to a determined protocol, making its inputs evolve and recovering its outputs [6].

Simulator or Simulation Platform. A simulation platform (or simulator for short) is a computer program that simulates a real phenomenon on a computer. In other words, a simulator enables the virtual reproduction of an environment or process.

Model Input/Output Parameters. The inputs of a dynamic model are parameters whose values are defined outside the model and which represent what the simulator can perturb. The outputs of a dynamic model are also parameters that express what we want to measure in response to these disturbances [6].

Ontology. Ontologies are interested in representing the knowledge of a domain. They consist more precisely in the identification of concepts and their relations, and in proposing their formal representation for resource annotation and semantic reasoning. Based on these representations, an autonomous agent will have the ability to understand and effectively manage a system, reason and make deliberations [10].

2.2 Related Works

In the literature, we have found a large number of works in line with the study we are proposing in this project, particularly in the areas of infectious disease model warehousing, sharing, reuse and reproducibility of models:

Models of Infectious Disease Agent Study (MIDAS)[1]. MIDAS is "a global network of scientists and practitioners who develop and use computational, statistical and mathematical models to improve understanding of infectious disease dynamics". MIDAS provides an organized collection of resources (data and software) relevant to the field of infectious disease modeling in a catalog form[2] to enable searches for specific resources on a disease, topic, location or temporal coverage. In 2008, the MREP (Model REPository) [11] tool was developed under the auspices of MIDAS to catalog models, model run results and store them in a relational database for future use and referencing.

World Health Organization's Disease Outbreak News (WHO's DON). DON is an online news service [12] through which WHO informs the international community about

---

[1] https://midasnetwork.us/.
[2] https://midasnetwork.us/catalog/.

disease outbreaks. It is the only official online registry of epidemic reports, maintained by WHO since 1996. In [13], the authors noted some limitations of this tool in terms of its analytical utility, which "is severely hampered by its unstructured, text-based system". To make the DON more operational and improve its performance, the authors developed a metadata "skeleton" that stores key information about DON reports (the identity of the report itself, the disease referred to in the report, the geographical area, the raw epidemiological data, the time of epidemic progression and any additional information) in order to constitute a fully-fledged data warehouse on disease epidemics.

Framework for Infectious Disease Analysis (FIDA). FIDA is a software environment and conceptual architecture for the integration of data and knowledge on infectious diseases, visualization, prediction and evaluation of control interventions [14]. To this end, it ensures:

- Automatic and autonomous collection of biomonitoring data (from various sources such as social media, news feeds, websites, etc.) using automatic natural language processing (NLP);
- The integration of structured and unstructured data on the history of disease emergence, endemic strains, environmental conditions, wildlife populations, land-use policies, human habitation and culture, local health infrastructures, etc.;
- The application of advanced machine learning for prediction;
- Multi-modeling, with the integration of several modeling approaches (mathematical, computational, compartmental, agent-based, etc.) to meet different requirements for analyzing the dynamics of infectious diseases.

In [5], the issue of the reproducibility of results of computer models of infectious diseases is addressed. Indeed, in publications relating to infectious disease models, even if input data and model source codes are available, it is notoriously difficult, if not impossible, to reproduce study results [15], because "other essential details such as information on software versions and dependencies, or on the required operating system and computing environments, are often missing" [4]. To address these limitations, [5] proposes "An implementation framework to improve the transparency and reproducibility of computational models of infectious diseases", which can be used by scientific communities to develop usable tools for sharing computer models in a reproducible way.

3 Presentation of Our Project

3.1 Theoretical Background

Our works focuses on three themes:

- **Epidemiological monitoring systems** are used to control the spread of disease by proposing action plans to prevent identified risks [1]. The advantage of an epidemiological monitoring system is that it enables and facilitates risk prediction and decision-making based on quantitative analyses, carried out on the basis of numerical model simulations. These models, built from epidemiological studies, help to explain the dynamics of disease propagation and validate hypotheses.

- **Computational epidemiology** is a discipline whose main objective is the application of computational (including modeling and simulation techniques, approaches and tools) and geographic (including tools for representing and visualizing complex geospatial data) concepts and resources to provide epidemiologists with user-friendly tools, to enable them to better understand the fundamental problems of epidemiology, such as the spread of disease, the effectiveness of a public health intervention, the prediction and analysis of disease manifestations and their spread in a given population, [2, 16].
- **Ontology Driven Simulation (ODS)** is a process that uses the knowledge encoded in ontologies to dynamically and automatically design simulation models. This involves having domain or application ontologies on the one hand, and modeling ontologies on the other (encoding modeling information such as model components, different modeling phases and activities, etc.). Next, domain ontology concepts are mapped to modeling ontology concepts, and modeling ontology instances are created to represent a model. Once the ontology instances representing the model have been created, additional tools are used to translate them into executable simulation models [10].

The platform we present in this work has its roots in these three themes. Indeed, it is an ontology-based platform for integrating infectious disease simulation models, which autonomously orchestrates the simulation process by guiding the selection, comparison and eventual composition (also called coupling) of models.

In terms of epidemiological monitoring systems, the platform offers the services of a numerical model simulation engine with a large "warehouse" of infectious disease simulation models. It is invoked, by providing a "simulation request", by a human user with numerical data or queries on a particular disease, or by any epidemiological monitoring system collecting field epidemiological data.

In terms of "Computational epidemiology", the platform aims to integrate, as far as possible, recent solutions resulting from advances in computer science research to meet the new contemporary epidemiological challenges of modeling and simulating the spread of infectious diseases. These include:

- The use of Multi-Agent Systems (MAS) as an additional modeling and simulation approach to capture the complexity inherent in the spread of infectious diseases, which is partly involved in human interactions and behaviors that are apprehended through social and spatial interaction networks.
- The use of new graphic representation and visualization techniques (e.g., Geographic Information Systems and virtual reality) for simulation input and output data.

In terms of ODS, the platform integrates a domain ontology for the semantic annotation of simulation models, data and resources. Based on this ontology and the simulation model repository, the platform orchestrates the simulation process by guiding the comparison, selection and composition of simulation models in response to a "simulation request".

3.2 Objectives

The overall aim of the project is to propose an ontology-based platform for integrating infectious disease simulation models and automating the simulation process of these models. This general objective is broken down into three specific objectives:

- **Objective 1.** Set up a library (warehouse) of infectious disease simulation models.
- **Objective 2.** Build a domain ontology of infectious disease simulation models to annotate the models in the warehouse.
- **Objective 3.** Implement a platform for model integration, orchestration and simulation automation.

3.3 Expected Results

Among other things, the platform will make it possible to:

- **Run simulations.** Simulate a single model at a time or by model composition (several models and several simulators).
- **Facilitating collaboration.** The platform will enable interoperability of simulation tools, model reuse and data sharing between researchers in the field of infectious disease modeling. This will enhance collaboration opportunities.
- **Serve as research support.** Articles published around infectious disease simulation models can be linked to the ontology to help researchers find more relevant research articles more quickly.
- **Share models and simulation model components.** By providing an ontology, an infrastructure is created for storing and retrieving executable simulation model components. This will facilitate the modeling exercise.
- **Reproduce the results of model simulations.** By hosting dedicated simulators and setting up the conditions for their execution, the platform should enable a model to be simulated under the conditions in which it has been presented in a scientific publication.

4 Microservices Architecture of Our Platform

4.1 Platform Architecture

We propose a microservices architecture for our platform. Definitions, advantages and challenges of a microservices architecture for applications such as the one we propose can be found in these articles [17–20] (Fig. 2).

This is a "data-driven" microservices architecture similar to those presented in [21] and [22]. In [21], knowledge extraction techniques such as data mining, classification and visualization are used to generate graphs enabling actors in a network of researchers to discover the thematic relationships between the various existing publications. A data-driven microservices architecture is proposed. It takes a publication as input and returns a graph containing all publications in the research network having themes in common with this publication. In [22], from a set of microservices that share common topics (functionality, input object, parameters, etc.), the system returns to the user the list of microservices that correspond to the topics requested in his query.

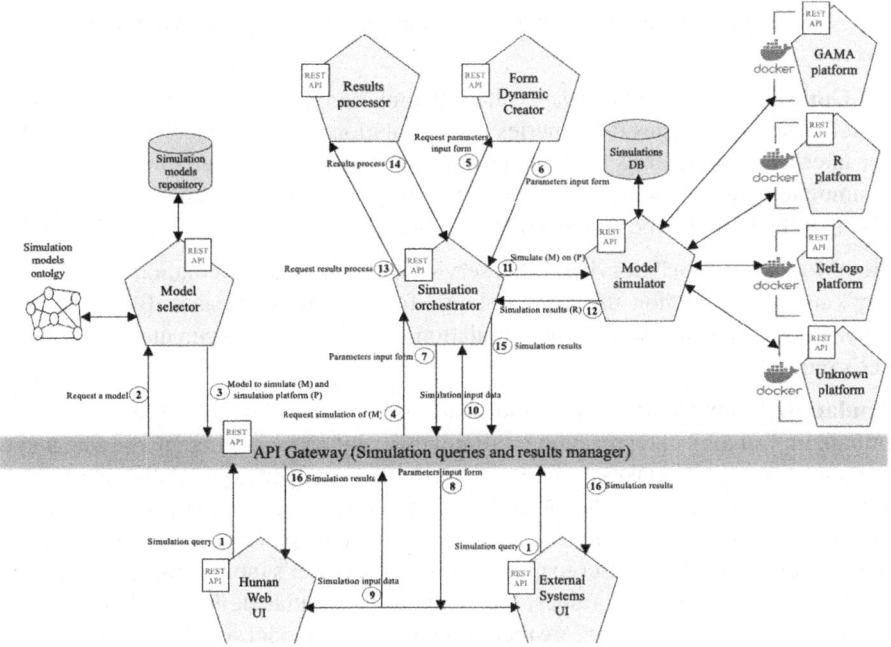

Fig. 2. Workflow for fulfilling a "simulation request" (first version).

The idea of publication discovery in [21] and microservices in [22] is similar to our approach which, starting from what we call a "simulation query", must select, in the best case, the appropriate simulation model to satisfy the query and, in the least, a list of simulation models to compose. In the worst case, if no simulation model can satisfy the user's query, the system must guide the user to formulate one. Once a simulation model has been found, the system should proceed to simulate it with the appropriate simulator and return the simulation results to the user.

4.2 The Different Services of Our Platform

This architecture[3] is generally composed of a "model selection" service, a "Gateway API" support service, user interfaces, a "simulation manager" module comprising a simulation "orchestrator", a "model simulator" service, a "dynamic form creator" service and a "simulation results exploitation" service.

User Interfaces. In our architecture, "user interfaces" are also microservices. They are divided into 2 parts: interfaces consisting of web pages for human users, and interfaces for external systems. These enable users (human or software) to interact with the assistance module using predefined functionalities via "simulation requests" (1). User requests can be accompanied by model simulation input data (9), which will always be supplied as

---
[3] This first version of the architecture does not yet take into account aspects related to model composition.

input via these interfaces. Simulation results are returned to users via these interfaces too (16).

API Gateway. The API Gateway, called "Simulation queries and results manager", is the helpdesk that handles user queries and simulation results. It receives requests from user interfaces and queries the "model selector" service (2) to determine the model to be simulated and the dedicated simulator. It then queries the simulation orchestrator, passing it the model to be simulated and the simulator (4).

The "Model Selector" Service. This service is based on a "Simulation models repository" and a "Simulation models ontology" for infectious diseases. Based on a user query, it identifies and selects the simulation model to be implemented to satisfy the user's request (3).

Simulation Orchestrator. The simulation orchestrator plays the role of conductor, "initializing" an object representing a simulation, and orchestrating the running and use of simulation results. It takes as input a model to be simulated, a simulation platform and initializes the simulation. If the model to be simulated requires input parameter data, the simulation orchestrator queries the "Form dynamic creator" service (5) to dynamically create a form enabling the user to give values to the model's input parameters (steps 6 to 10). These simulation input values, the model to be simulated, the simulation platform and the initialized "simulation" are then supplied to the "model simulator" service (11) to run the simulations. After simulations (12), the "simulation" object is saved in a database ("Simulation DB"). It is then supplied to the "Results processor" service (13) to define how the simulation results are to be used. These results are then retrieved and returned to the user (14) via the API Gateway (15).

The "Form Dynamic Creator" Service. The role of the "Form dynamic creator" service is to dynamically create forms according to user requirements. It can be used to create forms for simulation input parameters and forms for simulation output evaluation. Indeed, when a model is to be simulated with values to be supplied by the user, a form is dynamically created according to the model's input parameters. To exploit the raw data output from a simulation (which can sometimes be numerous and complex), a form can be created to allow the user to filter the data according to certain criteria in line with the model's simulation output.

The "Model Simulator" Service. It enables the simulation of a model in a dedicated simulator with input data supplied by the user. It is based on a set of dedicated simulators with their different versions. Each simulator is a microservice in a Docker container.

The "Results Processor" Service. It allows the user to exploit simulation results, for example, by visualizing simulation data via a user interface. Data can be loaded in their raw state or visualized with graphs.

5 Conclusion and Perspectives

In this article, we present an ongoing project that aims to make a contribution to facilitating the infectious disease modeling exercise for beginners in the field and non-experts, simplifying the model discovery and simulation process for practitioners, fostering collaboration between researchers (practitioners and "modelers") and in model reproducibility and reuse. We also presented the microservices architecture of a platform currently being implemented to implement this project. This architecture comprises a simulation model repository, an ontology for annotating these models, and a set of services for autonomously orchestrating simulations in dedicated simulators.

Our future works will focus on the details of each of the components of the architecture presented, notably the infectious disease simulation model ontology, the simulation model repository and the autonomous model simulation orchestration services. They will also focus on enhancing our microservices architecture to take into account aspects related to model composition and simulation platform integration.

References

1. Camara, G.: Conception d'un système de veille épidémiologique à base d'ontologies: application à la schistosomiase au Sénégal. Thèse de doctorat, Paris (1971–2017). Université Pierre et Marie Curie, France, Sénégal (2013)
2. Cissé, P.A.: Simulation à base d'agents de la propagation de la Schistosomiase : une approche de composition et de déploiement de modèles. P.hd. thesis, Université Pierre et Marie Curie - Paris VI (2016)
3. Moigne, J.-L.: La modélisation des systèmes complexes. Dunod, Paris (1990)
4. Stodden, V., et al.: Enhancing reproducibility for computational methods. Sci. **354**, 1240–1241 (2016). https://doi.org/10.1126/science.aah6168
5. Pokutnaya, D., Childers, B., Arcury-Quandt, A.E., Hochheiser, H., Van Panhuis, W.G.: An implementation framework to improve the transparency and reproducibility of computational models of infectious diseases. PLOS Comput. Biol. **19**, e1010856 (2023). https://doi.org/10.1371/journal.pcbi.1010856
6. Treuil, J.-P., Drogoul, A., Zucker, J.-D.: Modélisation et simulation à base d'agents: exemples commentés, outils informatiques et questions théoriques. Dunod, Paris (2008)
7. Ferber, J.: Les Systèmes multi-agents: vers une intelligence collective. InterEditions (1995)
8. Siebert, J.: Approche multi-agent pour la multi-modélisation et le couplage de simulations. Application à l'étude des influences entre le fonctionnement des réseaux ambiants et le comportement de leurs utilisateurs. Ph.d., thesis, Université Henri Poincaré - Nancy I (2011)
9. Fianyo, Y.E.: Couplage de modèles à l'aide d'agents: le système OSIRIS. Paris 9 (2001)
10. Cisse, P.A., Camara, G., Dembele, J.M., Lo, M.: An ontological model for the annotation of infectious disease simulation models. In: Bassioni, G., Kebe, C.M.F., Gueye, A., Ndiaye, A. (eds.) Innovations and Interdisciplinary Solutions for Underserved Areas. LNICS, Social Informatics and Telecommunications Engineering, pp. 82–91. Springer, Cham (2019). https://doi.org/10.1007/978-3-030-34863-2_8
11. Cooley, P.C., et al.: The model repository of the Models of Infectious Disease Agent Study. RTI International (2008). http://www.rti.org. https://doi.org/10.1109/TITB.2007.910354
12. Carlson, C.J.: cghss/dons: Preprint version of the data (version v0.1). Zenodo (2022). https://doi.org/10.5281/ZENODO.6374495
13. Carlson, C.J., et al.: The World Health Organization's disease outbreak news: a retrospective database. PLOS Global Public Health **3**, e0001083 (2023). https://doi.org/10.1371/journal.pgph.0001083
14. Erraguntla, M., Zapletal, J., Lawley, M.: Framework for infectious disease analysis: a comprehensive and integrative multi-modeling approach to disease prediction and management. Health Inform. J. **25**, 1170–1187 (2019). https://doi.org/10.1177/1460458217747112

15. National Academies of Sciences, Engineering, and Medicine; Policy and Global Affairs; Committee on Science, Engineering, Medicine, and Public Policy; Board on Research Data and Information; Division on Engineering and Physical Sciences; Committee on Applied and Theoretical Statistics; Board on Mathematical Sciences and Analytics; Division on Earth and Life Studies; Nuclear and Radiation Studies Board; Division of Behavioral and Social Sciences and Education; Committee on National Statistics; Board on Behavioral, Cognitive, and Sensory Sciences; Committee on Reproducibility and Replicability in Science (2019). Reproducibility and Replicability in Science. Washington (DC): National Academies Press (US)
16. Cisse, P.A., Dembele, J.M., Lo, M., Cambier, C.: Multi-agent systems for epidemiology: example of an agent-based simulation platform for schistosomiasis. In: Bajo, J., et al. (eds.) Highlights of Practical Applications of Cyber-Physical Multi-agent Systems. CCIS, pp. 157–168. Springer, Cham (2017)
17. Viggiato, M., Terra, R., Rocha, H., Valente, M.T., Figueiredo, E.: Microservices in Practice: A Survey Study (2018). arXiv. https://doi.org/10.48550/arXiv.1808.04836
18. Dragoni, N., Lanese, I., Larsen, S.T., Mazzara, M., Mustafin, R., Safina, L.: Microservices: How To Make Your Application Scale (2017). arXiv. https://doi.org/10.48550/arXiv.1702.07149
19. Dragoni, N., et al.: Microservices: yesterday, today, and tomorrow (2017). arXiv. https://doi.org/10.48550/arXiv.1606.04036
20. Hassan, S., Bahsoon, R., Kazman, R.: Microservice Transition and its Granularity Problem: A Systematic Mapping Study (2019). arXiv. https://doi.org/10.48550/arXiv.1903.11665
21. Thiele, T., Sommer, T., Stiehm, S., Jeschke, S., Richert, A.: Exploring research networks with data science: a data-driven microservice architecture for synergy detection. In: 2016 IEEE 4th International Conference on Future Internet of Things and Cloud Workshops (FiCloudW), pp. 246–251 (2016). https://doi.org/10.1109/W-FiCloud.2016.58
22. Caron, E., Houmani, Z.: Architecture Microservices pilotée par les données 1 (2018)

AI-Based Control Approach of .SN Reserved Domain Names (aIDN.SN)

Evrard Cabrel Nguemeyou Tchouangang[✉], Ahmadou Ndiaye,
Bassirou Kassé, Alex Corenthin, and Idrissa Sarr

Université Cheikh Anta Diop de Dakar, Dakar, Senegal
{evrard.nguemeyoutchouangang,ahmadou14.ndiaye,bassirou.kasse,
alex.corenthin,idrissa.sarr}@ucad.edu.sn
https://fst.ucad.sn/

Abstract. DNS (*Domain Name System*) is the distributed computer service that associates Internet domain names with their IP addresses. For the sake of business or malicious actions, some persons can make various DNS abuses such as squatting, typosquatting, and so on. To prevent such abuses, DNS managers elaborate a couple of policies and tools to double-check whether a domain name is compliant or not. Some existing solutions rely on identifying a list of reserved terms and proceed to syntactic verification before allowing the record of a new domain name. Such an approach, unfortunately, does not prevent typosquatting and Soundsquatting. To overcome such a drawback, we introduce a control approach made of both syntactic and phonetic verification supported by a classification module for decision-making. Our approach is validated over a set of 9726 domain names and around 5200 reserved terms. Results show the effectiveness of our approach and how it overcomes the existing algorithms devised for terms-reserved compliance check.

Keywords: DNS · DNS abuses · Intelligent domain names systems · squatting · typosquatting · cybersquatting · Soundsquatting

1 Introduction

DNS (*Domain Name System*) is the distributed computer service that associates Internet domain names with their IP addresses. Domains are organized in a hierarchical structure where the top is called root and represented by a dot. The domains immediately below the root are called Top Level Domains (TLDs). To simplify, TLD can be categorized as follow: Country Code Top-Level Domain (ccTLD), consisting of two letters identifying an independent country or territory (*e.g.* sn for Senegal, cm for Cameroon, fr for France); generic Top-Level Domain (gTLD), consisting of three or more letters generally identifying the sector of activity in which the individuals or organisations using them operate (.com, .org, .info). ccTLDs are managed by countries. For instance, NIC Senegal is the registry operator of .sn. To fulfill its mission, NIC Senegal has defined a naming policy and a set of services. Compliance with the legal policy is checked using the domain name management platform, which enables *a priori* checks to be carried out to ensure that created domain names cope with the naming framework. Additional checks can also be performed *retrospectively* for specific needs.

However, the existing control system suffers from two drawbacks. Firstly, a priori control is carried out based on a set of reserved terms that refer either to prohibited names (terms with sexual connotations or contrary to public decency, terms that may offend religious or gender sensitivities, etc.) or to names subject to conditions. Thus, the efficiency of the control depends on the consistency of the reserved terms list, which is currently updated manually and not regularly. As a result, some words can violate the legal framework sometimes without being detected even during subsequent checks. Secondly, the a priori control algorithm is based on a strict syntactic similarity. Then, only domain names that are literally identical to those already listed in the database of reserved terms are rejected. As a result, some person with malicious intent, commonly known as "abusers", may use terms that are syntactically different but phonetically identical. This type of abuse, more known as "squatting", consists of registering a domain name similar to another in order to profit from the latter. Unfortunately, this type of abuse is more difficult to control in advance. For example, some deep checking have revealed that certain people had registered names such as **fatik.sn** or **fatic.sn** to pass the filter set on **fatick.sn**, which is a city in Senegal and should only be registered as a domain name by the mayor's office. Even though it is possible to detect such squatting abuses, it is important to point out that they are often costly in terms of time and financial resources.

In addition, artificial intelligence is more and more used to face abuses on Internet and to optimise the management of registry services. For instance, one can rely on work done in [1,2] which generates domain names to update the database of reserved terms. Additional works [3,4] have used artificial intelligence to detect domains supplied by DGAs (Domain Generation Algorithm). Unfortunately, there is no one-size-fit-all solution that can be used to face all abuses. This is more true with the variety of sociolinguistic context and the fact that numerous African languages are poorly represented in AI solutions.

The aim of this article is to extend existing AI solution to address the problem of legal framework control in Senegal. To this end, we start from the assumption that the guarantee of both syntactic and phonetic difference is sufficient to semantically dissociate two names and, in turn, will enhance the control squatting-type abuses. We plan to use similarity metrics based on phonetics and domain name classification to pre-analyse compliance and determine what action to take. Due to this classification, creation requests can be automatically rejected or subjected to further checks.

The remainder of this document is divided into five sections. In the second section, we present related works on DNS and abuse management. In the third section, we present the problem statement, i.e. the details of the problem to be solved. In the fourth section, we present our approach, which includes language detection, phonetisation and domain classification. In the fifth section, we present the evaluation of the results obtained before concluding and presenting our research perspectives in the sixth section.

2 Related Work

Squatting are abuses linked to domain name registration and consist of registering a domain name similar to another in order to take advantage of the latter. In the remainder of this section, we address cybersquatting abuses [5,6] while focusing more specifically on typosquatting abuses [7] and DNS response hijacking such as DNS spoofing [8,9]. We present these works according to its evolution since the 90s.

From 1990 to 2000, the problems of domain name squatting emerged without any real solution. G. Andrew Barger proposed a hierarchical model of the registration and Internet architecture for domain names in order to resolve disputes of this type [10]. With no further solutions, in 1998 ICANN was created to intervene in the resolution of domain name disputes. Then, in 1999, the UDRP (Uniform Domain Name Dispute Resolution Policy) was adopted to effectively resolve disputes and also manage trademark rights violations.

From 2001 to 2010, the abuses did not change much, they just intensified, claiming more victims. In 2001, a new paradigm for intellectual property was defined by Susan Thomas Johnson. At first, several solutions were proposed to counter these abuses, such as the use of the federal trademark registration procedure proposed by John [11], to create a broader and fairer solution, and the application of the Trademark Act 194 of 1993 and/or the Unlawful Competition Act to cases of cybersquatting [12,13]. Later, around 2009, players began to look for solutions that would make it possible to prevent these abuses [14].

From 2011 to 2023, there was a big wave of interest in resolving DNS abuse. We have the soundsquatting approaches, which are approaches based on the pronunciation of the domain name. Nikiforakis et al. [15] use their approach to generate and deploy a series of domains to test their effectiveness. In the same vein we have the works [16,17] which propose approaches based on artificial intelligence to generate possible squatting domains. We also have work that, by analysing the recurring typing errors of Internet users, manages to generate possible malicious domains. In addition to this work, we can add the work done in relation to DGA (Domain Generation Algorithm). These involve using methods such as N-grammes [18], machine learning [19] or, more specifically, neural networks [20] to detect the domains produced by DGA algorithms.

Existing studies show the relevance of DNS abuse problem, however, we have noticed that they are usually based on the generation of abusive domain names and associate it with a syntax check. This may raise a problem since abusive domain name is sometimes different or even very close semantically to those generated, then they would not be able to be detected. To overcome this, our approach uses similarity metrics based on phonetics to prevent all words with strong similarity to the prohibited ones.

3 Problem Statement

As stated in the introduction, the main problem of our study is to check the compliance of domain names using a more intelligent strategy in order to better deal with abuse. In addition, we recall that verification of the legal framework conformity is carried out using a set of rules. These can be summarised and formalised as follows.

Let N be the set of all domain names already registered, $N = \{n_1, ..., n_n\}$. Given R, the list of all reserved terms in such a way that $R = \{r_1, .., r_m\}$, we define $Gen(r_i) = R - \{r_i\}$ the function that lifts the restriction on r_i. A new domain name (n_i) can be registered if one of the following two rules is met:

- **Rule 1:** $\forall r \in R, \forall n \in N, n_i \neq r \land n_i \neq n$.
- **Rule 2:** $\exists r \in R \mid r = n_i, \forall n \in N, n_i \neq n \land Gen(r)$.

In other words, a name is added if it is neither registered nor listed in the reserved terms. If the name is on the reserved list, generating a code to lift the restriction is a necessary condition for registration. Unfortunately, this approach only blocks the registration if a new unregistered domain name n_i is syntactically identical to a reserved term r_i, i.e., if $Sim(n_i, r_i) = 0$.

As a consequence, one might find a domain name $n'_i \mid Sim(n'_i, r_i) \leq \epsilon \land \epsilon \approx 0$. This situation reflects cases where someone records a name by removing a silent character or a character that does not change its phonetisation or semantics when pronounced. Therefore, problem statement is twofold. To specify them, we start from the assumption that the guarantee of a double syntactic and phonetic difference is sufficient to semantically dissociate two names and, in turn, will enhance the control of squatting abuses.

1. Let Γ be the set of domain names eligible for registration and $\bar{x}$ the phoneme of the name x, i.e. the phonetic pronunciation of x. The first question addressed is to know to what extent x should be added to Γ in order to guarantee that for any $x \in \Gamma$, $\bar{x}$ is enough distant from any $\bar{r}, \forall r \in R$.
2. The second question is how to ensure that any domain name x added to N through the answer to the previous question is not removed subsequently for the same reasons we were trying to avoid.

4 Proposed Solution

We propose a mechanism that detects any new domain name close to reserved terms. The main goal is to leverage the existing control algorithm that relies entirely on verifying syntactically the new domain name with reserved terms. By doing so, we aim to verify the eligibility of new domain name request by integrating both syntaxic and phonetic controls. This will avoid typosquatting abuses by ensuring that any new domain is different syntactically and phonetically with existing domain names. To this end, we define a similarity function based on the phonetics of words. Basically, two words are considered as close if their phonetics are quite similar. Moreover, our solution is made of two main building blocks: a domain eligibility checker and a domain name classifier.

4.1 Domain Name Eligibility Check (EligCheck)

Eligibility is checked in two phases: a preparation phase, which consists of phonetising the name, followed by a measurement of its similarity to the reserved terms.

Phonetization of Domain Names. As a reminder, phonetization, or the act of phonetizing, consists in basing the spelling of a word, text or language on its pronunciation. Graphical representation of a word is called a phoneme. In general, it involves the correspondence between the graphemes (writing units) and phonemes (sound units) of a language. To choose a phonetization tool, we found several solutions in the literature, three of which caught our eye after certain conditions had been met. The choice of solutions to be used is based on a comparative study and is presented in Subsect. 5.2. It should also be noted that the phonetisation process varies according to the languages and systems used. This is why we precede phonetisation with language detection. For this purpose, we assume that every domain name is either in French or in English. By doing this, we assume that even Wolof words, written in the Latin alphabet, can be read in French. We plan to test this hypothesis in future work. To carry out language detection, we rely on existing tools. In the Subsect. 5.1, we make a comparative study of these tools in order to choose the most appropriate in our context.

Similarity Calculation. Once the word has been phonetised, we calculate its similarity to the reserved terms. In fact, calculating the similarity between two strings of characters involves measuring how similar or close they are to each other. In machine learning, one of the simplest and most popular distances [21,22] is levenshtein's distance [23]. This will be used in this work to calculate the similarity between two domain names. It is defined by the following formula.

$$lev(a,b) = \begin{cases} max(|a|,|b|) & : \text{if } min(|a|,|b|) = 0 \\ lev(a-1,b-1) & : \text{if } a[0] = b[0] \\ 1 + min \begin{cases} lev(a-1,b) \\ lev(a,b-1) \\ lev(a-1,b-1) \end{cases} & : \text{else-if} \end{cases} \quad (1)$$

In the formula 1, for two domain names a and b, the levenshtein distance $lev(a,b)$ is the measure of the difference between two domain names. In other words, the minimum number of characters to be inserted, replaced or deleted to move from one domain name to another. This distance is defined with the two strings a and b; $|a|$ the cardinal of a (or its number of letters); and $a - 1$ the string a truncated by its first letter i.e. $a[0]$.

Identify the Eligibility of a Domain Name. To determine whether a new domain name, x, is eligible, we denote by $\bar{x}$ the phonetic of x and $Sim(\bar{x}, \bar{r})$, the similarity function used to calculate the distance separating $\bar{x}$ from the reserved term $\bar{r}$ the phonetics of x and r respectively. We declare x to be eligible if:

- $x \notin N$ and
- $\forall r \in R, \quad Sim(\bar{x}, \bar{r}) \in [0, 1]$ avec $\quad Sim(\bar{x}, \bar{r}) = lev(\bar{x}, \bar{r})/max(|x|, |r|)$

In other words, a name is eligible if it is not already registered and its phoneme is not similar to any word reserved up to a threshold.

4.2 Domain Name Classifier (DNClass)

This is the second component of our approach. It implements a variant of the KNN Machine Learning algorithm with k = 1. Actually, the relative algorithm evaluates the distance between the phonetic of any new domain name to the phonetics of all reserved domain names. Based on the result, the new domain is inserted in one of the predefined classes. In fact, theses classes can represent predefined actions to run in order to ensure that any new domain name is complaint with the registry's policies. Based on the Senegalese registry framework, we have identified three classes in which any new domain name can be placed. Let us assume Γ being the set of eligible domain names and α and β as two variables. Then the three classes are represented by Γ_α, $\Gamma_{\alpha\beta}$ and Γ_β with $0 \leq \alpha < \beta \leq 1$. We define these three classes as follows:

- **Class 0** (Γ_β): This is the class representing eligible domain names that must be registered directly. This class includes all domain names that comply with the registry's policy. $\forall \gamma \in \Gamma, \ c \in \Gamma_\beta$ si $\forall r \in R, \ Sim(\bar{\gamma}, \bar{r}) \in]\beta, 1]$.
- **Class 1** ($\Gamma_{\alpha\beta}$): This is the class of domain names requiring a second check by another filter before validation. $\forall \gamma \in \Gamma, \ \gamma \in \Gamma_{\alpha\beta}$, si $\exists r \in R$, such that $Sim(\bar{\gamma}, \bar{r}) \in]\alpha, \beta]$.
- **Class 2** (Γ_α): This is the class of domain names that must be blocked. This class represents domain names that are very close phonetically to the reserved domain names. $\forall \gamma \in \Gamma, \ \gamma \in \Gamma_\alpha$, si $\exists r \in R$, such that $Sim(\bar{\gamma}, \bar{r}) \in [0, \alpha]$.

One can notice that the numbers of classes can vary from one registry to another based on the policies. Bearing this in mind, the numbers of variables is set accordingly to numbers of classes that depicts mostly the implemented registry policies. In other words, our solution can be considered enough generic to be applied easily on other TLD registries.

5 Evaluation of the Proposed Solution

In this section, we conduct an evaluation of our solution to demonstrate its effectiveness. We began by conducting a comparative study of language detection and phoneticization solutions to select the most suitable one for our purposes. Following the comparative studies, we proceeded to evaluate the solution. For the latter, we used the two complete databases for the .SN TLD: the registered domain names database, containing 9726 domain names, and the reserved terms database, containing 4097 domain names. These two databases have 201 domain names in common, corresponding to reserved domain names with registration authorizations.

5.1 Language Detection Tools

There are various language detection tools based on AI process that can be ranged from natural language processing algorithms (Googletrans, FastText) to probabilistic statistics (Langdetect), linguistic features (Langid) or linguistic dictionaries (Dictionnaire CMU). We can have tools that are not intended for basic language identification but can be used as such. This is the case with Eng_to_ipa, whose basic purpose is English phonetisation, but which will be used here as a language detection tool. To choose a tool, we first rely on free accessibility criteria. Bearing this in mind, we compare the following solutions: CMU [24], Langid [25], Langdetect [26] and the Eng_to_ipa [27] tool. Afterward, we use the two sets of data (13622 domain names with 11186 names in French and 2436 names in English) to assess which tools is best to detect the language. Precisely we evaluate the different tools based on the following metrics: Elements detected per language, true positives (TP), false positives (FP).

$$Accuracy = \frac{TP + TN}{All\_elements} \qquad (2)$$

Table 1. Test results for selected language detection tools

Tools	French elements	TP French	FP French	English elements	TP English	FP English
CMU	11241	11189	28	2381	2378	3
Eng_to_ipa	11186	11186	0	2436	2430	6
Langid	4985	4411	574	8637	1856	6780
Langdetect	12324	10123	2201	1298	229	1069

Table 1 shows the results obtained from the language detection tools on the whole dataset. We can see that Langid and Langdetect tools produce more false positives compared to CMU and Eng_to_ipa tools.

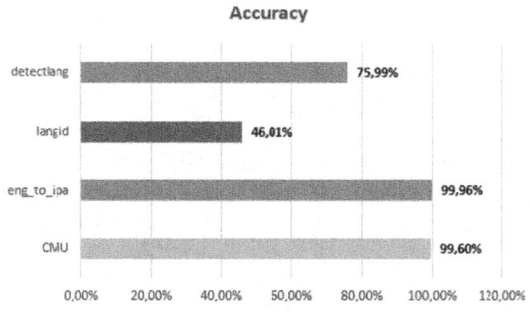

Fig. 1. Accuracy of different language detection tools

Figure 1 illustrates the results of the accuracy calculation given by the formula 2. We can see that the eng_to_ipa and CMU tools provide the best results with over 99% accuracy. However, when we add up the number of false positives for the two solutions as shown in Table 1, the CMU method accumulates thirteen-one false positives while the method with eng_to_ipa accumulates six false positives. Finally, to evaluate our solution, we will use the Eng_to_ipa tool for language detection.

5.2 Phonetization Tools

As previously, we rely on free tools to consider the following ones: eng_to_ipa [27], Espeak [28], and epitran [29]. Since the phonetisation tool depends tightly to the language, we have Eng_to_ipa tool, which is dedicated to English words, and Espeak and Epitran tools for both languages (English and French). We conducted an empiric evaluation around thousands of domain names for both french and English words. A rigorous analysis had let us know that Epitran and Espeak give best results than others respectively in french and english. Due to lack of space, we skip details of this evaluation.

5.3 Overall Solution Evaluation

In this section, we evaluate our overall solution against the existing solution. To achieve this, we will first determine the optimal α, β threshold values using an adaptive approach. Once the thresholds have been determined, we'll calculate the gains of our solution compared with the results of the existing solution.

To evaluate the gain, we introduce a fourth class (class 3) which represents the class of reserved domain names that have been registered by lifting the restriction using the $Gen()$ function. This class allows us to correctly evaluate the gain because it represents all the domain names that were blocked by the existing solution. We declare r in class 3 if $r \in R \wedge Gen(r)$. We use the first dataset which represents all registered domain names (9726 domain names). It is divided into four classes. We have 8664 in *class 0 domain names*, 288 in *class 1 domain names*, 573 in *class 2 domain names* and 201 in *class 3 domain names*. We use the Score F1 given by the Table 2 to optimize the α and β thresholds.

Table 2. Evaluation measures

Details	Measures	Formula
TP: True Positive	Precision	$\frac{TP}{TP+FP}$ (4)
FP: False Positive		
TN: True Negative	Recall	$\frac{TP}{TP+FN}$ (5)
FN: False Negative		
	Score F1	$\frac{2 X Precion X Recall}{Precision+Recall}$ (6)

- **Precision**: Measures the proportion of positive instances correctly identified among all instances identified as positive by the model.
- **Recall**: Measures the proportion of correctly identified positive instances among all the truly positive instances in the data.
- **Score F1**: Harmonic mean of precision and recall.

Optimization of α and β Thresholds: We set up an approach to determine the best pair of thresholds (α, β) to use to evaluate our solution. First, we fix α and vary β. This step allows us to identify the best value of β for which we have the best *Score F1* for class 1 (representing the category of abuse defined by β). Once this value has been found, we fix β at this value and vary α to determine its optimal value. In this way, we obtain the optimal value for the pair (α, β).

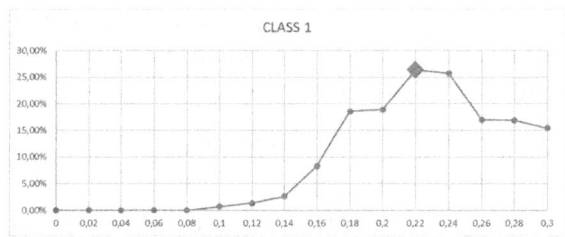

Fig. 2. Variation of *Score F1* for class 1 with $\alpha = 0.00$

Figure 2 illustrates the variation of the *Score F1* on all the data for class 1. We set (α) to 0.0 and we vary (β) from 0.0 to 0.30 with a step of 0.02. Here we only look at class 1 because it is the only class directly impacted by the variation of the β threshold. Choosing the best value for the β threshold means taking the value for which the *Score F1* is highest for class 1. By observing Fig. 2, we note that the value for which the curve is the highest is **0.22** which corresponds to the best value of β.

For the rest, we set the value of β to 0.22 and determine the best value of α. Knowing that the value of α must be strictly lower than the value of β, we vary the value of α from 0.0 to 0.2 with a step of 0.02. In this case, the classes affected are classes 1 and 2. We calculate the value of the *Score F1* for each of the classes and take the average. Figure 3 illustrates the variation of the average *Score F1* between class 1 and 2, in relation to α. We can see that the best value for α is 0.10, which gives a final *(0.10, 0.22)* for the pair of (α, β). After that,

Fig. 3. Variation of *Score F1* for classes 1 and 2 with $\beta = 0.22$

Calculating the Solution Gain: Once the thresholds have been chosen, our aim is to evaluate the contribution of our solution. This step enables us to assess the effectiveness of our approach by quantifying the gain in misuse detection compared with the existing method. To this end, We use the Gain and *Score F1* given by the formula 3 and the Table 2 to evaluate our solution.

$$Gain(total) = \frac{TP(c1) + TP(c2)}{TP(c3)} \qquad Gain(ci) = \frac{TP(ci)}{TP(c3)} \qquad (3)$$

with *TP(ci)* set of true-positives of the class *i*. In order words, the gain is calculating by making the ratio of all True positive of the new solution over the True positive of the existing solution $TP(c3)$. The Table 3 illustrates the calculation of the gain of our solution compared to the existing solution using the formula 3. Looking at the table, we see a gain of *45.27%* for class 1 and *217%* for class 2, totalling an overall gain of *262.69%* in terms of detecting additional abusive domain names. These results clearly indicate that the proposed solution can detect more than twice as many abusive domain names as the existing solution. This significant improvement underlines the increased effectiveness of our model in identifying abuse, positioning our solution as a significantly better performing alternative.

Table 3. Evaluation results of the solution

Details	Measures	Results
$\alpha = 0.10$	Class 1 gain	**45.27%**
$\beta = 0.22$	Class 2 Gain	**217.41%**
	Total Gain (class 1,2)	**262.69%**

6 Conclusion

In this article, we present a solution for managing reserved terms by introducing a dual syntactic and phonetic check. Our approach is based on the calculation of phonemes and the measurement of the distance between a new domain name and previously defined reserved domains. We used a dataset comprising 9726 domain names, 201 of which were reserved with authorisations. Our approach produced significant results, with gains of around *262.69%* of additional domain names detected as not compliant or under risk of violating the legal framework. However, our solution suffers with two drawbacks which are the time consuming of our algorithm and the lack of automatically integrating new additional reserved terms obtained by the phonetic checking process. The latter drawback has the disadvantage of requiring to run the algorithm indefinitely even though a previous word was already detected as not compliant phonetically with reserved terms rules. Ongoing works are conducted to face such drawbacks.

References

1. Tahir, R., et al.: It's all in the name: why some URLs are more vulnerable to typosquatting. In: IEEE INFOCOM 2018-IEEE Conference on Computer Communications, pp. 2618–2626. IEEE (2018)
2. Ahmad, I., Parvez, M.A., Iqbal, A.: TypoWriter: a tool to prevent typosquatting. In: 2019 IEEE 43rd Annual Computer Software and Applications Conference (COMPSAC), vol. 1, pp. 423–432. IEEE (2019)
3. Moubayed, A., Aqeeli, E., Shami, A.: Detecting DNS typo-squatting using ensemble-based feature selection & classification models. IEEE Can. J. Electr. Comput. Eng. **44**(4), 456–466 (2021)
4. Moubayed, A., et al.: DNS typo-squatting domain detection: a data analytics & machine learning based approach. In: 2018 IEEE Global Communications Conference (GLOBECOM), pp. 1–7. IEEE (2018)
5. Mercer, J.D.: Cybersquatting: blackmail on the information superhighway. BUJ Sci. Tech. L. **6**, 290 (2000)
6. Bhusari, R.V., Rampure, K.R.: Cybersquatting: a threat to the globalising world. Indian J. Law Legal Res. **3**(2), 2283–2304 (2022). ISBN 2582-8878
7. Moubayed, A., et al.: DNS typo-squatting domain detection: a data analytics & machine learning based approach. In: 2018 IEEE Global Communications Conference (GLOBECOM), Abu Dhabi, UAE, pp. 1–7. IEEE, December 2018. ISBN 978-1-5386-4727-1. https://doi.org/10.1109/GLOCOM.2018.8647679. https://ieeexplore.ieee.org/document/8647679/. Accessed 20 July 2023
8. Viegas, E.K., Lopez, M.A., Monteiro, R.M.: Method for detection of DNS spoofing servers using machine learning techniques. Google Patents (2022)
9. Hanley, S.: DNS overview with a discussion of DNS spoofing, November 2000
10. Barger, G.A.: Cybermarks: a proposed hierarchical modeling system of registration and internet architecture for domain names. J. Marshall L. Rev. **29**, 623 (1995)
11. Papavasiliou, J.: Using the federal trademark registration process to create a broader yet fairer solution to domain name contacts. U. Balt. Intell. Prop. LJ **11**, 93 (2002)
12. Ebersohn, G.: Cybersquatting, typosquatting and trade mark law (Part 1). J. S. Afr. Law/Tydskrif vir die Suid-Afrikaanse Reg **2006**(2), 315–329 (2006)
13. Ebersohn, G.: Cybersquatting, typosquatting and trade mark law (Part 2). J. S. Afr. Law/Tydskrif vir die Suid-Afrikaanse Reg **2006**(3), 551–563 (2006)
14. Moore, M.: Cybersquatting: prevention better than cure? Int. J. Law Inf. Technol. **17**(2), 220–231 (2009)

15. Nikiforakis, N., Balduzzi, M., Desmet, L., Piessens, F., Joosen, W.: Soundsquatting: uncovering the use of homophones in domain squatting. In: Chow, S., Camenisch, J., Hui, L., Yiu, S.M. (eds.) ISC 2014. LNCS, vol. 8783, pp. 291–308. Springer, Cham (2014). https://doi.org/10.1007/978-3-319-13257-0_17
16. Valentim, R., et al.: AI-based sound-squatting attack made possible. In: IEEE European Symposium on Security and Privacy Workshops (EuroS & PW), pp. 448–453. IEEE (2022)
17. Valentim, R., et al.: Lost in translation: AI-based generator of cross-language sound-squatting. In: 2023 IEEE European Symposium on Security and Privacy Workshops (EuroS&PW), pp. 513–520. IEEE (2023)
18. Selvi, J., Rodríguez, R.J., Soria-Olivas, E.: Detection of algorithmically generated malicious domain names using masked N-grams. Expert Syst. Appl. **124**, 156–163 (2019)
19. Almashhadani, A.O., et al.: MaldomDetector: a system for detecting algorithmically generated domain names with machine learning. Comput. Secur. **93**, 101787 (2020)
20. Congyuan, X., Shen, J., Xin, D.: Detection method of domain names generated by DGAs based on semantic representation and deep neural network. Comput. Secur. **85**, 77–88 (2019)
21. Quelle distance choisir en machine learning - Pensée Artificielle. https://penseeartificielle.fr/choisir-distance-machine-learning/. Accessed 15 Jan 2024
22. NLP: les techniques et les algorithmes préférés des data scientists- LeMagIT. https://www.lemagit.fr/conseil/NLP-les-techniques-et-les-algorithmes-preferes-des-data-scientists. Accessed 15 Jan 2024
23. Levenshtein, V.I., et al.: Binary codes capable of correcting deletions, insertions, and reversals. Soviet Phys. Doklady **10**(8), 707–710 (1966)
24. The CMU Pronouncing Dictionary. http://www.speech.cs.cmu.edu/cgi-bin/cmudict. Accessed 15 Jan 2024
25. langid on Pypi. en, April 2016. https://libraries.io/pypi/langid. Accessed 11 Jan 2024
26. Shuyo, N.: Language Detection Library for Java (2010). http://code.google.com/p/language-detection/
27. Roberts, R.: English-to-IPA Transcription (2021)
28. eSpeak: Speech Synthesizer. https://espeak.sourceforge.net/index.html. Accessed 09 Jan 2024
29. Mortensen, D.R., Dalmia, S., Littell, P.: Epitran: precision G2P for many languages. In: Proceedings of the Eleventh International Conference on Language Resources and Evaluation (LREC 2018) (2018)

Efficient Combination of Deep Learning Models for Skin Disease Detection

Mohamed Massamba Sene[✉], Ndeye Fatou Ngom, and Michel Seck

LTISI Laboratory, Ecole Polytechnique de Thiès, Thies, Senegal
smmassamba@ept.sn

Abstract. Identifying skin diseases is challenging due to their similar visual appearance, making it difficult to select features. Despite significant progress in the effective identification of skin diseases, the problem remains unsolved. This paper presents a new method for accurate skin disease detection, which combines the Attention U-Net architecture for image segmentation and a customized Convolutional Neural Network (CNN) for image classification. The first step of the proposed approach is training the segmentation model on a dataset of segmented skin disease images. The resulting model is then used to segment images from a skin disease images classification dataset before training the customized CNN using the segmented images to classify skin diseases. With the proposed approach, we were able to achieve an accuracy of 99% as well as high precision, recall and F1 score of 99% on the HAM10000 dataset. Comparative analysis with other similar studies demonstrates its effectiveness in accurately identifying these diseases.

Keywords: Skin diseases identification · Image segmentation · Deep learning · Image classification · Computer vision

1 Introduction

The skin is an essential organ of the human body, protecting us from harmful radiation, injuries and infections caused by UV rays. The prevalence of skin cancer is increasing worldwide and represents a significant health risk. Skin diseases are generally detected by time-consuming procedures such as skin biopsy, clinical screening, dermoscopic analysis and histopathological diagnosis [1]. Melanoma is the most dangerous type of skin cancer and is responsible for the majority of skin cancer deaths. However, there are other diseases that are visually similar to malignant melanoma, such as blue nevus and spitz nevus. Dermoscopic images are essential for identifying skin cancer, but visual inspection can be challenging. The use of computerized automatic medical image segmentation technology will have a significant impact on the problem of diagnostic errors by clinicians as well as providing strong support for automatic classification [1]. In recent years, CNNs have shown promising results when it comes to computer vision tasks like pattern localization or features learning. In addition, semantic segmentation is proving to be well suited to biomedical image segmentation, allowing a more flexible and comprehensive approach to capturing the diverse structures within biomedical images.

This study aims to propose a new approach that improves the accuracy of skin disease identification using deep learning based techniques. The proposed workflow starts with segmentation using Attention U-Net to identify the region of interest, followed by the use of a customized CNN to identify skin disease. The key contributions of this paper are:

- A new skin disease detection model that combines the Attention U-Net and a customized Convolutional Neural Network.
- By using the Attention U-Net architecture instead of classical methods such as region growing [15] or other descriptors for segmentation, we enhance the model's ability to capture context, resulting in more accurate segmentation.
- By using a customized Convolutional Neural Network with optimized hyperparameters, we directly extract features and identify the skin disease without manual feature extraction.

With the proposed approach, we were able to achieve an accuracy of 99% on the HAM10000 dataset with high precision, recall and F1 score of 99%. Comparative analysis with other similar studies demonstrates its effectiveness in accurately identifying skin diseases.

The rest of this paper is organized as follows. Section 2 discusses previous work on skin disease classification. Section 3 discusses the Attention U-Net Architecture. In Sect. 4, we describe the design of the proposed approach, as well as the datasets and techniques used for segmentation and classification of the skin disease images. Section 5 examines the process used to build the models and discusses the results of the experiment. Finally we conclude our work in Sect. 6.

2 Related Work

The development of artificial intelligence technology has opened up many possibilities in the field of automated disease detection from image analysis.

Shetty et al. [12] applied machine learning and deep learning techniques using CNNs to classify the skin lesion images on the HAM10000 dataset, achieving an accuracy of 95.1% using a customized CNN. After training different state-of-the-art models (MobileNet, VGG19, ResNet50, InceptionV3) using transfer learning, Valasco et al. [2] found that MobileNet had the highest accuracy (94.1%) while VGG16 had the lowest accuracy (44.1%). In [11], Ali et al. trained the EfficientNets B0-B7 on the HAM10000 dataset by performing transfer learning on pre-trained weights from ImageNet and fine-tuning the Convolutional Neural Networks. Wei et al. [3] proposed an approach based on the combination of DenseNet and ConvNet. Compared to other state-of-the-art models, the proposed model achieved good results due to its accuracy and F1 score of 95.29%

and 89.99% respectively. However, it is computationally expensive, which limited it to performing classification on only three skin diseases.

In [13], Oktay et al. proposed a skin disease detection approach using pretrained Convolutional Neural Network features before multi-class SVM classification. Reddy et al. [1] proposed an approach that utilizes optimized region-growing-based segmentation and an autoencoder-based classification to identify skin diseases. The accuracy of the proposed system was 94.2%. However it was limited to detecting the presence or absence of skin disease and not identification on a wide range of diseases. Soh et al. [9] proposed a hybrid U-Net transformer to improve the efficiency of segmentation of single-modality lesion and multi-modality brain tumour images. Recently, the connection between the U-Net architecture and the attention mechanism has been the focus of many authors. The Attention U-Net architecture is based on the U-Net architecture which boasts an expansive symmetric path that effectively captures spatial context, enabling accurate edge detection and detailed segmentation [9]. By introducing the attention mechanism, it allows the network to focus on relevant image features and suppress irrelevant noise, resulting in cleaner and more accurate segmentation [13]. Hasrh et al. [18] use Attention U-Net for dental segmentation to further increase sensitivity and prediction accuracy with minimal computational overhead.

Based on these previous works, we propose a novel approach aimed at improving the accuracy of detection.

3 Attention U-Net Architecture

In this work, unlike in [1], we don't use optimized region growing segmentation. Instead, we use Attention U-Net segmentation. U-Net is a Fully Convolutional Neural Network designed for accurate and efficient biomedical image segmentation. Its name comes from its U-shaped architecture, which consists of two main pathways: a Contracting path (Encoder/Left side) and an Expanding path (Decoder/ Right side).

Contracting path: the upper part of the "U" is used to extract higher level features from the image through a gradual down-sampling of the image [6]. To achieve this, similar to a classical CNN architecture, we repeated the block of two 3×3 convolutions with step 1 and ReLu activation, separated by a Droupout layer with rate 0.1 and followed by a max pooling layer. We start with 32 filters for the first block, and in each step we double the number of filters we use. For the last block, which acts as a bottleneck, we use 5 encoder blocks with pooling removed.

Expanding path: the lower path of the "U" is used to restore the spatial resolution of the image while performing semantic segmentation. It uses transposed convolutions to increase the resolution of the image and up-sample the feature maps learned in the contracted path [6].

A key feature of the U-Net architecture is the use of skip connections. This bridges the gap between high-level and low-level features, improving segmentation accuracy with the advantage of preserving a large amount of spatial information. However, it also results in poor feature representation from the initial layers. In the Attention U-Net, soft attention is implemented at the skip connections with attention gates to actively suppress activation at irrelevant regions, as shown in Fig. 1. Two inputs are taken, a gating signal from the lower layer with better feature representation and the skip connection with better spatial information. The two inputs are passed through convolution layers, with the skip connection being down-sampled to allow it to be added. Aligned weights become larger while unaligned weights become smaller. The result is then passed to a ReLu activation before convolution with a filter that allows the weights to be retrieved. The resulting array is then up-sampled to the skip connection size before element by element multiplication [13].

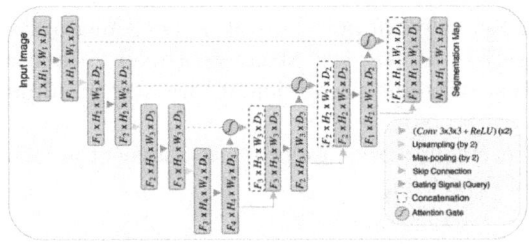

Fig. 1. Attention U-Net architecture as seen in [13]

4 Methodology

4.1 System Design

The proposed workflow consists of a combination of segmentation using the Attention U-Net and classification using a CNN, as shown in Fig. 2. Unlike in [1], we don't use optimized region growing segmentation. Instead, we use Attention U-Net segmentation. This is a crucial shift from traditional region growing segmentation, which is sensitive to noise and relies heavily on setting thresholds and seed points [15], which can be tedious. By replacing region growing with Attention U-Net, the proposed workflow enjoys significant advantages in terms of accuracy, robustness and automation [9].

We also remove manual feature extraction and rely on feature extraction provided by the CNN, as it is able to learn features from raw data in a hierarchical manner. In fact, manual feature definition requires domain expertise and meticulous effort, often becoming a bottleneck in the development process and struggling to adapt to new data or variations in existing data, hindering the generalizability of the model [14]. By doing so, we are able to reduce development time and effort and minimize the risk of human bias.

Finally, as seen in [3], we exploit the power of fusion models by combining the Attention U-Net and the CNN model. This improves the performance of the proposed model by exploiting the strengths of both architectures.

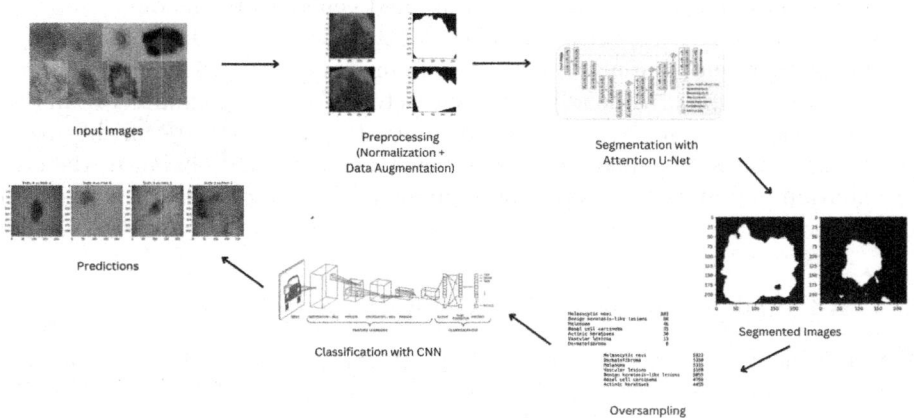

Fig. 2. Proposed skin disease classification model

4.2 Datasets

Two datasets are used in our study: the PH^2 dataset [4] for segmentation and the HAM10000 (Human-Against-Machine with 10000 training images) dataset for classification [5].

The PH^2 dataset was created for research and comparative analysis purposes and consists of a collection of 200 images acquired at the Dermatology Service of the Pedro Hispano Hospital (Matosinhos, Portugal). They are 8-bit RGB color images together with their segmentation masks at 768×560 pixels resolution [4].

The HAM10000 dataset is a collection of 10015 dermoscopic images from different populations, acquired and stored using different modalities. The cases include a representative collection of all major diagnostic categories of pigmented lesions: Actinic Keratoses and Intraepithelial Carcinoma (AKIEC), Basal Cell Carcinoma (BCC), Benign Keratosis-like Lesions (BKL), Dermatofibroma (DF), Melanoma (MEL), Melanocytic Nevi (NV) and Vascular Lesions (VASC) [5].

4.3 Data Preprocessing

Image normalization was applied to both datasets and the images were resized to a resolution of 224×224 pixels using OpenCV's resize function with the INTER_AREA strategy. This strategy prioritizes maintaining smooth transitions and minimizing aliasing effects, making it a preferred choice for downsampling images in applications where visual quality is important [7].

To increase the size of the PH^2 dataset to 600 images, we applied data augmentation by flipping and rotating the 200 images. Data augmentation helps to learn more robust features and reduces the risk of over-fitting by exposing our model to a wider range of data variations. This leads to better performance on unseen data, resulting in more accurate and generalizable models.

Class imbalance was present in the HAM10000 dataset, with the Melanocytic Nevi class represented in more than 70% of our images. We apply over-sampling random over-sampler, while adjusting the factor based on the number of images for each class. This simply duplicates the minority class by the specified factor in the training dataset to increase its representation, artificially balances the class distribution and gives the model more opportunities to learn from examples of the minority class.

4.4 Adapted Attention U-Net Architecture

We implement the encoder blocks of the attention U-Net architecture as seen in [13] with four repeated combinations of attention gates followed by decoder blocks. The attention gates consist of three convolution layers followed by an up-sampling layer and batch normalisation. For the first two layers we use a 3×3 convolution with ReLu activation. The first layer uses stride 1 to keep the dimension of the gating signal and the second uses stride 2 to reduce the dimension of the skip connection. The last layer uses 1×1 convolution with sigmoid activation. The decoder blocks use an up-sampling layer followed by two 3×3 convolutions with stride 1 and ReLu activation. We start with 256 filters and at each step we divide the number of filters by 2.

4.5 Convolutional Neural Network

Convolutional Neural Networks (CNNs), also known as ConvNets, are a class of a class of deep learning models specifically designed to solve computer vision problems such as image classification, object detection, and image segmentation. We propose a CNN model that is built from scratch and modified by fine-tuning the parameters to find the best classifier for skin disease classification. The architecture of the proposed CNN can be seen in Fig. 3. The network takes as input images of size 224×224 pixels and provides as output a probability distribution for the seven output classes. The preprocessing block implements the transformations described in Subsect. 4.3, such as normalization, data augmentation, and class balancing.

The rest of our CNN consists of two parts: the convolution module, which transforms the input images into feature vectors, and the classification module, which determines which class the input image belongs to. It is composed of

- **Convolution Layers**: serve as the backbone of a CNN. Filters also called kernels are used to perform operations on the input images. Each filter goes through the image and computes the weighted sum of the pixel values. The results are then stored in feature maps. Filters are then moved along the

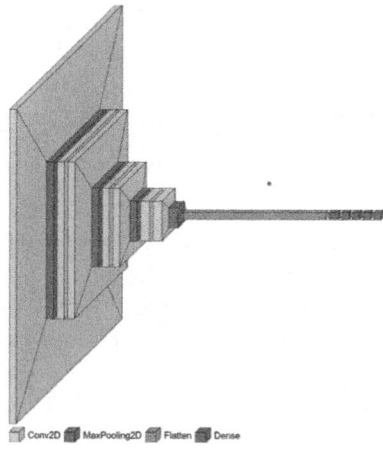

Fig. 3. CNN model architecture

images storing important features like edges, textures, shapes. The size of the Kernel used here is 3×3 with He-normal as kernel initializer.
- **Activation Layers**: after each convolution, an activation function is used on the resulting feature map. This allows the introduction of non-linearity allowing the capture of more complex relations between features [8]. The ReLu activation function was used for our Convolution layers.
- **Pooling Layers**: are used to reduce the dimensions of the feature maps while preserving the important information. Pooling reduces the model complexity and makes features insusceptible to small changes in position on the image [8]. The MaxPooling2D layer was used in our implementation. We use three blocks of double convolution followed by pooling.
- **Fully Connected Layers**: after repeated convolution and pooling, they are used to perform classification. These layers are similar to those of traditional Neural Networks and are used to combine the extracted feature maps to perform classification [8].

The features extracted from the convolutional module are passed on to the classification module, which consists of 5 Fully Connected Layers using Dense Layers. The number of neurons in the first and second layers is 64. The third and fourth layers have 16 neurons. The output layer consists of 7 neurons, corresponding to the number of output classes in the network. The ReLu activation is used for each of the Dense Layers, except for the last layer where a softmax activation function is used to provide a score for the 7 classes.

4.6 Evaluation Metrics

The metrics used in this study to evaluate the performance of our model are accuracy, precision, recall and F1 score.

Accuracy is simply the ratio of the number of correctly predicted observations to the total number of observations. It is calculated using

$$\text{Accuracy} = \frac{TP}{TP + FP + TN + FP}$$

where

- TP (True Positives) are correctly predicted positives, the actual class values are yes and prediction class values are also yes.
- TN (True Negatives) represent the correctly predicted negative values. This means that the value of the actual class is no and the value of the predicted class is also no.
- FP (False Positives) represent when the actual class is no and the predicted class is yes.
- FN (False Negatives) denotes when the actual class is yes but the predicted class is no [3].

Recall is the proportion of true positives that are correctly identified.

$$\text{Recall} = \frac{TP}{TP + FN}$$

Precision is the ratio of the correctly predicted positive observations to the total number of positive observations predicted.

$$\text{Precision} = \frac{TP}{TP + FP}$$

The F1 score takes into account both precision and recall.

$$\text{F1 score} = \frac{2 \times \text{Precision} \times \text{Recall}}{\text{Precision} + \text{Recall}}$$

We also use IoU (Intersect over Union) to evaluate our segmentation model, which allows us to compare our segmented masks with the ground truth masks. It calculates the overlap between the predicted and ground truth regions by calculating the ratio of the intersection area to the union area [19].

5 Experimental Results

The experiments were performed on the two datasets described in 4.2. The metrics described in the Subsect. 4.6 were used for performance evaluation. The effectiveness of the proposed methodology is compared with previous studies based on deep learning for skin disease classification.

5.1 Experimentation

The experiments were carried out on a 14" Macbook Pro M2 with an Apple M2 Pro chip with a combined 10-core CPU and 16-core GPU. The code was written using Tensorflow, OpenCV and NumPy libraries with Python 3.8 as the programming language.

We first load and preprocess the images from the PH^2 dataset using the steps described in Subsect. 4.3 such as normalization, data augmentation and class-balancing. We then build and train the segmentation model using the Attention U-Net architecture. Training lasted for 45 epochs, and the results shown in Fig. 4, Fig. 5 and Fig. 6 were obtained after training and evaluation.

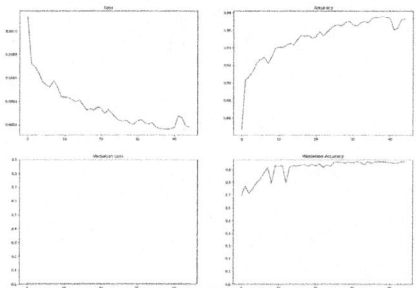

```
IOU:        |  82.61  |
Precision:  |  95.79  |
Recall:     |  90.19  |
Accuracy:   |  94.95  |
Loss:       |   3.64  |
```

Fig. 4. Loss and Accuracy on the train set with the Attention U-Net model

Fig. 5. Metrics on the test set with the Attention U-Net model

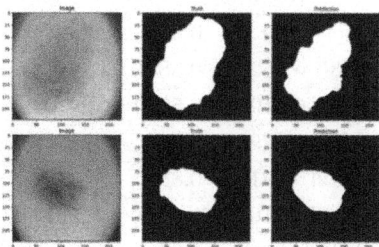

Fig. 6. Intermediate results obtained with the Attention U-Net model

The images from the HAM10000 dataset were then segmented using the trained model and used as input to train our CNN model for classification. To optimize the hyperparameters, we configure a search space with a define-by-run syntax and then use RandomSearch to find the best values for our models. After training and evaluation, the results obtained are shown in the Fig. 7 and Fig. 8 which provides a better understanding of the metrics of our model.

The proposed model has a higher accuracy compared to the model [3] which uses a transfer learning based approach. Experimental results also show that the proposed model achieves better performance than previous CNN based model [11], GAN based model [10] and models based on deep transfer learning with sparrow search algorithm [17]. It also shows similar results to the model based on deep ensemble learning [16]. The models were all tested on the HAM10000 dataset and the results can be seen in Table 1.

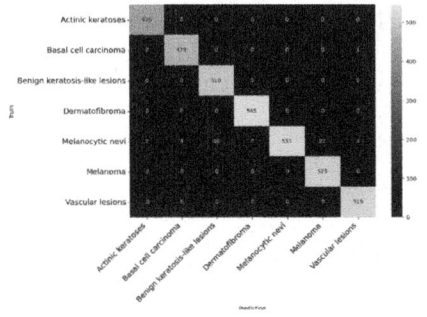

Fig. 7. Confusion matrix of the proposed model

	precision	recall	f1-score	support
0	1.00	1.00	1.00	436
1	0.99	1.00	0.99	480
2	0.97	1.00	0.98	510
3	1.00	1.00	1.00	545
4	1.00	0.92	0.96	582
5	0.96	1.00	0.98	525
6	0.99	1.00	1.00	519
accuracy			0.99	3597
macro avg	0.99	0.99	0.99	3597
weighted avg	0.99	0.99	0.99	3597

Fig. 8. Classification report of the proposed model

Table 1. Comparative performance analysis of the proposed model to other state-of-the-art models

Model	Accuracy	Precision	Recall	F1-score
Our model	0.99	0.987	0.988	0.987
model 1 [3]	0.9529	0.8835	0.9258	0.8999
model 2 [10]	0.9193	0.5050	0.9104	0.6497
model 3 [11]	0.879	0.88	0.88	0.87
model 4 [12]	0.9518	0.88	0.85	0.86
model 5 [16]	0.910	0.9938	0.9927	0.9932
model 6 [17]	0.9883	0.9883	0.9883	0.9883

5.2 Discussion

The proposed approach combines the strengths of Attention U-Net segmentation and CNNs to improve the accuracy of skin disease classification. U-Net architectures excel in semantic segmentation, making them well suited to medical image analysis. By adding the attention mechanism to the architecture, it leads to more accurate localization by focusing on the relevant regions. It can effectively distinguish between different classes of tissues or lesions, providing detailed segmentation maps. The end-to-end learning capability of CNNs allows the model to understand complex relationships within the data, enabling better representation of relevant features for classification. The combination of these two powerful architectures enhances the model's ability to accurately locate and classify lesions, ultimately contributing to more effective and reliable diagnostic support. Although similar architecture were previously explored in [1,3], our work highlights the importance of model choice when combining different deep learning models.

Although our proposed model approach achieved good classification performance on the HAM10000 dataset, which presents an extreme imbalance, it was not perfect and still had limitations. Therefore, for future work, we recommend applying a lightweight transformation to the proposed model to achieve better performance. We would also recommend trying out other segmentation models such as U-Net3+, V-Net, E-Net to verify their impact on the performance of the model.

6 Conclusion

In this paper, we propose an approach for skin disease classification based on a combination of segmentation using Attention U-Net and classification using a customized CNN. The classification performance of the proposed model was further improved by a series of preprocessing transformations such as data augmentation, oversampling and hyperparameters optimization. On the public dataset HAM10000, the accuracy and F1 scores of the proposed model were 99% and 98.7%, respectively. These results were also good compared to the other state-of-the-art models.

References

1. Reddy, D.A., Roy, S., Kumar, S., Tripathi, R.: A scheme for effective skin disease detection using optimized region growing segmentation and autoencoder based classification. Procedia Comput. Sci. **218**, 274–282 (2023). https://doi.org/10.1016/j.procs.2023.01.009
2. Velasco, J.S., Catipon, J.V., Monilar, E.G., Amon, V.M., Virrey, G.C., Tolentino, L.K.S.: Classification of skin disease using transfer learning in convolutional neural networks. arXiv (2023). https://doi.org/10.48550/ARXIV.2304.02852
3. Wei, M., et al.: A skin disease classification model based on DenseNet and ConvNeXt fusion. Electronics **12**(2), 438 (2023). https://doi.org/10.3390/electronics12020438
4. Mendonca, T., Ferreira, P.M., Marques, J.S., Marcal, A.R.S., Rozeira, J.: PH^2 - a dermoscopic image database for research and benchmarking. In: 2013 35th Annual International Conference of the IEEE Engineering in Medicine and Biology Society (EMBC). IEEE (2013). https://doi.org/10.1109/embc.2013.6610779

5. Tschandl, P., Rosendahl, C., Kittler, H.: The HAM10000 dataset, a large collection of multi-source dermatoscopic images of common pigmented skin lesions. arXiv (2018). https://doi.org/10.48550/ARXIV.1803.10417
6. Ronneberger, O., Fischer, P., Brox, T.: U-net: convolutional networks for biomedical image segmentation (Version 1). arXiv (2015). https://doi.org/10.48550/ARXIV.1505.04597
7. Team, L.: Image Resizing with OpenCV | LearnOpenCV. LearnOpenCV - Learn OpenCV, PyTorch, Keras, Tensorflow With Examples and Tutorials (2023). https://learnopencv.com/image-resizing-with-opencv/
8. Vancappel, K.: Deep Learning: le Réseau neuronal convolutif (CNN). Business & Decision (2023). https://fr.blog.businessdecision.com/tutoriel-deep-learning-le-reseau-neuronal-convolutif-cnn/
9. Soh, W.K., Yuen, H.Y., Rajapakse, J.C.: HUT: hybrid UNet transformer for brain lesion and tumour segmentation. Heliyon **9**(12), e22412 (2023). https://doi.org/10.1016/j.heliyon.2023.e22412
10. Gu, Y., Ge, Z., Bonnington, C.P., Zhou, J.: Progressive transfer learning and adversarial domain adaptation for cross-domain skin disease classification. IEEE J. Biomed. Health Inform. **24**(5), 1379–1393. https://doi.org/10.1109/jbhi.2019.2942429
11. Ali, K., Shaikh, Z.A., Khan, A.A., Laghari, A.A.: Multiclass skin cancer classification using EfficientNets - a first step towards preventing skin cancer. Neurosci. Inform. **2**(4), 100034 (2022). https://doi.org/10.1016/j.neuri.2021.100034
12. Shetty, B., Fernandes, R., Rodrigues, A.P., Chengoden, R., Bhattacharya, S., Lakshmanna, K.: Skin lesion classification of dermoscopic images using machine learning and convolutional neural network. Sci. Rep. **12**(1) (2022). https://doi.org/10.1038/s41598-022-22644-9
13. Oktay, O., et al.: Attention U-net: learning where to look for the pancreas (Version 3). arXiv (2018). https://doi.org/10.48550/ARXIV.1804.03999
14. Workgroup, T.G.M., et al.: SpecBit, DecayBit and PrecisionBit: GAMBIT modules for computing mass spectra, particle decay rates and precision observables. arXiv (2017). https://doi.org/10.48550/ARXIV.1705.07936
15. Iznita Izhar, L., Petrou, M.: Thermal imaging in medicine. Adv. Imaging Electron Phys. 41–114 (2012). https://doi.org/10.1016/b978-0-12-394297-5.00002-7
16. Shehzad, K., et al.: A deep-ensemble-learning-based approach for skin cancer diagnosis. Electronics **12**(6), 1342 (2023). https://doi.org/10.3390/electronics12061342
17. Balaha, H.M., Hassan, A.E.-S.: Skin cancer diagnosis based on deep transfer learning and sparrow search algorithm. Neural Comput. Appl. **35**(1), 815–853 (2022). https://doi.org/10.1007/s00521-022-07762-9
18. Lin, Z., Tsui, P.-H., Zeng, Y., Bin, G., Wu, S., Zhou, Z.: CLA-U-Net: convolutional Long-short-term-memory attention-gated U-Net for automatic segmentation of the left ventricle in 2-D echocardiograms. In: 2022 IEEE International Ultrasonics Symposium (IUS). IEEE (2022). https://doi.org/10.1109/ius54386.2022.9958784
19. Shah, D.: Intersection over Union (IoU): Definition, Calculation, Code. V7 (2024). https://www.v7labs.com/blog/intersection-over-union-guide

Agricultural and Land Management Using AI: A Case Study of Rice Plot Identification in Senegal

Mariama Drame(✉), Seydina Moussa Ndiaye, and Moussa Lo

Universite Numérique Cheikh Hamidou Kane, Pikine, Senegal
mariama.drame@unchk.edu.sn

Abstract. Agricultural yield improvement is important to handle food insecurity mostly for developing countries. Indeed accurate knowledge of the distribution of crops in the landscape is crucial for better management and monitoring of the agricultural sector. In recent years the combination of artificial intelligence (AI) and remote sensing data has been widely used for crop type mapping. Given the essential place of rice in the Senegalese diet, increasing its production can positively impact food security. Thus, having an estimate of its harvests can be useful to stakeholders for better management of the rice sector in Senegal. In this work, we aim to build an AI system with remote sensing data for rice crop mapping in Senegal. We exploit two AI models with Sentinel-2 images for rice mapping. The first model is based on Support Vector Machine (SVM) and a second model based on deep learning using the Deeplab V3+ model. Both models shows promising results even if they still very low. The results reveals that the deep learning model provides better performance at identifying rice crop than the SVM model which has a lower accuracy.

Keywords: Agriculture · AI · Machine Learning · Remote sensing · Crop type mapping

1 Introduction

The world's population has been growing for years and, according to the United Nations (UN), it will reach 9.7 billion in 2050 and around 11 billion in 2100[1]. In addition, climate change is becoming more and more noticeable, with harmful impacts on agricultural production. Seasonal irregularities, excess heat and changes in rainfall patterns reduce yields. Thus, food security is very threatened and becomes a subject of great importance. Therefore, crop monitoring must be improved for better crop yield. The main component of crop monitoring is crop mapping which is included in land cover/land use mapping. Crop mapping

---

[1] https://www.un.org/fr/un75/shifting-demographics.

is crucial for providing accurate agricultural statistics [5], improving crop yield estimation and water management.

Remote sensing plays an important role in agriculture monitoring and management. It has emerged as a cost-effective tool for crop type mapping over space and time, repeatedly, and consistently at various spectral, spatial and temporal resolutions [1]. Today, satellite data is publicly and freely available. Among them, Moderate-resolution Imaging Spectroradiometer (MODIS)[2], Landsat(7, 8)[3], and Sentinel(1, 2, 3, 5)[4] are advancing methodologies to solve environmental and societal challenges. The lunch of Sentinel-2A and 2B satellites by the European Space Agency (ESA) provides a 5 days revised time data with high spatial resolution(10 m for visible bands and 20 m for the remaining bands) and has shown their potential in agricultural applications [4].

In the past decades, machine learning algorithms (MLA) have been widely used in remote sensing as an inductive approach for pattern recognition. They are used to extract reliable information related to crop health, distribution, and acreage estimation. Earlier works has investigated classical MLA including Support Vector Machine (SVM), Random Forest, Decision Trees (DT) and Maximum Likelihood Classifier (MLC). In a first work, Saini et al. [27] used SVM on Sentinel-2 images to classify crops. Later they studied a comparison between Sentinel-2 and Landsat-8 by using random forest and MLC [26]. In [19], the authors explored the identification of sugarcane plantations using Landsat-8 images and SVM. Random Forest has also been used in [32] for crop type mapping with Sentinel-2 data. [12] investigate DT models for land cover mapping. These works rely on different bands from satellite images [26,27] and/or vegetation indices such as Normalized Difference Vegetation Indices (NDVI) [12], Green Vegetation Index (VIgreen), Renormalized Difference VI (RDVI) [24].

In recent years, deep learning applications with satellites images for land cover/land use (crop type mapping) mapping has emerged. Most of them are based on transfer learning [22]. Wu et al. [33] opted for an ensemble of convolutional neural networks (CNN) models including Resnet [13], Inception V4 [30], Densenet [16], MobileNet [15] which is also used in [10] and ShuffleNet [36]. A majority voting approach is used to classify images. In [8], Chew et al. used VGG16 [28] as backbone and add a feed-forward network for the crop identification. Transfer learning [22] has also been explored for land cover/land use mapping in [20] where the authors used GoogleNet [31] and VGG16 [28]. In [3], Bah et al. has used the Segnet model [2] for mapping crops. Recurrent neural network has also been used for crop mapping as in [23], which used an LSTM (Long Short-term Memory) [14] and [11] which employed a recurrent CNN.

This study constitute a first step towards our goal of building an AI system for rice crop management in Senegal which will include rice crop identification, rice yield estimation and disease detection on rice leaves. Here, we made a focus on crop type mapping in Senegal. We propose an ongoing work on identifying

---

[2] https://www.sciencedirect.com/topics/earth-and-planetary-sciences/modis.
[3] https://www.sciencedirect.com/topics/earth-and-planetary-sciences/landsat.
[4] https://www.sciencedirect.com/topics/earth-and-planetary-sciences/sentinel.

rice crops in Senegal using Sentinel-2 images and AI. We explore classical MLA such as SVM and deep learning model based on Deeplab V3+ [7] and Resnet [13]. The rest of this paper is structured as follow. We first will discuss about the study area in Senegal and explain why we are focusing on the rice culture. Then the data we used in this work will be explained. We will also talk about the models that we used in this work and finally we will discuss the results we obtained from these models.

2 Related Works

Land Use/Land Cover (LULC) based on remote sensing and machine learning (ML) has been an active topic of research for the last decades. First works have exploited classical ML algorithms including Random Forest (RF), Support Vector Machine (SVM), and Decision Trees(DT). Saini et al. [26] exploit the capabilities of RF and Maximum Likelihood Classifier (MLC) to classify different crop typ using Sentnel-2 and Landsat 8. They also investigated SVM on Sentinel-2 images. Their studies shows that RF performs better compared to SVM and MLC. Tran et al. [32] achieved higher accuracy with random forest and Sentinel-2 in South Dakota (94.24% against 90.05 in Roorkee city) and smaller accuracy in California (83.20%). More recent works such as [18] in 2020 has also explored the power of SVM and RF for LULC classification (with a focus on rice mapping). They made different combination of different features extracted from different satellite imagery (Sentinel-1, Sentinel-2, Landsat-8). SVM has provided higher accuracy on 2015 (90.16 against 88.6) dataset and RF gives better results in 2016 (95.0 and 92.7). DT algorithms have also been studied by Friedl et al. [12]. They presented a univariate DT, a multivariate DT and an hybrid DT. The latest gave higher accuracy on the different dataset they used. Zhang et al. [35] made a comparative study of several machine learning models included RF, XGBoost and SVM for rice mapping. Their experiment was carried out in two districts, and the XGBoost and SVM models performed best (0.7742 and 0.7538 F1 score). In 2022, [25] also used RF and XGBoost to identify rice type (Tarom-Hashemi and Shirodi) by combining Sentinel-1 and Sentinel-2 images, resulting in an overall accuracy of 84.0% and 80.8% respectively with XGBoost and RF. A study combining Sentinel-1 and Landsat images was also carried out by [21] for rice mapping in China using SVM and RF. In addition to these algorithms, [6] has also experimented with Naive Bayes (NB) and K Nearest Network (KNN) to map rice from Sentinel-1 images.

These works have achieved good results but requires tremendous work to manually extract multiple features that are then fit into the model for training. Therefore recent studies are mostly focused on using deep learning models that allow to extract deep and complex features from data and provides better results. Paris et al. [23] have used a Long Short Term Memory (LSTM) model for multiple crop classification and the highest accuracy they achieved was 85.87%. Attention with Recurrent Convolutional Neural Network (RCNN) was used by Feng et al. [11] for multi crops classification and achieved an OA (overall accuracy) of

92.8%. Attention with CNN has also been used in [25] for rice classification. The authors got an OA of 97.1% by combining Sentinel-1 and Sentinel6-2 datasets. CNN architecture is used in [10] for crop classification and achieved an F1 score of 88.1%. [20] has adopted two existing model (GoogleNet and VGG16) for crop mapping in Malawi and Mozambique and achieved an OA of 83% and 90% respectively in Malawi and in Mozambique. Likewise Chew et al. [8] used VGG16 for with a F1 score of 86%. Xu et al. [34] made a study where they compare different deep learning models (DeeplabV3, Unet and Swin Transformer [17]) for rice crop mapping using Sentinel-2 images. The highest accuracy is obtained from Swin Transforme with 95.47% followed by DeeplabV3 with 90.80% and Unet with 89.34%. However Unet and DeeplabV3 has lower number of parameters and inference time.

3 Study Area and Dataset

3.1 Study Area

Senegal is one of the most affected countries by the lack of food self-sufficiency and the rice constitutes the staple food. Indeed, to overcome the food insecurity problem, we are focusing on the monitoring and management of the rice crop in Senegal.

In this first part of our work, the study area is centered in the north of Senegal specifically at Dagana located between 16° 30′ 38.027″ North and 15° 30′ 12.524″ West. Rice cultivation is more developed in this area because of the Senegal River valley which allows cultivation throughout the year.

3.2 Dataset

Field Data: The ground truth data used in this study was provided by CER-AAS (Centre d'Etude Régional pour l'Amélioration de l'Adaptation à la Sécheresse), a Senegalese organisation. They provided us 3 with shapefiles containing rice fields coordinates for February, March and April 2018. Figure 1 shows an examples from the ground truth data. The attribute *Dates_de_s* indicates the date on which the field was sown. The harvest date is scheduled two months after sowing. In overall 3133 field coordinates were collected (490 for February, 2074 for March and 569 for April).

```
{'type': 'Feature',
 'id': '0',
 'properties': OrderedDict([('Dates_de_s', '2018-02-25')]),
 'geometry': {'type': 'Polygon',
  'coordinates': [[(378964.5507067973, 1820096.2766705956),
   (378927.8651713524, 1820079.3011205588),
   (378889.9047981091, 1820150.408893695),
   (378919.33975281473, 1820162.3151675034),
   (378964.5507067973, 1820096.2766705956)]]}}
```

Fig. 1. Example of field coordinates from the ground truth data.

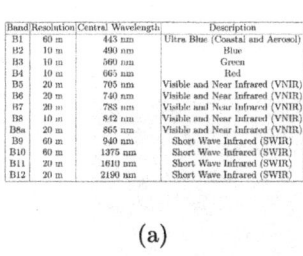
(a)

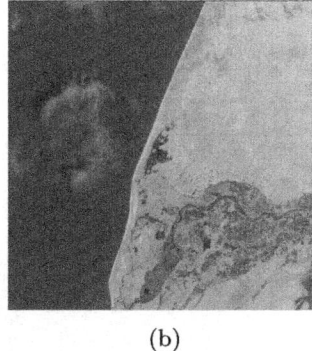
(b)

Fig. 2. (a) Sentinel-2 Bands specifications. (credit GisGeography). (b) Satellite images. (Color figure online)

Satellite Data: Sentinel-2 satellite images were used in this study. It provides medium resolution images for a revisit time of 5-days. Its specifications are given in Fig. 2a

We collected Sentinel-2 images using Earth Explorer[5] from April to June 2018 which correspond to the date on which the ground truth data were collected. Four images were collected in overall on the following dates: 03rd April, 28th April, 18th May and 22nd June. The original Sentinel-2 images were of size 5490 × 5490 × 3 where 3 is the number of bands we considered (Red, Green and Blue). Figure 2b shows an examples of a Sentinel-2 satellite image that was collected

In order to be able to process these images through a neural network, we had to split them into smaller sizes. Each image was split into several images of size 256 × 256 × 3. Given the original images extend were larger than the area of interest, we only kept images within this area after splitting. We ended up with a dataset of 203 images of size 256 × 256 × 3. Crop type mapping can be seen as an image segmentation problem. Indeed, a segmented label is needed for each input image. Following the DeepGlobe dataset [9], we used the ground truth coordinates of rice field to map them into an RGB mask image with two classes: Rice and Not Rice. Figures 3a and 3b shows an illustration of an image and its corresponding mask label.

4 Modeling

Several classical machine learning (including SVM, Random Forest and decision trees) and deep learning (Unet, Deeplab V3 and Deeplab V3+) models were trained. The best results was obtained with SVM for classical ML models and DeepLab V3+ for deep learning models. In the following parts, we will present those models and the results we obtained.

---

[5] https://earthexplorer.usgs.gov/.

Model	Accuracy
Random Forest	49.73%
Decision Trees	47.51%
SVM	50.64%

Model	IOU
Unet	66.03
DeeplabV3 +	67.87

(a)   (b)

Fig. 3. (a) Original Satellite images. (b) Mask: rice with yellow color and not rice purple (Color figure online)

4.1 SVM

To be able to train SVM on our data, we converted our image segmentation problem into a pixel wise classification problem. For each pixel in the satellite images, we associate a label (Rice = 1, Not Rice = 0) based on its color on the masks image. Figure 4 gives an illustration of the final dataset we used to train the SVM model.

R	G	B	class
62	70	73	0
69	75	87	0
87	109	88	1
59	66	74	0
61	69	72	0

Fig. 4. Tabular pixel data

The original dataset was too large (over 1 million data points) and unbalanced with more than not rice than rice pixels. To overcome this, we randomly sampled

50 000 pixels. The final dataset contains 25561 of not rice pixels and 24439 rice. 80% of the data was used for training and 20% for testing. We used SVM from Sklearn and trained multiple models with different kernels (Linear and polynomial) and C values (from 1.0 to 200). The best results was obtained with a linear kernel with 100.0 as C value.

SVM Results: The overall accuracy of the SVM model is 50.64% on the test set. Figure 5a and 5b give details of the evaluation results. They show that the precision and recall for the class 0 (not rice) are higher than those for the class 1 (rice) which has a very low recall. This can be explained by the fact that the model is better at identifying not rice pixels (4168 over 5051 correct prediction) than rice pixels (only 896 over 4949 pixels). Figures 6a, 6b and 6c show a predicted image from our SVM model.

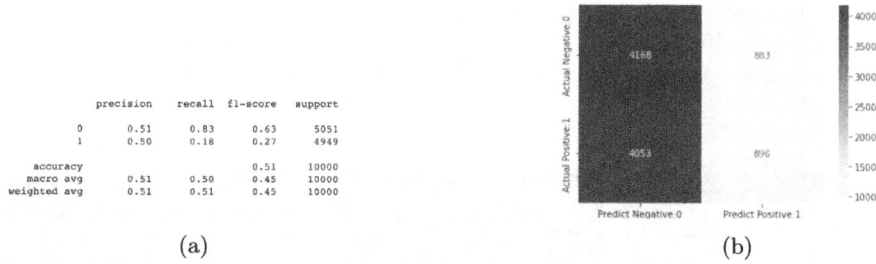

Fig. 5. (a) Classification report. (b) Confusion matrix

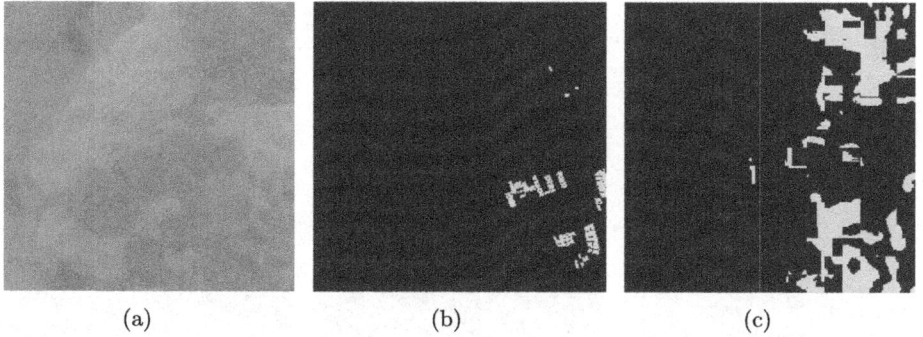

Fig. 6. (a) Original image, (b) Original mask and (c) Predicted image

4.2 DeepLab V3

DeepLab V3+ [7] is a convolutional neural network made of an encoder and a decoder for image segmentation. Given the size of our dataset (203 images) and the computation power that we have, we were not able to retrain the model from scratch. We did a transfer learning by considering Resnet [13] as backbone in the encoder part and retrain the decoder. Adam optimizer is used for training with a learning rate of 0.00008. Learning rate scheduler is also applied using the cosine annealing with a minimum learning rate of $5e^{-5}$. The model was trained for 10 epochs. DiceLoss [29] and Intersection over Union (IOU) were used to evaluate the model. The IoU is calculated by dividing the overlap between the predicted and ground truth annotation by the union of these.

$$IOU(A, B) = \frac{|A \cap B|}{|A \cup B|} = \frac{TP}{TP + FP + FN} \qquad (1)$$

- TP: True Positive
- FP: False Positive
- FN: False Negative

Given the size of our dataset only 20 images were kept for model evaluation and the IOU was 67.87%. Figures 7c and 7f shows an example of predicted image using our deeplab V3+ model along with their corresponding images and ground truth masks.

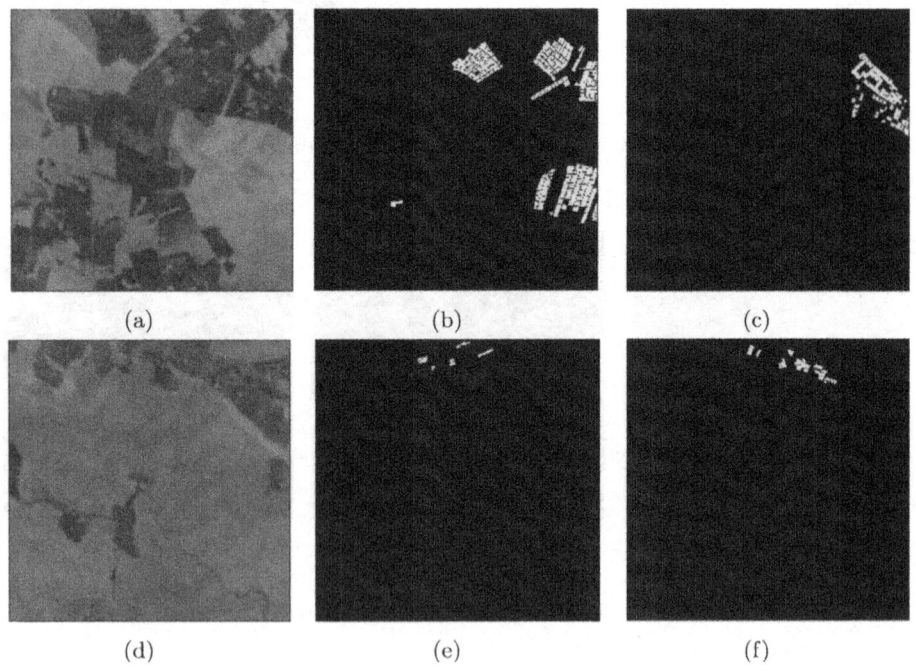

Fig. 7.

5 Discussion

The study reveals interesting results with both models (SVM and Deeplab V3+). They were able to identify some rice pixels even if there is a large room for improvement. The experiences we made show that Deeplab V3+ is more accurate and provide better results than the SVM model for which IOU is around 15 % on the test set. In both cases the performance still low. This can be due to two facts:

The Image Resolution. Sentinel-2 provides one of the free highest resolution for satellite images. However, this resolution still low for high performance images segmentation. To be convinced of this, we trained the same Deeplab V3+ model with the same hyperparameters on the DeepGlobe land cover classification dataset [9] which is 50 cm resolution. We sampled the same number of examples (203 images) and the IOU was about 80%.

Pixel Color Overlapping. Considering a binary classification(rice and not rice) can create more confusion for the model and make the pixels identification very hard. In fact, there is a lot of green pixels with very close values. Therefore, using multi-class instead of binary-class classification by differentiating other types of crop and vegetation to the rice crop may improve model performance on rice field mapping.

6 Conclusion

The development of AI and the availability of free satellite images have been widely used in the service of agriculture for a better yield management. In this study, we explored them for rice crop in Senegal. The first part of this work which is presented here shows that we can use AI and Sentinel-2 images to map rice field in the North of Senegal (Dagana). Two experiences have been conducted with an SVM model and a CNN model using Deeplab V3+. The outputs from these experiences show that the later model gives better results with 67.87% of IOU score. However, this still very low and leaves room for improvement. The main cause that might lead to this low performance are the resolution of the satellite images we considered here (Sentinel-2) and the pixel color overlapping. Indeed, for future work we first plane to handle the later problem by considering a multi-class problem instead of binary. We plan to collect data about other types of crops and vegetation in order to help the model to better map rice field. Then we will also build our own models that will fit better the data. If the outputs of this setting still low, we will consider collecting higher resolution satellite images which may requires some cost.

References

1. Atzberger, C.: Advances in remote sensing of agriculture: context description, existing operational monitoring systems and major information needs. Remote Sens. **5**(2), 949–981 (2013). https://doi.org/10.3390/rs5020949. https://www.mdpi.com/2072-4292/5/2/949
2. Badrinarayanan, V., Kendall, A., Cipolla, R.: Segnet: a deep convolutional encoder-decoder architecture for image segmentation. CoRR abs/1511.00561 (2015). http://arxiv.org/abs/1511.00561
3. Bah, M.D., Hafiane, A., Canals, R.: Crownet: deep network for crop row detection in UAV images. IEEE Access **8**, 5189–5200 (2020). https://doi.org/10.1109/ACCESS.2019.2960873
4. Bontemps, S., et al.: Building a data set over 12 globally distributed sites to support the development of agriculture monitoring applications with sentinel-2. Remote Sens. **7**(12), 16062–16090 (2015). https://doi.org/10.3390/rs71215815. https://www.mdpi.com/2072-4292/7/12/15815
5. Boryan, C., Yang, Z., Mueller, R., Craig, M.: Monitoring us agriculture: the US department of agriculture, national agricultural statistics service, cropland data layer program. Geocarto Int. **26**, 341–358 (2011). https://doi.org/10.1080/10106049.2011.562309
6. Crisóstomo de Castro Filho, H., et al.: Rice crop detection using LSTM, Bi-LSTM, and machine learning models from sentinel-1 time series. Remote Sens. **12**(16) (2020). https://doi.org/10.3390/rs12162655. https://www.mdpi.com/2072-4292/12/16/2655
7. Chen, L., Zhu, Y., Papandreou, G., Schroff, F., Adam, H.: Encoder-decoder with atrous separable convolution for semantic image segmentation. CoRR abs/1802.02611 (2018). http://arxiv.org/abs/1802.02611
8. Chew, R., et al.: Deep neural networks and transfer learning for food crop identification in UAV images. Drones **4**(1) (2020). https://doi.org/10.3390/drones4010007. https://www.mdpi.com/2504-446X/4/1/7
9. Demir, I., et al.: Deepglobe 2018: a challenge to parse the earth through satellite images. CoRR abs/1805.06561 (2018). http://arxiv.org/abs/1805.06561
10. d'Andrimont, R., Yordanov, M., Martinez-Sanchez, L., van der Velde, M.: Monitoring crop phenology with street-level imagery using computer vision. Comput. Electron. Agric. **196**, 106866 (2022). https://doi.org/10.1016/j.compag.2022.106866. https://www.sciencedirect.com/science/article/pii/S0168169922001831
11. Feng, Q., et al.: Multi-temporal unmanned aerial vehicle remote sensing for vegetable mapping using an attention-based recurrent convolutional neural network. Remote Sens. **12**(10) (2020). https://doi.org/10.3390/rs12101668. https://www.mdpi.com/2072-4292/12/10/1668
12. Friedl, M., Brodley, C.: Decision tree classification of land cover from remotely sensed data. Remote Sens. Environ. **61**(3), 399–409 (1997). https://doi.org/10.1016/S0034-4257(97)00049-7. https://www.sciencedirect.com/science/article/pii/S0034425797000497
13. He, K., Zhang, X., Ren, S., Sun, J.: Deep residual learning for image recognition. CoRR abs/1512.03385 (2015). http://arxiv.org/abs/1512.03385
14. Hochreiter, S., Schmidhuber, J.: Long short-term memory. Neural Comput. **9**, 1735–1780 (1997). https://doi.org/10.1162/neco.1997.9.8.1735
15. Howard, A.G., et al.: Mobilenets: efficient convolutional neural networks for mobile vision applications. CoRR abs/1704.04861 (2017). http://arxiv.org/abs/1704.04861

16. Huang, G., Liu, Z., Weinberger, K.Q.: Densely connected convolutional networks. CoRR abs/1608.06993 (2016). http://arxiv.org/abs/1608.06993
17. Liu, Z., et al.: Swin transformer: hierarchical vision transformer using shifted windows. CoRR abs/2103.14030 (2021). https://arxiv.org/abs/2103.14030
18. Mansaray, L., Wang, F., Huang, J., Yang, L., Kanu, A.: Accuracies of support vector machine and random forest in rice mapping with sentinel-1a, landsat-8 and sentinel-2a datasets. Geocarto Int. (2019). https://doi.org/10.1080/10106049.2019.1568586
19. Mulyono, S., Nadirah: Identifying sugarcane plantation using landsat-8 images with support vector machines. In: IOP Conference Series: Earth and Environmental Science, vol. 47, p. 012008 (2016). https://doi.org/10.1088/1755-1315/47/1/012008
20. Nowakowski, A., et al.: Crop type mapping by using transfer learning. Int. J. Appl. Earth Obs. Geoinf. **98**, 102313 (2021). https://doi.org/10.1016/j.jag.2021.102313. https://www.sciencedirect.com/science/article/pii/S0303243421000209
21. Onojeghuo, A., Blackburn, G., Wang, Q., Atkinson, P., Kindred, D., Miao, Y.: Mapping paddy rice fields by applying machine learning algorithms to multitemporal sentinel-1a and landsat data. Int. J. Remote Sens. **39**, 1042–1067 (2018). https://doi.org/10.1080/01431161.2017.1395969
22. Pan, S.J., Yang, Q.: A survey on transfer learning. IEEE Trans. Knowl. Data Eng. **22**, 1345–1359 (2010)
23. Paris, C., Weikmann, G., Bruzzone, L.: Monitoring of agricultural areas by using sentinel 2 image time series and deep learning techniques, p. 18 (2020). https://doi.org/10.1117/12.2574745
24. Peña-Barragán, J.M., Ngugi, M., Plant, R., Six, J.: Object-based crop identification using multiple vegetation indices, textural features and crop phenology. Remote Sens. Environ. **115**, 1301–1316 (2011). https://doi.org/10.1016/j.rse.2011.01.009
25. Saadat, M., Seydi, S.T., Hasanlou, M., Homayouni, S.: A convolutional neural network method for rice mapping using time-series of sentinel-1 and sentinel-2 imagery. Agriculture **12**(12) (2022). https://doi.org/10.3390/agriculture12122083. https://www.mdpi.com/2077-0472/12/12/2083
26. Saini, R., Ghosh, S.: Exploring capabilities of sentinel-2 for vegetation mapping using random forest. ISPRS - Int. Arch. Photogrammetry Remote Sens. Spatial Inf. Sci. **XLII-3**, 1499–1502 (2018). https://doi.org/10.5194/isprs-archives-XLII-3-1499-2018
27. Saini, R., Ghosh, S.K.: Crop classification on single date sentinel-2 imagery using random forest and support vector machine. Int. Arch. Photogram. Remote Sens. Spatial Inf. Sci. (2018)
28. Simonyan, K., Zisserman, A.: Very deep convolutional networks for large-scale image recognition (2014). https://doi.org/10.48550/ARXIV.1409.1556
29. Sudre, C.H., Li, W., Vercauteren, T., Ourselin, S., Cardoso, M.J.: Generalised dice overlap as a deep learning loss function for highly unbalanced segmentations. CoRR abs/1707.03237 (2017). http://arxiv.org/abs/1707.03237
30. Szegedy, C., Ioffe, S., Vanhoucke, V.: Inception-v4, inception-resnet and the impact of residual connections on learning. CoRR abs/1602.07261 (2016). http://arxiv.org/abs/1602.07261
31. Szegedy, C., et al.: Going deeper with convolutions. CoRR abs/1409.4842 (2014). http://arxiv.org/abs/1409.4842
32. Tran, K.H., Zhang, H.K., McMaine, J.T., Zhang, X., Luo, D.: 10 m crop type mapping using sentinel-2 reflectance and 30 m cropland data layer product. Int. J. Appl. Earth Obs. Geoinf. **107**, 102692 (2022). https://doi.org/10.1016/j.jag.2022.102692. https://www.sciencedirect.com/science/article/pii/S0303243422000186

33. Wu, F., Wu, B., Zhang, M., Zeng, H., Tian, F.: Identification of crop type in crowdsourced road view photos with deep convolutional neural network. Sensors **21**, 1165 (2021). https://doi.org/10.3390/s21041165
34. Xu, H., Song, J., Zhu, Y.: Evaluation and comparison of semantic segmentation networks for rice identification based on sentinel-2 imagery. Remote Sens. **15**(6) (2023). https://doi.org/10.3390/rs15061499. https://www.mdpi.com/2072-4292/15/6/1499
35. Zhang, W., Liu, H., Wu, W., Zhan, L., Wei, J.: Mapping rice paddy based on machine learning with sentinel-2 multi-temporal data: model comparison and transferability. Remote Sens. **12**(10) (2020). https://doi.org/10.3390/rs12101620. https://www.mdpi.com/2072-4292/12/10/1620
36. Zhang, X., Zhou, X., Lin, M., Sun, J.: Shufflenet: an extremely efficient convolutional neural network for mobile devices. CoRR abs/1707.01083 (2017). http://arxiv.org/abs/1707.01083

Beqi: Revitalize the Senegalese Wolof Language with a Robust Spelling Corrector

Derguene Mbaye[1,2](✉) [iD] and Moussa Diallo[2]

[1] Baamtu, Dakar, Senegal
[2] Université Cheikh Anta Diop, Dakar, Senegal
{derguenembaye,moussa.diallo}@esp.sn
https://www.baamtu.com/

Abstract. The progress of Natural Language Processing (NLP), although fast in recent years, is not at the same pace for all languages. African languages in particular are still behind and lack automatic processing tools. Some of these tools are very important for the development of these languages but also have an important role in many NLP applications. This is particularly the case for automatic spell checkers. Several approaches have been studied to address this task and the one modeling spelling correction as a translation task from misspelled (noisy) text to well-spelled (correct) text shows promising results. However, this approach requires a parallel corpus of noisy data on the one hand and correct data on the other hand, whereas Wolof is a low-resource language and does not have such a corpus. In this paper, we present a way to address the constraint related to the lack of data by generating synthetic data and we present sequence-to-sequence models using Deep Learning for spelling correction in Wolof. We evaluated these models in three different scenarios depending on the subwording method applied to the data and showed that the latter had a significant impact on the performance of the models, which opens the way for future research in Wolof spelling correction.

Keywords: Spelling correction · Spell checking · Deep Learning · LSTM · Transformer · Low-resource languages · African languages · Wolof

1 Introduction

Spelling mistakes are common in language usage and can be due to a lack of language skills or carelessness. They can become an important element to take into account when writing emails, speeches or when searching on the internet. This

---

Supported by the Google PhD Fellowship program.

is the reason why automatic correctors can be found in various NLP applications such as Summarization [1], Machine Translation [2] and Search Engines [3]. Regarding Wolof specifically, it is a language that is more spoken than written, like most African languages. The Wolof alphabet has been defined by presidential decree since 1971[1] as well as spelling and word separation in 2005[2] but its adoption remains weak. Although it is the predominant language spoken in Senegal (statistically), Wolof is not taught in school as it has been supplanted by French, the official language since colonization. All these aspects contribute to the fact that the majority of the population has a weak grasp of the writing of this language and it is common to note spelling mistakes on social networks, advertising posters and even in television programs. Nevertheless, in recent years there has been a significant resurgence of interest in the language and several initiatives to revitalize it have been launched. A group of linguists called WAX ("Wolof Ak Xamle" meaning Wolof and knowledge sharing) has been created and is working on the popularization of Wolof[3] by content creation and the launch of an e-learning platform[4], among other things. All these initiatives contributed greatly to the acceleration of the adoption of the written form of this language.

However, incorrect writing has become so widespread that it can be considered as an orthographic system to which we will refer in this article by the term "conventional form". The one based on the official spelling will be called "Official Form". The existence of these two forms of writing creates a gap that can greatly hinder the performance of NLP applications designed for Wolof. In fact, the datasets collected to date in Wolof [4–7] are based on the official alphabet and the spelling used is different from the conventional form that is commonly used by the population. NLP applications designed from these datasets will therefore have a lot of trouble working once in production due to this gap. Figure 1 and Fig. 2 illustrate this problem with the translation system designed in [8] by Meta researchers[5].

It is thus crucial to have a spell checker in Wolof in order to bridge the gap between the conventional form and the official one. Wolof being a low-resource language, it makes this task even more challenging.

It is in this context that we introduce BEQI[6]: the first Deep Learning-based Wolof spelling corrector for end-to-end learning. We structured the paper as follows:

- We begin by presenting the work done in automatic spell correction in Wolof and other low-resource languages in Sect. 2.
- Data collection and synthetic data generation are discussed in Sect. 3.

---

[1] *Decree No. 71-566 of May 21st, 1971 concerning the transcription of national languages. Republic of Senegal, 1971.*

[2] *Decree no. 2005-992 of October 21st, 2005 concerning the spelling and separation of words in Wolof (currently effective).*

[3] *Senegal: The Titan work of Wolof language academics, by le360 Afrique (French).*

[4] https://jangwolof.com/.

[5] *The translations were performed with the NLLB model distilled to 600M parameters.*

[6] *A Wolof word meaning the action of correcting.*

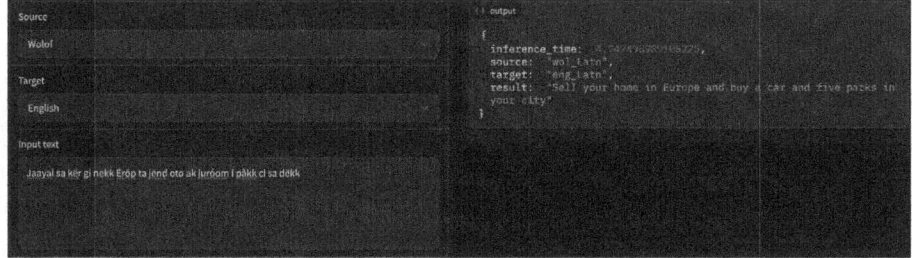

Fig. 1. A correctly done translation when the sentence in Wolof is written with the official form. The correct translation of pàkk would be plot of land but the overall meaning is maintained.

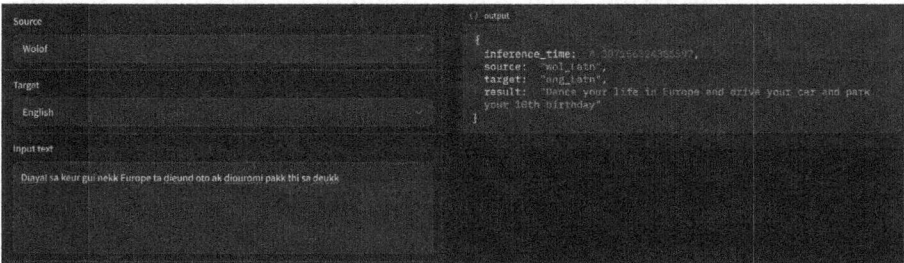

Fig. 2. A totally wrong translation when the same sentence is written with the conventional form.

- In Sect. 4, we present the model used and the experiments.
- Sect. 5 presents the results and perspectives.
- The conclusion is presented in Sect. 6.

2 Related Work

Several approaches have been studied to address the problem of automatic spelling correction in general. The study in [9] divides these approaches into three groups:

1. One that is based on expert rules;
2. One that adds a context model to rearrange candidate corrections;
3. One that learns error patterns from a set of training data.

A portable spellchecker for the Amharic language, spoken in Ethiopia, was developed in [10]. The system uses a corpus-driven approach that uses a noisy channel to derive linguistic knowledge to correct spelling errors. Grammatical error correction in low-resource scenarios was studied in [11] with a focus on the Czech language. The researchers modeled the correction task as a machine translation task with a Transformer-based model [12]. Indian languages have also been studied in the spelling correction task in particular in [13] which uses a Deep Learning based approach and targets Hindi and Telugu languages. Their approach also leverages the machine translation framework and uses a sequential encoder-decoder model based on the Long short-term memory (LSTM) architecture [14].

Although significant work has been done in spelling correction in low-resource languages, little work has been done in this area for Wolof specifically. Several dictionaries were developed in the context of the Dictionnaires Langue Africaine-Français (DiLAF) project which covered five other African languages in addition to Wolof [15]. The implementation of a spellchecker for Wolof was studied in [16] with an approach based on a French-Wolof dictionary studied in [17] as a lexicon and a morphological analyzer of the Wolof language explored in [18]. But the work did not go as far as the actual implementation of a functional corrector and was limited to the state of the art of methods based on the first two previously mentioned approaches i.e. those based on expert rules and those using a context model based on n-gram language models. In addition, at the time of writing this article, all dictionaries developed in [15] are available online[7] except Wolof, which prevents us from exploring a dictionary-based approach. These are also difficult to maintain (the number of rules can quickly increase and their update is tedious), are limited by the size of the dictionary and do not take into account the context. The latter can be included thanks to a context model which is generally an n-gram language model [19] that defines the probability according to the history of the words. This language model thus only takes into account the previous words in addition to the current word, which limits the context considered. Although additional classifiers can be used to bridge this gap in context [9], the use of neural networks allows the inclusion of a broader context on both sides of a word.

Deep Learning is thus a promising approach that has been studied for the spelling correction task and for different languages. But to the best of our knowledge, this is the first attempt applied to the Wolof language.

3 Data Collection

We have collected an in-house dataset of 154,000 correctly written sentences in Wolof which is an extension of the dataset presented in [20]. These sentences were obtained by first collecting monolingual French data from various sources: Coran, Bible, books and news sites as illustrated in Fig. 3. Since Senegal is a French-speaking country, it is easier to find linguists who master both languages (Wolof and French) in order to make the best possible translations. We thus collaborated with a team of linguists from the Linguistic Department of the Cheikh Anta Diop

---

[7] Website of the DILAF project.

University of Dakar to manually translate the collected French corpus into Wolof. The Wolof corpus thus collected and written in the official form constitutes the "target language" that we wish to have as output. To obtain the data of the "source language" written in conventional Wolof, we scraped data on Twitter from accounts that generally publish in Wolof in order to detect recurrent spelling error patterns. Indeed, Twitter is a micro-blogging platform where people write casually about various topics. This makes it an ideal candidate for collecting data that may contain spelling errors and the platform is much in demand for data collection for NLP tasks such as Sentiment Analysis [21]. Author accounts of Wolof publications were identified using Twitter's advanced search functionality by searching for conventional Wolof keywords that appear in tweets and picking up the corresponding authors. From there, we scrape a sample of tweets and identify patterns of errors that we will subsequently reproduce on our corpus written in official form. The overall collection process is illustrated in Fig. 4.

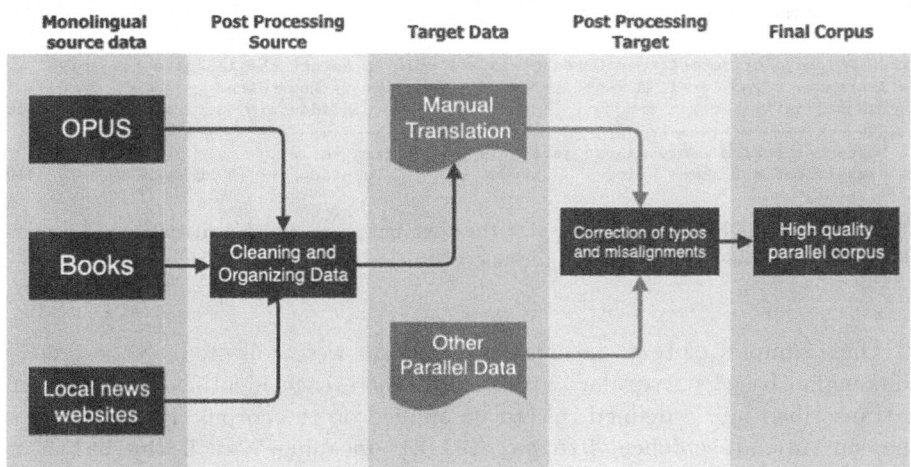

Fig. 3. Data collection pipeline

However, since people are generally bilingual, many publications are also written in French which includes artifacts in the collected data. To filter them, we first used the language identification model [22] included in the polyglot library[8] in its *16.7.4* version to detect the languages of the tweets in order to remove those in French. However, we encountered the problem illustrated in Fig. 2 where the model struggles to detect the language when the text is written in conventional form as illustrated in Fig. 5. We thus had to do the filtering manually.

---

[8] http://www.polyglot-nlp.com/.

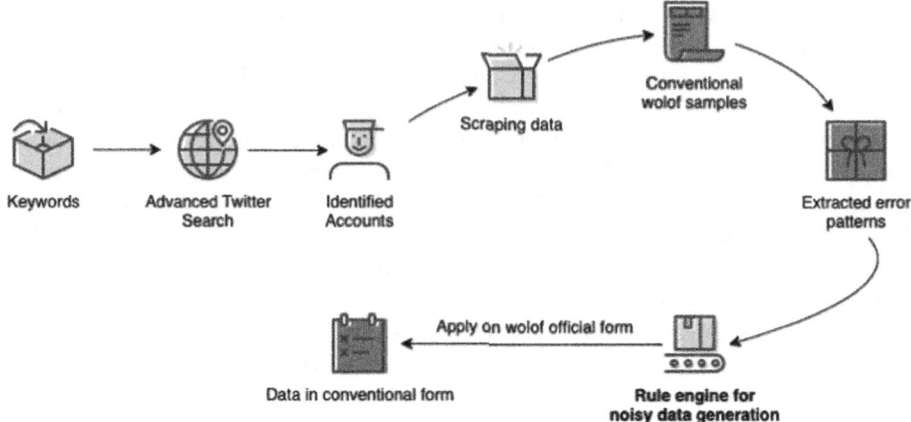

Fig. 4. The collection steps that led to the generation of the parallel corpus with noisy data as source and correctly written data as target.

```
WARNING:polyglot.detect.base:Detector is not able to detect the language reliably.
- Sentence: balma leral ma yane diafei diafei nga am fi mou tolou?
- Classification: name: Tongan       code: to       confidence: 98.0 read bytes:   208
----------------------------------------------------------------
- Sentence: baalma leeralma yan jafe-jafe nga am fimu tollu?
- Classification: name: Wolof        code: wo       confidence: 97.0 read bytes:   490
```

Fig. 5. The model failing to recognize the text language when written in the conventional form (above the dash line) and succeeding when written in the official form.

Once samples of texts in conventional form were collected, we designed a rule engine based on regular expressions[9] where each identified error pattern is transcribed into a defined rule to be applied on the corpus. For example, in the conventional sentence "Diappal bal bi" meaning "Catch the ball", we derive the rule that the "J" followed by a vowel (except "i") is often wrongly replaced by the string "Di". Thus the correct writing of the previous sentence is "Jàppal bal bi". We reproduce this error in our corpus by replacing all the times where the letter "J" is followed by a vowel that is not "i", by the string "Di". The Table 1 presents the rules used in the engine when pre-processing the data. Two other rules were applied in a post-processing phase: one to remove spaces between a word and a vowel (used in formal Wolof to express a plurality for example) and another one to replace occurences of 'g' followed by vowels by 'gu'. All this process allowed us to collect as much synthetic data as formal data i.e. 154,000 parallel sentences of noisy text on one side and well written text on the other, that will be used to train the final spelling correction model. Some examples of the resulting output of this transformation are shown in Table 2.

---

[9] Patterns used to match character combinations in strings.

Table 1. Patterns used in regular expressions to map the correct writing to manually identified errors on the collected data ("f/b" means "followed by").

Patterns	Replacement	Description
ñ+	gn	Replace occurences of 'ñ' by 'gn'
η+	ng	Replace occurences of 'η' by 'ng'
ë+	eu	Replace occurences of 'ë' by 'eu'
u+	ou	Replace occurences of 'u' by 'ou'
u([blt]+)	ou\1	Replace occurences of 'ub/l/t' by 'oub/l/t'
q	kh	Replace every 'q' character by 'kh'
x	kh	Replace every 'x' character by 'kh'
u\b	ou	Replace words ended with 'u' by 'ou'
c([aeiouy]{1,})	th\1	Replace occurences of 'c' f/b vowels by 'th'
c{2}\b	thie	Replace 'cc' at the end of a word by 'thie'
[Jj]([eao]1,2)	di\1	Replace 'j' f/b a vowel (except i and u) by 'di'
[Jj]([i]+)	dj\1	Replace 'j' f/b occurences of 'i' by 'dj'
[Jj]([u]+)	dio\1	Replace 'j' f/b occurences of 'u' by 'dio'
th([aeouy]+)	thi\1	Replace occurences of 'th' f/b vowels (except i) by 'th'

Table 2. Examples of sentences in the official form converted to conventional form by the rule engine.

Official form	Conventional form
Nàngul kula raw, kula ëppalé	Nangoul koula raw, koula euppale
Kula gën a taaru ak kula mag	Koula gueuna taarou ak koula mag
Yii yëpp dula wàññi dara	Yii yeupp doula wagni dara
Wànté bul nangu mukk kula gën	Wante boul nangou moukk koula gueun
Lilakoy may, mooy nga sàmm sa ngor	Lilakoy may, mooy ngua samm sa ngor

4 Experiments

When designing the spelling correction system we considered two architectures commonly used in sequence-to-sequence mapping tasks: the LSTM [14] and the Transformer [12]. LSTMs are a particular type of Recurrent Neural Networks (RNNs) [23], consisting of several gates that allow them to manipulate the information flow. This manipulation is performed by forgetting or selectively memorizing the information of the previous temporal sequence in a dynamic memory as shown in Fig. 6[10].

---

[10] LSTMs Explained: A Complete, Technically Accurate, Conceptual Guide with Keras.

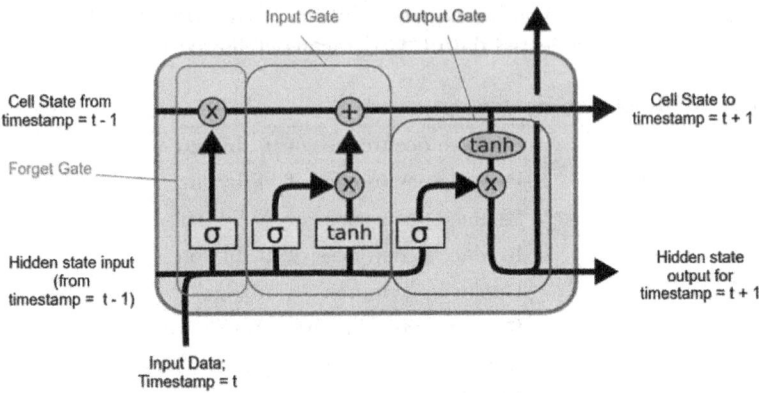

Fig. 6. Illustration of an LSTM cell

The LSTM is a sequential model in which one element of the sequence is processed at a time, which is not the case for the Transformer, illustrated in Fig. 7. The Transformer is a Deep Learning model (i.e. a neural network) of the seq2seq type (takes a sequence as input and returns a sequence as output) which has the particularity of only using the attention mechanism and no recurrent

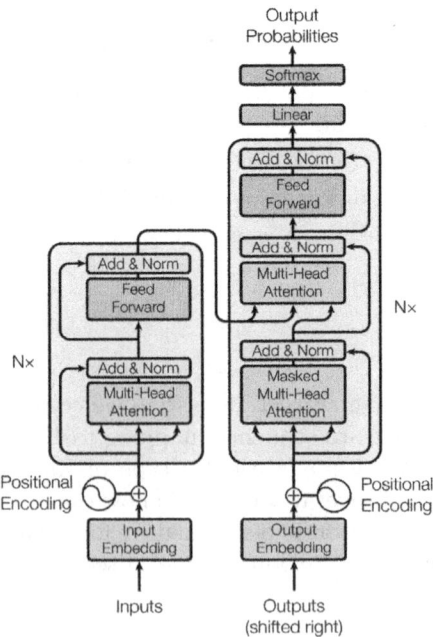

Fig. 7. Illustration of a Transformer architecture as presented in [12]

or convolutional network. The Transformer is more efficient in tracking remote dependencies but is however more data intensive.

To implement them, we used the OpenNMT library [24] which is an open source ecosystem for neural machine translation and neural sequence learning. Our implemented LSTM consists of two layers of encoders and two layers of decoders with 500 hidden units, an embedding of size 500 and a dropout layer associated with a rate of 0.3. As optimizer we defined the Stochastic Gradient Descent [25] with a learning rate of 1.0 as recommended in the OpenNMT documentation[11]. We added a global attention layer [26] which is a simplification of the "classic" attention mechanism proposed in [27] and which may achieve better results. Regarding the Transformer-based architecture, we have reproduced the same features as those defined in the base paper (Vanilla Transformer) [12]. To adapt it to our low-resource context, we reduced some parameter values such as the number of training steps, the early-stopping threshold, the number of validation steps and the warmup steps.

We then divided our dataset into train, validation and test sets with 140,000 sentences for the train set and 7,000 sentences for each of the remaining sets. We applied stratified sampling to ensure that each subset is representative of the overall dataset. This enables a fairer evaluation of the model's performance and limits the biases that can creep into the process. We then applied two different types of segmentation[12] on the data: SentencePiece [28] and Character-Level Subwording which has been shown in [29] to be very effective in translation tasks. All models are trained until convergence, which we consider as reached when no improvement on the validation set is observed after 04 epochs. In the case where the model does not converge, we set a limit of 30k epochs to stop the training. We then compared the performance of the models on the raw data (not subworded) and on the subworded data to evaluate the impact of this process on the models performance. The vocabularies used on the datasets are generated on all segments of training sets and models are evaluated with Accuracy[13] as a metric calculated on test sets at a sentence level. All experiments took place on a virtual machine with a Tesla V-100 GPU with 16 GB of RAM.

5 Results and Perspectives

We compared the two models on the same dataset in different subwording scenarios and Table 3 shows their performances in accuracy given in percentage. We notice that the LSTM model greatly outperforms the Transformer one when no subwording is applied with accuracies of 50.09% and 9.46% respectively which are the lowest performances. We observe a similar pattern with the Sentence-Piece subworded data where the LSTM still outperforms the Transformer with an accuracy of 69.14% versus 6.99%. The highest scores were achieved with character-level subworded data where the Transformer performed the best with

---
[11] https://opennmt.net/OpenNMT-py/options/train.html.
[12] Task of dividing a text into coherent and semantically meaningful segments.
[13] The percentage of correct predictions made by a model.

an accuracy of 81% compared to the LSTM which achieved an accuracy of 77.67%. In fact, when no tokenization is applied, it tends to reduce the size of the vocabulary to the total number of words in the corpus. This has the effect of limiting the occurrence of words and reduces the ability of the model to learn these words [30]. The models are thus very sensitive to rare or out-of-vocabulary words (OOV), which results in the generation of <unk> tags during predictions and greatly hinders models' capabilities. In addition, since the Transformer has significantly more parameters than the LSTM, it requires much more data to capture the most error patterns. This may explain why it performs poorly than LSTM under these conditions. This problem is therefore alleviated by tokenizing into subwords or at a character level and the latter has the great advantage to make the model usable on all languages. Furthermore, since most spelling errors occur at the character level (omission, addition and replacement), a model that processes text under these conditions will have a greater ability to capture these kinds of errors.

Table 3. Performance of LSTM and Transformer models evaluated with Accuracy on synthetic Wolof data depending on the type of subwording applied.

Model Architecture	Accuracy (%)	
LSTM	No Subword	50.09
	SentencePiece	69.14
	Character-level	77.67
Transformer	No Subword	09.46
	SentencePiece	06.99
	Character-level	**81.00**

Table 4 and 5 show some predictions of the LSTM and Transformer models on character-level subworded data. We notice that both models are able to learn the errors while considering the context. This can be attributed to the attention module which integrates information from surrounding words into the embedding of the current word. The other advantage of these models over dictionary-based models is that they are very robust to out-of-vocabulary words. They are also scalable in the sense that their performance increases as they are used when live data is collected back, corrected and then re-injected as training data, which makes them very powerful. However, we note that the LSTM model fails in some cases such as the last two rows of Table 4 where it seems to have trouble correcting accents while the Transformer model did a perfect job on the considered extract. The latter nevertheless still seems to have concerns about handling accents as shown in Table 5. The first row of this table also illustrates an error on the reference side, which suggests the presence of artifacts in the training data that may explain this phenomenon. The last two rows illustrate an interesting problem related to the rule engine. Some rules appear to be too generic, so that some errors that are generated by them would never occur in "real" text (e.g., some types of character replacements may only occur in certain contexts, such as the beginning, middle or end of words, etc.). We observe this phenomenon in the first row of Table 4, where the word "juin" (French word meaning June) is changed to "diouin", representing an error that would never occur in a real context. Such over-generation could lead the model to make corrections when it should not, as in the case of proper nouns (e.g. Kouchner, last line of Table 5) or with some common nouns such as Espagnol (second last line).

Table 4. Qualitative evaluation of the Character-level LSTM predictions on few conventional Wolof inputs along with corresponding correction (prediction) expected outputs (reference).

Input	Prediction	Reference
Ndieekhitaloum diouin bi	Njeexitalum juin bi	Njeexitalum juin bi
Daa nourou kou beg	Daa nuru ku bég	Daa nuru ku bég
Dougnou leen dakh	Duñu leen dàq	Duñu leen dàq
Gnoo and ak orob	ñoo ànd ak **orob**	Ñoo ànd ak **órób**
Bignouy oubbi bank bi	Biñuy ubbi **bank** bi	Biñuy ubbi **bànk** bi

Table 5. Qualitative evaluation of the Character-level Transformer predictions on few official Wolof sentences (model's outputs) along with references (expected outputs)

Input	Prediction	Reference
Nitou loot ya weddi woon nagnou	Nitu Lóot ya weddi woon nañu	Nitu **Loot** ya weddi woon nañu
Yeena nou moucthial noun gnepp	**Yeen** a nu muccal nun ñépp	Yéen a nu muccal nun ñépp
Yakkamti naa degg lignouy wakh	Yàkkamti naa dégg liñuy wax	**Yakkamti** naa dégg liñuy wax
Espagnol bi dooleel na kou gnoul ki	**Espagnol** bi dooleel na ku ñuul ki	**Español** bi dooleel na ku ñuul ki
Na dem te yobbaale Bhl ak Kouchner	Na dem te yóbbaale Bhl ak **Kuchner**	Na dem te yóbbaale Bhl ak Kouchner

This paper is an initial work opening the way to investigate Deep Learning based approaches to address the spelling correction problem in Wolof. The Transformer model already shows promising performances and can be further improved to better adapt to low-resource scenarios as studied in [31]. In perspective, we will further analyze the nature of the errors made by the model in order to study the appropriate solutions.

We will also improve our noisy data generator by collaborating with linguists to better identify common errors and create corresponding rules. The e-learning platform of the WAX group of linguists would be very useful to collect data from dictated exercises performed by students. A similar approach has been taken in [32] which has resulted in a high quality, real-world corpus. We will also explore unsupervised approaches to learn common errors from a noisy corpus instead of a rule engine like the one used in this paper. We also plan to extend the polyglot language identification model on the collected synthetic data to improve its performance in detecting conventional Wolof. This will allow us to later scrape real data from social networks, have it corrected by linguists and then use the resulting parallel corpus to fine-tune our spelling correction model on it. This is particularly important in order to take into account sensitive phenomena such as code-switching, which refers to the passage from one language to another in the same conversation. This phenomenon is very characteristic of everyday Wolof which is strongly influenced by French. We will thus explore NLP approaches addressing this phenomenon of code-switching as studied in [33] in order to make the model more robust to real-world cases. We will also explore other tokenization mechanisms specific to Wolof that could be more efficient than the Character-Level one used here and extend the current system to a model that can make the correspondence in both directions between the two forms of writing.

6 Conclusion

We presented the first dataset for spelling correction in Wolof to date, as well as the first approach that addresses the issue from a Deep Learning and Machine Translation perspective. The corpus contains 154,000 sentences, making it the largest parallel corpus collected to date for wolof spelling correction. As the collection is still in progress, the datasets are not yet publicly available. In addition, we have performed experiments on the two most used NLP architectures, namely the LSTM and the Transformer, on the collected synthetic data. We implemented these architectures using the OpenNMT library and built baseline models. We evaluated these models based on the Accuracy metric computed at a sentence level and we compared their performance regarding the type of subwording applied to the data. We then showed that the Vanilla Transformer model used on character-level subworded data performed the best. We ended by proposing possible improvements that could broaden the scope of such systems and greatly boost their performance.

We have also shown that such a system is crucial for the proper working of NLP applications for Wolof that are being built and will be built in the future. It could also be a major asset in the adoption of the written form of Wolof through large-scale integration into the keyboards of smartphones and other devices.

References

1. El-Kassas, W.S., Salama, C.R., Rafea, A.A., Mohamed, H.K.: Automatic text summarization: a comprehensive survey. Expert Syst. Appl. **165**(113), 679 (2021). https://doi.org/10.1016/j.eswa.2020.113679. https://www.sciencedirect.com/science/article/pii/S0957417420305030
2. Yang, S., Wang, Y., Chu, X.: A survey of deep learning techniques for neural machine translation (2020). https://doi.org/10.48550/ARXIV.2002.07526
3. Sudeepthi, G., Anuradha, G., Babu, M.S.P.: A survey on semantic web search engine (2012)

4. Tiedemann, J.: Parallel data, tools and interfaces in opus. In: Chair, N.C.C., et al. (eds.) Proceedings of the Eight International Conference on Language Resources and Evaluation (LREC 2012) European Language Resources Association (ELRA), Istanbul, Turkey (2012)
5. Strassel, S., Tracey, J.: LORELEI language packs: data, tools, and resources for technology development in low resource languages. In: Proceedings of the Tenth International Conference on Language Resources and Evaluation (LREC 2016), European Language Resources Association (ELRA), Portorož, Slovenia, pp. 3273–3280 (2016). https://aclanthology.org/L16-1521
6. Adelani, D.I., et al.: MasakhaNER: named entity recognition for African languages. Trans. Assoc. Comput. Linguist. **9**, 1116–1131 (2021). https://doi.org/10.1162/tacl_a_00416. https://aclanthology.org/2021.tacl-1.66
7. Goyal, N., et al.: The Flores-101 evaluation benchmark for low-resource and multilingual machine translation. Trans. Assoc. Comput. Linguist. **10**, 522–538 (2022). https://doi.org/10.1162/tacl_a_00474. https://aclanthology.org/2022.tacl-1.30
8. NLLB Team, et al.: No language left behind: scaling human-centered machine translation (2022). https://doi.org/10.48550/ARXIV.2207.04672
9. Hládek, D., Staš, J., Pleva, M.: Survey of automatic spelling correction. Electronics **9**(10), 167 (2020). https://doi.org/10.3390/electronics9101670
10. Gezmu, A.M., Nürnberger, A., Seyoum, B.E.: Portable spelling corrector for a less-resourced language: Amharic. In: Proceedings of the Eleventh International Conference on Language Resources and Evaluation (LREC 2018), European Language Resources Association (ELRA), Miyazaki, Japan (2018). https://aclanthology.org/L18-1651
11. Náplava, J., Straka, M.: Grammatical error correction in low-resource scenarios. In: Proceedings of the 5th Workshop on Noisy User-Generated Text (W-NUT 2019), Association for Computational Linguistics, Hong Kong, China, pp. 346–356 (2019). https://doi.org/10.18653/v1/D19-5545. https://aclanthology.org/D19-5545
12. Vaswani, A., et al.: Attention is all you need. In: Guyon, I., et al. (eds.) Advances in Neural Information Processing Systems, vol. 30. Curran Associates, Inc. (2017). https://proceedings.neurips.cc/paper/2017/file/3f5ee243547dee91fbd053c1c4a845aa-Paper.pdf
13. Etoori, P., Chinnakotla, M., Mamidi, R.: Automatic spelling correction for resource-scarce languages using deep learning. In: Proceedings of ACL 2018, Student Research Workshop, Association for Computational Linguistics, Melbourne, Australia, pp. 146–152 (2018). https://doi.org/10.18653/v1/P18-3021. https://aclanthology.org/P18-3021
14. Hochreiter, S., Schmidhuber, J.: Long short-term memory. Neural Comput. **9**, 1735–1780 (1997). https://doi.org/10.1162/neco.1997.9.8.1735
15. Mbodj, C., Enguehard, C.: Production et mise en ligne d'un dictionnaire électronique du wolof 2 (2015). https://talaf.imag.fr/2016/Actes/MBODJ_ENGUEHARD%20-%20Production%20et%20mise%20en%20ligne%20d%E2%80%99un%20dictionnaire%20%C3%A9lectronique%20du%20wolof.pdf
16. Lo, A., et al.: Correction orthographique pour la langue wolof : état de l'art et perspectives. In: JEP-TALN-RECITAL 2016: Traitement Automatique des Langues Africaines TALAF 2016, Paris, France (2016). https://hal.archives-ouvertes.fr/hal-02054917
17. Khoule, M., Mangeot, M., Nguer, E.H.M., Cissé, M.T.: ibaatukaay : un projet de base lexicale multilingue contributive sur le web à structure pivot pour les langues africaines notamment sénégalaises (2016)

18. Dione, C.M.B.: A morphological analyzer for Wolof using finite-state techniques. In: Proceedings of the Eighth International Conference on Language Resources and Evaluation (LREC 2012), European Language Resources Association (ELRA), Istanbul, Turkey, pp. 894–901 (2012). http://www.lrec-conf.org/proceedings/lrec2012/pdf/572_Paper.pdf
19. Goodman, J.: The state of the art in language modeling. In: Proceedings of the 2003 Conference of the North American Chapter of the Association for Computational Linguistics on Human Language Technology: Tutorials - Volume 5, Association for Computational Linguistics, USA, NAACL-Tutorials 2003, p 4 (2003). https://doi.org/10.3115/1075168.1075172
20. Mbaye, D., Diallo, M., Diop, T.I.: Low-resourced machine translation for Senegalese Wolof language (2023). arXiv2305.00606
21. Drus, Z., Khalid, H.: Sentiment analysis in social media and its application: Systematic literature review. Procedia Comput. Sci. **161**, 707–714 (2019). https://doi.org/10.1016/j.procs.2019.11.174. https://www.sciencedirect.com/science/article/pii/S187705091931885X
22. Hughes, B., Baldwin, T., Bird, S., Nicholson, J., MacKinlay, A.: Reconsidering language identification for written language resources. In: Proceedings of the Fifth International Conference on Language Resources and Evaluation (LREC 2006), European Language Resources Association (ELRA), Genoa, Italy (2006). http://www.lrec-conf.org/proceedings/lrec2006/pdf/459_pdf.pdf
23. Rumelhart, D.E., Hinton, G.E., Williams, R.J.: Learning Internal Representations by Error Propagation, pp. 318–362. MIT Press, Cambridge (1986)
24. Klein, G., Kim, Y., Deng, Y., Senellart, J., Rush, A.: OpenNMT: open-source toolkit for neural machine translation. In: Proceedings of ACL 2017, System Demonstrations, Vancouver, Canada, pp. 67–72. Association for Computational Linguistics (2017). https://www.aclweb.org/anthology/P17-4012
25. Kiefer, J., Wolfowitz, J.: Stochastic estimation of the maximum of a regression function. Ann. Math. Stat. **23**(3), 462–466 (1952). https://doi.org/10.1214/aoms/1177729392
26. Luong, M.T., Pham, H., Manning, C.D.: Effective approaches to attention-based neural machine translation (2015). arXiv:1508.04025
27. Bahdanau, D., Cho, K., Bengio, Y.: Neural machine translation by jointly learning to align and translate (2016). arXiv:1409.0473
28. Kudo, T., Richardson, J.: SentencePiece: a simple and language independent subword tokenizer and detokenizer for neural text processing. In: Proceedings of the 2018 Conference on Empirical Methods in Natural Language Processing: System Demonstrations, Association for Computational Linguistics, Brussels, Belgium, pp. 66–71 (2018). https://doi.org/10.18653/v1/D18-2012. https://aclanthology.org/D18-2012
29. Lee, J., Cho, K., Hofmann, T.: Fully character-level neural machine translation without explicit segmentation. Trans. Assoc. Comput. Linguist. **5**, 365–378 (2017). https://doi.org/10.1162/tacl_a_00067
30. Domingo, M., Garcıa-Martınez, M., Helle, A., Casacuberta, F., Herranz, M.: How much does tokenization affect neural machine translation? arXiv e-prints arXiv:1812.08621 (2018)
31. Araabi, A., Monz, C.: Optimizing transformer for low-resource neural machine translation. In: Proceedings of the 28th International Conference on Computational Linguistics, International Committee on Computational Linguistics, Barcelona, Spain (Online), pp. 3429–3435 (2020). https://doi.org/10.18653/v1/2020.coling-main.304. https://aclanthology.org/2020.coling-main.304

32. Mizumoto, T., Komachi, M., Nagata, M., Matsumoto, Y.: Mining revision log of language learning SNS for automated Japanese error correction of second language learners. In: Proceedings of 5th International Joint Conference on Natural Language Processing, Asian Federation of Natural Language Processing, Chiang Mai, Thailand, pp. 147–155 (2011). https://aclanthology.org/I11-1017
33. Çetinoğlu, Ö., Schulz, S., Vu, N.T.: Challenges of computational processing of code-switching. In: Proceedings of the Second Workshop on Computational Approaches to Code Switching, Austin, Texas, p. 1. Association for Computational Linguistics (2016). https://doi.org/10.18653/v1/W16-5801. https://aclanthology.org/W16-5801

Important Predictors for Covid-19 Vaccine Hesitation

Mireille Fangueng[✉], Mamadou Thiongane, Idrissa Sarr, and Bitsha-kitime D. Kabkia

Department of Mathematics and Computer Science, University Cheikh Anta Diop, Dakar, Senegal
{mireille.fangueng,mamadou.thiongane,idrissa.sarr}@ucad.edu.sn,
dieudone.kabkia@eismv.org

Abstract. Hesitation to take the Covid-19 vaccine is one of the main obstacles to the establishment of a general vaccination program that would quickly achieve mass immunity. Identifying the human and societal factors that lead to hesitancy toward the Covid-19 vaccine can be very useful in raising awareness about vaccine acceptance. In this work, we are interested in finding these factors for the African universities population (students and professors). Surveys are conducted in several universities and some information that we believe may influence vaccine hesitancy, vaccine acceptance, and vaccine rejection are collected from individuals in this community. Three classes of people are observed in these data: the vaccinated, the non-vaccinated, and the hesitant. We propose a Bernoulli Mixture Model with conditional class dependency that can estimate the importance candidate predictor variables for a class. We used this model and determined the most important variables to predict Covid-19 vaccine hesitancy in the study population.

Keywords: Bernoulli Mixture Model · Covid-19 · Vaccine Hesitancy

1 Introduction

1.1 Context and Problem

According to the Strategic Advisory Group of Experts on Vaccination (SAGE), vaccine hesitancy is the term used to describe the delay in acceptance or refusal of vaccination despite the availability of vaccination services [10]. Complacency, confidence, and convenience are conducive to this attitude [17]. Complacency denotes a low perception of disease risk, so vaccination is deemed unnecessary. Confidence or lack of confidence refers to the assurance of safety produced by vaccination and generally to the competence of health systems. Convenience involves the availability, affordability and delivery of vaccines in a comfortable setting. Vaccines developed against Covid-19 are particularly in the spotlight for vaccine hesitancy. This disease discovered in Wuhan, China in December 2019 was officially declared by the World Health Organization as a public health emergency of international concern in January 2020. The high infectivity of this disease has led to various measures to limit its spread: social distancing, wearing a face mask in public places, regular hand washing, etc. At the same time, several research teams around the world have started to develop vaccines against the disease. Although the social measures helped to reduce transmission, they were not without consequences for the social structure of the population, their psychological balance, and the world economy. In addition, there is little evidence to suggest that the spread of Covid-19 will be halted by natural immunity of the population. A general vaccination is therefore an option for overcoming the health crisis. Indeed, the higher the number of people vaccinated, the lower the exposure to the virus. This artificially leads to collective immunity. Hesitation about the Covid-19 vaccine is one of the main obstacles to the establishment of a general vaccination program. This hesitancy is due, in part, to the fact that the development of these vaccines has been particularly rapid compared to the duration of standard protocols. Identifying the behavioral and societal factors leading to hesitancy about the Covid-19 vaccine can be used to understand this attitude and to assess its dangerousness in relation to the overall plan to contain or at least control this pandemic. Our study is conducted on the population of some African universities. Students and professors are the targets of this study.

1.2 Literature Review

Vaccine hesitancy in the case of Covid-19 has been of particular interest to the community in recent months. Several approaches based on statistical and/or machine learning models have already been proposed in the literature to study the elements (predictors) likely to influence the decision in favour or not of a Covid-19 vaccine. A predictor or predictive variable or explanatory variable designates an input used to predict the values of an output variable, or target, or explained variable. In Riad and al [15], decision trees are used to model Covid-19 vaccine hesitancy, with 23 demographic and psychological predictors on a population of dental students from around the world. The results highlight five important predictors of willingness to receive the Covid-19 vaccine: the economic level of the country where the student lives and studies, the individual's trust in the pharmaceutical industry, the individual's misconception of natural immunity, the individual's belief in the risk-benefit ratio of vaccines, and the individual's attitude towards new vaccines. Figueiredo et al. [6] propose a Bayesian ordinal logistic regression model to identify socio-demographic determinants of Covid-19 vaccine acceptance, on a population of 26,759 individuals over 18 years of age across 32 countries worldwide. Ruiz et al. [16] use a community detection and semantic network analysis (SNA) approach for identifying pro- and anti-vaccine influencers through the social network Twitter, and also identify online communities formed around Covid-19 vaccine hesitancy. Lyu et al. [13] use a multinomial logistic regression model and counterfactual analysis to identify sociological factors of importance for vaccine acceptance through tweets as well. In Lombo et al. [12], a Bayesian ordinal logistic regression model is used to establish whether exposure to misinformation has a differential impact on subjects' intention to accept a vaccine for themselves, depending on their socio-demographic background. Lange et al. [11] combine a multivariate regression model and a random forest model to quantify the factors contributing to vaccine hesitancy at the county level in the continental United States. The joint effects of several variables (race/ethnicity, politics, age, etc.) are considered simultaneously to capture and quantify the factors that affect vaccination rates. Bouguila et al. [2] address the problem of unsupervised selection of binary features using finite mixture models of multivariate Bernoulli distributions. Pires [1] does a review of works that identify and analyse the predictors of Covid-19 vaccine acceptance and/or hesitancy in different studied populations. In these studied groups as in ours, the most predominant predictors of vaccine hesitancy were a lower perceived risk of getting infected, a lower level of institutional trust, not being vaccinated against influenza, lower levels of perceived severity of Covid-19, or stronger beliefs that the vaccination would cause side effects or be unsafe. Syed et al. [14] examine state-level features and policies that are most important in achieving a threshold level vaccination rate to curve the effects of the Covid-19 pandemic.

1.3 Motivation and Objective

Most of the works presented in the previous section, attempt to develop models capable of capturing the importance of each predictor (selected a priori in an intuitive way) in the choice of vaccine hesitancy. The main objective of these works is not to predict whether an individual will be vaccinated or not, but rather to identify the factors (the predictors) that would most or least guide the choices. A wide range of relevant factors to predicting Covid-19 vaccine hesitancy for several population categories have been identified in these work. However, the above methods look at the importance of predictors for classification in general. They do not look at the importance for discrimination of specific classes. Indeed, looking specifically at the importance of a predictor in relation to a class provides more information, and therefore understanding.

In this paper, we propose a method that captures the importance of predictors variables conditional on classes for any classification dataset. It is a mixture model for supervised classification which estimates the importance of predictors as a function (conditional) of classes. We assume a Bernoulli distribution for our predictors that are independent of each other. The activation of a predictor is modeled as a binary latent variable, whose distribution parameter provides information on its importance in the classification. We use a fully frequentist approach, unlike Bouguila et al. [2] where a Bayesian approach to clustering is used. We estimate a conditional dependence model of class importances that allows us to obtain the predictor importances for specific class by using the Expectation-Maximisation (EM) algorithm [4]. This model can capture variables importance for any classification dataset. Thus, the validation of our model is done with a well known dataset from the literature and information given by our model confirms well known knowledge that are not given by existing models [2].

We conduct surveys in several African universities and collect some information (from students and professors) that we believe may influence Covid-19 vaccine hesitancy, acceptance, or rejection. We used our proposed method to determine the most important predictors for Covid-19 vaccine hesitancy for the africain universities population. Indeed, academics have a strong voice among other segments of the population and can influence others to accept the Covid-19 vaccine. Knowing the factors that cause professors and students to be reluctant to take the Covid-19 vaccine can help in their awareness of vaccine acceptance.

1.4 Structure of the Paper

The remainder is organized as follows. Section 2 presents our Bernoulli Mixture Model Method and it validation with a well know dataset. Section 3 describes the collected dataset with surveys. Numerical result for variables importance in the Covid-19 dataset are reported in Sect. 4. Finally, concluding remarks are given in Sect. 5.

2 The Bernoulli Mixture Model Method and Validation

2.1 Bernoulli Mixture Model

On an independent and identically distributed sample (i.i.d.) of n individuals from a population structured in K classes, we observe D binary variables supposed to determine the class to which each individual belongs. The dataset is then presented in the form:

$$\mathcal{D}_n = \{(x_i, y_i)\}_{i=1}^n \tag{1}$$

$x_i = (x_{i,d})_{d=1:D}$ is the vector of D binary predictors of individual i; $(y_i)_{d=1:D}$ is the vector of D binary predictors of individual i; $(y_i)_{d=1:D}$ $(y_i)_{i=1:n}$ the observed class (output variable) for individual i, such that: y_i^K, $\sum_{k=1}^{K} y_{i,k} = 1$. This is a common representation of classes as K-lists where each position in the list represents a class, the value 1 indicates the activation of a specific class while the values 0 obviously indicate the disactivation of all other classes, since an individual belongs to only one class. We note respectively $(\omega_k)_{1:K}$ and $(\theta_{k.})_{1:K}$ the proportions of the classes and the parameters of the distributions of the variables within the classes.

We begin by making the basic assumptions without which it would be impossible to infer the laws of a sample on the global population [3]. Two individuals of "close" variables belong to the same class. The classification boundary runs through the low density areas. We also make the assumptions that the data come from a Bernoulli mixture distribution. Indeed, according to the maximum entropy principle, the multivariate Bernoulli distribution is the best model for binary vectors [7–9]. Thus $y_i = (y_{i,k})_{k=1}^{K} \sim \mathcal{M}(1; \omega_{1:K}) \sim \prod_{k=1}^{K} \omega_k^{y_{i,k}}$; multinomial distribution with one trial and K possible outcomes of probability ω_k each; and

x is Bernoullian conditional on y and s; i.e. $x_{id}|(y_{ik} = 1, s_{id} = 0) \sim \mathcal{B}(\beta_d)$ et $x_{id}|(y_{ik} = 1, s_{id} = 1) \sim \mathcal{B}(\alpha_{dk})$;.

We add here an assumption of heterogeneity of the variables with respect to the classes because of the conditional dependence with respect to the classes; ie, $s_{id}|y_{ik} = 1 \sim s_{ikd} \sim \mathcal{B}(\gamma_{kd}) \sim \gamma_{kd}^{s_{ikd}}(1-\gamma_{kd})^{1-s_{ikd}}$; $s_{ikd} = 1$ (i.e. $s_{id} = 1|y_{ik} = 1$) if the variable x_d is discriminating for the classification of the individual i with respect to the class k, $s_{ikd} = 0$ otherwise.

1. Likelihood of observations

The likelihood of the observations in this case is given by:

$$P(D_n, \theta) = \prod_{i=1}^{n} \prod_{k=1}^{K} \left\{ w_k \prod_{d=1}^{D} \left[(1 - \gamma_{kd}) p(x_{id}; \beta_d) + (\gamma_{kd}) p(x_{id}; \alpha_{kd}) \right] \right\}^{y_{ik}} \quad (2)$$

2. The complete log-likelihood

The full likelihood is found in:

$$p(D_n^c; \theta) = \prod_{i=1}^{n} \prod_{k=1}^{K} w_k^{y_{ik}} \times \prod_{i=1}^{n} \prod_{k=1}^{K} \prod_{d=1}^{D} \gamma_{kd}^{s_{ikd} y_{ik}} (1 - \gamma_{kd})^{(1-s_{ikd}) y_{ik}}$$

$$\times \prod_{i=1}^{n} \prod_{k=1}^{K} \prod_{d=1}^{D} p(x_{id}; \beta_d)^{(1-s_{ikd}) y_{ik}}$$

$$\times \prod_{i=1}^{n} \prod_{k=1}^{K} \prod_{d=1}^{D} p(x_{ik}; \alpha_{kd})^{s_{ikd} y_{ik}} \quad (3)$$

The full log-likelihood is thus deduced:

$$\ln p(D_n^c; \theta) = \sum_{k=1}^{K} \left(\sum_{i=1}^{n} y_{ik} \right) \ln w_k + \sum_{k=1}^{K} \sum_{d=1}^{D} \left(\sum_{i=1}^{n} y_{ik} s_{ikd} \right) \ln \gamma_{kd}$$

$$+ \sum_{k=1}^{K} \sum_{d=1}^{D} \left(\sum_{i=1}^{n} y_{ik}(1 - s_{ikd}) \right) \ln(1 - \gamma_{kd})$$

$$+ \sum_{i=1}^{n} \sum_{d=1}^{D} \left(\sum_{k=1}^{K} (1 - s_{ikd}) y_{ik} \right) \ln p(x_{id}; \beta_d)$$

$$+ \sum_{i=1}^{n} \sum_{d=1}^{D} \sum_{k=1}^{K} s_{ikd} y_{ik} \ln p(x_{id}; \alpha_{kd}) \quad (4)$$

This time, we have $x|y$ as the marginal distribution of $x, s|y$. We are still looking for the maximum likelihood estimator, and the idea remains to use the Log of the likelihood obtained in Eq. (4). But the sum brought by the marginal distribution makes it difficult to calculate by the classical differentiable optimisation methods. A way of getting around this difficulty is proposed in Dempster et al. [4] and known as the Expectation-Maximisation algorithm, or EM algorithm.

A distinction is made between the observations $\mathcal{D}$ and the so-called complete data $\mathcal{D}^c$ made up of observations and the latent variable s.

The classical EM algorithm is as follows:

Input: Dataset
Output: Parameter and latent variable estimates
1 Initialization ; $t \leftarrow 0$
2 **while** *no-convergence* **do**
3   Step E:
      $Q(\theta|\theta^{(t)}) = \mathbb{E}_s[lnp(\mathcal{D}^c; \theta)|D = \mathcal{D}; \theta = \theta^{(t)}] = \mathbb{E}_{s|\mathcal{D};\theta^{(t)}}[lnp(\mathcal{D}^c; \theta)]$
4   Step M: $\theta^{(t+1)} = \underset{\theta}{argmax}\ Q(\theta|\theta^{(t)})$
5 **return**

Thus,
Step E of the EM algorithm

Using the expectation of the complete log-likelihood following the distribution of the latent variable s conditional on the observations and parameters, we have:

$$\gamma_{ikd} = \frac{\left[\gamma_{kd}p(x_{id}, \alpha_{kd})\right]^{y_{ik}}}{\left[\gamma_{kd}p(x_{id}, \alpha_{kd})\right]^{y_{ik}} + \left[(1-\gamma_{kd})p(x_{id}, \beta_d)\right]^{y_{ik}}} \quad (5)$$

Step M of the EM algorithm

Using the full log-likelihood expectation:
Estimation of $w_k\ \forall k = 1 \cdots K$:

$$w_k = \frac{1}{n}\left(\sum_{i=1}^{n} y_{ik}\right) \quad (6)$$

Estimation of γ_{kd} $\forall k = 1 \cdots K$ and $\forall d = 1 \cdots D$:

$$\gamma_{kd} = \frac{\sum_{i=1}^{n} \gamma_{ikd} y_{ik}}{\sum_{i=1}^{n} y_{ik}} \quad (7)$$

Estimation of α_{kd}
$\forall k = 1 \cdots K$ and $\forall d = 1 \cdots D$:

$$\alpha_{kd} = \frac{\sum_{i=1}^{n} \gamma_{ikd} y_{ik} x_{id}}{\sum_{i=1}^{n} \gamma_{ikd} y_{ik}} \quad (8)$$

Estimation of β_d
$\forall d = 1 \cdots D$:

$$\beta_d = \frac{\sum_{i=1}^{n} \left(\sum_{k=1}^{K} (1 - \gamma_{ikd}) y_{ik} \right) x_{id}}{\sum_{i=1}^{n} \sum_{k=1}^{K} (1 - \gamma_{ikd}) y_{ik}} \quad (9)$$

2.2 Validation of the Model

The validation of our model was done with the "Zoo dataset" [5]. The later is constituted of 101 animals of a zoo described by 16 traits or attributes supposed to allow to classify them according to the following 7 classes: mammals, birds, reptiles, fish, amphibians, insects and invertebrates. The common use is to predict the class of animals on the basis of the variables. The observed attributes and their types are: name (unique for each instance), hair (boolean), feathers (boolean), eggs (boolean), milk (boolean), aerial (boolean), aquatic (boolean), predator (boolean), toothed (boolean), spine (boolean), breathes (boolean), venomous (boolean), fins (boolean), legs (set of values: 0,2,4,5,6,8), tail (boolean), domestic (boolean), cat size (boolean), class (integer values in the range [1–7]). Except for the "legs" variable, all predictors are binary. To make the dataset suitable for our model, we have eliminated the "legs" column as in Bougila et al. [2]. The dataset we use is thus made up of 101 individuals described by 15 binary predictors and structured in 7 classes.

The average success rate for the classification is 0.85 ± 0.04 for the classical model [2], 0.91 ± 0.02 for the model with class independent importance [2], and 0.90 ± 0.04 for the model with class dependent importance (our model) on this dataset. For the variable importance, the model with class independent importance show that "tooth" possession or "egg" laying are discriminating criteria for the different classes of animals, without further clarification. However, our model with class-dependent importance goes further and indicates that "milk" production is more discriminating for the mammalian class; "tooth" possession is strongly discriminating for insects, invertebrates and birds; and "egg" laying is strongly discriminating for mammals. This is perfectly consistent with our knowledge of these categories of animals. Let us also note, for example, that the "venomous" character is weakly discriminating for any class; this is also intuitive, since venomous animals are found in each of these categories. Figure 1 and 2 show the result for the importance of the predictors, and the probabilities of membership for each class according to the discriminant variables respectively.

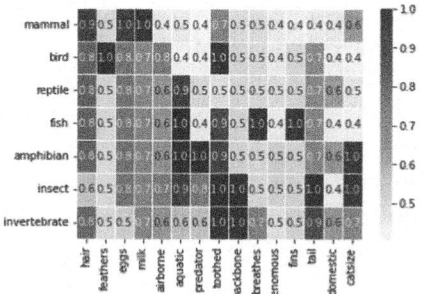

Fig. 1. Importance of the predictors

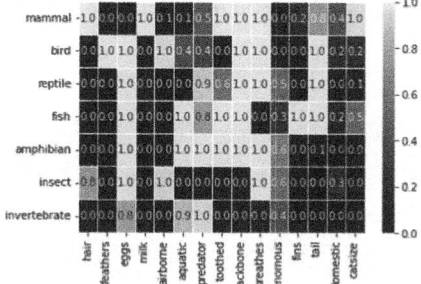

Fig. 2. Class membership probabilities for class-predicting variables

3 The Collected Covid-19 Dataset

We conducted surveys from six African universities to get data on factors that we believe may influence the choice to accept, reject, or be hesitant to take the vaccine against Covid-19. Our candidate variables are: profession of the individu, gender, age, level of education, place of residence, risk or danger associated with Covid-19, number of prevention methods used (the prevention methods are: wearing a mask in public places, use of disinfectant gel to clean hands, respecting barrier measures, regular hand washing), intentions of the vaccine manufacturers (good or bad), and effectiveness of the vaccines. The universities concerned by the surveys are Université Cheikh Anta Diop de Dakar (Sénégal), Université de Thiés (Sénégal), Université de Yaoundé 1 (Cameroon), Université de Yaoundé 2 (Cameroon), Université Alassane Ouattara (Ivory Coast), and Université de Lomé (Togo). As mentioned earlier in the introduction, the target population was professors and students. These surveys are done in two phases, the first one from June 2 to July 31, 2021, and the second one was done between

May 28 and June 15, 2022. Forums and social networks were used to distribute the questionnaires and 1882 people have completed the questionnaires. Table 1 shows the survey questionnaires and the possible answers for each question.

Table 1. Questionnary and possible answers of the surveys

1. What is your profession ? (a) Professor (b) Student	2. What is your gender ? (a) Female (b) Male
3. Are you under 35 years old ? (a) Yes (b) No	4. Is your level of education below Master 2? (a) Yes (b) No
5. Do you live outside the university campus ? (a) Yes (b) No	6. Do you think there are any risks/dangers associated with Covid-19 ? (a) Yes (b) No
7. Do you practice more than two preventive methods ? (a) Yes (b) No	8. Do you think there are bad intentions in the design of vaccines ? (a) Yes (b) No
9. Is the Covid-19 vaccine a prevention measure ? (a) Yes (b) No	10. Have you take a COVID 19 vaccine? (a) Yes (b) No (c) I am still hesitating

Here are some statistics summary on collected data. We notice that $44,98\%$ of the people who responded to the surveys are not vaccinated, $25,08\%$ of people are vaccinated, and $29,92\%$ of people are hesitant. We observe that $13,52\%$ of the respondents are professors and $86,47\%$ are students, $56,04\%$ are men and $43,95\%$ are women. For the age of the persons, $26,51\%$ of the respondents are over 35 years old and $73,48\%$ are under 35 years old. For intentions on the manufacture and preventability of the Covid-19 vaccine, so $56,93\%$ of people thinks that there is no bad intentions with the vaccines but $43,06\%$ thinks there is a bad intentions with vaccines, and $51,95\%$ of people thinks that vaccines are not preventive and $48,04\%$ thinks that there are preventive.

4 Experiment and Result

Based on the collected and preprocessed dataset, we use our Bernoulli mixture model for classification to determine the importance of each variable in predicting vaccine hesitancy. We also determine the importance variable in predicting vaccine acceptance or rejection. The evaluation is done in a 5-fold cross-validation context. The dataset is partitioned into 5 subsets, each of which will be used for testing, the remaining 4/5 will be used for training. An average of the inter-fold results allows an overall assessment of the model performance.

Figure 3 and Fig. 4 report the results of the importance of the variables, and probabilities of membership for each class according to the discriminant variables. For the hesitant class, we observe that the scores importance of the variables varies between 0.5 and 0.68. The variable "prevention" with a score of 0.68 stands out the most in terms of importance compared to the other variables. We notice that hesitant people tend to increase preventive actions other than vaccination (see Fig. 4). The variable "age" with score of 0.52 arrives in second position. The "sex" and "effectiveness" arrive in third position with a score of 0.51. The "profession", "study level", "risk" and "intention" variables are the least discriminating. If we combine these importances with probabilities of membership for each class according to the discriminant variables values, we notice that the hesitant individuals are less likely to think that there are bad intentions in the design of the vaccines, believe more that there are risks and dangers associated with Covid-19, and believe a little in the effectiveness of the vaccine. These elements are likely to justify their "hesitant" position.

We can also see that the "effectiveness" of Covid-19 vaccines character is discriminating for the class of the vaccinated. So vaccinate people believe in the effectiveness of the vaccine.

We notice that the character "prevention" is also discriminating for the non-vaccinated, and vaccinated class.

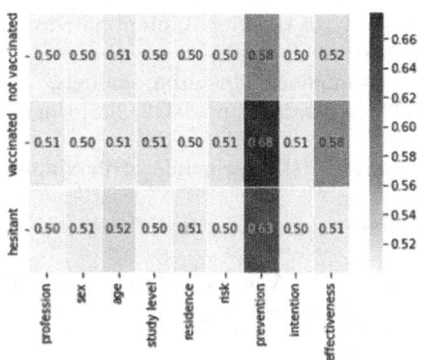

Fig. 3. Importance of the predictors

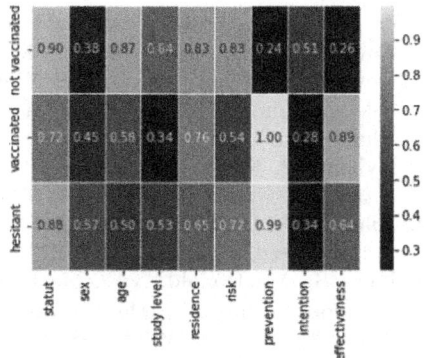

Fig. 4. Class membership probabilities for class-predicting variables

5 Conclusion

We introduced the assumption of class dependencies in a Bernoulli mixture model to estimate the importance of the predictors in a classification model. We proposed to define latent variables to model these class dependencies and we used the Expectation-Maximisation algorithm to compute variables importance. This class dependence hypothesis proved to be effective in providing finer-grained explanations. The method was validate with a an animal dataset. The later was able to provide well known knowledge with these data. This gives confidence in the model. This model has allowed us to identify some factors that drive the African university population to be reluctant to be vaccinated against Covid-19. For example, we learn that the age of the person, and the number of prevention methods used are determining factors in predicting vaccine hesitancy.

References

1. Carla, P.: Global predictors of Covid-19 vaccine hesitancy: a systematic review. Vaccines (Basel). MDPI **10**(8), 1349 (2022). https://www.mdpi.com/2076-393X/10/8/1349
2. Bouguila, N.: On multivariate binary data clustering and feature weighting. Comput. Stat. Data Anal. **54**(1), 120–134 (2010)
3. Chapelle, O., Scholkopf, B., Zien, A.: Semi-supervised learning. IEEE Trans. Neural Netw. **20**(3), 542–542 (2009). (Chapelle, O., et al. (eds.) 2006)[book reviews]
4. Dempster, A.P., Laird, N.M., Rubin, D.B.: Maximum likelihood from incomplete data via the EM algorithm. J. Roy. Stat. Soc.: Ser. B (Methodol.) **39**(1), 1–22 (1977)
5. Dua, D., Graff, C.: UCI machine learning repository (2017). http://archive.ics.uci.edu/ml
6. de Figueiredo, A., Larson, H.J.: Exploratory study of the global intent to accept Covid-19 vaccinations. Commun. Med. **1**(1), 1–10 (2021)
7. Govaert, G., Nadif, M.: Block Bernoulli parsimonious clustering models. In: Selected Contributions in Data Analysis and Classification, pp. 203–212. Springer, Cham (2007)
8. Gyllenberg, M., Koski, T.: Numerical taxonomy and the principle of maximum entropy. J. Classif. **13**(2), 213–229 (1996)
9. Juan, A., Vidal, E.: On the use of Bernoulli mixture models for text classification. Pattern Recogn. **35**(12), 2705–2710 (2002)
10. Lane, S., MacDonald, N.E., Marti, M., Dumolard, L.: Vaccine hesitancy around the globe: Analysis of three years of WHO/UNICEF joint reporting form data-2015–2017. Vaccine **36**(26), 3861–3867 (2018)
11. Lange, C., Lange, J.: Applying machine learning and AI explanations to analyze vaccine hesitancy. arXiv preprint arXiv:2201.05070 (2022)
12. Loomba, S., de Figueiredo, A., Piatek, S.J., de Graaf, K., Larson, H.J.: Measuring the impact of Covid-19 vaccine misinformation on vaccination intent in the UK and USA. Nat. Hum. Behav. **5**(3), 337–348 (2021)
13. Lyu, H., et al.: Social media study of public opinions on potential Covid-19 vaccines: informing dissent, disparities, and dissemination. Intell. Med. **2**(1), 1–12 (2022). https://doi.org/10.1016/j.imed.2021.08.001. https://www.sciencedirect.com/science/article/pii/S266710262100036X

14. Osman, S.M.I., Sabit, A.: Predictors of Covid-19 vaccination rate in USA: a machine learning approach. Mach. Learn. Appl. **10**, 100408 (2022). https://doi.org/10.1016/j.mlwa.2022.100408. https://www.sciencedirect.com/science/article/pii/S2666827022000834
15. Riad, A., et al.: IADS-SCORE: Universal predictors of dental students' attitudes towards Covid-19 vaccination: machine learning-based approach. Vaccines **9**(10), 1158 (2021)
16. Ruiz, J., Featherstone, J.D., Barnett, G.A.: Identifying vaccine hesitant communities on twitter and their geolocations: a network approach. In: Proceedings of the 54th Hawaii International Conference on System Sciences, p. 3964 (2021)
17. Sallam, M.: Covid-19 vaccine hesitancy worldwide: a concise systematic review of vaccine acceptance rates. Vaccines **9**(2), 160 (2021)

Ensemble Machine Learning Methods to Predict Oil Production

M. D. Adewale[1(✉)], I. A. Adeyanju[2], J. Oju[1], O. C. Ubadike[1], U. I. Muhammed[1], and S. T. Omisakin[3]

[1] Africa Centre of Excellence On Technology Enhanced Learning, National Open University of Nigeria, Abuja, Nigeria
mdadewale@gmail.com, ace22140007@noun.edu.ng
[2] Department of Computer Engineering, Federal University of Oye-Ekiti, Oye, Nigeria
[3] DaraTom Consulting Incoporated, Toronto, ON, Canada

Abstract. This research unveils an ensemble prediction model tailored for Nigeria's oil production, addressing the need for accurate forecasting in a critical economic sector. Nigeria, a leading oil producer in Africa, relies heavily on its oil sector, necessitating robust prediction models for economic planning and stability. This study aims to create a predictive model integrating pivotal factors such as oil reserves, oil consumption, oil prices, and political stability. These factors were chosen due to their significant impact on oil production dynamics, encompassing economic, political, and consumption-related influences that critically determine production outcomes. Using data from 1980 to 2016, we employed advanced machine learning algorithms—including Extra Trees Regressor, XGBoost Regressor, and Random Forest Regressor—to enhance prediction accuracy. The Extra Trees Regressor emerged as the superior algorithm, demonstrated by a correlation coefficient of 0.8155, a mean absolute error of 0.2812, and a root mean squared error of 0.3929. Our findings confirm the model's predictive power, highlighting the significant influence of critical variables on Nigeria's oil production trends. This study offers indispensable insights to stakeholders, aiding in informed decision-making and showcasing the significant capabilities of ensemble machine learning in improving oil production forecasts. Ultimately, this work enhances understanding of the factors affecting oil production and supports strategic planning within Nigeria's oil sector, promoting economic stability and growth.

Keywords: Oil Price · Machine Learning · Oil Consumption · Oil Production · Oil Reserve

1 Background of the Study

Developing a predictive model for oil production in Nigeria is essential due to its significant economic implications. Nigeria, a leading oil producer in Africa, relies heavily on its oil sector, which contributes substantially to its GDP. Accurate oil production forecasts enable the government and stakeholders to make informed decisions about fiscal budgeting, infrastructure investments, and long-term economic policies, which are crucial for managing global oil market volatility that affects national revenue and economic health (Obite et al., 2021).

Such a model can enhance operational efficiency by anticipating fluctuations in oil production and allowing for proactive strategies in drilling operations, maintenance, and workforce management. This foresight is essential for maintaining competitiveness in the global oil market, especially amidst growing environmental concerns and the shift towards renewable energy sources (Gbakon et al., 2022).

A predictive model aids in forecasting production trends, facilitating effective environmental protection measures and sustainable resource management and addressing issues like oil spillage and environmental degradation in Nigeria (Asumadu-Sarkodie & Owusu, 2016; Gbakon et al., 2022).

The model also promotes socio-economic stability by informing labour market strategies, bolstering job security, and supporting workforce development. A predictive model for Nigeria's oil production is crucial for economic optimisation, sustainable development, environmental stewardship, and socio-economic stability (Asumadu-Sarkodie and Owusu, 2016; Falode & Udomboso, 2021; Gbakon et al., 2022).

However, the inherent volatility of global oil markets and Nigeria's fluctuating political and economic conditions present significant challenges for accurate oil production forecasting. Traditional models often fail to capture the complex interplay of socio-economic and political factors influencing oil production, leading to suboptimal forecasting accuracy and unreliable policy decisions.

This study aims to develop a more accurate and reliable forecasting model for Nigeria's oil production by incorporating various socio-economic and political factors using ensemble machine learning techniques. The goal is to improve forecasting precision, supporting informed decision-making and strategic planning in Nigeria's oil sector. The central aim is to create a system capable of processing socio-economic data and converting it into meaningful insights for future oil production forecasting using ensemble machine learning algorithms to attain high accuracy levels.

The following research inquiries are addressed to clarify the contributions of this work through the developed model:

(**R.Q.1**) *Which variables directly influence the value of oil production?*

(**R.Q.2**) *Can the Ensemble Machine Learning Model effectively forecast oil production values based on various factors?*

These questions guide the study's focus on creating a predictive model that leverages the latest technological advancements to address the complexities of oil production forecasting in Nigeria.

1.1 Identifying Key Variables Influencing Oil Production Value

(R.Q.1) Which variables directly influence the value of oil production?

This study acknowledges several critical factors in exploring the variables significantly impacting oil production. These include oil consumption levels, oil reserves, global exchange rates, environmental considerations, political dynamics, and oil market speculation. These elements play a vital role in shaping oil supply and demand. For instance, oil consumption, directly correlated with demand, increases production as consumption levels rise (Karakurt, 2021). Oil reserves, a primary supply determinant, can enhance production capabilities when abundant (Falode & Udomboso, 2021). Exchange rates also influence oil prices and, by extension, supply and demand, particularly in significant oil-importing and exporting countries (Salisu et al., 2020). As the global energy landscape shifts towards sustainability, environmental policies to reduce carbon emissions significantly impact oil demand (Asumadu-Sarkodie & Owusu, 2016). Political factors, including stability and government policies, significantly affect oil supply and demand (Gbakon et al., 2022). Financial market speculations can also cause oil price fluctuations, affecting perceived supply and demand (Obite et al., 2021; Salisu et al., 2020).

The need for a predictive model in Nigeria that encompasses oil reserves, consumption, oil price, and political stability is highlighted by several studies. These models demonstrate the complexity of forecasting oil production and the importance of various interacting factors. Cavallo (2004) notes the role of stable markets, demand growth, import availability, and accurate reserve estimates in predicting oil production, which is particularly relevant given Nigeria's fluctuating political and economic conditions (Cavallo, 2004). Moroney and Berg (1999) show that integrating physical reserves with economic variables like exchange rates yields more accurate forecasts than models based solely on reserves or economic data (Moroney & Berg, 1999). The importance of considering political, economic, and resource-related variables is underscored by Duhu (2019), especially pertinent for Nigeria, where political stability influences both domestic and global market perceptions. Karakurt (2021) emphasises the need to model and forecast oil consumption, a critical factor in oil production, highlighting the importance of understanding consumption patterns for accurate forecasting (Karakurt, 2021).

These studies collectively indicate the necessity of a comprehensive predictive model that includes oil reserves, consumption, oil price, and political stability. Such a model is critical for Nigeria to aid in economic planning and effectively navigate the complexities of the global oil market.

1.2 Efficacy of the Ensemble Machine Learning Model

(R.Q.2) Can the Ensemble Machine Learning Model effectively forecast oil production values based on various factors?

This inquiry evaluates the efficacy of ensemble machine learning models, explicitly incorporating XGBoost, Random Forest, and Extra Trees Regressor, in accurately forecasting Nigerian oil production. The strength of these ensemble models lies in their sophisticated ability to process and analyse complex datasets, identifying nuanced patterns crucial for precise prediction tasks. XGBoost is renowned for its efficiency and accuracy across various prediction challenges. It is a scalable ensemble technique that has demonstrated reliability and efficiency in solving complex machine-learning challenges. Random Forest Regressor builds upon bagging multiple decision trees to reduce variance and improve prediction accuracy. It effectively captures nonlinear relationships without the need for extensive parameter tuning. The Extra Trees Regressor introduces additional randomness compared to Random Forest by randomising thresholds for feature splits, leading to more diversified tree ensembles. This approach enhances the model's generalisation ability, making it suitable for complex regression tasks. This research aims to assess how effectively these models can utilise inputs such as oil reserves, consumption patterns, exchange rates, and political stability to forecast oil production accurately.

The significance of employing ensemble machine learning models, which amalgamate the predictive power of multiple algorithms, has been underscored in recent literature. Studies by Sagi and Rokach (2018) and Shahhosseini et al. (2020) have shown that ensemble models surpass the predictive performance of individual models in complex data environments. The adaptability and robustness of ensemble approaches, highlighted in research by Sagi and Rokach (2018) and further supported by Shahhosseini et al. (2020), advocate for their application in dynamic and complex markets such as the oil sector. These attributes are precious in addressing Nigeria's oil sector's unique and challenging aspects, which may not align with global oil production trends.

Given the distinct characteristics and challenges inherent to Nigeria's oil industry, there is a critical need for a predictive model custom-fitted to the Nigerian context. This model must capture the general predictors of oil production and account for local nuances that influence Nigeria's production outcomes. Therefore, this study proposes using an ensemble machine learning framework that leverages the combined strengths of XGBoost, Random Forest, and Extra Trees Regressor. By integrating these advanced algorithms, the model aims to offer a more refined and context-sensitive tool for forecasting. This approach is expected to yield more accurate, reliable predictions, facilitating better-informed decision-making and strategic planning within Nigeria's oil sector.

In essence, by harnessing the capabilities of these ensemble machine learning models, this research seeks to advance the accuracy and relevance of oil production forecasts in Nigeria, thereby contributing to the optimisation of production strategies and broader economic planning within the country.

1.3 Gaps in the Previous Studies

Previous works on forecasting oil production have left significant gaps that this study aims to address. Firstly, traditional models have often focused narrowly on physical and economic factors, neglecting broader socio-economic and political influences on oil production (Moroney & Berg, 1999). Additionally, these models struggle to adapt to the dynamic nature of the global oil market, especially in regions like Nigeria, known for market volatility (Falode & Udomboso, 2021). Moreover, existing models lack the predictive accuracy and efficiency needed in today's fast-paced energy sector, often failing to capture the nonlinear relationships between factors affecting oil production (Obite et al., 2021). Policy decisions in Nigeria's oil sector have relied on historical data rather than contemporary insights, leading to delayed responses to market changes (Gbakon et al., 2022). Furthermore, traditional forecasting models have overlooked environmental and socio-economic considerations, highlighting the need for a more holistic approach to promote sustainable practices (Asumadu-Sarkodie & Owusu, 2016). Finally, generalised models developed with a global perspective may not adequately address the unique complexities of the Nigerian oil market (Karakurt, 2021).

1.4 Novelty in the Current Work

This study introduces an advanced predictive model for forecasting Nigerian oil production using the Ensemble Machine Learning Approach, including the Extra Trees Regressor, Random Forest Regressor, and XGBoost algorithms. The model integrates socio-economic, political, and environmental factors, providing a holistic analysis of influences on Nigeria's oil production. It adapts to market dynamics through adaptive algorithms like Extra Trees Regressor, capturing the global oil market's complexities. The ensemble machine learning algorithms ensure high predictive accuracy by handling complex data relationships. Additionally, the model offers real-time, data-driven insights for informed decision-making, crucial for strategic planning in Nigeria's oil industry. It assesses oil production's environmental and socio-economic impacts and aligns with sustainable development goals. Custom-tailored for Nigeria, this approach offers practical forecasting solutions specific to the country's challenges. This work significantly advances predictive modelling in the oil industry, addressing gaps and introducing tailored solutions for Nigerian oil production forecasting.

2 Methods and Techniques

In our study, we adopted a comprehensive approach to forecasting Nigeria's oil production using advanced machine-learning techniques. Our initial step involved gathering secondary data from several authoritative sources, including Worldometer, Statista, and TheGlobalEconomy.com, focusing specifically on Nigeria's oil reserves, production, consumption statistics, and political rights. Following the data acquisition phase, we began data preprocessing to ensure compatibility with our machine learning models. Given the diverse scales and units across our dataset's features, we normalised the data to a range of [0, 1]. This normalisation was crucial for accommodating our data's non-Gaussian distribution and optimising the performance of the selected algorithms, particularly for models like Extra Trees Regressor and XGBoost, where feature scale uniformity enhances model training efficiency. Although Random Forest Regressor is inherently scale-invariant, normalisation facilitated a consistent preprocessing pipeline across all models (Huangi et al., 2018; Li, 2019; Mrabet et al., 2022). The dataset was then partitioned into training and test sets (70/30), employing a 5-fold cross-validation method to maximise the use of our data in a robust evaluation framework. This approach is beneficial for datasets of limited size because it ensures comprehensive training and validation across multiple folds while mitigating the risks of overfitting and variance, which can compromise model reliability.

The core of our analysis involved the application of three distinct machine learning models: Extra Trees Regressor, XGBoost, and Random Forest Regressor. Each model was chosen for its unique strengths in predictive accuracy and handling complex datasets. We meticulously trained these models on the normalised data and then conducted an exhaustive evaluation phase. This phase utilised a suite of performance metrics, including Mean Absolute Error, Relative Absolute Error, Root Mean Squared Error, Root Relative Squared Error, and the Correlation Coefficient, to assess and compare each model's predictive accuracy and reliability. The final stage of our research focused on leveraging the trained models to predict Nigeria's oil production, showcasing the potent application of machine learning in forecasting within the energy sector. The procedural flow of our research, from data collection to oil production forecasting, is detailed in Fig. 1, providing a visual overview of the methodological steps undertaken in our analysis.

Fig. 1. Steps Followed in Oil Production Prediction

2.1 The Ensemble Algorithms Approach

Predicting Nigerian oil production with advanced ensemble machine learning models offers a nuanced understanding and higher accuracy in prediction tasks. This section elaborates on using XGBoost, Random Forest Regressor, and Extra Trees Regressor, each bringing unique strengths to the ensemble approach.

2.1.1 Extra Trees Regressor (Extremely Randomised Trees Regressor)

The Extra Trees Regressor introduces additional randomness compared to RandomForest by randomising thresholds for feature splits. This approach can lead to more diversified tree ensembles, enhancing the model's generalisation ability. We highlight the effectiveness of the Extra Trees Regressor in feature importance extraction and regressor fitting for predictive modelling, providing valuable insights into influential factors affecting outcomes. The adaptability and efficiency of the Extra Trees Regressor make it an essential tool for predictive modelling across various fields (M. Devi et al., 2019).

The selection of splits in the Extra Trees Regressor can be represented as a randomised process, differing from the optimal split selection in traditional decision tree algorithms. This randomised process described by Geurts, Ernst, and Wehenkel (2006) could be visualised through algorithmic descriptions, highlighting the randomness in split selection. The process can be summarised in pseudo-code, as shown in Fig. 2:

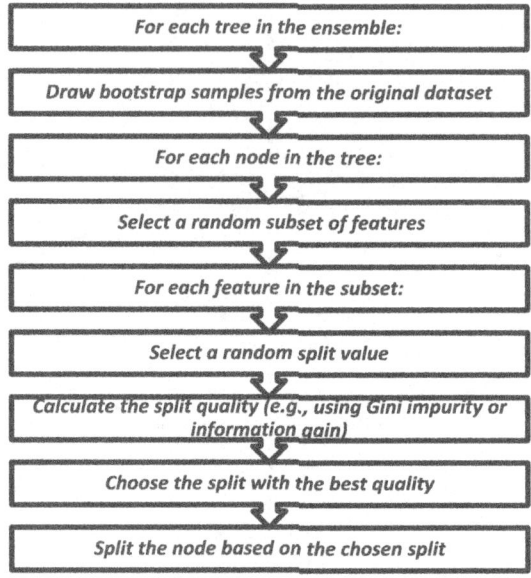

Fig. 2. Pseudo-code for ExtraTrees Regressor

2.1.2 XGBoost (Extreme Gradient Boosting)

XGBoost, standing for Extreme Gradient Boosting, is recognised for being a powerful and efficient ensemble learning framework that excels in a wide range of predictive modelling tasks. It distinguishes itself by simultaneously optimising predictive accuracy and computational efficiency, which makes it exceptionally suitable for handling complex data sets. At the heart of XGBoost's approach is an objective function it seeks to minimise, which artfully combines a loss function with a regularisation term to enhance model performance and robustness. The objective function is formulated as:

$$\text{Obj} = \sum_{(i)} L(y_i, \hat{y}_i) + \sum_{(k)} \Omega(f_k) \qquad (1)$$

where L is the loss function that measures the difference between the predicted $\hat{y}_i$ and actual y_i values and Ω represent the regularisation term to prevent overfitting (Chen & Guestrin, 2016). XGBoost is an ensemble method, precisely a type of boosting, where it builds models sequentially, each new model correcting errors made by previous models and combining them to produce a final, more accurate prediction (Adewale et al.,

2024a; Shi et al., 2021). This method effectively improves the model's performance by integrating the strengths of multiple learners.

2.1.3 Random Forest Regressor

Random Forest Regressor builds upon bagging multiple decision trees to reduce variance and improve prediction accuracy. It is particularly effective in capturing nonlinear relationships without extensive parameter tuning. The effectiveness of the Random Forest Regressor in various applications, including the prediction of train arrival delays, demonstrates its reliability and adaptability in handling complex datasets and achieving high accuracy in predictions (Ji et al., 2020).

Incorporating these advanced ensemble models for forecasting Nigerian oil production promises higher accuracy and provides a methodologically sound and innovative approach adaptable to the domain's complexities. Integrating recent studies and mathematical formulations will further strengthen the research, offering a scientifically rigorous foundation for these predictive models.

2.2 Empirical Validation

The metric of accuracy—five well-established statistical evaluation measures (see Eqs. 2 to 6—forms the basis of our validation process. The selection of these metrics is informed by the work of notable researchers in the application of machine learning to solve practical problems, including Adewale et al., 2024a, Adewale et al., 2024b, and Yao et al. (2010). By integrating a comprehensive suite of evaluation criteria, our approach ensures a robust and multidimensional assessment of the hybrid model's forecasting capabilities.

The mean absolute error (MAE) measures the average magnitude of the absolute differences between predicted and actual values, representing the average error magnitude.

$$\text{Mean Absolute Error (MAE)} = \frac{1}{n}\sum_{i=1}^{n}|y_i - \hat{y}_i| \qquad (2)$$

The root mean squared error (RMSE) calculates the square root of the average of the squared differences between predicted and actual values, indicating the standard deviation of the errors.

$$\text{Root Mean Squared Error (RMSE)} = \sqrt{\frac{1}{n}\sum_{i=1}^{n}(y_i - \hat{y}_i)^2} \qquad (3)$$

The relative absolute error (RAE) compares the total absolute error of the predictions to the total absolute error of a naive baseline model, which always predicts the mean of the actual values.

$$\text{Relative Absolute Error (RAE)} = \frac{\sum_{i=1}^{n}|y_i - \hat{y}_i|}{\sum_{i=1}^{n}|y_i - \overline{y}|} \qquad (4)$$

The root relative squared error (RRSE) is similar to the RMSE but is normalised by the variance of the actual values.

$$\text{Root Relative Squared Error (RRSE)} = \sqrt{\frac{\sum_{i=1}^{n}(y_i - \hat{y}_i)^2}{\sum_{i=1}^{n}(y_i - \bar{y})^2}} \tag{5}$$

The correlation coefficient (Pearson's r) evaluates the linear relationship between predicted and actual values, ranging from −1 to 1.

$$\text{Correlation Coefficient (Pearson's } r) = \frac{\sum_{i=1}^{n}(y_i - \bar{y})(\hat{y}_i - \bar{\hat{y}})}{\sqrt{\sum_{i=1}^{n}(y_i - \bar{y})^2 \sum_{i=1}^{n}(\hat{y}_i - \bar{\hat{y}})^2}} \tag{6}$$

where:

- n is the total number of observations.
- y_i denotes the actual outcome for the ith observation.
- $\hat{y}_i$ is the predicted value for the ith observation.
- $\bar{y}$ is the mean of the actual values.
- $\bar{\hat{y}}$ is the mean of the predicted values.

The proximity between predicted and actual values is directly proportional to the decrease in error values. These metrics allow us to gauge the accuracy of our predictions against actual outcomes, with lower error values and a correlation coefficient closer to 1, indicating better model performance.

2.3 Research Model

This research crafted a unique model targeting oil production (OPR), weaving together four pivotal predictors: oil reserves (OR), oil consumption (OC), oil prices (OP), and political rights (PR). Central to the model, these factors define OPR as the outcome of interest. Figure 3 shows the conceptual model of the oil production prediction system. The investigation aimed to unravel the nexus between OPR, a metric of the nation's energy sector prowess, and its influencing predictors, such as reserves, consumption rates, exchange rate shifts, and political rights, often seen as a foundation for political stability. When citizens can express their opinions, participate in free and fair elections, and engage in the political process, it can lead to a more satisfied populace. The study employed these predictors to forecast OPR, utilising machine learning techniques to fine-tune the estimation of model parameters. The essence of this research model is succinctly captured in fundamental Eq. 7, which is in line with the strategy delineated by Gareth et al. (2017), as shown in Eq. 7.

$$OPR = f(OR, OC, OP, PR) \tag{7}$$

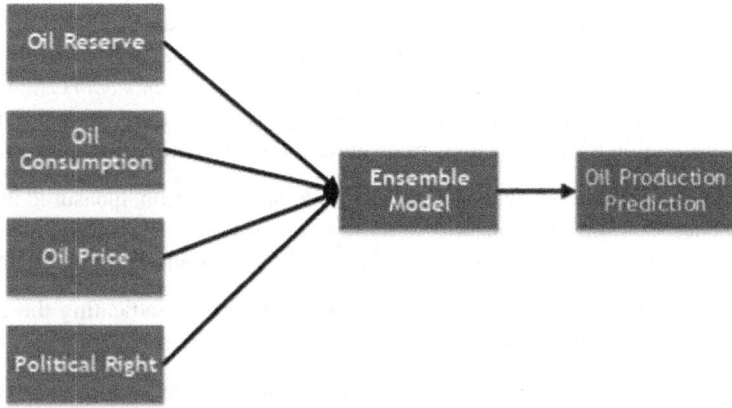

Fig. 3. Conceptual model showing the oil production prediction system

2.4 Hypothetical Case Study Application

This case study applies our research model to predict Nigeria's oil production, utilising historical data to demonstrate its efficiency and practical implications. By focusing on key variables—oil reserve (OR), oil consumption (OC), oil price (OR), and political rights (PR)—the model assesses how these factors collectively influence oil production trends.

The parameters for the study are set as follows:

- **Oil Reserve (OR):** This is measured in billions of barrels.
- **Oil Consumption (OC):** This is recorded in millions of daily barrels.
- **Oil Price (OR):** This is represented in USD.
- **Political Right (PR):** This is scored based on the electoral process, political diversity and engagement, and government effectiveness. Ratings range from 1 (high rights) to 7 (low rights).

Using machine learning algorithms, the model predicts oil production and highlights the potential impact of policy adjustments in these areas. By analysing the practical implications, we demonstrate how adjustments in oil reserves, consumption, pricing policies, and political reforms can enhance Nigeria's oil output. For example, expanding oil reserves through exploration and investment can boost production capacity. Similarly, policies to stabilise oil prices and improve political rights can create a more favourable environment for oil production.

This approach offers policymakers a compact yet comprehensive tool, showcasing the model's utility in guiding strategic decisions. The model helps formulate policies that optimise oil production and stimulate economic growth by providing actionable insights and demonstrating their practical implications in real-world scenarios.

2.5 Data Sources, Definitions and Measurement of Variables

The dataset under examination extends from 1980 to 2016, incorporating a broad spectrum of data across several years to analyse socio-economic factors (Nigeria Oil

Reserves, Production and Consumption Statistics - Worldometer (2024); *Nigeria: Oil Production 2022 | Statista* (2023); *Brent Crude Oil Price Annually 1976–2024 | Statista* (2024); *Nigeria Political Rights - Data, Chart | TheGlobalEconomy.com* (2024). Table 1 offers a glimpse into a segment of this dataset, covering the years 1999 to 2004, and illustrates a selection of key variables relevant to the study. These variables include:

Oil Production (OPR): The country's daily crude oil production, measured in millions of barrels, encapsulating both onshore and offshore activities. This metric is pivotal for assessing a nation's contribution to the global energy sector and economic vitality.

Oil Reserves (OR): This is quantified in billions of barrels, indicating the estimated quantities of crude oil that are anticipated to be commercially recoverable.

Oil Price (OP): The cost of crude oil, expressed in USD, reflects the global market valuation.

Political Rights (PR): Evaluated on a scale from 1 (indicating high levels of political rights) to 7 (signifying low rights), this score is derived from an analysis of the electoral process, political pluralism, participation, and the functionality of government.

Oil Consumption (OC): This is measured in millions of barrels daily, representing the total domestic oil volume.

This subset of the dataset, as outlined in Table 1, provides a concise overview of these critical indicators within the specified timeframe, enabling a focused analysis of the trends and patterns that emerge from these variables.

Table 1. Part of the Dataset used for modelling

Year	OPR	OR	OP	PR	OC
1999	2136263.00	22500000000.00	17.90	4.00	252000.00
2000	2169135.00	22500000000.00	28.40	4.00	227354.00
2001	2261416.00	22500000000.00	24.45	4.00	286822.00
2002	2123323.00	24000000000.00	25.01	4.00	292196.00
2003	2278592.00	24000000000.00	28.83	4.00	280225.00
2004	2331696.00	25000000000.00	38.10	4.00	280188.00

3 Results and Discussion

3.1 Descriptive Statistics

The descriptive statistics in Table 2 detail various indicators related to oil dynamics and governance in Nigeria, covering 37 instances, and provide insights into the critical variables analysed in this study. Indicators include oil production (OPR), oil reserve

(OR), oil price (OP), political rights (PR), and oil consumption (OC). The average oil production (OPR) of 2,001,529 barrels, with a standard deviation of 385,432.20, highlights variability in output, reflecting differing capacities across oil fields and its critical economic role. The oil reserve (OR) data, normalised around a mean of 0 and a standard deviation of 1.01, suggests a wide range of recoverable crude oil, emphasising strategic reserves. Oil Price (OP), averaging 41.70 USD with a standard deviation of 30.63, illustrates global price fluctuations impacting Nigeria, driven by supply-demand dynamics, geopolitical tensions, and economic conditions. Normalised political rights (PR) scores reveal a range of political climates crucial for understanding governance and its effect on oil production policies. Also, normalised oil consumption (OC) shows varied usage levels, indicating domestic energy demand and economic activity. This analysis offers insights into the interplay between oil production, reserves, pricing, consumption, and political governance, underscoring the complexities of managing oil resources and the importance of political stability for sustainable energy production and economic growth.

Table 2. Descriptive Statistics

	OPR	OR	OP	PR	OC
count	37.00	37.00	37.00	37.00	37.00
mean	2001529.00	0.00	41.70	0.00	0.00
std	385432.20	1.01	30.63	1.01	1.01
min	1246000.00	−0.97	12.80	−1.74	−1.80
25%	1817000.00	−0.86	19.10	−0.49	−0.70
50%	2060000.00	−0.40	28.70	−0.49	−0.09
75%	2278592.00	1.34	54.38	1.39	0.40
max	2630860.00	1.45	111.63	1.39	3.14

3.2 Test for Multicollinearity

The Variance Inflation Factor (VIF) is a measure used to identify the presence of multicollinearity among independent variables in a regression analysis. Using the rule of thumb that a VIF greater than 10 indicates significant multicollinearity, as stated by Forthofer et al. (2007), our analysis of the VIF factors for features related to oil production, as shown in Table 3, demonstrates that none of the predictors—oil reserve, oil price, political right, and oil consumption—exceed this threshold. Specifically, oil reserve and oil price, with VIFs of 7.314537 and 5.235808, respectively, indicate moderate multicollinearity, which, under this stricter criterion, does not present a significant concern for the regression model's stability or its interpretability concerning predicting oil production. Similarly, political rights and oil consumption, with VIFs significantly below 10, show minimal to low multicollinearity, reinforcing their suitability as predictors without necessitating immediate corrective measures to address multicollinearity.

As Cripps and Nguyen (2001) note, multicollinearity does not affect the model's predictive capacity within the observed data range, although it complicates identifying individual variable impacts. This aspect, while important, is less critical for our research objectives. In light of this and considering the more conservative approach to managing multicollinearity, our findings suggest that the current variables can remain within the model. The lack of significant multicollinearity, as evidenced by VIF values not exceeding the ten thresholds, suggests that our model maintains sufficient robustness for the intended analysis. This finding is in harmony with our research objectives, which emphasise the model's overall predictive accuracy and understanding of each independent variable's specific impact on Oil Production. Consequently, this reduces the urgency for immediate modifications to diminish multicollinearity within the model.

Table 3. VIF for each feature

S/N	Features	VIF Factor
1	Oil Reserve	7.314537
2	Oil Price	5.235808
3	Political Right	1.196773
4	Oil Consumption	2.035931

3.3 Performance Evaluation of Extra Trees, XG Boost, and Random Forest Regressor

In the endeavour to predict Nigeria's Oil Production (OPR) using a combination of economic and non-economic indicators, Table 4 delineates the performance metrics of three distinct machine-learning models. We rigorously evaluated each model's efficacy across a spectrum of metrics, including the relative absolute error (RAE), mean absolute error (MAE), root relative squared error (RRSE), root mean squared error (RMSE), and correlation coefficient. These metrics offer a holistic view of each model's predictive accuracy. Figure 4 graphically contrasts the performance of the models, providing a visual interpretation of their effectiveness.

The Extra Trees Regressor emerged as the most accurate model, as evidenced by its superior correlation coefficient of 0.8155, indicating a solid alignment between the predicted and actual OPR values (See Fig. 5). It also maintained the lowest error margins, with an MAE of 0.2812 and an RMSE of 0.3929, suggesting high precision in its predictions. Conversely, the XGBoost Regressor, while demonstrating reasonable accuracy with a correlation coefficient of 0.6434, showed higher error rates (MAE of 0.4032 and RMSE of 0.5222) compared to the Extra Trees Regressor. Although a robust model in various contexts, the Random Forest Regressor exhibited a relatively lower correlation coefficient of 0.4362 in this scenario. Its error metrics, with an MAE of 0.5607 and RMSE of 0.6211, further indicated its limitations in accurately forecasting Nigeria's OPR.

Table 4. Model's Evaluation

Performance Metrics	Extra Trees Regressor	XGBoost Regressor	Random Forest Regressor
Correlation coefficient	0.8155	0.6434	0.4362
Mean absolute error	0.2812	0.4032	0.5607
Root mean squared error	0.3929	0.5222	0.6211
Relative absolute error	0.3481	0.5055	0.5431
Root relative squared error	0.4044	0.5440	0.5757

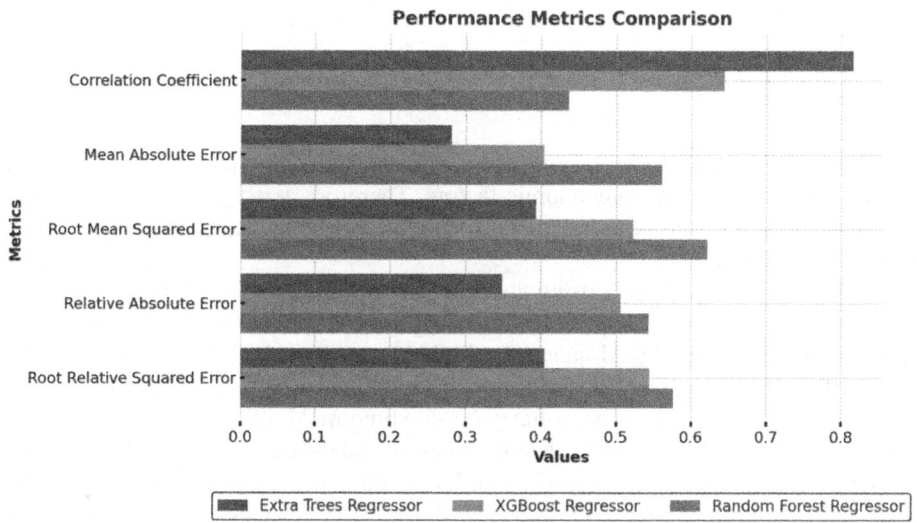

Fig. 4. Performance Metrics of Machine Learning Algorithms

These findings underscore the importance of model selection in machine learning tasks. The choice of algorithm has a profound impact on the accuracy and reliability of predictive analyses, as demonstrated by the varied performance of the evaluated models in the context of this study. Regarding R.Q.2, the Extra Trees Regressor has proven to be the most effective model, providing accurate forecasts based on the selected variables.

3.4 Comparative Analysis and Validation

Considering the comparative analysis in Table 5, our findings align with the 'No Free Lunch' theorem, which asserts that no single algorithm excels universally (Sterkenburg & Grünwald, 2021). This principle is evident in the varied performance of algorithms across different studies. Our application of the Extra Trees Regressor yielded a mean absolute error (MAE) of 0.2812, demonstrating notable accuracy within our Nigerian dataset.

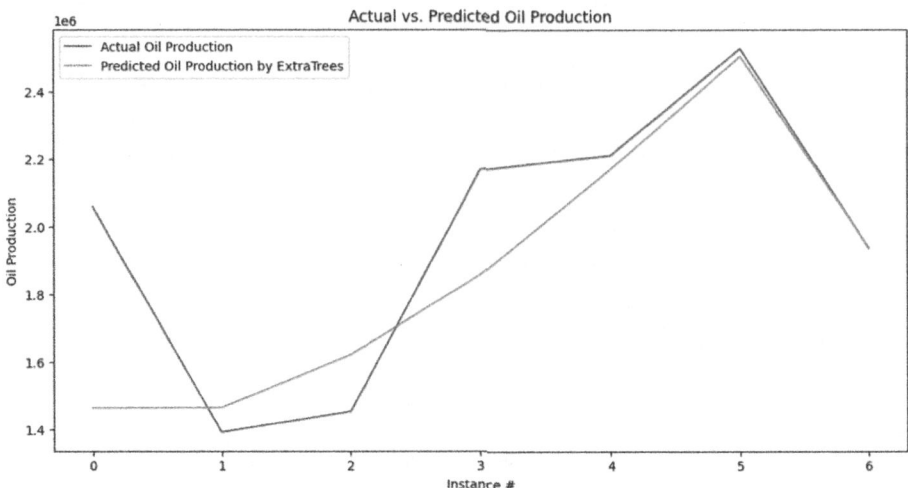

Fig. 5. Actual vs Predicted Oil Production by ExtraTrees Model

However, this success does not guarantee similar results in other economies due to varying sensitivities to socio-economic factors. Therefore, testing and validating these algorithms in diverse contexts is crucial for tailored machine-learning applications in economic forecasting.

Table 5 includes our study using the Extra Trees Regressor, which focuses on variables such as oil reserve, oil price, political rights, and oil consumption over the past 37 years. Another study by Al-qaness et al. (2022) employs the Modified Aquila Optimizer with Opposition-Based Learning, analysing oilfield production data over 11 years. AlRassas et al. (2021) use a neurofuzzy-based slime mold algorithm on similar data. Each study's methodology, independent variables, and dataset size uniquely contribute to understanding oil production prediction. The Extra Trees Regressor's low MSE in our study signifies its effectiveness in capturing socio-economic nuances within our dataset. The Extra Trees Regressor excels at handling high-dimensional data and offers valuable insights into feature importance, making it particularly useful for policymakers.

While the MAE reported by Al-qaness et al. (2022) is lower than our model's, it is important to note several contextual factors. First, the dataset size and composition in Al-qaness et al.'s study differ, focusing on various oilfields' production data over 11 years, which may present different dynamics compared to the broader 37-year dataset used in our study. Additionally, the Modified Aquila Optimizer with Opposition-Based Learning employed by Al-qaness et al. (2022) may be particularly well-suited to their specific dataset characteristics, potentially explaining the lower MAE.

However, our approach has several strengths that extend beyond the MAE metric. The Extra Trees Regressor offers robustness in handling high-dimensional data and provides insights into feature importance, highlighting critical predictors like 'Oil Reserve' and 'Oil Consumption.' This transparency in the decision-making process is particularly valuable for policymakers who require understandable and actionable insights.

Moreover, our model incorporates a broader range of socio-economic and political factors, providing a comprehensive view of the determinants affecting oil production. This enriched model can better inform strategic decisions and policy formulations.

Furthermore, our methodology's application of rigorous cross-validation techniques ensures that the model's performance is consistently reliable across different subsets of the data, minimising the risks of overfitting and enhancing its generalizability. Incorporating diverse predictors such as exchange rates and political stability also broadens the analytical lens, offering a more holistic understanding of the factors driving oil production. While the MAE of our model may not be the lowest compared to some other studies, the Extra Trees Regressor's robustness, transparency, and comprehensive analytical approach provide significant advantages. These strengths highlight the model's potential for practical application in policy development and strategic planning within Nigeria's oil sector.

3.5 Feature Importance

Figure 6 highlights the varying impact of different attributes within the Extra Trees model. The feature importance graph for the Extra Trees model indicates that 'Oil Reserve' and 'Oil Consumption' are the most influential variables when predicting oil production, with 'Oil Reserve' being the most significant. 'Oil Price' and 'Political Right' have less importance in the model, with 'Political Right' being the least influential. This suggests that while market factors like oil price and political stability play a role, the physical availability of oil and consumption patterns are stronger predictors in this model's context. Our findings indicate that 'Oil Reserve' and 'Oil Consumption' are the most significant predictors of oil production, addressing R.Q.1.

Table 5. Comparing our best result with other models used to predict Oil production

S/N	Reference	Top Performing Model	Independent variables used	The size of the dataset	Mean Absolute Error
1	Our Investigation	ExtraTrees Regressor	Oil reserve, oil price, political rights, and oil consumption	37 years	0.281
2	Al-qaness et al. (2022)	Modified Aquila Optimizer (AO) with the Opposition-Based Learning (OBL) technique	Various oilfields' production data	11 years	0.080
3	AlRassas et al. (2021)	Neuro fuzzy-based slime mould algorithm	Various oilfields' production data	11 years	0.693

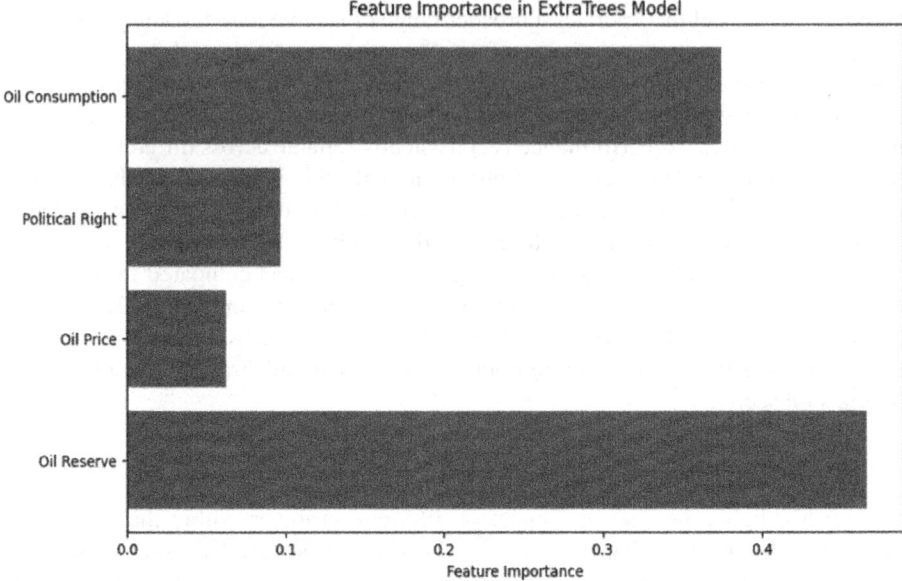

Fig. 6. The Features Importance of the Extra Trees Model.

3.6 Limitations of the Methodologies and Models Used in the Study

While extra trees regressor models effectively handle complex, high-dimensional data, they have certain limitations. High computational demands can limit scalability, and the model's performance may vary significantly across different economic contexts, necessitating careful localisation and data adaptation. The model's accuracy depends heavily on data quality; incomplete or biased datasets can impair performance. Furthermore, the model may not generalise well to other regions without significant modifications, limiting its immediate applicability to broader contexts.

Future work should focus on enhancing the robustness and generalizability of the proposed method. This can be achieved by exploring and integrating other machine learning algorithms to complement the strengths of the Extra Trees Regressor, developing hybrid models to address specific weaknesses, and implementing transfer learning approaches to adapt the model to new regions or contexts with minimal retraining. Additionally, extending the methodology to other economic forecasting tasks beyond oil production and incorporating additional data sources, such as real-time market data, can improve the model's resilience and predictive capabilities. These steps can make the model more versatile and practical for various economic forecasting applications.

4 Conclusion

In conclusion, our study enhances the precision of Nigeria's oil production forecasts by comparing the Extra Trees Regressor, XGB Regressor, and Random Forest Regressor using performance indicators such as MAE, RAE, RMSE, RRSE, and the Correlation

Coefficient. The Extra Trees Regressor emerged as the most accurate model, effectively capturing socio-economic nuances and reducing forecasting errors. Key predictors identified include 'Oil Reserve' and 'Oil Consumption,' highlighting the model's robustness in economic forecasting. By incorporating variables like Oil Reserves, Oil Consumption, Exchange Rates, and Political Stability, our approach comprehensively analyses Nigeria's oil production, emphasising the influence of economic policies, market dynamics, and political stability. This challenges the traditional reliance on direct production and economic indicators alone, proposing a more nuanced prediction model. While acknowledging the study's limitations, such as reliance on a specific dataset and limited algorithm selection, our findings advocate for diversified algorithmic exploration to support insightful and practical policy development in the oil industry, aligning with the "No Free Lunch" theorem (Sterkenburg & Grünwald, 2021).

4.1 Recommendations

Building on the findings of this study, which utilised the Extra Trees Regressor for predicting Nigeria's oil production, future research should embrace a broader spectrum of socio-economic and environmental factors. It is recommended that analyses across global oil-producing countries, comparative model evaluations, and sensitivity tests be conducted under varying market conditions. Additionally, it is crucial to explore other nonlinear machine learning algorithms, such as neural networks and deep learning models. These advanced algorithms can capture complex patterns and interactions within the data, potentially enhancing prediction accuracy. Incorporating case studies from diverse oil economies and examining their unique socio-economic and geopolitical influences will further sharpen forecasting accuracy. This approach aims to deepen insights into global oil production drivers, supporting crafting more refined oil sector policies.

Disclosure of Potential Conflict of Interest. The authors confirm that no financial or personal relationships among them could appear to bias the findings presented in this manuscript

Authors Contributions
M.D. Adewale spearheaded the concept, methodology, and data collection and drafted the initial manuscript. Other authors contributed to validation, project management, and manuscript editing. All authors approve this submission to the journal.

Data Availability Statement. The datasets utilised in this research were obtained from multiple sources, including Nigerian Oil Reserves, Production, and Consumption Statistics from Worldometer (2024), Oil Production in Nigeria as reported by Statista (2023), Annual Brent Crude Oil Prices from Statista (2024), and Nigerian Political Rights data available at TheGlobalEconomy.com (2024). For additional inquiries, please contact the lead author.

Author Statement. The authors of this piece affirm their commitment to the guidelines and stipulations set forth by the Journal of Forecasting publication.

References

Adewale, M.D., et al.: Comparative performance evaluation of random forest, extreme gradient boosting and linear regression algorithms using Nigeria's gross domestic products. In: Seeam,

A., Ramsurrun, V., Juddoo, S., Phokeer, A. (eds.) Innovations and Interdisciplinary Solutions for Underserved Areas. InterSol 2023. LNICS, Social Informatics and Telecommunications Engineering, vol. 541, pp. 131–150. Springer, Cham (2024a). https://doi.org/10.1007/978-3-031-51849-2_9

Adewale, M., et al.: Predicting gross domestic product using the ensemble machine learning method. Syst. Soft Comput. **6**, 200132 (2024b). https://doi.org/10.1016/j.sasc.2024.200132

AlRassas, A.M., et al.: Advance artificial time series forecasting model for oil production using neuro fuzzy-based slime mould algorithm. J. Pet. Explor. Prod. Technol. **12**(2), 383–395 (2021). https://doi.org/10.1007/s13202-021-01405-w

Al-qaness, M.A.A., Ewees, A.A., Fan, H., AlRassas, A.M., Elaziz, M.A.: Modified aquila optimiser for forecasting oil production. Geo-spatial Inf. Sci. **25**(4), 519–535 (2022). https://doi.org/10.1080/10095020.2022.2068385

Asumadu-Sarkodie, S., Owusu, P.A.: Forecasting Nigeria's energy use by 2030, an econometric approach. Energy Sources Part B **11**, 990–997 (2016). https://doi.org/10.1080/15567249.2016.1217287

Brent crude oil price annually 1976–2024 | Statista. (2024, February 12). Statista. https://www.statista.com/statistics/262860/uk-brent-crude-oil-price-changes-since-1976/. Accessed 18 Feb 2024

Cavallo, A.: Hubbert's petroleum production model: an evaluation and implications for world oil production forecasts. Nat. Resour. Res. **13**, 211–221 (2004). https://doi.org/10.1007/S11053-004-0129-2

Chen, T., Guestrin, C.: XGBoost: a scalable tree boosting system. In: Proceedings of the 22nd ACM SIGKDD International Conference on Knowledge Discovery and Data Mining (2016). https://doi.org/10.1145/2939672.2939785

Devi, M., Mathew, R., Suguna, R.: Regressor fitting of feature importance for customer segment prediction with ensembling schemes using machine learning. Int. J. Eng. Adv. Technol. (2019). https://doi.org/10.35940/ijeat.f8255.088619

Duhu, I.G.: Democratic stability in mitigating the impact of corruption on economic growth in Nigeria. Eur. Sci. J. ESJ **15**(31) (2019). https://doi.org/10.19044/esj.2019.v15n31p106

Falode, O., Udomboso, C.: Efficient Crude Oil Pricing Using a Machine Learning Approach. Day 2 Tue, 03 August 2021. https://doi.org/10.2118/207152-ms

Forthofer, R.N., Lee, E.S., Hernández, M.: Linear regression. Elsevier eBooks, pp. 349–386 (2007). https://doi.org/10.1016/b978-0-12-369492-8.50018-2

Gareth, J., Daniela, W., Trevor, H., Robert, T.: An introduction to statistical learning. Springer, New York (ISL) (2017)

Gbakon, K., Ajienka, J., Gogo, J., Iledare, O.: Oil Production Forecasting Models and Oil End-Use Optimization Framework under Global Energy Transition Dynamics. Day 2 Tue, 02 August 2022. https://doi.org/10.2118/211967-ms

Geurts, P., Ernst, D., Wehenkel, L.: Extremely randomised trees. Mach. Learn. **63**, 3–42 (2006). https://doi.org/10.1007/s10994-006-6226-1

Huangi, L., Yang, D., Liu, B., Deng, J.: Decorrelated batch normalisation. In: 2018 IEEE/CVF Conference on Computer Vision and Pattern Recognition (2018). https://doi.org/10.1109/cvpr.2018.00089

Ji, Y., Zheng, W., Dong, H., Gao, P.: Train delays prediction based on feature selection and random forest. In: 2020 IEEE 23rd International Conference on Intelligent Transportation Systems (ITSC), pp. 1–6 (2020). https://doi.org/10.1109/ITSC45102.2020.9294653

Karakurt, I.: Modelling and forecasting the oil consumptions of the BRICS-T countries. Energy **220**, 119720 (2021). https://doi.org/10.1016/j.energy.2020.119720

Li, C.: Preprocessing Methods and Pipelines of Data Mining: An Overview. arXiv (Cornell University) (2019). https://doi.org/10.48550/arxiv.1906.08510

Moroney, J.R., Berg, M.: An integrated model of oil production. Energy J. **20**, 105–124 (1999). https://doi.org/10.5547/ISSN0195-6574-EJ-VOL20-NO1-6

Mrabet, Z.E., Sugunaraj, N., Ranganathan, P., Abhyankar, S.: Random forest regressor-based approach for detecting fault location and duration in power systems. Sensors (2022). https://doi.org/10.3390/s22020458

Nigeria: Oil Production 2022 | Statista. (2023, August 25). Statista. https://www.statista.com/statistics/265195/oil-production-in-nigeria-in-barrels-per-day/. Accessed 18 Feb 2024

Nigeria oil reserves, production and consumption statistics - Worldometer. (2024). Worldometer.info. https://www.worldometers.info/oil/nigeria-oil/. Accessed 18 Feb 2024

Nigeria Political rights - data, chart | TheGlobalEconomy.com. (2024). TheGlobalEconomy.com. https://www.theglobaleconomy.com/Nigeria/political_rights/. Accessed 19 June 2024

Obite, C.P., Chukwu, A., Bartholomew, D.C., Nwosu, U.I., Esiaba, G.E.: Classical and machine learning modeling of crude oil production in Nigeria: identification of an eminent model for application. Energy Rep. **7**, 3497–3505 (2021). https://doi.org/10.1016/J.EGYR.2021.06.005

Sagi, O., Rokach, L.: Ensemble learning: a survey. WIREs Data Min. Knowl. Discov. **8**(4) (2018). https://doi.org/10.1002/widm.1249

Salisu, A.A., Cuñado, J., Isah, K.O., Gupta, R.: Oil Price and Exchange Rate Behaviour of the BRICS. Emerg. Mark. Financ. Trade **57**, 2042–2051 (2020). https://doi.org/10.1080/1540496X.2020.1850440

Shahhosseini, M., Hu, G., Archontoulis, S.: Forecasting corn yield with machine learning ensembles. Front. Plant Sci. **11** (2020). https://doi.org/10.3389/fpls.2020.01120

Shi, R., Xu, X., Li, J., Li, Y.: Prediction and analysis of train arrival delay based on XGBoost and Bayesian optimisation. Appl. Soft Comput. **109**, 107538 (2021). https://doi.org/10.1016/J.ASOC.2021.107538

Sterkenburg, T.F., Grunwald, P.: The no-free-lunch theorems of supervised learning. Synthese, 4 June 2021. https://doi.org/10.1007/s11229-021-03233-1

Yao, W., Chen, X., Van, Tooren, M., Wei, Y.: Euclidean distance and second derivative based widths optimisation of radial basis function neural networks. In: International Joint Conference on Neural Networks (IJCNN) (2010). https://doi.org/10.1109/ijcnn.2010.5596528

AI-Powered Corn Disease Classification Using Deep Transfer Learning

Moussa Mahamat Boukar[1,2], Assia Aboubakar Mahamat[1,3](✉), Hassane Hamdan[4], and Usman Abubakar Bello[5]

[1] Nile University of Nigeria, Abuja, Federal Capital Territory, Nigeria
aassia@aust.edu.ng
[2] Université Virtuélle du Tchad, N'djamena, Tchad
[3] Ecole Nationale Superieure des Travaux Publics (ENSTP), N'djamena, Tchad
[4] Université de N'djamena, N'djamena, Tchad
[5] Baze University, Abuja, Federal Capital Territory, Nigeria

Abstract. Corn, a vital agricultural crop, and essential food source, plays a crucial role in the global food chain and serves as a raw material for various industrial applications like biofuels. Small-scale corn cultivation sustains livelihoods in developing nations, but these crops are highly susceptible to diseases. Extreme weather conditions can exacerbate these diseases, leading to significant declines in agricultural yields.

Advancements in artificial intelligence (AI), particularly deep learning algorithms, offer promising solutions. This study explores the application of deep transfer learning for classifying three distinct corn leaf conditions: rust, northern leaf blight, and healthy plants. By utilizing corn leaf images as input and leveraging convolutional neural networks, the proposed approach eliminates the need for complex pre-processing or manual feature extraction.

Employing well-established deep learning models (VGG19, GoogleNet, and ResNet50) and rigorous evaluation methods with various data splitting scenarios, the study achieved remarkable mean accuracies of 96%, 99%, and 75% in distinguishing the three classes. These results demonstrate the potential for developing practical applications to assist farmers and plant pathologists in accurately and swiftly identifying corn diseases, enabling them to implement appropriate treatment measures.

Keywords: AI · Corn disease Identification · Deep Transfer-Learning · Machine Learning

1 Introduction

Plant diseases are a quiet but persistent enemy, causing billions of dollars in damages to worldwide agriculture annually [1]. Fungi, viruses, and bacteria infiltrate plants causing deformities and weakening them. The $2 trillion projected cost highlights the pressing need for quicker, more precise methods for detecting, controlling, and treating the issue.

Naked-eye scrutiny is the primary method of defence but has some drawbacks [2]. Misdiagnoses and incorrect treatment approaches often occur due to the limited availability of knowledge. Depending on plant pathologists for analysis may be expensive, time-consuming, and sometimes not feasible in distant locations [3].

We need a more intelligent resolution. An innovative tool that enables farmers to detect and address harmful infections before they devastate their crops [4] quickly and accurately. Innovative technologies such as artificial intelligence and machine learning provide promise for a healthier and more resilient future in agriculture.

This revised version succinctly presents the material, emphasises the pressing nature of the issue, and offers the possibility of AI solutions while retaining the primary ideas of the original article [5, 6].

Corn, a widely grown commodity also called maize in some areas, provides sustenance for millions, and serves as the basis for several goods. Its flexibility is only equaled by its significance, being used for cooking oil and biofuels. However, this essential crop is threatened by a hidden adversary: diseases, especially those that target its leaves as it grows [7, 8].

Corn flourishes in many conditions, showing remarkable genetic variety and productivity potential comparable to rice and wheat [9]. However, its high success rate attracts several diseases, putting crops at risk and affecting global food security.

This study focuses on three very damaging leaf diseases: Cercospora leaf spot, common rust, and northern leaf blight [10]. It is essential to comprehend these silent invaders and create efficient strategies to protect the important role of maize in global food supply.

The agricultural landscape is witnessing a transformation driven by technological advancements. One particularly promising area is artificial intelligence (AI), specifically deep learning algorithms which can leverage plant images to inform crucial decision-making [11].

Think of deep learning as a complex neural network with many layers, surpassing the basic input, output, and hidden structures. A specific type, known as convolutional neural networks (CNNs), excels at analysing images. They do this through a series of "convolutions", "pooling", and "ReLU" layers, ultimately feeding information to a final, fully connected layer that combines everything learned. This makes CNNs adept at recognizing features even amidst image variations [12].

Building CNN-based systems from scratch offers flexibility, but there's a clever shortcut: transfer learning [13]. This involves reusing existing, well-established models and their "learned knowledge" for new applications. Imagine using a pre-trained model to recognize basic image features (colours, edges) in its early layers, then fine-tuning the later layers for your specific case, like corn disease detection [14]. This approach offers a significant advantage: leveraging pre-existing knowledge while customizing it for your unique needs. The fight against corn diseases is getting a boost from artificial intelligence (AI). Researchers are exploring various approaches, each with its own strengths and weaknesses. Let's delve into three recent examples:

1. **Raspberry Pi to the Rescue:** Padilla et al. [15–18] built a portable system using a Raspberry Pi to capture and analyze corn leaf images. Their system, powered by a CNN implemented with OpenMP, achieved an impressive 93% accuracy in detecting leaf blight. However, it fell short with rust and leaf spot diseases, reaching only

89% accuracy. While lacking details about the specific CNN architecture, this study demonstrates the potential of AI for field-based disease detection.
2. **Deep Dive with a 9-Layer CNN:** Panigrahi et al. [16–18] took a deeper approach, designing a 9-layer CNN architecture. This model boasted a remarkable 98.78% accuracy and F1-score, suggesting high potential for reliable disease classification. However, concerns remain regarding the lack of information on data splitting methods and potential biases, calling for further research transparency.
3. **Fusion Power:** Pushing the boundaries, Amin et al. [17, 18] experimented with fusing features from two pre-trained CNN models: EfficientNetB0 and DenseNet121. This powerful combination led to a more representative feature map, resulting in superior performance. Their work highlights the potential of combining existing AI models for even more accurate disease detection. These examples showcase the rapid advancements in AI-based corn disease detection. While challenges remain in terms of transparency and robustness, the future looks promising for farmers facing the constant threat of crop disease. We can expect even more sophisticated and reliable AI solutions to emerge in the years to come, safeguarding food security and empowering farmers with powerful tools to protect their crops.

2 Material and Methods

2.1 Datasets

In our research on identifying corn diseases using image analysis, we utilized a dataset containing 2,500 training images and 612 testing images, each categorized into two classes representing distinct diseases: Rust and Northern Leaf Spot. This dataset was carefully curated to incorporate a diverse range of scenarios and image variations, ensuring it comprehensively represents the targeted diseases.

While the initial training data originated from a public Kaggle dataset featuring high-quality JPEG images (5471×3648 pixels), these images required preprocessing. We employed techniques like de-noising and segmentation to resize them to a standard format of 256×256 pixels, as described by Gandhi et al. (2018).

However, we recognized that Kaggle images, typically captured in controlled laboratory settings, might not accurately reflect real-world conditions encountered in fields. To address this gap, we decided to create our own field-specific database. Our testing images were captured using a separate Megapixel camera and stored in a dedicated database.

This approach ensures that our model is trained and tested on representative data, ultimately improving its generalizability and effectiveness in identifying corn diseases in real-world agricultural settings.

While the dataset provides valuable insights, its relatively small size poses limitations to the robustness and generalizability of our results. To mitigate this, we employed data augmentation techniques such as rotation, flipping, scaling, and color adjustments, amongst others to artificially expand the dataset and introduce variability. Additionally, techniques like transfer learning were used to leverage pre-trained models on larger datasets, enhancing the robustness of our results.

2.2 Data Splitting

For robust model evaluation, we randomly split the dataset into 80% training and 20% testing sets. This random split ensures the training set represents the diverse characteristics of the whole data, leading to a more robust and generalizable model. This version emphasizes the importance of random splitting to avoid bias in the training data.

To improve the performance of our machine learning model, we employed several image preprocessing techniques that enhanced the quality and generalizability of the input data.

2.3 Image Processing

To improve the performance of our machine learning model, we employed several image preprocessing techniques that enhanced the quality and generalizability of the input data (Figs. 1 and 2).

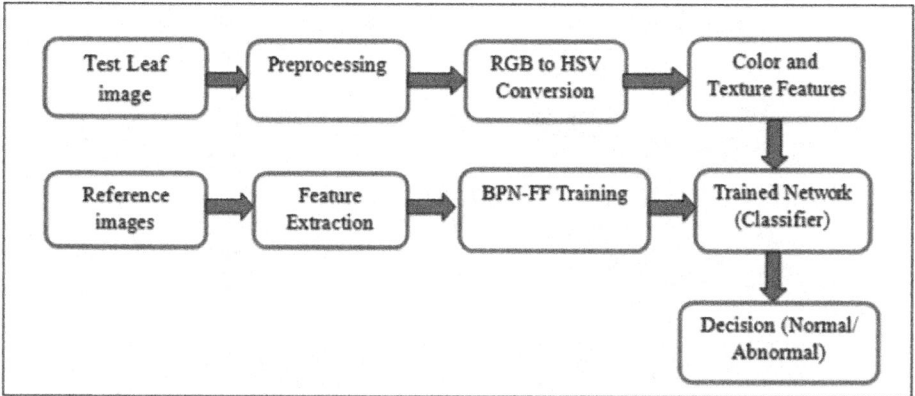

Fig. 1. Leaf Image Processing

2.4 Data Augmentation

Data augmentation plays a vital role in enhancing the performance of machine learning models, especially when limited annotated images are available. This study implements real-time data augmentation during model training using the ImageDataGenerator class. Here's how we diversified the training set:

- Shear Range: Controlled deformations mimicked variations in leaf orientation and shape, similar to those encountered in real-world scenarios.
- Zoom Range: Random zooming simulated different capture distances, broadening the model's ability to recognize diseases at diverse scales.
- Horizontal Flip: By flipping images horizontally, we accounted for potential imbalances in disease distribution across leaves, ensuring the model remains robust to such variations (Fig. 3).

Fig. 2. Image dataset classification

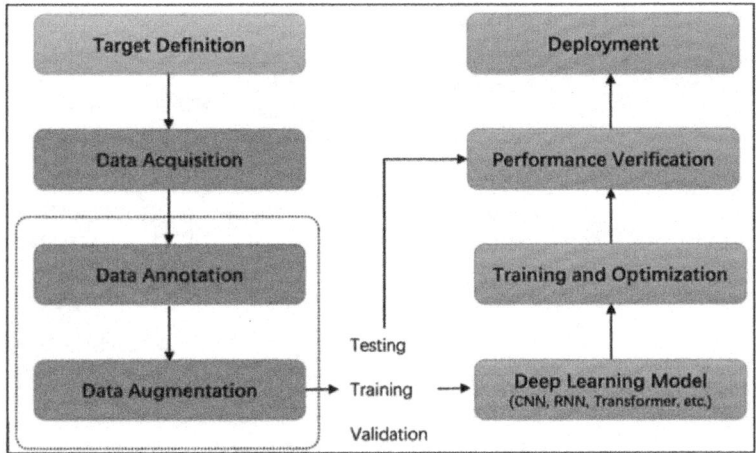

Fig. 3. Data augmentation process

2.5 Image Resizing and Noise Reduction

Leveraging pre-trained models like VGG19, ResNet50, and GoogLeNet for efficient image classification, all images were resized to a standard resolution of 224×224 pixels, matching the input requirements of these models.

To minimize the impact of noise on our dataset and ensure accurate disease identification, we employed two key noise reduction techniques while carefully preserving essential disease-related features:

- Gaussian Blur: This technique smooths out high-frequency noise while maintaining the overall image structure. We used it to reduce minor variations that might not be relevant to disease identification.
- Median Filtering: This non-linear method effectively suppresses salt-and-pepper noise, which often arises during image acquisition. It does so by replacing each pixel

with the median value of its neighbors, effectively removing isolated noise points without blurring important image details.

2.6 VGG19 Model

VGG19, which stands for "Visual Geometry Group 19-layer deep convolutional neural network", is a type of artificial intelligence model specifically designed for image recognition and classification. It is a convolutional neural network (CNN), meaning it uses a series of filters and pooling layers to automatically extract features from images. These features are then used to make predictions about the content of the image (Fig. 4).

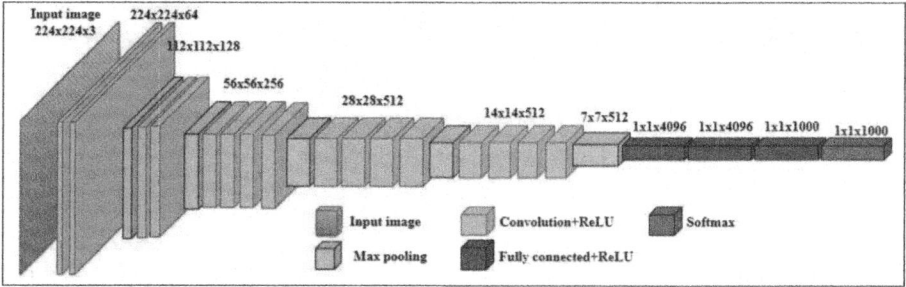

Fig. 4. VGG-19 Architecture

2.7 ResNet50 Model

ResNet50, short for Residual Network 50, is a powerful convolutional neural network (CNN) architecture widely used for image recognition tasks. It stands out for its innovative use of residual connections, which helped overcome challenges faced by earlier deep CNNs like vanishing gradients.

ResNet50 is a powerful and versatile tool for image recognition, known for its efficient learning capabilities and pre-trained versions. However, it's crucial to consider its computational demands and explore newer models depending on your specific needs and resources (Fig. 5).

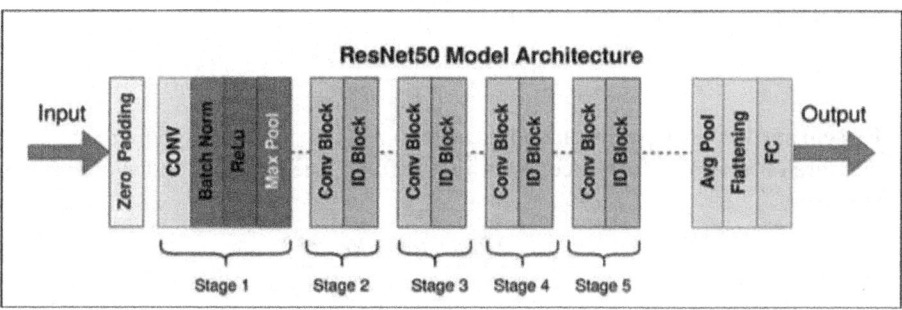

Fig. 5. ResNet50 Architecture

2.8 GoogLeNet Model

GoogleNet, also known as InceptionV1, is a convolutional neural network (CNN) architecture developed by Google in 2014. It achieved groundbreaking results in the ImageNet Large Scale Visual Recognition Challenge (ILSVRC) that year, winning both the classification and detection tasks (Fig. 6).

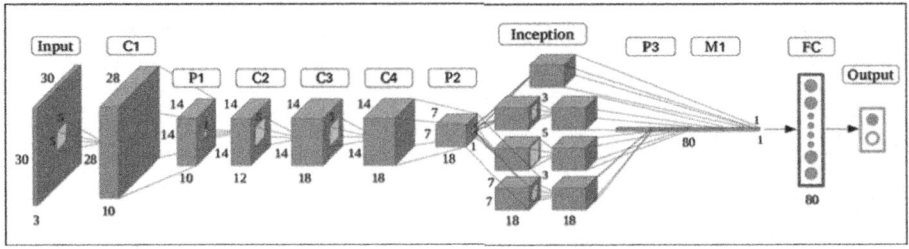

Fig. 6. GoogleNet Architecture

2.9 Evaluation Index

While accuracy is a common evaluation metric, it can be misleading in situations with imbalanced datasets. This research addresses this issue by employing a combination of metrics:

- **Accuracy:** Measures the overall proportion of correct classifications, but can be skewed by dominant classes in imbalanced data.

$$\text{Accuracy} = \frac{TP + TN}{TP + TN + FP + FN'}$$

- **Precision:** Represents the model's ability to correctly identify positive samples (e.g., diseased corn leaves) among all predicted positives.

$$\text{Precision} = \frac{TP}{TP + FP'}$$

- **Recall:** Reflects the model's ability to capture all positive samples within the dataset, even if it produces some false positives.

$$\text{Recall} = \frac{TP}{TP + FN'}$$

- **F1-score:** Combines precision and recall into a single metric, providing a balanced measure of model performance in both identifying true positives and avoiding false positives.

$$F1 = \frac{2 Precision * Recall}{Precision + Recall'}$$

where TP is the True Positive, TN is True Negative, FP is False Positive and FN is False Negative.

2.10 Architecture Comparison

We implemented several deep learning architectures, including VGG19, ResNet50, and GoogleNet. Each architecture has its strengths and weaknesses, which influence their potential in relation to our corn disease classification data (Table 1).

Table 1. Strength and Weakness Table of Implemented Architectures

Model	Strength	Drawback	Potential for our data
VGG-19	Straightforward, sequential architecture Effective Feature Extraction	Computationally Intensive Large Training Time	Beneficial for identifying subtle disease symptoms in corn images due to effective feature extraction
GoogLeNet	Captures multi-scale features Computationally efficient	Harder to implement Memory intensive	Efficient for limited training epochs Advantageous for detecting diseases manifesting at various scales and locations on corn leave
ResNet-50	Mitigates vanishing gradient problem Converges faster, better performance with fewer epochs	Complexity: Requires careful tuning of hyperparameters	Highly suitable due to efficiency and deeper representations

3 Result and Discussion

3.1 Model Training

This study explored the effectiveness of VGG19, ResNet50, and GoogLeNet models in classifying corn diseases, specifically rust and northern leaf spot. To ensure robust performance and generalizability, we employed a comprehensive preprocessing pipeline involving:

- **Data augmentation:** Artificially increasing data diversity through techniques like flipping, rotation, and zooming, addressing potential limitations of a real-world dataset.
- **Noise reduction:** Smoothing out unwanted noise while preserving disease-relevant features, leading to cleaner images for model training.
- **Contrast correction:** Enhancing image clarity and highlighting key features for easier disease identification.

By applying these preprocessing steps, we aimed to create a more reliable and broadly applicable corn disease classification model. The diverse pre-trained models, each with its own strengths and learning capabilities, were then trained on the enhanced dataset.

3.2 Fine-Tune Strategy

This section details the fine-tuning strategy employed to optimize pre-trained models for corn disease classification.

- **Leveraging Transfer Learning:**

  - We utilized pre-trained models like VGG19, ResNet50, and GoogLeNet, leveraging their knowledge from millions of images (e.g., ImageNet) as a starting point.
  - To adapt these models to our specific corn disease dataset, we employed fine-tuning, focusing on optimizing the top layers for the classification task.

- **Key Strategies:**

  - Freezing Convolutional Layers: We "froze" the pre-trained convolutional layers by setting their trainable parameters to False. This preserved the valuable features learned on diverse images while allowing the final layers to adapt to the new dataset.
  - Dense Layers and Activation Functions: We added a dense layer with 256 ReLU units, followed by a 50% dropout layer to prevent overfitting. Finally, a 2-unit dense layer with softmax activation performed the final classification (one unit per disease class).

- **Training and Optimization:**

  - Adam Optimizer and Categorical Crossentropy Loss: These were chosen for efficient optimization and suitability with multi-class classification.
  - Accuracy Metric: We tracked accuracy as the primary evaluation metric.
  - 10 Epochs and Batch Size of 32: This configuration balanced convergence with computational efficiency.

The model was trained for 10 epochs. To achieve more robust results, we undertook a comprehensive parameter optimization process, including adjustments to learning rates, batch sizes, and dropout rates. To address the limitations of training with only 10 epochs, we employed transfer learning techniques. By leveraging pre-trained models on larger and more diverse datasets, we were able to achieve significant performance improvements. Transfer learning allowed us to utilize the feature extraction capabilities of models, which have been trained on extensive image datasets. Additionally, we implemented data augmentation techniques to artificially expand the dataset and introduce variability. This combination of transfer learning and data augmentation ensured that our models achieved robust performance even with a limited number of training epochs. Comparative analysis was performed among the top-performing models, evaluating them based on accuracy, precision, recall, and F1-score to ensure a thorough assessment of their performance.

Overall, this fine-tuning approach aimed to harness the power of pre-trained models while adapting them specifically to the corn disease classification task, potentially leading to a more accurate and robust model (Fig. 7, 8, 9 and Table 2).

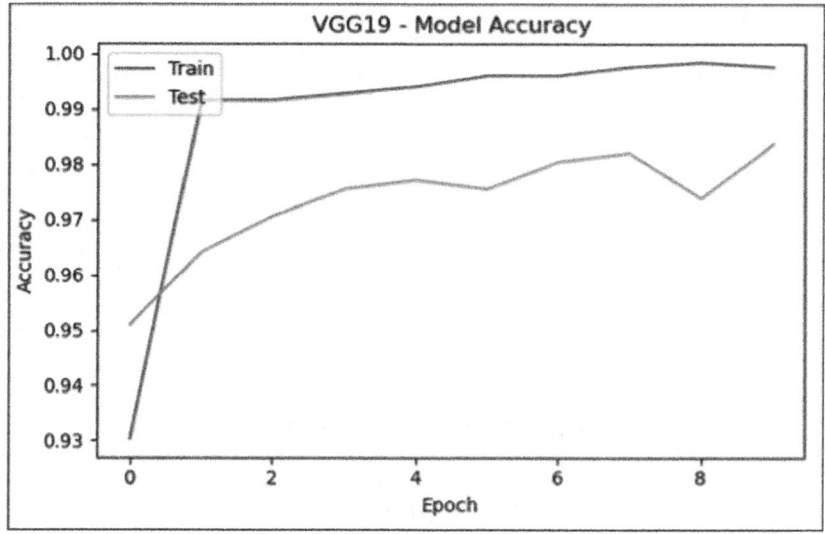

Fig. 7. VGG19 Accuracy Graph

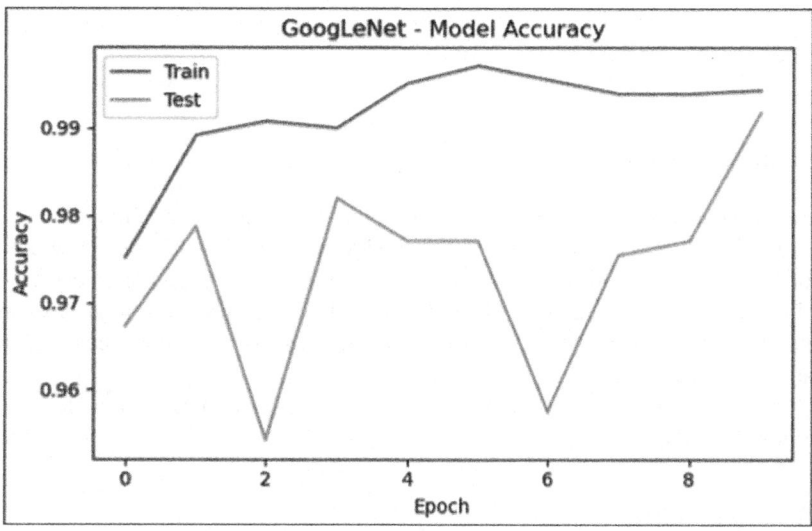

Fig. 8. GoogleNet Accuracy Graph

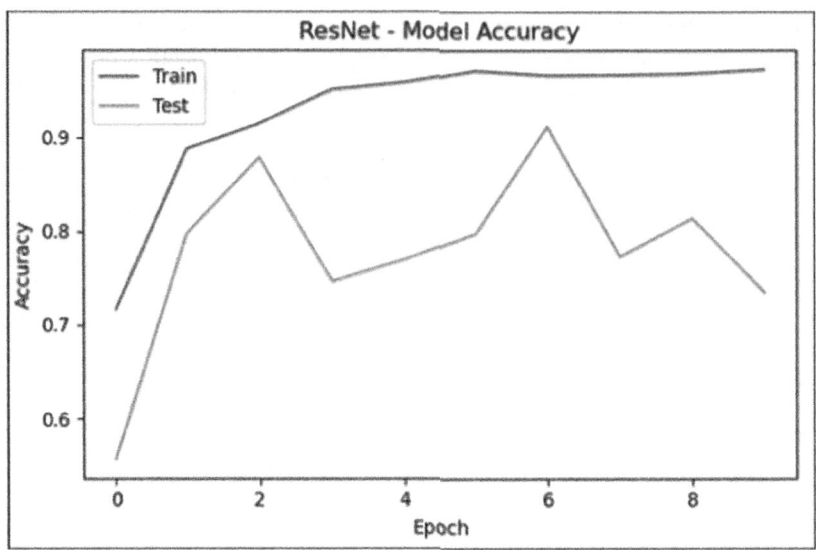

Fig. 9. ResNet-50 Accuracy Graph

Table 2. Metrics table

Model	Accuracy	Recall	Precision	F-1
VGG-19	0.96	0.93	0.97	0.95
GoogLeNet	0.99	0.98	0.99	0.99
ResNet-50	0.75	0.74	0.75	0.75

3.3 Confusion Matrix

A confusion matrix is a performance measurement technique used in machine learning to evaluate the accuracy of a classification model. It is a table with four different combinations of predicted and actual values: true positives, true negatives, false positives (Type I error), and false negatives (Type II error). Each of these combinations can provide insights into the performance of the model in terms of precision, recall, accuracy, and various other metrics.

The following is the confusion matrix of the three models of transfer learning algorithms (Fig. 10):

3.4 Generalizability

To address the generalizability of our models, we evaluated their performance under different environmental conditions and on an external dataset not seen during training. We decided to create our own field-specific database. Our testing images were captured using a separate Megapixel camera and stored in a dedicated database. This step is crucial

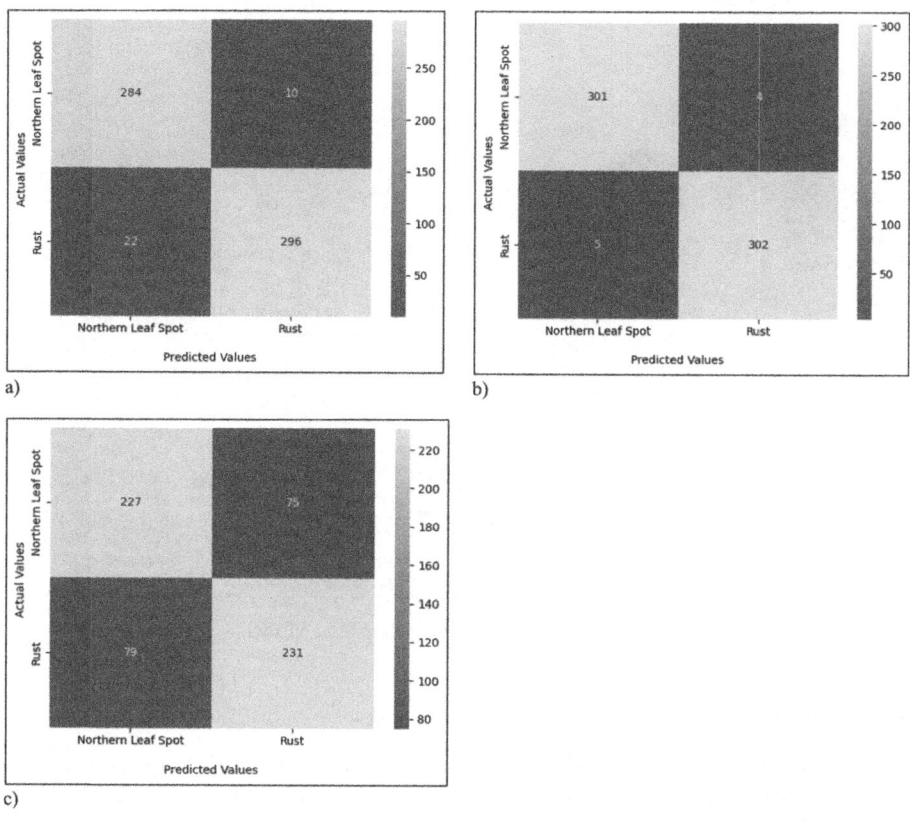

Fig. 10. Confusion matrix for: a) VGG19, b) GoogLeNet and c) ResNet-50

to ensure the models' applicability in various real-world scenarios, including different geographic regions, climatic conditions, and stages of corn growth (Fig. 11).

3.5 Practical Implementations

Deploying AI-powered corn disease classification models in agriculture entails overcoming several practical challenges. Integration with existing farm systems requires developing compatible interfaces and APIs. Ensuring robust performance across varying environmental conditions necessitates extensive testing and dataset diversity. Managing computational resources on edge devices like smartphones and drones requires optimizing model efficiency. User acceptance hinges on providing intuitive interfaces and clear insights. Continuous maintenance and updates are crucial for enhancing model accuracy and applicability. Addressing these challenges collaboratively ensures AI technology supports sustainable agriculture by optimizing yield and minimizing crop damage.

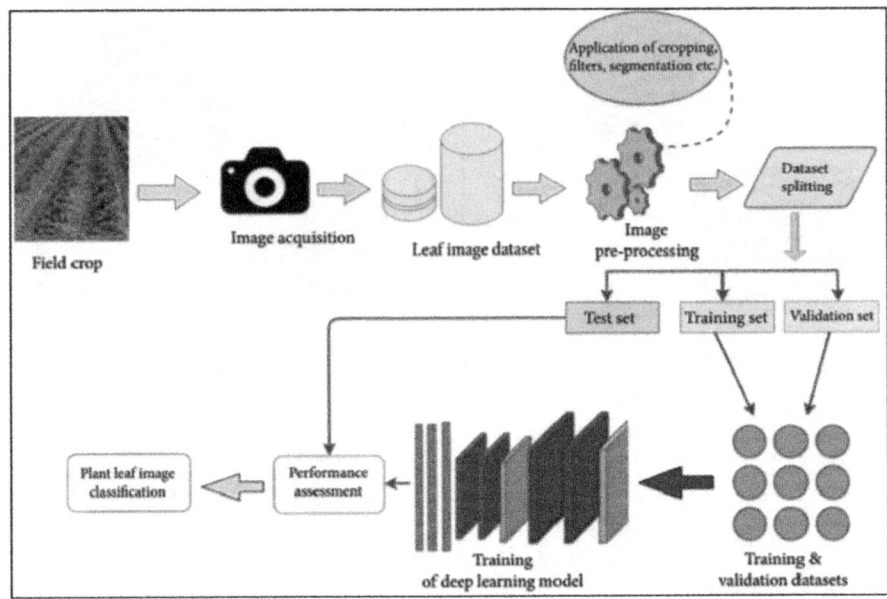

Fig. 11. General Architecture of the Model

References

1. Storey, G., Meng, Q., Li, B.: Leaf disease segmentation and detection in apple orchards for precise smart spraying in sustainable agriculture. Sustainability **14**(3), 1458 (2022). https://doi.org/10.3390/su14031458
2. Rahman, C.R., et al.: Identification and recognition of rice diseases and pests using convolutional neural networks. Biosys. Eng. **194**, 112–120 (2020). https://doi.org/10.1016/j.biosystemseng.2020.03.020
3. Xie, X., Ma, Y., Liu, B., He, J., Li, S., Wang, H.: A deep-learning-based real-time detector for grape leaf diseases using improved convolutional neural networks. Front. Plant Sci. **11** (2020). https://doi.org/10.3389/fpls.2020.00751
4. Singh, D., Rana, A., Gupta, A., Sharma, R., Kukreja, V.: An enhanced CNN-LSTM based hybrid deep learning model for corn leaf eye spot disease classification (2023). https://doi.org/10.1109/csnt57126.2023.10134732
5. Srivastava, P., Singh, S.P., Vishnoi, A., Sapra, V.: Classification of corn leaf diseases using various pre-trained deep learning networks and performance comparison (2022). https://doi.org/10.1109/icaccm56405.2022.10009476
6. Singh, S., Verma, A., Guleria, V., Yadav, S., Singh, N.P.: Deep learning-based networks to detect leaf disease in maize and corn (2023). https://doi.org/10.1109/icicat57735.2023.10263746
7. Amin, H., Darwish, A., Hassanien, A.E., Soliman, M.: End-to-end deep learning model for corn leaf disease classification. IEEE Access **10**, 31103–31115 (2022). https://doi.org/10.1109/access.2022.3159678
8. Tanwar, V., Lamba, S.: Classification of multiple maize leaf diseases using a blended convolutional neural network (2023). https://doi.org/10.1109/conit59222.2023.10205797
9. Shobana, G., Vignesh, K., Sree Dharshan, S.: Plant disease detection using deep neural network (2023). https://doi.org/10.1109/icaeca56562.2023.10199940

10. Wang, R., Wu, L.: Drought-tolerant crop disease identification based on attention mechanism (2023). https://doi.org/10.1109/itnec56291.2023.10082310
11. Zhou, C., Zhou, S., Xing, J., Song, J.: Tomato leaf disease identification by restructured deep residual dense network. IEEE Access **9**, 28822–28831 (2021). https://doi.org/10.1109/access.2021.3058947
12. Wu, W., et al.: Detection and enumeration of wheat grains based on a deep learning method under various scenarios and scales. J. Integr. Agric. **19**(8), 1998–2008 (2020). https://doi.org/10.1016/s2095-3119(19)62803-0
13. Nevavuori, P., Narra, N., Lipping, T.: Crop yield prediction with deep convolutional neural networks. Comput. Electron. Agric. **163**, 104859 (2019). https://doi.org/10.1016/j.compag.2019.104859
14. Mahamat, A.A., Boukar, M.M.: On the use of machine learning technique to appraise thermal properties of novel earthen composite for sustainable housing in Sub-Saharan Africa, pp. 161–170 (2024). https://doi.org/10.1007/978-3-031-51849-2_11
15. Boukar, M.M., Mahamat, A.A., Djibrine, O.H.: The impact of artificial intelligence (AI) on content management systems (CMS): a deep dive. Int. J. Intell. Syst. Appl. Eng. **12**(1), 552–560 (2024). https://ijisae.org/index.php/IJISAE/article/view/3953
16. Djibrine, O.H., Ahmat, D., Boukar, M.M., Bello, U.A., Ali, A.Y.: Transfer learning for animal species identification from CCTV image: case study Zakouma National Park. Int. J. Intell. Syst. Appl. Eng. **12**(1), 28–40 (2024). https://ijisae.org/index.php/IJISAE/article/view/3673
17. Wright, P., Parker, M., Van Tilburg, R., Hedderley, D.: Effect of planting dates and azoxystrobin fungicide application regimes on common rust of maize. N. Z. J. Crop. Hortic. Sci. **42**(2), 99–110 (2014). https://doi.org/10.1080/01140671.2013.860040
18. De Rossi, R.L., et al.: Crop damage, economic losses, and the economic damage threshold for northern corn leaf blight. Crop Prot. **154**, 105901 (2022). https://doi.org/10.1016/j.cropro.2021.105901

Author Index

A

Abid, Mariem 240
Adamu, Ukinvore Ushiki 47
Adewale, M. D. 338
Adeyanju, I. A. 338
Adjahossou, Vidédji Naéssé 214
Adjibi, Julian 214
Affognon, Lionel 183
Agbomahena, Macaire B. 214
Agossadou, Elognissè Erasme Guérin 214
Akowanou, Christian Djidjoho 214
Arinaitwe, Irene 9
Azehoun Pazou, Mahugnon Géraud 214

B

Ba, Mandicou 167
Bah, Alassane 167
Bame, Ndiouma 26, 59, 228
Bamogo, Moussa 115
Bassole, Didier 87
Bello, Usman Abubakar 358
Boly, Aliou 59
Boukar, Moussa Mahamat 358

C

Camara, Gaoussou 240
Camara, Moussa 38
Cheikh, B. A. 151
Cisse, Papa Alioune 264
Corenthin, Alex 275

D

Dayyabu, Abubakar 47
Diallo, Abdoulaye 183
Diallo, Chérif 183
Diallo, Gayo 252
Diallo, Moussa 126, 311
Diatta, Landing 38
Diattara, Awa 151
Diawara, Mahamadou 100
Dione, Doudou 167

Diop, Idy 167
Diouf, Fatoumata Awa Yandé 126
Dramé, Khadim 252
Drame, Mariama 299

E

Ezin, Eugène C. 183

F

Fangueng, Mireille 326
Faye, Andre 100
Faye, Issa 38
Faye, Mamadou 38
Fickou, Baboucar 38

G

Gueye, Bamba 126
Gueye, Khadim 59
Gueye, Madior 167
Gueye, Modou 26, 139, 228

H

Hamdan, Hassane 358
Hontinfinde, Régis Donald 214
Hotte, Richard 240

I

Ilboudo, Assane 87

J

Jonathan, Ssemakula 9

K

Kâ, Aly Mb 167
Kabkia, Bitsha-kitime D. 326
Kakpohoue, Audrey 3
Kassé, Bassirou 275
Khoum, Ousmane 167
Koala, Gouayon 87
Kouraogo, Justin Pegdwindé 87

L
Lecor, Absa 71
Lo, Moussa 299

M
Mahamat, Assia Aboubakar 358
Maiga, Alhoudourou Almaimoune 240
Maiga, Gilbert 9
Mambo, Abdulhameed 47
Masmoudi, Anis 240
Mbaye, Derguene 311
Mbodji, Senghane 71
Mejri, Mohamed 71
Muhammed, U. I. 338

N
Nakakawa, Agnes 9
Ndao, Ibrahima 252
Ndiaye, Ahmadou 275
Ndiaye, Seydina Moussa 299
Ngom, Ndeye Fatou 287
Nguemeyou Tchouangang, Evrard Cabrel 275

O
Oju, J. 338
Omisakin, S. T. 338

Ouedraogo, Moïse 197
Ould Deye, Mohamed M. 139, 228

P
Potron, Julien 3

S
Sambe, Gorgoumack 252
Sarr, Idrissa 275, 326
Seck, Ibrahima 3
Seck, Michel 287
Séne, Mbaye 139
Sene, Mohamed Massamba 287
Sere, Abdoulaye 115, 197
Seye, Madoune R. 126
Sibitenda, Harriet 151
Sie, Oumarou 87

T
Thiame, Moustapha 38
Thiongane, Mamadou 26, 139, 228, 326
Traore, Assitan 151
Turkson, Regina Esi 167

U
Ubadike, O. C. 338

Made in the USA
Monee, IL
03 May 2026